# Communicative Reason

The book examines philosophical and sociological approaches within critical theory and more widely from the vantage point of communicative reason. It seeks to revitalize the sociological dimension of critical theory by advancing a critical sociology of reason. It does so fully in the knowledge that reason is a contentious concept in sociology and other disciplines. Nonetheless, building on Habermas's original insight, it argues that an extensively modified version of communicative reason is indispensable. This modified approach will draw extensively from Peirce's pragmatist semiotics and critical cognitive sociology. Such a focus has significant implications for meta-theoretical, theoretical-empirical, and methodological approaches in critical theory, critical sociology, and related disciplines. This book will be of interest to readers in the social sciences, humanities, and philosophy who value the importance of a social theory of a reasonable society for their disciplines and for increasingly essential interdisciplinary activities. The book will also appeal to many in critical theory and beyond who are interested in the cognitive foundations of normative orders, including unjust or pathological as well as actually or potentially just foundations. The book emphasizes both validity and critique within communicative reason and critical theory and accordingly presents a distinctive perspective on critical-reconstructive research.

**Patrick O'Mahony**, Department of Sociology and Criminology, University College, Cork, Ireland, is the author of *The Contemporary Theory of the Public Sphere*, the editor of *Nature, Risk and Responsibility: Discourses of Biotechnology*, the co-author of *Rethinking Irish History: Nationalism, Identity and Ideology* and *Nationalism and Social Theory*, co-editor of *Irish Environmental Politics after the Communicative Turn*, and guest editor of the Special Issue on The Critical Theory of Society for the European Journal of Social Theory (2023).

# Routledge Studies in Social and Political Thought

This series explores core issues in political philosophy and social theory. Addressing theoretical subjects of both historical and contemporary relevance, the series has broad appeal across the social sciences. Contributions include new studies of major thinkers, key debates and critical concepts. The full series can be viewed here.

**Regimes of Capital in the Post-Digital Age**
*Edited by Szymon Wróbel and Krzysztof Skonieczny*

**The Not So Outrageous Idea of a Christian Sociology**
*Joseph Scimecca*

**Against the Background of Social Reality**
Defaults, Commonplaces, and the Sociology of the Unmarked
*Carmelo Lombardo and Lorenzo Sabetta*

**The Cognitive Foundations of Classical Sociological Theory**
*Ryan McVeigh*

**Social Theory and the Political Imaginary**
Practice, Critique, and History
*Craig Browne*

**Being a (Lived) Body**
Aesthesiological and Phenomenological Paths
*Tonino Griffero*

**Revisiting Social Theory**
Challenges and Possibilities
*Edited by D.V. Kumar*

**Alfred Schutz, Phenomenology, and the Renewal of Interpretive Social Science**
*Besnik Pula*

**Communicative Reason**
A Sociological Restatement
*Patrick O'Mahony*

# Communicative Reason
A Sociological Restatement

## Patrick O'Mahony

LONDON AND NEW YORK

First published 2025
by Routledge
4 Park Square, Milton Park, Abingdon, Oxon OX14 4RN

and by Routledge
605 Third Avenue, New York, NY 10158

*Routledge is an imprint of the Taylor & Francis Group, an informa business*

© 2025 Patrick O'Mahony

The right of Patrick O'Mahony to be identified as author of this work has been asserted in accordance with sections 77 and 78 of the Copyright, Designs and Patents Act 1988.

All rights reserved. No part of this book may be reprinted or reproduced or utilised in any form or by any electronic, mechanical, or other means, now known or hereafter invented, including photocopying and recording, or in any information storage or retrieval system, without permission in writing from the publishers.

*Trademark notice:* Product or corporate names may be trademarks or registered trademarks, and are used only for identification and explanation without intent to infringe.

*British Library Cataloguing-in-Publication Data*
A catalogue record for this book is available from the British Library

ISBN: 978-0-367-18293-9 (hbk)
ISBN: 978-1-032-84680-4 (pbk)
ISBN: 978-0-429-06057-1 (ebk)

DOI: 10.4324/9780429060571

Typeset in Times New Roman
by KnowledgeWorks Global Ltd.

# Contents

| | |
|---|---|
| *List of Figures* | *vi* |
| *Preface* | *vii* |

Introduction: Communicative Reason: A Sociological Restatement   1

1  Habermas, Communicative Reason, and the Social Sciences   18

2  Sociology and Reason: General Considerations   49

3  Reason and the Reflexive Turn in Sociology   69

4  The State of Reason in Sociology   114

5  Peirce, Reason, and Signification   135

6  Reasoning and Schemata in a Societal Frame   159

7  Towards a Sign-Mediated Societal Ontology   194

8  Reason, Communication, and Validity   216

9  Validity, Schemata, and Reasoning on Moral-Political Issues   238

10  Reasoning and Validity Standards   255

11  Reason and Critique   279

12  Critique and Reasoning Pathologies   293

*Index*   *315*

# List of Figures

| | | |
|---|---|---|
| 7.1 | Sign-mediated Societal Ontology | 199 |
| 8.1 | Validity and Societal Ontology | 228 |

# Preface

This book has been long in the making. It responds to a deeply rooted sense that sociology needs to revisit and build on the critical theoretical goal of an integrated approach spanning philosophy and the social sciences, a goal that is also only fitfully pursued in contemporary critical theory. It has been accompanied by the further sense that the way normative issues are addressed in sociology is far from satisfactory and that this, in turn, is inextricably bound up with its relation to reason.

This constellation of thoughts has been maturing for some time. It has been greatly aided by various seminar contexts that have enriched its development. The most local and small-scale has been the Harbour View seminar series, whose focus has overlapped with the core issues of the book. I would like to thank my colleagues there, Piet Strydom, Roddy Condon, Ronan Kaczynski, and Richard Milner, and a visitor, Hauke Brunkhorst, for important interventions, criticisms, and suggestions for reorientation.

I have also been a regular attendee over the duration of the research and writing process at the annual Prague Colloquium on Philosophy and the Social Sciences. There, I had regular opportunities to present aspects of the work in progress. Out of that context, I would particularly like to thank Rainer Forst for his sustained interest in the project over time.

Over the duration of the writing process, I am very grateful for the assistance of first, Suzy Renwick, and then, Sarah Bologna. They each provided me with encouragement and support for the project. Suzy's support at the outset was invaluable in reading and commenting on drafts, attending to matters of style and argument, and arranging a productive presentation of the book to her young son, Oscar. My thanks are also extended to Oscar for his interest and questions. I am extremely grateful to Sarah for helping to push the project to completion over the course of the last few years, keeping an eye on deadlines and providing a regular context that inspired me to further efforts when I was flagging. Thanks are also due to Klair van Haght for important organizational support to the writing project. Ronan Kaczynski not only provided intellectual analysis and criticism, but he also played a pivotal role in helping me with technical aspects of the project. I would also like to thank Joseph Kelleher for extensive questions and comments on the overall arguments of the book.

I would sincerely like to thank Piet Strydom, my intellectual companion and friend for many years, for providing an indispensable context for writing a book of

viii   *Preface*

this kind. I would also like to thank Gerard Delanty for agreeing to and supporting a special issue on the Critical Theory of Society in his journal, *European Journal of Social Theory*, over the course of the writing project. The special issue proved an important forum for the deepening of the ideas that underpin the book.

Finally, I want to extend my deepest gratitude to the wonderful non-human companions who have accompanied me along the way, always on the job and always ready to forgive my tendency to sit in front of screens for far too long. There are many of them, both residents and visitors; some passed on their way, some present. Their inestimable contribution has been deeply treasured.

Harbour View, Kilbrittain, December 14th, 2023.

I dedicate this book to my beloved canine companions of many years, Ayana, Bart, Benny, Dudley, Emerald, H/ee, Lena, Leo, Lola, Ochi, Ozzie, Ruby, and Sooty.

# Introduction
## Communicative Reason: A Sociological Restatement

The overall rationale of this book is to explore the relationship between a contemporary concept of reason, communicative reason, and potentials for a normative, democratic sociology. The concept of reason casts a dark shadow on the social sciences. The import of much of the intellectual tradition of sociology – notably its strongly objectivist and strongly subjectivist poles – leads to constant questioning of reason's claims, a questioning that has been pronounced in the last half-century. Yet, sociology's overall commitment to a universally justifiable social order has also been deeply embedded in its classical and neoclassical elaboration. Frequently, there has been acknowledgement of the role of reason, even if it was never properly developed beyond the extensive sociological writings of the early Frankfurt School. The ambivalent and highly fragmentary reception of the Enlightenment in the discipline meant that the explicit concept of reason itself played a submerged status. Nevertheless, *rational natural law* ideas, variously drawn from Kant and Hegel and taken on in different ways by Marx, Durkheim, Weber, and Parsons, played a critical part in embedding the ideal of universal justice in the discipline.

Such an ideal is losing traction today as sociology and related disciplines are increasingly preoccupied by the critique of reason, a reason whose claims are thought to lie in a false universalism that merely disguises partial interests and established hegemony. The constant self-critique could even be said to be leading to antagonism to the very idea of reason, up to the point where to invoke reason in any positive register is to invite suspicion. What Schnadelbach describes as the critique of functionalist reason the claim that since Nietzsche 'reason' can be explained by forces other than reason, for example, technologies of power, the instinct for survival, expressive competence, and social systems, has fully come into its own (Schnadelbach, 1998). Yet, important strands of sociology have always at least latently depended on a concept of reason insofar as it has been concerned with the general normative well-being of society. Even before critical theory, the thrust of the classics was to offer a diagnosis of modern society that saw it as divorced or alienated from a possible state of reasonableness. However, this formulation was ambivalent in Weber and Durkheim, if less so in Marx. Yet it remained latently present in Parsons's interpretation of these traditions and, in particular, his accounts of the regulative role of ultimate values and its normative, anti-utilitarian thrust.

DOI: 10.4324/9780429060571-1

## 2 Introduction

Nonetheless, what did not happen in classical and neoclassical sociology, and has not happened since, is the full articulation of a *democratic* idea of reason. At a manifest level, emphatically in much contemporary sociology, such an idea of reason is treated as suspicious and is variously accorded 'negative' terms such as idealized, supra-contextual, elitist, ethnocentric, masculine, and rootless. In part, this emphasis may be explained by the history of the use of reason, and the traditions of knowledge, such as early critical theory, that sought to show how forms of reason, notably formalized, subjective reason, can be used against the very possibility of a reasonable society. Yet the option of pursuing reason in another way, taken up in early critical theory, was not much pursued in the social and cultural sciences. Such a pursuit of reason has, in varying forms, run through first- and second-generation critical theory, addressing the appropriate balance of those forms of reason that might lead to a reasonable society in the light of standards of freedom, equality, and responsibility. If sociology were somehow to embrace this task, it would no longer be the prisoner of some parts of its own history in denying the indispensable relationship between reason and any prospect of a just, modern society. In so doing, it would at last begin to affirmatively centre itself on what up to now has been largely absent in the discipline, or only negatively present, that is, a concern for radical, popular democracy. With this orientation, it might also begin a wider interdisciplinary embrace of its divided moments, functional, aesthetic, and normative, with the realization that if they remain divided, sociology will forever dissolve its energies in the spaces between them and deny its primary purpose, that of contributing to the building of reasonable social arrangements.

Sociology has multiple strands. In the philosophy of social science, it has now become commonplace to identify three main historical ones that, in more recent times, inform a wider variety of traditions and schools. The three are the empirical-analytic strand concerned with the 'scientification' of sociology, the interpretive strand opposing it concerned with separating out from scientific concerns a distinctive domain of human meaning, and a third, critical or critical reflexive, that seeks to engage and partially incorporate dimensions of the other two while emphasizing its own norm-critical and reflexive-learning oriented perspective. Each of these strands has classically acquired a distinctive relation to reason and the Enlightenment transformation of our understanding of the world that lies behind it. The empirical-analytic tradition has tended to focus on scientific *rationalism* and a concept of reason that seeks to be detached and logically formal. The interpretive tradition, which historically has often been suspicious of the Enlightenment and often emphasizes instead the virtues of 'primordial' human cultural legacies in religions, national communities, or other 'non-rational' cultural forms, directs much of its animus to the critique of reason. It understands reason as canonically lying in the sphere of purposive or means-end, formal logical and scientific rationality, the reason of its historically long-established empirical-analytical adversary. Finally, the critical tradition has classically emerged from the Enlightenment, and indeed, reason's emphasis on the self-critique of individuals and collective social forms, with a type of grounding in the idea of critique associated with Kant. However, critical sociology and Enlightenment reason have still exhibited a tension-laden history, with sociology from its origins displaying both a latent affinity to the idealist legacy and a desire to transform it by drawing attention to reason's false promises.

It is in the critical tradition that this text is largely anchored, though very much mindful that the various traditions of thinking about reason, or, indeed, against reason, require much more than simply standing in one tradition or even one discipline. Moreover, the complexity of contemporary society in a multitude of ways has taken elements of these traditions and combined them in new ways. So much so that, over time, various sociologies have drawn extensively off traditions of thinking about reason to which they might not mainly subscribe but still find a way to utilize. All of this has become latterly expressed in a variety of new philosophies of sociology that combine multiple motifs connected with reason or its denial and that have the effect of making the contemporary social scientific landscape particularly hard to decipher from the standpoint of any more encompassing account of reason.

In some contrast, contemporary 'normatively relevant' scholarship in what is often called the ideal theoretical tradition continues to be concerned with reason, even if often quite obliquely, because for the goal of forming anything like a just and well-ordered society, nothing else could be conceived that might work. Hence, some diagnosticians of the modern conditions do incline more emphatically to restore the significance of the idea of reason. Philosophers like Habermas, also, of course, a sociologist, and Rawls are among many to advance theories of reason, respectively communicative reason and public reason. These accounts of reason are indeed concerned with the idea of a normatively well-governed and hence just society. Prominent sociologists such as Bourdieu, Alexander, and Archer have developed a sociological variation on the 'space of reason' over the last 30 to 40 years when they speak in various ways about reflexivity, a concept that has become extensively used in the social sciences to emphasize the significance of cognitive capacities to change action orientations. Yet, as will be shown, this latter sociological treatment still retains an ambivalent relation to any affirmation of reason, even democratic reason. The relation of this type of sociological thinking to the reason concept of the Enlightenment is rarely made manifest and, where it is done, what stands forth more is the effort to achieve distance from its idealist legacy rather than its critical embracing.

The above naturally forces the question of why might this be so, why has sociological thinking, especially in the last half-century, found it easier to criticize reason – while using it obliquely – than to consider why it might in crucial ways still depend on it? Partly, without doubt, it is because the legacy of reason has become seen as complicit with power and ideology. Certain assertions of what reason consists of have historically been used to dismiss the capacity of others to reason differently and to install regimes of domination. Reason has therefore come to be seen by many sociologists as too positive in its emphasis and too friendly to those who would unjustly impose regimes of domination on others. Partly it lies in the sense that the emphasis on reason, regarded by certain self-interested groups as

4   *Introduction*

somehow complete in itself, is construed as a means of denying what lies beyond their own particular version of 'reason'. Thus, impure forms of self-interested reason are advanced with the claim that this version of reason is complete and final in relation to what we now have and all that we can have, that it defines the actuality of reason. In this dogmatic, often technical, power-saturated, and partial form, such constrained reason may be used to obviate what reason as learning ultimately depends on, the capacity for reflective, public self-critique. Without this, what is claimed as reason becomes arrogant, imagining itself to have solutions to social problems it does not have. It also becomes an easier target for those who want to dismiss democratic reason altogether and, with it, democracy itself.

In identifying reason as a whole with the unjust assertion of interests or the justification of particular emotions and the blocking of others, for example, greed over empathy, sociology generally rejects reason, mostly by simply ignoring it, and accepting the case against it to be well-founded. In other words, sociology identifies the absence of self-critique built into the actual operation of reason by self-interested or pathologically disoriented groups, but in many cases, it then goes on to extend that to the very idea of reason itself. As against this tendency to dismiss reason, it will be argued here that reason must be a core concept of sociology, and here that also means a critically theoretically revised account of sociology. Reason involves an affirmation of a possible state of the world. Such affirmation is paradoxically essential to the critical enterprise as a whole, dating back to Kant, even if modified in a multitude of ways. Such affirmation not only allows the specification of how justified standards of validity must operate in society but also how these standards guide critical insight into needless societal suffering.

Against much of its recent treatment in many disciplines, the idea of reason should stand in its own name and not be denied or hidden behind other concepts whereby the intellectual legacy of reason could be surreptitiously used, what Apel calls performative contradiction (Apel, 2001; Habermas, 2007). From Kant through Peirce and beyond, the conscious and controlled use of reason is essential for the building of what Honneth calls rational societal universals (Honneth, 2004), while also acknowledging that reason is constantly engaged with, and also frequently in tension with, that which lies beyond it in the way of feelings and natural and social forces. What counts as reasonable at a given time may well be found deficient in the light of learning processes accomplished and ultimately consolidated through reasoning, in the dual context of existing knowledge, and its phenomenal reconsideration. Learning, understood as collective learning, is indispensable to reason, already implicit in Kant's transcendental ideas of reason as species-wide capacities. Yet, collective learning is another neglected concept in the social sciences, and its contribution accordingly is not recognized, in spite of some suggestive sociological work in the critical theory tradition (Eder, 1985; 1999; Miller, 1986; 1992; 2002; Rosa, 2019; Strydom, 1987; 2009). None of this must deny the need to be mindful of potentials for its abuse in regimes of domination when asserting the positive power of reason. According to Kant, reason was conceptualized as constantly necessitating its own self-critique, asserting that at its core it consisted of the practice of critique and that therefore reasoned critique was essential. By contrast, contemporary forms of social thought regularly decouple critique from reason.

On the basis, as supposed in the foregoing, of the intrinsic relatedness of reason and the possibility of a reasonable society, the question underlying this book is how can a self-critical but still collectively orienting use of reason be envisaged, given that the activity of reasoning is intrinsic to human forms of life and that forms of reasoning even about the same object domain have different and often opposing normative implications? It is from this premise that the book turns to Habermas's concept of communicative reason in the wider context of the history of reason in both philosophy and sociology. I leave the details of the architecture and implications of Habermas's theory to later chapters. For now, I want to say that in the light of requirements of validity as well as critique, the orientation to communicative reason is fundamental in offering a concept of reason that is intrinsically self-critical and designed to be, in appropriate ways, both general and universal while at the same time differentiated. Only a concept of reason that can demonstrate its own modalities of self-creation and dissolution, that is intrinsically and evidently self-critical and fallible, could both make manifest the human dependence on reason and also make its permanently self-critical function inescapable. To even begin to utilize Habermas in this manner is challenging in the light of the deafness of the social sciences, by and large, to the concerns of *The Theory of Communicative Action* (hereafter *TCA*) (Habermas, 1984; 1987). Many obstacles lie in the way in the form of the reception of the theory in the social sciences, but also in philosophy, and not least in critical theory, as well as some intrinsic problems with the theory itself.

These latter problems, faced with the task of showing how reason is one way or another intrinsic to the many expressions of contemporary social sciences, lead in the text to follow to going backwards in time to Peirce in order to deepen and expand Habermas's communicative epistemology in a thoroughly sign-mediated direction. Such a move pushes the account of reason in a more radical cognitive direction, showing how the operations of individual and extended social 'minds' make use of sign-mediated reasoning capacities that cannot be dogmatized into one, enduring, and unassailable canon of what is reason. The sign-mediated approach clarifies issues of the relation between consciousness and reason, the ontology of reason within the idea of a reasonable society, and the different facets of reasoning and world creation in a way with similarities but yet considerable differences from Habermas, who like his great collaborator, Apel, himself drew off Peirce. The use of Peirce's sign-mediated approach also clarifies matters with which contemporary social philosophy and the philosophy of social sciences have commenced a renewed grappling, matters to do with the relation between ontology and epistemology, and between them both and methodology.

The adjustment of focus arising from putting the theory of communicative action in a more definite relation to Peirce's sign-mediated approach opens the theoretical-methodological path to a modern form of critical cognitive sociology in which reason is placed at the centre. While Peirce, as suggested, offers the

## 6   Introduction

means to deepen Habermas's approach, and while, conversely, Habermas places his approach instructively in proximate relation to both classical and modern sociology, the account of cognitive sociology provided here tries to blend them both in the service of a societal theoretical architectonic through an account of a sign-mediated, communicative, fallible demonstration of the operations of reason, including its perverse and pathological manifestations. Included in this approach, whose first task is to make manifest the various sources and operations of reason, is the second task of portraying how, from this basic cognitivist societal architecture, a normative theory can be advanced that addresses what kinds of reasoning in what kinds of contexts could bring about 'progressive' social change, where the validity standards for such change must also be defined.

Such standards should be both procedural in the sense of how a reasonable society should democratically organize itself and substantive in the sense of what should be goals of concrete reasonableness. In the relevant critical theoretical literature, the former is addressed from an intersubjective, deliberative perspective, and the latter is generally more concerned with the actual state of society, specifically the degree to which it could be regarded as concretely reasonable. These divided moments are often interpreted along the lines of a conflict between ideal procedural theories and non-ideal accounts of actual societal arrangements. This in turn mirrors the long-held distinction between the potential of reason and the bad rationality of existing society. This distinction characterizes much of the latent controversy of modern critical thought. It encapsulate show critical theorists respectively emphasize an intersubjective epistemology that might hold the key to bringing about a better society, or an ontological critique of existing society in whose interstices potentials for a better society can be discerned, and accordingly whether critique should be grounded immanent-transcendently or 'merely' immanently. Read in terms of reason, such distinctions ask whether the modernity-long shift from a metaphysical objective reason towards subjective reason, including the intersubjective form of the reason we can 'give ourselves', has eliminated any prospect of an objective reason? Such an objective reason would attest to the reasonableness of societal arrangements, that is, a justifiable, society-immanent, rationalization process. Certainly, the distancing of sociology from reason can be partly explained by the apparent impossibility of any longer advancing an encompassing objective reason of 'the whole', a goal that early critical theory in the Marxist tradition could still negatively assert by bemoaning its absence while also asserting its potentiality. Any possibility of such an objective reason today rests on the relationship between democratization and society. If neither the fact of democracy in the narrow sense nor that of a dispersed and polycentric society is given predominance, then the hope of objective reasonableness lies in the nature of the cognitive principles and process forms that could carry their appropriate mediation. For this task, quite a different kind of meta-theoretical account of the dynamics and – relative – statics of contemporary society is needed than sociology on the whole has provided. The book will outline the elementary features of such an account.

## Critical Cognitive Sociology, Second-Generation Critical Theory, and Peirce

In the text to follow, to pursue the above goals, a number of intersecting branches of knowledge will be related. The most insistent such branch will be a critical cognitive sociology – first to be outlined in Chapter 2 and then revised and deepened multiple times more –, the second-generation critical theory of Apel and Habermas, and the semiotic tradition developed first by Peirce. The aim is to address how the mature advancement of a sociology that incorporates the logic of inquiry in the Peirce tradition, oriented towards reason, reasoning, and reasonableness, would significantly benefit the furtherance of both critical theory and sociology generally. Much has stood against the realization of such a vision of sociology, ultimately built on the substantial, though not full, de-transcendentalization of German idealism. A good deal of the explanation for the limited adoption of a manifest concern with reason in sociology has emanated from the way in which the idea of reason has been generally diffused in the last two centuries, that is, as a technical, repeatable, rule-governed accomplishment. Such an account was influentially criticized by early critical theory – Horkheimer's *Eclipse of Reason* being a symptomatic text – and then a little later in the influential writing of Toulmin, to name just a few important currents of a rethinking process that contributed to important intellectual change in the second half of the 20th century (Horkheimer, 1982; Toulmin, 2003). Yet, while these texts offered a powerful critique of the dominant understanding of reason as formal and instrumental, they also envisaged its necessary rehabilitation in the wider register of an equilibration of forms of reason and rationality. Within a wide swathe of later critical theory that continues to be inspired by the first generation, and more broadly still in post-structuralism, the step to the rehabilitation of the idea of reason by contrast has not been emphasized. Within critical theory, the original Marx-inspired diagnosis supplemented by Weber's rationality theory has consolidated itself, become extended beyond the initial cultural Marxism of the theory, and taken on an ever more encompassing critique of western 'scientistic' thinking, utilizing critical concepts like alienation, reification, and estrangement in multiple forms. Though this critique remains an important moment in diagnosing and addressing the problems and iniquities of our contemporary world civilization, it is necessary to take distance from it in certain important respects if a critical sociology is to be able to balance the negative dialectic with what Badiou calls the 'affirmative dialectic' (Badiou and Nancy, 2018, 104), a step Habermas also emphasized in *TCA* but a step laden with the potential for ambivalence.

Nonetheless, the form of communicative critical theory advanced by the second generation of Apel and Habermas is of intrinsic inspiration for the task of rehabilitating the affirmative dialectic. This intellectual movement also opens the way for a potential transformation of sociology. This path has thus far not been extensively followed by the several generations of sociology that accompanied or followed the clear definition of this stir of thought in *TCA*. In critical theory itself, the idea of communicative action has had significant import, though far from decisively so, and this import has been more prominent in philosophy and law, though it is also

8  *Introduction*

in sociology (Miller, 1992; Eder, 2007; Strydom, 2011; O'Mahony, 2013; Brunkhorst, 2014). More generally than in the reception of the second generation, the tilt to political and social philosophy, as well as to political and legal theory, has come to encompass much of what is generally understood as critical theory among critical theorists themselves, with consequent damage to Horkheimer's original ideal of the co-elaboration of philosophy and the social sciences. Though often alluded to, in fact, this ideal has very little traction in contemporary critical theory. This leaves a noticeable sociological deficit in the current form of institutionalization of critical theory.

As is by now reasonably well-known as a basic fact, but not widely understood or incorporated, both Apel and Habermas built much of their second-generation departure through an innovative reception of Peirce, stemming from Apel's pioneering book (Apel, 1995). There were a number of compelling attractions in Peirce. Through the theory of abductively guided reasoning, it could combine the phenomenological hermeneutic and Wittgensteinian emphasis on disclosing meaning with the Kantian concern for validity. Through its modal logic, it could present the Hegelian emphasis on potentiality and becoming in a form compatible with the linguistic turn. Further, through this modal logic, it could get beyond the Kantian restriction to possible experience by taking on Peirce's experimental testing of validity against reality. Through the emphasis on both Peirce's derivation of his categories and his account of the long-run discovery of the true or right, it could develop an immanent-transcendent methodology of inquiry. Through his category of thirdness as mediation by means of signs, it could escape the besetting and limiting dualisms of various knowledge traditions by combining formal communicative mediation of subject perspectives of external objects with recognition of the mind-independence – relatively for social objects – of these objects. On this basis, a critical-reflexive theory of argumentation could be advanced, formally grounded in the structure and process of mediation and yet in a way that at least potentially could be made substantively relevant. This would also mean a decisive move beyond post-Cartesian philosophy of consciousness. Through developing Peirce's version of intersubjectivity, deriving from his interactive, inferential pragmatism, in the later light of social phenomenology, it could follow him in the direction of social, objective ethics of rational justification. Through Peirce's doubt-belief model, favouring 'really socially present' doubt as opposed to radical paper doubt, it could advance the Hegelian-Marxist project of social integration based on justice. It will already be clear that in these commonalities, I have blended out different emphases of Habermas and Apel – especially from the 1990s onwards – on various matters in the interests of showing the general relation of second-generation critical theory with Peirce. Though the two towering second-generation figures do differ on certain matters, there is still sufficient overall consistency to speak of a distinctive second generation and to draw out the importance of their combined reception of Peirce.

Even if the legacy of the second generation has actively continued in critical theory, though in recent times more hesitantly, the relation to Peirce has languished. At least it has done so in the sense of a direct relation to Peirce's own thought. One of the key objectives of this text is to put that relation once again on the agenda and to take as its decisive import a normatively and empirically salient account of sign-mediated reasoning, where such reasoning is understood in the double sense of general, societal reasoning and intellectual reasoning about society. Yet, for all the remarkable erudition, Apel's widely recognized contribution to Peirce studies, and Habermas's extended essays on him, it is necessary in certain respects to go beyond this path-breaking second generation.

The broad lines of the idea of advancing the communicative innovation of second-generation critical theory take on board the following themes that also serve as a more detailed list of the book's aspirations. These various themes are far from separate, and it is indeed difficult to separate them even for expository purposes, though it has its value. The first theme, addressing the theme of inferential reasoning, involves the application of Peirce's semiotic frame to the theoretical-methodological task of analyzing issues on a societal scale. The fulfilment of this task will require elaborating on both Peirce and second-generation critical theory in the direction required by a theory of society with both normative and theoretical-empirical claims. This ineluctably needs attention to be given to the wider societal contexts of reasoning through argumentation, where the latter is understood through all of subjective, intersubjective, transsubjective, and objective frames. The semiotic architecture of Peirce allows for the intermeshing of different feelings, reasons, and facts along the rails of the process of signification. Along similar lines to Adorno, it is not a nominalist classifying exercise in which manifest observations can be classified within conceptual containers (Adorno, 2019). In fact, while concepts remain fundamental, their operations and effects cannot be grasped without consideration of the wider semiotic process that ever impels them forward. Such a semiotic architecture, critically theoretically elaborated, also allows for a wider and more dynamic account of the complex relations between meaning, validity, and critique.

The second theme is the emphasis on the distinctive modal theorizing of critical theory drawn down from the idealist tradition (O'Mahony, 2023; Strydom, 2023). This entails attending not only to the factual reconstruction of existing societal trends but also to identifying tendencies within the trends, including tendencies that oppose the direction of the trends. In this way, a normative moment is interjected between the factual and the potential, where normative commitments to desired changes are justified by identifying suppressed potentials. The task is not simply to gesture imaginatively towards a possible different future but to show how interfering conditions that block a better future could conceivably be overcome. Such a modal frame is critical to a theory with reconstructivist intentions, but it is also critical to provide a better sense of what reconstructivist critique might entail for actual states of society, in the light of the normative commitments of critical theory and in the light of the various kinds of critique it utilizes. It is also critical to the realization of the immanent-transcendent form of the theory.

A third theme is to offer more thorough-going cognitive foundations to modify the dominant 'asociological' normativism of critical theory. Such a revision should not deny the necessity of normative commitments, but attempt to show what is

## 10   Introduction

normatively discernible and justifiable amidst the vortex of contemporary social change in the light of general validity standards. It does not attempt to show this in some once-for-all sense, but only within the necessary fallibilism and learning orientation of the theory. Such a theme is designed to explore both cognitive processes of the genesis of normative conjectures that could be validated and the roles of cognitive structuring in the validation process at different societal levels. So far as sociology and cognate disciplines have been communicatively transformed, and the significance of discourse increasingly emphasized, it needs some form of higher-level theoretical scaffolding. Its absence, or insufficiency, indicates the need for an elaborated social ontology towards which the book attempts some modest steps. Such a social ontology should be able to show the nature of the procedural aspirations of the theory, both in relation to democratization and in the logic of inquiry, while also being able to criticize and propose actual normative arrangements. Further, in relation to procedures, Habermas's account of the democratic and wider societal implications of different normative political philosophies – from liberalism, through republicanism, to deliberative theories – does not adequately reflect their societal anchoring and the constitutive powers of the kind of theorizing currently being proposed (O'Mahony, 2013). As a type of democratic theorization of the appropriate rationalization of the lifeworld, Habermas, while pointing in the right direction, leaves unclear the relationship between reasoning, good and bad, and forms of rationalization. The proposed architectonic in the book seeks to correct for that in various ways, above all, by exploring a methodologically productive path between ideal and fact by means of a semiotic epistemology.

The following chapters take up the challenge raised by these themes. Its goal is to offer an approach on how to take forward ideas of the second generation with a view to exploring the adequacy of their normative foundations. A guiding assumption is that critical theory evinces a degree of consistency over its various generations but that the second generation remains distinctive in fully embracing the communicative turn and intrinsically building this dimension from Peirce fortified by other traditions. It can be disputed to what extent Habermas, in the end, follows Peirce relatively closely or gives equal or higher place to speech act pragmatics and social phenomenology within his overall 'idealist-realist' type of position. Nonetheless, it is contended here that overall the Peirce-type position, coming from the joint project of discourse ethics with Apel, had the more determining influence viewed over his entire oeuvre. There is no doubt that the balance in Apel lies with the Peirce tradition in spite of his immense philosophical and social theoretical erudition in the way he also draws variously from analytic, phenomenological, and, more diffusely, sociological sources. There is much productive that remains to be said on the relationship of Apel and Habermas to Peirce. However, that is not the present goal. It is rather to take forward key dimensions of the second-generation project within the framework of a cognitive sociology that itself builds substantially on Peirce and associated intellectual developments. Inevitably, Habermas's version of communicative reason, especially the social theoretical framework of *TCA*, provides a backdrop to pursuing such a goal. The essence of the goal is to advance societal theoretical conceptualization by developing an account of communicative reason within critical cognitive sociology, that is, a sociology that understands itself as lying within the tradition of critical theory. The book will also examine how adequately recent theorists in sociology have addressed the intellectual space of reason and reasoning, with a view both to incorporating such resources and to address the wider aim of suggesting a new kind of departure in critical sociology that better aligns it with critical theory.

Through all of this, a number of key semiotically mobilized concepts for understanding the role of reason will be central. The basic concepts will first be outlined in Chapter 2 as a prelude to the survey of contemporary sociological approaches to reason in Chapter 3. They will then undergo further development throughout the text. In considering the relation between sociology and reason, it will be argued that the development of reason within sociology, at least in terms of any kind of 'affirmative dialectic', is disappointing. Nonetheless, it will also be claimed that adapted sociological ideas are essential to grasping the societal operation of reason both as it is and as it could be. Much of sociology, and at least some parts of the other social and human sciences, have followed a particular version of the linguistic turn. However, they have not been strongly orientated towards a version of communicative reason. Sociology remains indebted in most of its major traditions to a variety of nominalism, what Adorno describes as classification of facts that excludes the autonomy of generals (Adorno, 2019 (1964), such as the evolutionarily produced and transcendentally anchored principles of the cognitive order. In most branches of sociology, such generals, that is, general concepts that by virtue of their evolutionary necessity have a cognition-directing a priori status, are set aside in the pursuit of either structural or phenomenological theory development. Often today, the two are brought together in an inexplicit tandem, for such theories share the desire to distance themselves from autonomous generals.

The point of unity in much of contemporary social science is to work up from 'below', to confer status on individual instances that either can – apparently – be fruitfully aggregated into explanatory causal theory or generate knowledge on the ramifications of a local situation or the horizons of a subject. Over the last half-century or so, the once confident capacity for generalization of the first tradition, the causally oriented analytic one, became progressively weakened in at least academic sociology by attacks on the very idea of the general by the interpretive-phenomenological tradition, leading to strong relativist tendencies in the discipline generally. This is so even in those many cases where these relativist tendencies have a kind of normative underpinning associated with modern movements for social change. The success of this relativist tendency undoubtedly moved the discipline away from the previous characteristic kind of emphasis on the general. Neither society-integrating functional assumptions nor social class constituting societal conditions were subsequently accorded anything like the same authority to explain social outcomes. At best, they appeared to belong to a time of greater societal stability, respectively theoretically secured by either order-conferring institutions or by the inhibiting effect of class domination.

This state of affairs is particularly troubling for critical sociology, and all the more so for critical theoretical sociology. Critical theory advances the standard of

12  *Introduction*

the normative well-being of society as a whole, increasingly recognizing institutional and identity plurality and with a pronounced emphasis on law and democracy. The rule of democracy is the rule of reason, understood democratically.
However, how can the fragmented world of the social be grasped in terms sufficiently general to allow for normative evaluation and for the reflexive feeding back
of normative conjectures about a better possible future to reflective publics? This
latter goal of a reasonable society requires the capacity to comprehend its actuality
and its possible tendencies in order to seek to influence or change them. Already
present in second-generation critical theory in the 20th century was the beginning
of an answer. Neither the differentiated institutional order nor a collective class
actor was the key to understanding what was general in society. That instead lay
in the Peirce-inspired idea of a communication community that could indefinitely
pursue the ideal of reasonableness, an idea that also inspired Dewey. It could not
do so on the basis of empirical generalization of societal trends, for these were
evanescent and contradictory and formed no basis on their own for a judgement of
reasonableness. However, it could at least imagine doing so on the basis of a reading of the effects of reason. Such a reason could be used to demonstrate the contradictory, dysfunctional, and unjust playing out of partial rationalities that do not join
up, and yet also show how such rationalities could be joined up on a different basis
as part of the democratic implications of a communicatively understood reason.
Nonetheless, beyond this signal statement, the Peirce-derived idea of the general
as a continuum of meaning for social scientific application still needs considerable
further work, towards which some beginnings are made later in this text

## Sociology and Communicative Reason

These ideas have generally not gone down well in sociology and related disciplines. Under the general negative connotation of the widely used designation of
'ideal theory', specifying normative principles a priori is assumed to be opposed to
ideas of struggle, materiality, embodiment, factual contingency, and the inescapable
relativism of modern societal orders. For critical sociology and a range of related
disciplines concerned with critique, a priori principles, no matter how understood,
were assured to occlude concern for mechanisms and experiences of domination
of all kinds. Rejection of ideal theory often goes hand in hand with the rejection of
ideals per se. What characterizes much of modern critical thought are two poles:
forces that conduce to domination and agencies that try to act against it. Mediation
through cognitive generals, the complex infrastructure of sense-making through
signs, is neglected or opposed in favour of a concentration on either causal forces,
phenomenal experience, or their combination. If, to the contrary, cognitive principles, reasoning processes, ideal-forming capacities, and other mediating cultural
powers are brought to the centre, then the perspective that animated sociology for
a long time regarding the societal consequences of the dominant configuration of
reason is altered. It becomes a question of assessing to what extent societal rationalization processes conform or deviate from their normative implications, where
these implications can only be made manifest as a consequence of the reflexive

operations of democratic discourse. Without consideration of such discourse in the widest sense of the societalization of democratic ideas, the evolutionary implications of communicative coordination cannot be grasped. From this vantage point, sociology's concern for generalization had commenced too low down based on the attachment of normative validity, good and bad, to factual trends. It only addressed questions of validity on an observational basis without being able to adequately justify either the normative criteria underpinning this assessment of trends or, increasingly, the specification of the trends themselves in the context of increasing societal complexity.

Thus, in sociology and the social sciences, the idea of reason is generally either disregarded or opposed on the grounds that it is a priori regarded as epistemically untenable and also as indiscriminately legitimating forms of domination. Dominant actors, embedded in social systems and status hierarchies they wish to maintain and extend, are assumed to canalize the power of 'reason' for their own ends. They specify formal means-end operations of subjective reason and associated ideas of rational coordination of pivotal economic and political institutions that secure the interests of the powerful. Actors who espouse faith in political liberalism are often seen as the worst offenders from this vantage point in that they continue to hold to the perceived empty promises of bourgeois-liberal ideology. This is also, of course, in part the critique of Adorno and Horkheimer, but there it is not a question of giving up on reason as a whole. Instead, taking up specifically Horkheimer's account, the need to balance the problematic dominance of the means-end logic of subjective reason with the broader ends of objective reason, reason in the world, is advanced as a desideratum. The question then arises: What might be the form of objective reason, and what are the implications of this form of reason in society in the light of modern pluralism and complexity at multiple levels?

This question underpins the book, though the answer is not in the form of any reversion to an objective reason that has been discredited so far as it is assumed to reveal the 'teleological' destiny of society. Rather, objective reason has to be aligned not simply with subjective reason but also with intersubjective reason. From the standpoint of objective reason within these forms, issues arise as to what is general in society, since generality is intrinsic to it. In the account offered here, what is ultimately general in society emerges through communicatively achieved normative coordination mediated through cognitive generals, for example, Habermas's universal pragmatic validity standards. The normative complex that emerges in appropriate circumstances in the light of such standards may have the potential to bring about a just coordination of social relations. This is, broadly conceived, the formula of the second generation of critical theory. Perhaps the most besetting challenge for such an account is to advance ideas of potentially just societal coordination in the context of societies and inter-societal relations that regularly appear to have little trace of it. The affirmative potential has, therefore, to be squared with the negative consequences of how the world has gone on and is still going on. The challenge of theorizing by means of coordinative cognitive generals is that general consequences of a negative kind must be addressed as much as those that are advocated for the societal good. The theoretical implication is that a societal ontology

14    *Introduction*

is needed that can plausibly explain one or the other set of outcomes, or, very commonly, mixed forms combining the reasonable and unreasonable. Normative accounts that depend on reasonable ideal standards, as opposed to the fixed principles of justice that are used in the stereotype of ideal theory, must advance such an ontology. Ineluctably, this means that the cultural endowment of human forms of life needs attention, since it may be assumed to hold the key to understanding the possibilities of societal reasonableness. It is at least widely agreed now that it must be reflexively applicable postulates of such reasonableness and not the adaptive causal laws of nature-dominating evolution that lie at the heart of just social change. Of course, there are many different views on what or who could carry the necessary postulates, what material forms and agentic powers might block them, and what contradictory and self-defeating genealogies characterize them.

### The Societal Ontology of Critical Reason: Key Concepts

Not surprisingly, a significant range of key concepts arise in any attempt to characterize the societal ontology of reason. These concepts will be introduced gradually as part of the task of building such an ontology, a task that becomes more explicit as the book progresses. A number of them, however, will receive explicit mention at this point as the main steps in building that ontology. These are, respectively, that of a sign-mediated societal ontology itself, validity, and critique. Regarding the first, the concept of a societal ontology of reason, what is to come is an attempt to build an account of the structured yet dynamic interplay of key elements of signification that both enable reason and decide on its societal prospects. These elements vary dramatically not only in space but also in time, from the fraction of a second of a moment of consciousness to the millennia of evolutionary time. What is critical here is the attempt to frame such an ontology within the Peirce-inspired idea of the three categories underlying signification, firstness, secondness, and thirdness, categories that will be properly introduced in due course (Chapter 5). In this attempt, the dimension of rational mediation through the category of thirdness will be shown to be critical. Yet, the ontology places reason in this sense of rational mediation within the broader contexts of feelings, with its affinity to the category of firstness, and facts, with its affinity to secondness, which are also essential to signification. Such an ontological framework is socially theoretically elaborated over a number of chapters, Chapters 5 through 7, and allows variously for the defence of valid forms of reason, the self-critique of reason, and the critical identification of unreason.

A second key concept is validity, which will be linked to Peirce's concept of interpretant, how a sign determines another sign within a discourse – or culminates in a habit. By extension, validity arises from the interpretation path that signs follow or should follow in interpretation. It involves the channelling of signs through schemata composed of relevant interpretants. These schemata, composed of paths of 'interpretantation', provide a warrant to act in various possible ways. These possible ways encompass a variety of possible cultural ends or motives that underpin human action and the forms of their expression. Successive processes of validation, understood as following prescribed patterns of interpretation or introducing innovative ones, are at the very heart of Peirce's concept of reasoning. Validity is, of course, systematically addressed in *TCA* by means of validity claims arising from different kinds of speech acts. Here, the account is developed differently than from speech act theory, operating instead through an account of inferences, even if the premises of speech act theory and pragmatics remain important in the background. The concept of validity thus extends from Habermas's emphasis on cognitive and intersubjective validation processes ('validity claims') all the way down to validated conceptions or actions on the normative plane. Validity is understood as a series of standards that delineate the steps of reasoning and its outcomes, steps of reasoning that are woven together into the overarching logic of relations that characterize Peirce's account of thirdness. Such a relational logic modally encompasses both the recognition of endless possible paths of validity and the communicative means to select actual paths from these possibilities.

A third key concept is that of critique. Its relation to validity is intrinsic. Critique ranges from small-scale but cumulatively significant adjustments to instituted regularities of any possible kind right up to radical criticism and reformulation of what was previously deemed generally valid. It is the latter kind of critique that is most of interest to critical theory, but it is nonetheless bound up in various ways with the former kind. If the former kind can be understood as the inevitability of incremental deviation from regularities over time in routinized situations, it can also encompass the protracted building up of perceptions of injustice in the consciousness of groups such as women, workers, and the colonized to name but three examples. Such consciousness, if it is to beget social change, has to become explicated, become in some way or other cognitively powerful and resonant. Frequently, when consideration is given to the concept of critique, it is assumed to be confined to emancipatory movements and the legitimacy of their claims. However, the lesson of the Enlightenment is that critique is a ubiquitous and essential component of human mental life. The Enlightenment itself simply shifted the level of universality of critique so that it was understood as intrinsic to human powers of learning and the ability to change social arrangements. Critique became inextricably linked with the capacity for change and learning at various levels and of various kinds. In this way, critique and the impulse to learn that it animates became understood as a universal cognitive capacity. Of course, critical theory has an intrinsic interest in radical emancipatory critique, but this should not be supposed to mean that critique is confined to emancipation only, as in the reflexive critique of reason. Critique that seeks to block Enlightenment or proposes anti-emancipatory norms still utilizes the universal critical capacity, albeit in a way that negates its emancipatory import. Critique at some level and of some kind is unavoidable. Moving forward from this, critique is embedded, following the outline of validity, into the evolving societal ontology for the potential generation of a reasonable society. Validity standards give form to critique and potentially become reconstructed as a result of their operations, which will here be presented as sign-mediated in form.

These basic concepts will be embedded in the overall immanent-transcendent architecture that is central to critical theory, whose form and implications will be

## 16  Introduction

developed at various stages in the book. There are a whole range of other concepts that will enter into the account as it proceeds, such as, in no particular order, alienation, reification, freedom, learning, pathology, justice, discrimination, solidarity, democracy, and others. These concepts have enormous scope in their own right, and it is no exaggeration to say that to address them 'properly' would take many books. The intention here is to contribute to the development of critical theorizing by not focusing exhaustively on encompassing theoretical articulation at all levels, nor to demonstrate the theoretical-empirical value of the exercise. It is rather to contribute to essential meta-theoretical elements of an account of communicative reason. A book with this kind of ambition is inevitably going to leave much out. In this case, I must leave out, for example, in-depth illustrative cases of critical cognitive sociology, in-depth analysis of social and institutional structures in the light of the theory, and the contributions of multiple intersecting intellectual traditions, to name but a few. All of this further work will have its time, but for now, the task is to make sufficiently visible a certain kind of meta-theoretical approach that ultimately bears on the relationship of modern sociological critical to critical theory generally. As a sociological theory, such an approach also aims to have wider implications for sociology beyond its immediate employment in critical theory. Ultimately, sociology is not understood as a defined and final disciplinary space in which the validity of certain kinds of knowledge can be contained. It is instead viewed as a distinctive contribution to knowing and knowledge beyond specific individual disciplines altogether. Sociology is only one sphere of knowledge, and for that sphere to properly make its contribution, it must put itself forth in inter- and trans-disciplinary spaces in activities of reciprocal and general learning.

## References

Adorno, T (2019 (1964)) *Philosophical Elements of a Theory of Society*. Cambridge: Polity.

Apel K-O (1995) *Charles Peirce: From Pragmatism to Pragmaticism*. New York, NY: Prometheus.

Apel K-O (2001) Regarding the Relationship of Morality, Law and Democracy: On Habermas's Philosophy of Law (1992) from a Transcendental-Pragmatic Point of View. In: Aboulafia MBM and Kemp C (eds) *Habermas and Pragmatism*. London: Routledge.

Badiou, A and Nancy, J-L (2018) *German Philosophy: A Dialogue*. Cambridge, MA: MIT Press.

Brunkhorst H (2014) *Critical Theory of Legal Revolutions: Evolutionary Perspectives*. New York, NY: Bloomsbury.

Eder K (1985) *Geschichte als Lernprozeß? Zur Pathogenese Politischer Modernität in Deutschland*. Frankfurt: Suhrkamp.

Eder, K (1999) Societies Learn and Yet the World is Hard to Change. *European Journal of Social Theory*. 2(2): 195–215

Eder K (2007) Cognitive Sociology and the Theory of Communicative Action: The Role of Communication and Language in the Making of the Social Bond. *European Journal of Social Theory* 10(3): 389–408.

Habermas, J (1984) *The Theory of Communicative Action, Volume 1. Reason and the Rationalization of Society*. Boston, MA: Beacon.

Habermas, J (1987) *The Theory of Communicative Action, Volume 2. Lifeworld and System: A Critique of Functionalist Reason*. Boston, MA: Beacon.

Habermas J (2007) *Moral Consciousness and Communicative Action*. Cambridge: Polity Press.

Honneth A (2004) A Social Pathology of Reason: On the Intellectual Legacy of Critical Theory. In: Rush FL (ed) *The Cambridge Companion to Critical Theory*. Cambridge: Cambridge University Press.

Horkheimer M (1982) *Critical Theory: Selected Essays*. London: Continuum.

Miller M (1986) *Kollektive Lernprozesse: Studien zur Grundlegung einer Soziologischen Lerntheorie*. Frankfurt: Suhrkamp.

Miller M (1992) Rationaler Dissens. zur Gesellschaftlichen Funktion Sozialer Konflikte. In: Giegel HJ (ed) *Rationaler Dissens. zur Gesellschaftlichen Funktion Sozialer Konflikte*. Frankfurt: Suhrkamp.

Miller, M (2002) Some Theoretical Aspects of Systemic Learning. *Sozialer Sinn.* 3(3): 379–422.

O'Mahony P (2013) *The Contemporary Theory of the Public Sphere*. Oxford: Peter Lang.

O'Mahony P (2023) Critical Theory, Peirce and the Theory of Society. *European Journal of Social Theory* 26(2): 258–281.

Rosa Hartmut. *A Sociology of Resonance*. Wiley and Sons. New Jersey, NJ. 2019.

Schnadelbach H (1998) Transformations of the Concept of Reason. *Ethical Theory and Moral Practice* 1: 3–14.

Strydom P (1987) Collective Learning: Habermas's Concessions and Their Theoretical Implications. *Philosophy and Social Criticism* 13(3): 265–281.

Strydom, P (2009) *New horizons of Critical Theory: Collective Learning and Triple Contingency*. New Delhi: Shipra Publications.

Strydom P (2011) *Contemporary Critical Theory and Methodology*. London: Routledge.

Strydom P (2023) The Critical Theory of Society: From Its Young-Hegelian Core to Its Key Concept of Possibility. *European Journal of Social Theory* 26(2): 153–179.

Toulmin SE (2003) *The Uses of Argument*. Cambridge: Cambridge University Press.

# 1 Habermas, Communicative Reason, and the Social Sciences

In the late 1970s and early 1980s, Habermas began to give more systematic attention to a theory of communicative reason, a theory that in some form or other had underlain his writing from his first major work on the public sphere in the early 1960s. While previously in those earlier writings up to the late 1970s, he had come to speak of a two-pole social theory built upon the twin categories of work and interaction, now the interactionist part began to subsume the labour part; the latter was redefined as either a specific kind of systemic communication or a category of instrumental action that stood beyond communication, though not with the normative connotations that the category of work had previously enjoyed.

There are many detailed accounts in the literature on Habermas of how this more developed communicative interactionist architectonic takes shape. Most of them follow Habermas closely and then, in various ways, qualify, criticise, or seek to extend the perceived achievement. Looking back on this process of consolidation of a paradigm from the distance of several decades, it does not, broadly speaking, appear to have succeeded. More striking, viewed from the standpoint of its reception, is the sense of uncertainty and inconsistency in the overall account, even if there is also for some a clear sense of a radical breakthrough in key respects. While for these, especially certain kinds of critical philosophers, there is a sense of belonging to a paradigm that still appears ongoing or progressive, for others in the critical theory tradition whose main roots are in the social sciences the paradigm did not in the end appear truly fruitful. Though mindful of the continuing significance of the breakthrough, I belong more to the latter orientation, troubled by the inability of modern critical theory of society in the Habermas tradition to really take flight within the social sciences. But, unlike many in the social sciences who more or less completely reject it, my view is different. What is needed is to build on this theory, as it remains the pre-eminent attempt to join philosophy and the social sciences in the common pursuit of an account of democratic reason. Where necessary, it should also be reconstructed, in some respects quite radically. Even if few, in the social sciences at least, explicitly concern themselves with an account of democratic reason, few would discount the importance of this theory if they were among those to accept the centrality of reason to modern society. No adequate social scientific response to the contemporary state of society can cut remotely deep enough without addressing this

DOI: 10.4324/9780429060571-2

*Habermas, Communicative Reason, and the Social Sciences* 19

centrality, though exactly what kind of response is offered will depend on how democratic reason is elaborated.

This chapter will try to capture what Habermas understands by communicative reason, the building block first adumbrated in *The Theory of Communicative Action* (hereafter *TCA*), to what would become an extended theory of democratic reason in the later *Between Facts and Norms* (*BFN*) and beyond (Habermas, 1984; 1987; 1996). It will, at the same time, indicate where the challenges lie for developing the theory to reach the goal of influentially engaging with the contemporary social sciences, both as they are and still more as they could be. In this light, it might perhaps be beneficial to first expend a few words on the apparent mutual opacity between Habermas's account of communicative reason and those social sciences as they currently stand. This relationship is, of course, complex, and its full explication would comfortably take a book of its own. However, the term 'mutual opacity' already tells much of the story. Social scientists in the main found – still find insofar as they at all take the theory into account – the various signature moves of the theory to be unconvincing where not baffling. The quasi-transcendent idea of idealizing presuppositions of communication, the emphasis on rationalization, familiar from Weber but now conceived in a new way, the introduction of a universalistic, symbolic background frame such as lifeworld, and the determination to de-emphasize the category of consciousness just when the concern with agency or the subject appeared to be a pressing matter for much social scientific consideration, all appear inconsistent with various directions of travel of the social sciences.

This identification of mutual opacity can, of course, be comprehended in two ways. It can, on the one hand, indicate that Habermas's theory is too far from the concerns of the social sciences and, indeed, that it fails in its intentions to be relevant in this regard. On the other hand, it may be that it is the intellectual limits and dispositions of the social sciences themselves that should be called into question, especially the awkward and confusing transition from a mainstream positivism to the relative dominance of a mostly inexplicit, determinedly intra-mundane social phenomenology of various kinds.[1] Let me now outline a little more systematically how this mutual opacity, or, maybe expressing it a little more tractably, mutual non-transparency, might be grasped as part of the wider project of bridging the distance lying between. Once this preliminary outcome has been completed, I will then turn back to a specific treatment of Habermas's theory.

The idea of communicative reason does not begin with Jurgen Habermas, but rather as Habermas himself acknowledges with Peirce's semiotizaton of idealist philosophy. Yet, his two-volume *TCA* is the most identifiable text in its contemporary sociological and wider interdisciplinary reception (Habermas, 1984; 1987). These volumes, the later *BFN* and a range of other contributions, comprise Habermas's voluminous contribution to the subject (Habermas, 1996). The later work after TCA developed communicative reason as *democratic* communicative reason and, more generally, his conceptualization of reason was increasingly articulated as a philosophical project. Nonetheless, the often-repeated narrative of Habermas's abdication from the social sciences after *TCA* is often overstated, as he never lost his preoccupation, both normative and empirical, with the relationship

20   *Habermas, Communicative Reason, and the Social Sciences*

between democracy as the privileged site of normative reason and society generally. With his remarkable sociological imagination, he reads very differently from most philosophers concerned with the question of reason and democracy, as, for example, his account of the role of the public in the core-periphery model in *BFN*.

*TCA* remains important to the understanding of communicative reason in the general sociological community, even if its reception remains relatively limited. This applies both to the critical sociological community, which in some way aligns with Habermas and seeks to strengthen the sociological dimension of critical theory, and to the diffuse general understanding of this work within the discipline and the broader social sciences. Speaking from the vantage point of those who have broad sympathies with the project, and who are not surprisingly mostly to be found in sociological critical theory, the approach beginning in *TCA*, subsequently extensively elaborated by Habermas, has a range of achievements, where 'achievement' is here understood more as a productive opening of a path rather than something established:

- It marks an important step from the primacy of the paradigm of consciousness to that of intersubjective communicative processes located in trans-subjective culturally structured contexts, and it also clearly differentiates the various possible dimensions of communication, moving away from the dominance of discourses of truth to address the equal importance of discourses of right (normativity) and authenticity (subjectivity, ethics).
- It opens up a multi-level architectonic that interrelates the historically dominant traditions in social science and places them, through the theory of validity, in an intrinsic relation to critique; it, therefore, interrelates both the objectivating perspective (system) and the 'subjective' or action-oriented perspective (lifeworld); it also incorporates the relation between the quasi-transcendental – those presuppositions of reason essential for world-making that arise in the world and yet can reach beyond its existing state – and the immanent, the possible or actual realization of reason as fully justified norms; and, finally, it incorporates the relation between emancipation and domination, actual or potential.
- In this spirit, and animated by a reading of the development of philosophy of social science, it moves away from one-dimensional sociologies – for example, the empirical-analytical frameworks that dogmatize the factual world of the external 'is'; the many sociologies today focussed non-critically on 'symbolic structures' and processes; and the demiurgic nature of a critique only negatively directed at structures of domination – to a multi-dimensional critical communicative theory, characterized by a differentiated, complex, social ontology that variously incorporates transcendent society-enabling pragmatic meaning orientations, convergent immanent normative horizons (democracy), multi-facetted symbolic lifeworld structures with associated communicative practices, objectively experienced systems, and subjects that are – at least potentially – competent in reasoning but also blocked from its utilization by inhibiting power structures and societal misalignments.

*Habermas, Communicative Reason, and the Social Sciences* 21

- Communicative reason is at the core of developing an emphatic social episte-mology in the pragmatist tradition, which remains Kantian in its universalism – through discourse ethics – but breaks with Kant's transcendental subjectivity and the 'direct normativity' of practical reason towards the 'detranscendental-izing' necessity of reconstructing the communicative presuppositions and net-work of discourses that condition perspectives of all kinds, including political ones. Habermas, therefore, detranscendentalizes[2] Kant's noumenal realm, em-phasizing instead the formal pragmatic, contestable presuppositions of commu-nicative interaction and, on this basis, developing a procedural understanding of morality and law.
- Habermas's multi-perspectival vision of sociology – and the assertion of a com-municative social epistemology – remains a normative sociology, identifying *general* social conditions that produce either domination or emancipation, in-cluding 'realistic utopian projections' as deliberative democratic collective learning projects; hence, while identifying both the factual and normative significance of the communicative rationality at work in society, it privileges normativity – rightness – in the form of the action-coordinating, democratic normative moment, and, accordingly, advances the idea of an inextricable re-lationship between communicative reason – and unreason – and a normative sociology.

Overall, through these epistemological, ontological, and methodological orien-tations, Habermas significantly contributes to the theory of society. Nonetheless, as indicated, his theory has not been particularly resonant within the contemporary social sciences, especially sociology, where his social scientific work was most concentrated, leaving aside the minority tendency to affirm some dimensions of it. In fact, both explicitly and implicitly, there has been a general sociological scepti-cism towards the project of communicative reason over the last nearly four decades. To understand the potential for a more fruitful relationship between communicative reason and sociology, in part going beyond Habermas, it is important to recognize the degree of enhanced scepticism towards the idea of reason in sociology and the social and human sciences more generally. A few general theses can be advanced here to give a sense of this scepticism and its sources:

**Suspicion of reason:** Much of sociology, inspired by parallel developments in other disciplines, now dedicates itself to the critique of reason, viewing that which stands in the name of reason as actually a cloak for various forms of hegemony. This is coupled with a lack of attention in sociology to democracy, often conceptualized as a mere rationality of power-based governance of either Weberian or Marxist provenance, a general hostility to transcendental argu-ments, and, often coupled with this hostility, antipathy to any form of utopian-ism. In some contrast and for some time, there has been increasing interest in situated social experience hermeneutically accessed through investigations of subjectivity in context, an interest associated with a preference for 'the other of reason' as a type of non- or anti-reason in different combinations, and greater

## 22  Habermas, Communicative Reason, and the Social Sciences

importance attributed to the practical experience of embodiment. Generally, this is exhibited in various ways, both internally complementary and contradictory, in post-modernism, post-structuralism, new social movement theories, feminist theory, and practice theory, including habitus theory, among other sources. Contemporary sociology, in a rather dramatic contrast to its traditional orientation, exhibits a concern for the new, especially the process of 'subjective' becoming, as it is concretely manifested and tentatively present in subjects and their relations, inducing it to turn away from a project such as that of communicative reason, understood as a variation of a discredited, a priori enlightenment reason, and as consensual, even affirmative, and normative 'in the wrong way'.

**The negative critical model:** There is a widely shared perception in sociology that the 'affirmative' moment in communicative reason pays insufficient attention to the implications of sociocultural structures, especially structures such as capitalism and other racial, gendered, and further imputed forms of structured hegemony that deny subjugated groups the necessary freedom to be or act differently. This concentration of sociology on domination, empirically and especially normatively, fuels a critical perception of its attributed absence in Habermas. This is closely connected to sociology's general preference for exclusively negative critique in which social arrangements are criticized according to various standards, a type of critique that does not imply commitment to disclosing a different possible future, or, rather, only doing so in an implicit and indirect manner. This is supplemented by a suspicion of critical theory's reconstructive methodology, geared towards an encompassing normative redirection of society, that understands itself, at least as regards Habermas, as a critique of an assumed transcendent asocial idea of reason.

**Turn away from macro-sociology:** Within contemporary sociology, with its emphasis on bodily experience and the situated context of action, there is scepticism of those sociologies that, like Habermas, emphasize the indirect, collectively operating, and mediated nature of social orders, in his case comprising of both systemic steering media and the cultural structures of the lifeworld. Sociological approaches generally, even where not stated explicitly, tend to favour the dialectical paradigm of structure and action, which, while not different in all respects, does operate with a significantly different combination of ontology, epistemology, and methodology to Habermas. The relative lack of resonance of *TCA* was perhaps secured by the perceived unacceptability of its reconstructive critique of functionalist reason. Instead of being interpreted as a form of critique of functionalism, Habermas's recourse to Parsons was taken to be its rehabilitation and, together with its supra-subjective assumptions, to remove sociological understanding too far from actors' horizons and/or situated contexts of action (Joas, 1988). This contradicts what has become widespread in sociology, where attempts at normative diagnosis and prognosis are contemplated not in terms of societal reconstruction but in terms of actors' perceptions of states of affairs and associated critical sentiments understood through hermeneutical interpretation of actions or lived experience. Insight in this latter register is generally accomplished without the perceived need of an encompassing, formal, structured social ontological framework. It is thus a critique of Habermas's systematic intentions in *TCA*, especially his development of Parsons, from whom most sociology has long sought to radically distance itself, but which, as at least a systematic theory of society, in some respects remains attractive to the normative reconstructive goals of critical theory (Honneth, 2011). Instead, for much contemporary sociology focussed on the paradigm of the subject, ontological perspectives can be brought in 'selectively' on an 'as needed' basis, giving rise to a type of latent a priori of the differentiated, actor-carried, forms of the social as opposed to the a priori of society to be found in Habermas – and classical and neoclassical social theory too. But still, big structural categories such as capitalism *are* brought into play in sociology where perceived to be needed, even if, in contemporary sociology, they are generally not systematically theorized.

In various ways, these evaluations of sociology hold a certain substance over against Habermas's account, even though they are not fully explicated in the critical discourse of sociology, either specifically towards Habermas or more generally in the critical theory of that provenance. For example, Habermas's move away from the paradigm of consciousness to that of communication, while not ignoring, certainly elides the issue of the subject and does indeed open the question of how he addresses the other of reason, especially because he does not systematically or consistently address intra-psychic communication or the communicative mediation of 'inside' and 'outside' over time.[3] Furthermore, the elaboration of negative critique in Habermas suffers for the above reason – the presumption of achievable reasonability by subjects in the present – and for other reasons, the relative neglect of interfering structures, such as, the multiple structural sources of inequality.

Nonetheless, the paradigmatic emphasis on the dialectic of structure and action within sociology leaves it with many problems, for example, there is little or no general synthesis of the implications of actual or possible forms of subjectivity and intersubjectivity. This is partly due to the absence of a comprehensive social ontology, and, correspondingly, no adequate *genetic* account of the formation and transformation of structures. In general, the contemporary sociological field offers insights into plural, symptomatic situations of social action and interaction without macro-social synthesis, insights that cumulatively tend to produce confusing and piecemeal knowledge. This is manifested in syndromes in sociology that are symptomatically related to the dismissal of dimensions of communicative reason present in Habermas's account, such as:

- At most, a hesitant embrace of any form of the communication paradigm, even beyond Habermas, and certainly no will to extend it to adequate treatment of mediated multi-level semiosis with a corresponding inability to understand and explain mechanisms of social variation; it operates – mostly – as forms of constructivism that lack a cognitive-communicative, semiotic core.[4]
- A lack of interest in collective and societal learning processes, especially disregarding those cultural-evolutionary formed collective cognitive structures that undergird society and any form of societal change; sociology remains overall

# 24   *Habermas, Communicative Reason, and the Social Sciences*

attached to a paradigm of societal semantics that inhibits understanding of the *processes* of cultural variation and resultant normative stabilization taking place through, roughly articulated, progressive or regressive collective learning.[5]

- Sociology frequently utilizes a confusing and over-drawn all-or-nothing kind of normative judgement where, in its different formulations, either structures overwhelm actors or actors appear to have extensive and unrealistic levels of freedom to construct structures. Ultimately, the cognitive-communicative and immanent-transcendent type of understanding of normativity present in much second – for example, Habermas – and third generation – for example, Honneth – critical theory remains largely absent in sociology. In general, there has been a penetration of a totalizing critique of logos into sociological thinking with no real estimation of the costs, ontologically, epistemologically, methodologically, and normatively, nor adequate consideration of alternatives that would advance an account of a better, logically grounded rightness.

Hence, sociology struggles to incorporate the insights of Habermas's *version* of communicative reason, even where willing to consider it, partly because of the discipline's self-imposed limitations and partly because of limitations in Habermas's account – to follow below. This is either – or both – a result of general constitutive problems or specifically the relative non-development of a communicative perspective within sociology, despite a loosely formulated communicative turn within the discipline.[6] But if this is the case for general sociology, what about the fate of communicative reason within critical theory, especially where critical theory addresses classical sociological problems? This exhibits a very mixed story. In one sense, considerable time and attention have been given to general accounts of Habermas's position, including various kinds of critical attention. Indeed, it could be said that relevant books and journals have copious and, in their way, valuable materials of this kind. However, in another sense, it is not easy to discern any significant shifts beyond Habermas in the foundations of the theory. In other words, for all the attention given to the elaboration of the theory, there is very little attention given to fundamental questions such as the epistemic value of the speech act theory on which his account of reason rests, to the sufficiency or otherwise of his account of Peirce – noting especially the lack of an account of inference in Habermas –, to the balance he strikes in his incorporation of analytic philosophy into a communicative theory, and to the potential for the theory's *application* within a critical reconstructive approach to societal issues and social change generally.

This observation stands although critical theory has undergone something of a sociological turn in and through Axel Honneth, among the most influential of the third generation's theorists. Honneth's extensive use of sociology, even more pronounced and systematic in his later work, is embedded in a Hegelian framework that allows very little room for the further development of an emphatic idea of communicative reason. His extensive utilization of the neoclassical theory of Parsons, for all the insight he is still able to derive from it, is not a road to the furtherance of communicative reason. Rainer Forst's theory of justification, whose Kantian architecture is closer to Habermas, does develop an insightful sociologically informed account of noumenal power; however, it does this largely from a standpoint that does not fully do justice to the original sociological – for example, the contexts of lifeworld and system – and linguistic-theoretical architectures – for example, the speech act account, of communicative reason (Forst, 2015). More generally, in critical theory, a turn against the concept of communicative reason may be discerned, whether in the form of its post-colonial and feminist critique or simply by its quiet sidelining, often in favour of a return to first-generation motifs of alienated subjectivity inspired by a sense of the other of reason. Finally, the outstanding philosophical contribution of Habermas's close colleague, Karl Otto-Apel, to the elaboration of communicative reason is very infrequently introduced into contemporary debates in critical theory, indicating, as clearly as anything else, a lack of comfort for good or bad reasons with the core status of the theory (Apel, 1998).

The reception of the theory of communicative reason within critical theory has some points in common with the sociological reception, for example, the concern with power and with structural domination, the emphasis on motifs associated with the other of reason in some cases, and the quite widespread emphasis on identity in civil society, but in one key respect, it has a different focus. Unlike sociology viewed overall, critical theory cannot even go on without consideration of the overall normative state of society. For this reason, it is more inclined, as exemplified in the influential case of Honneth, to consider such a state through the theory of society. Moreover, critical theory from its very outset is bound to consider such a normative judgement beyond merely the negative critical standard dominant in critical sociology but also through a disclosing critique that could identify societal potentials that could be actualized. For these reasons, in the light of the great practical urgency in contemporary times of advancing a more coherent normative sociology, the relationship between reason and sociology has much to gain from exploring how it is received in critical theory, which, of course, also has a strong sociological dimension. The cumulatively unfolding question of by what means a reconciliation can be achieved between a sociology with critical intentions and the key tenets of communicative reason will thus be further advanced by such consideration.

In the remainder of this chapter, I turn to address three main motifs within Habermas's theory that throw light on these issues. In the outline of these sections, respectively on his communicative epistemology, the strategy of detranscendentalization of transcendental philosophy, and the formulation of a new kind of social ontology, I will seek to follow Habermas's argument, with occasional indications of the need for critical elaboration, both in relation to the theory itself and its further relation to the social sciences. I will conclude with some critical points that indicate tasks that must yet be taken up to develop the intentions of the theory. Yet, for the gaining of any insight into what communicative reason might mean today and for its further development through the vast capability of sociology – even if much of this capability is only latent in its contemporary articulation – Habermas's contribution is taken here to be indispensable.

## The Communicative Epistemology of Reason

With the advent of the TCA, Habermas began in earnest the task of what he would later call the 'cultural embodiment of reason' (Habermas, 2003, 218). This cultural embodiment of reason was premised upon the task of the detranscendentalization of reason, that is to say, stripping from reason the particular kind of transcendental foundations that Kant had outlined in his critical philosophy, especially the assumption of the incognizability of the thing-in-itself. After the various strands of the linguistic turn, beginning in the late 19th century with its gradual displacement of the philosophy of the rational subject, epistemology should now instead assume the potential cognizability of everything that is a reasonable object of knowledge, even if not currently knowable. Habermas indeed associates this 'desublimation' of reason with the impact of the linguistic turn. What counts as knowledge is mediated through the supra-individual linguistic forms implicated in its construction rather than through the minds of isolated, rational subjects. How knowledge of any kind could be asserted through this process depended both on the semantic idealization of common social meaning making possible the frame of reference, and on pragmatic idealizations whereby interlocutors understood how to coordinate their respective validity claims bearing on potential common social meaning.

The emphatic moving of the foundations of reason in a social, intra-mundane direction through the linguistic turn also allowed Habermas to breathe new life into Weber's account of rationality in *TCA*. He claims that any sociology concerned with the theory of society is bound to address meta-theoretically the rationality implications of the guiding concepts of action, methodologically, the rationality entailed in gaining access to the object domain, and, empirical-theoretically, in the account of modernization as rationalization (Habermas, 1984, 7). The core innovation is the expansion of Weber's rationality types away from the latter's predominant focus on means-end rationality towards communicative rationality. The teleological implications of the means-end concept of rationality are retained in Habermas's acceptance of the monological quality of 'cognitive-instrumental' rationality, but, beyond this type of rationality, it is essential to properly recognize the communicative rationality that coexists with it and, in key respects, has precedence over it. Communicative rationality has this precedence since it is indispensable to securing the motivational and coordinating foundations of a feasible common life, from which monological rationality is, in a certain sense, derived. Hence, from this vantage point, Weber's rationality theory appears doubly truncated. Truncated in its own terms by virtue of its concentration on two rationality types, purposive and value rationality, from which in the end the first emerges as completely dominant, and effectively ignoring the role of others that he identifies, traditional and affective rationality. From Habermas's point of view, it is also truncated in its failure to incorporate a concept of communicative rationality, how human agents relate to one another and how they might accordingly consensually coordinate their understanding and actions. This is a decisive shortcoming for grasping society as an achievement of *social* coordination. It also echoes, in certain respects, Horkheimer's critique of subjective reason as formal and solipsistic when taken

*Habermas, Communicative Reason, and the Social Sciences* 27

in isolation (Horkheimer, 1974 (1947)). However, while Horkheimer principally sought to mediate subjective and objective reason, Habermas's primary goal is to mediate subjective and intersubjective reason and to give the latter primacy. Objective reason, in the sense of the rationalization of the lifeworld, a rationalization that in turn makes possible symbolically generalized steering media, is not excluded but is now understood to emerge from communicative processes.

Habermas's general intention is to add the action and knowledge coordinating features of communicative action to other kinds of action types and their corresponding rationality that can be utilized non-communicatively, viz., the 'cognitive' rationality bearing on the factual status of states of affairs and the teleological rationality embedded in the intentional statements underpinning plans of action. However, the ultimate standpoint that crystallizes in TCA is that non-communicative rationality must ultimately be understood as secondary to communicative rationality. For it is through the latter kind of rationality that socially operating validity can be attached to the interlocking plans of action of actors. This type of rationality would also be properly intersubjective, hence, following Mead, neither reducible to the individualistic bias of the theory of action nor the intention-less determination of social structures (Joas, 1997).

Habermas's account of communicative rationality is thereby set against the cognitive-instrumental rationality that, though empiricism, has deeply marked the modern era with, as he puts it, its 'connotations of successful self-maintenance made possible by informed disposition over, and intelligent adaptation to, conditions of a contingent environment' (Habermas, 1984, 10). On the other hand, if we start from the communicative employment of propositional knowledge in assertions, 'we make a prior decision for a wider concept of rationality connected with the ancient concept of logos.' (ibid). This concept of communicative rationality brings with it 'the central experience of the unconstrained, unifying, consensus-bringing force of argumentative speech in which different participants overcome their merely subjective views and, owing to the mutuality of rationally motivated conviction, assure themselves of both the unity of the objective world and the intersubjectivity of their lifeworld.' (ibid).

Communicative rationality, including its basic and enduring distinction from cognitive-instrumental rationality, is understood in terms of the evolutionist sequence of the emergence and development of modern societies. With their advent, the unity of an encompassing worldview becomes dispersed into three formal world concepts: those relating to the objective world accessed through a concept of truth, the social world accessed through a concept of rightness, and a subjective world accessed through a concept of sincerity. These three basic concepts are described as 'formal pragmatic', and they serve as the indispensable criteria for the raising and redemption of validity claims in communicative action. Communicative action accordingly entails the intersubjective coordination of validity claims occurring within the social relations of communication. With regard to three criteria, he says that under 'the functional aspect of reaching understanding, communicative action serves the transmission and renewal of cultural knowledge; under the aspect of coordinating action, it serves social integration and the establishment of group

## 28  *Habermas, Communicative Reason, and the Social Sciences*

solidarity; under the aspect of socialization, it serves the formation of personal identities' (Habermas, 1984, xxiv).

These three criteria are consistent with the validity claims of truth, rightness, and sincerity/authenticity, and they also correspondingly delineate the three structural dimensions of the sociocultural lifeworld. The lifeworld, for Habermas, is a trans-individual, social phenomenological structure that forms a background to all communication. Normally, however, the lifeworld does not operate through communicative action in the strong sense. It instead facilitates the routinized reproduction of valid knowledge, solidarities, and personal identities by means of its established structures of orientation. Communicative action only properly comes into play when an aspect of this 'taken for granted' lifeworld is problematized. Habermas's idea of the lifeworld appears to be in part drawn from or at least to have some analogies with Peirce's concept of thirdness[7] in that, firstly, the lifeworld is a collective structure intrinsic and essential to the social enablement of meaning. Meaning, one might say, is stored ready for use in the lifeworld and then brought down into practical situations to impart sense to practices. Secondly, the lifeworld is ordinarily reproduced through habits of sense-making that do not always require communicative action in the emphatic sense of problematization, learning, and cultural reorientation. Thirdly, this 'problematization' through communicative action is analogous to Peirce's idea of the radical operation of the logical interpretant in the form of habits of habit change (West, 2017). Nonetheless, these analogies can only be offered to serve explication of the concept of lifeworld, for, as will be seen later, there are also significant differences between the categories of lifeworld and thirdness, most notably the non-appearance of logical relations of reasoning in Habermas's account.

The account of communicative rationality in *TCA* is of an 'evolutionist' kind. The critical learning process leading to the societal instantiation of communicative action arises in the transition to modern society, notably the transition from unified magical worldviews to formal world concepts. These formal world concepts, respectively, the differentiated sense of objective, social, and subjective worlds, are both the source and context of validity claims. Modern societies in this account appear as being at the top of the pyramid of societal types, both requiring a special kind of communication and, by virtue of that communication, capable, when organized correctly, of institutionalizing life-supporting and life-enriching competences. In developing his account of modernity in *TCA*, Habermas drew off Parsons's frames of references – typified concepts that must be made coherent in their interrelation –, including the four elements of the AGIL scheme, adaptation, goal attainment, integration, and latency, the three spheres respectively of culture, society (institutions), and personality that made their way into the lifeworld concept, and the dynamic phases of societalization ranging from primitive society to hierarchical societies organized around a state, and, finally, to modern societies. In effect, Habermas builds his description of society on Parsons and thereby runs the associated risk of adopting an evolutionist understanding of the ineluctable superiority of modern societies. It should be stressed that Habermas does not merely take over Parsons's schema. His social phenomenological account of the lifeworld and adoption of a corresponding Luhmannian phenomenological concept of systems actually build a missing reflexivity into Parsons framework, an issue identified as a problem with Parsons's theory from as early as the 1940s in his debate with Alfred Schutz (see chapter 3). Yet, TCA is substantially dependent on these Parsonian frames of reference even with the added dimension of communicatively achieved reflexivity. It creates a distinct uneasiness as to their theoretical compatibility, as the objectivism of Parsons meets the intersubjectivity of communicative reason.

One further dimension of Habermas's theory of communicative rationality is its strong pragmatic or interactionist quality. Communicative action, and hence communicative reason, occurs between co-present interlocutors, nearly always understood as two such interlocutors who raise and test validity claims in their speaker/hearer roles. Though the validity claims encompass not just the normative orientations that underpin their communicative relation but also its propositional or semantic dimension and its sincerity or truthfulness dimension, it is nonetheless the intersubjective *relation* to these validity claims that is emphasized. In other words, to speak in relation to one validity sphere, what is emphasized by Habermas is that the given locution is intersubjectively assumed to be valid – or not – in relation to its claim to truth by the interlocutors rather than how such a claim to truth might arise in the first place or what it might consist of. In arriving at this perspective, Habermas in *TCA* builds upon Austin's distinction in his speech act theory between locutions, illocutions, and perlocutions, where locutions refer to the content of what is said, illocutions refer to the act of saying it, and perlocutions refer to the consequences or force of it having been said. Of these three, Habermas emphasizes the illocutionary component, the actual commitment made by the speaker and assessed by the hearer in the *speech act* itself. The component of perlocutionary force is understood by him to be associated with strategic communication based on the intentions of the speaker. Both perlocutions, with their intentional dimension, and locutions, with their relation to substance, are dissociated from the focus on illocutionary, manifest meaning in his account of communicative action, where all that can be at issue between two interlocutors is communicating in strict good faith.

This account has a strongly normative interactionist quality. The good faith interaction between co-present interlocutors is at the core of communicative reason, and, accordingly, for Habermas must also be at the core of societal learning processes, including democratization. In later work, Habermas turns this insight in a deliberative direction in *BFN* and elsewhere. Communicative action, as the highest form of communication and learning, is now additionally transposed into deliberation in the political and legal systems. Of course, such transposition is not in principle different from the earlier treatment of communicative action, but the focus on deliberation produces a more pluralistic range of interlocutors and expanded institutional implications. Though the scale of communication has expanded, Habermas nonetheless holds to the co-present interactionist model in his account of deliberation.

The contribution of discourse ethics also becomes more apparent in line with the later deliberative focus. While I will eschew more extended treatment of the various technical aspects of discourse ethics, especially the operation of the Discourse and Universalization principles, it is important to note certain facets

30  *Habermas, Communicative Reason, and the Social Sciences*

of great importance to the overall theory. In line with the threefold core validity claims of communicative action, but especially in this respect those of rightness and sincerity/authenticity, in the discourse ethics frame there are certain unavoidable yet counterfactual 'pragmatic presuppositions' that are fundamental to argumentation. These are that (i) no one capable of making a relevant contribution has been excluded; (ii) participants have equal voice; (iii) they are internally free to speak their honest opinion without deception or self-deception; and (iv) there are no sources of coercion built into the process and procedures of discourse (Habermas, 2008). Habermas means by 'counterfactual' the meta-standards to be applied to ordinary discourses while aware that such ordinary discourses will rarely meet these elevated standards. Such claims are analogous to truth claims, where Habermas follows Dummett's idea of the standard of 'justified assertibility' (Habermas, 2018, 50–51).[8] The question arises as to whether these counterfactual standards have an immanent-transcendent grounding or are just higher-level immanent, a question I will take up in the next section. What is clear, though, is that the interactionist paradigm is extended and, at least in principle, made society-side by these universalistic presuppositions of discourse, a move that proved indispensable for the extension of the theory into legal-political contexts of societal coordination.

### The Turn to Detranscendentalization

Habermas is associated with a project of the detranscendentalization of reason or, put differently, the cultural embodiment of reason (Habermas, 2003). The concept of detranscendentalization is, in some respects, deliberately ambivalent. It points to the 19th and 20th centuries attempts to move away from Kant's transcendental emphasis on the capacity of the knowing subject to make sense of the world of appearances. Detranscendentalization appears in this light as a decentering of the essential powers of the knowing subject in this sense in favour of a medium-theoretical type of weak transcendentalism as that which underpins – for Habermas – the conditions of rational linguistic communication. This weak transcendentalism takes expression in the form of the counterfactual pragmatic presuppositions already discussed above. In *BFN*, Habermas is careful to separate communicative from practical reason. Communicative reason is a means of engaging in argumentation guided by the 'weak' transcendental necessity of a range of idealizations, viz., ascribe identical meaning to expressions, connect utterances with context-transcending validity claims, and assume that addressees are accountable, that is, autonomous and sincere with both themselves and others. However, practical reason goes beyond this to the 'must' of a rule of action, whether, as he puts it, 'the latter "must" can be traced back deontologically to the normative validity of a moral law, axiologically to a constellation of preferred values, or empirically to the effectiveness of a technical rule.' (Habermas, 1996, 4).

Hence, communicative reason makes an orientation to validity claims possible, but it does not supply any practical orientation for managing practical tasks. It thus falls short of a practical reason aimed at motivation, that is, a guiding of the will. It may be inferred, then, that participants engage in communicative reason as a type

*Habermas, Communicative Reason, and the Social Sciences* 31

of open-ended exploration of options. In discourse ethics, a relevant distinction is made between the kinds of procedural norms underpinning such explorations from the 'material' norms that might emerge from practical reason. As Wellmer explores in *The Persistence of Modernity*, the communicative rationality of the procedure is no guarantee that the right norms will actually be arrived at, for this depends on the appropriateness of the reasoning, not just its communicative conditions (Wellmer, 1991, 160–161). Such a procedural account of communicative rationality also has the tendency to preclude innovative forms of perception that tend to run ahead of normative deliberation. This applies even in those not-so-many cases where the deliberation is institutionally adequate in the first place to fully address the substantive innovation being explored.

Reflecting on immanent transcendence in BFN, Strydom observes on the deliberate tension between idea and reality, between validity and facticity, in Habermas's understanding (Strydom, 2015). This tension operating variously through what he calls 'validity operators' such as presuppositions, idealizations, and counterfactuals creates the effect of 'innerwordly transcendence' within social practice. Innerworldly transcendence is understood by Habermas as the basis of any possible learning process. These learning processes, activated by the validity operators, are made possible by 'transcendental' leaps beyond what is immanently known to be the case, but leaps that must also return to the immanent in the sense of rationally evaluating what could be possible. They thus facilitate understanding where it did not previously exist, the immanent outcome of transcendentally enabled learning, and the realization of potentiality in the sense of Hegel. Strydom accordingly understands the difference between facticity and validity as that between immanence and immanent transcendence. Validity, standing on the transcendental side, is therefore to be understood as the regulator of meaning; only through explorations of validity in learning processes can fundamental leaps between existing immanent understandings and hitherto unrealized but possible capacities be accomplished. This transcendental validity structure is therefore at the heart of the constitution of the social, subjective, and objective conditions of human social life.

The transcendental validity structure emphasized by Habermas is a formal pragmatic one. The transcendental validity operators of truth, rightness, and sincerity/ authenticity are a context-independent set of validity claims that guide learning processes. In *Truth and Justification*, he describes himself as sharing a Kantian pragmatism with Hilary Putnam based on the transcendental fact that subjects capable of learning cannot not learn (Habermas, 2003, 213–235). If so, for Habermas, the learning occurs through the coordination of the three basic validity claims, whose formal possibility lies beyond the situation of co-present communicative interaction. In fact, the other way round, they make such interaction possible in the first place. When operating in the right conditions, the learning is associated with a good-willed search for inclusive and non-coercive agreement, whose most basic *orientation* emerges from the context-independent, 'weak' transcendental foundations of formal pragmatics.

This social or collective learning has two distinct characteristics. The first is that it has in itself, so to speak, and to a greater or lesser extent, a quality of egalitarian

32   *Habermas, Communicative Reason, and the Social Sciences*

coordination of social life through communication. When this coordination is extended to democratic communication, one can speak of the learning of this type as having the quality of learning how to achieve democratic coordination. Taking the span of Habermas's work into account, including the internal changes of emphasis, the greatest burden of this first kind of learning is in the register of democracy, with the emphasis on democracy moving from latent to manifest in Habermas's work over time. Given the nature of the initial weak transcendental premises of the theory, this democratic learning has a procedural quality that is compatible with its normative interactionist premises.

The second kind of potential learning is more ambivalently constructed. Its outcomes, actual changes in the logics underlying social practices, are located in symbolic structures of the lifeworld. The mechanism is that of rationalization of the lifeworld. While this rationalization is said to take place through the lifeworld, social systems organized around general media of communication, money, and power separate themselves out from this lifeworld and continue another kind of purposive rationalization. This second kind of learning is generally treated by Habermas as secondary to and supportive of the first kind. The very organization of the lifeworld understood according to the neo-Kantian, Parsonian frames of culture, society, and personality ultimately underpin communicative action, and, since communicative rationalization is basic to the constitution of the lifeworld in the first place, the process of rationalization of the lifeworld has no evident independence from communicative action. Hence, this characteristic 'deontological' feature of the general theory of communicative action was already well established in TCA. This created problems for the theory, already apparent in *TCA*, where the lifeworld itself appears as normatively 'positive', yet subject to colonization by a system that has separated itself out from it and reverse colonizes it. By contrast, problems internal to the lifeworld itself are not directly addressed, leading to significant limitations in the critical thrust of the theory.

An interesting aspect of this question of learning, bearing on Habermas's account of detranscendentalization and the cultural embodiment of reason arises in debate with his great collaborator, Karl Otto Apel (Apel, 2001). Apel's more emphatic transcendental-pragmatic view disputes the importance Habermas attaches to the principle of democracy and his concomitant dependence on an optimistic reading of the degree of 'post-conventional' rationalization of the lifeworld that, as Habermas understands it, meets communicative action half-way. Such a construction allows Habermas to understand the rationalization of the lifeworld as, in principle, democratization, hence the assertion of the dominance of the principle of democracy, the view that democracy could be fully realized in modern societal conditions. Habermas is, therefore, able to propose that the principle of democracy operating through communicative rationalization of the symbolic foundations of all social practice, the lifeworld, could take on a universalistic aspect, that is to say, the full realization of democracy could be envisaged as a result of communicative learning processes of the first kind sketched above, fundamental *democratic learning*, and supported by the second kind, the post-conventional rationalization of the lifeworld. The post-conventional emphasis, which Habermas

## Habermas, Communicative Reason, and the Social Sciences   33

takes from the developmental psychology of Piaget and Kohlberg, arises, notably in Kohlberg's stages model, from the capacity to reason according to principles rather than – merely conventionally – through perceptions of the consequences of action. This idea of reasoning according to principles closely articulates with the idea of communicative rationality and with the *principle* of democracy.

By contrast with this, Apel thinks that the immanent realization of the principle of democracy is quite far away given the multiple problems that beset contemporary societies, problems that generate a frequently unjust or pathological, even if still essential, operation of democratic institutions. In these circumstances, the idea of a thoroughgoing post-conventional rationalization of the lifeworld appears untenable. At this point, he invokes the continuing necessity of a final philosophical grounding, a Letzbegrunding, of the moral fundamentals of democracy. Such a final grounding would depend not on the immanent operations of democratic discourse as it now stands but upon transcendental philosophical reflection on the issue at hand. Such reflection would not ultimately depend on, even if it would be shaped by, any empirical state of affairs, but instead on a post-conventional, transcendentally guided, process of reaching beyond existing, immanent reasoning. Of course, Habermas's deontological emphasis similarly involves going beyond the situation, but, for him, addressed within the framework of communicative rationality, it has taken on a procedural, legal-political form, and, accordingly, such 'going beyond' could only be achieved by the subjects themselves. In this way, Habermas distinguishes himself from the transcendental pragmatic emphasis of Apel with its premise of the power of an intellectual avant-garde to clarify what must be the moral core of democratic action in each situation, though, for Apel, this does not have the connotation of them acting entirely separately from public reason more generally. Echoes of German history appear to be latent in this difference of views. What the difference brings to the fore from the point of view of a philosophically informed sociology of reason is what constitutes a collective learning process, who might be its carriers, and how the structure of immanent transcendence enters into it?

Further to detranscendentalization, in *Truth and Justification*, the validity claim of truth is decoupled from that of rightness (Habermas, 2003). This occurs because Habermas breaks with his own earlier epistemic conception of truth that he claimed to take from Peirce. In breaking with this conception, he attributes to Peirce the epistemic idea that all engaged in the process of inquiry might agree in the long run to a factual construction of things or states of affairs and that this construction is truth. Habermas's new position, as in *Truth and Justification*, is that a proposition should be agreed to by all concerned because it is true, not be regarded as true as the result of an ideal consensus within the scientific community of investigators or, indeed, any other community concerned with questions of truth. In this way, he takes his leave from his own earlier consensus theory of truth. In this later move, truth acquires a different kind of transcendental structure to that of rightness, which he feels can continue with the older epistemic concept of consensual agreement within the relevant community since rightness lacks the ontological connotation of the facticity of states of affairs that reaches 'beyond itself'. This ontological

## 34 *Habermas, Communicative Reason, and the Social Sciences*

connotation is transcendentally significant, because it goes with the idea of truth as something that exists independently of us and which we can only fallibly grasp, whereas rightness is something that is the product of our actions. Something that might exist can only be grasped transcendentally as possible, and hence truth becomes a transcendental validity standard that orients us towards what might be true in the world. For Habermas, this transcendental quality of possibility takes truth as an idea of reason to potentially stand beyond what we might currently know immanently, though what we do know about the external world is still subject to the immanent standard of 'rationally warranted acceptability'. Warranted acceptability in this sense is no longer to be understood epistemically, that is, as a consensual idealization, in the case of truth, but as a fallabilistic outcome of a discourse built upon nominalistically generated perceptions of an external world. On this basis, the rational discursive moment of truth enters in as this warranted assertibility, but it rests on something else, the nominalistic observation of the world. In other words, echoing Habermas himself, the discursive moment is ontologically constrained by the fact of an external world that we did not construct, and which is independent of us.

Habermas at the same time understands the standard of rightness differently from that of truth, here retaining an epistemic standard of justification, that is, the justification standard of that to which all could agree given the discourse ethical standard of inclusivity, sufficient time, fair argumentation, and freedom from coercion. Accordingly, rightness becomes an immanent matter that does not have a transcendental standard equivalent to that of truth, but it still – somehow – retains for Habermas the unconditionality of a context-transcending validity claim. In an incisive and textually precise way, Strydom outlines what, in the end, appears as a contradictory position in Habermas. Strydom (Strydom, 2019), as above, distinguishes between a validity concept and an achievement concept, where the validity concept is of an unconditioned nature and refers to an infinite cognitive process on some dimension of reality regarding which the mind imposes certain kinds of limits. In the above discussion, truth would be an infinite-limit validity concept in that sense. Such concepts are to be distinguished from what he calls achievement concepts, in which infinite limit concepts are transposed into finite limit concepts such as that of warranted assertability in the case of truth or, as he proposes, warranted judicability in the case of rightness. He argues that, even in the case of truth, Habermas confuses an *achievement standard*, concerned with finite limit concepts, that is, goals in immanent forms of life, with a *validity standard* concerned with the infinite cognitive continuum that lies in part beyond our current cognitive competences, but stimulated by new conjectures, we might utilize to generate new competences in the future.

As Strydom also points out, without the clear articulation of limit concepts and their relations, it is not clear what exactly is Habermas's understanding of immanent transcendence (Strydom, 2019). As a strictly immanent matter for Habermas, how can rightness at all be understood as a form of weak transcendence in the formal pragmatic sense? In this light, what does the kind of context-independent validity that Habermas attributes to it signify? Habermas's account in *Truth and*

*Justification* has the further connotation that, since rightness is something that humans themselves generate, it does not have the ontological implications that truth has, and, accordingly, does not operate by means of a transcendental regulative idea (Habermas, 2003). In this account, rightness does not have objective correlates either, given the procedural emphasis on separating morality and inclination in the deontological purity of norm formation. The emphasis is on separating the horizons of actors from empirical contingencies, interests, and specific dispositions so that they can deliberate impartially. While the search for impartiality is essential to democracy, it is commonly far from clear in norm-formation processes what the right norm is and even how to go about ascertaining it. The epistemic process must be able to assess the consequential implications of rightness norms in the light of their deontological standing. Moreover, such deontological standing in episodes of contested normative innovation is precisely what is at issue. It is in these contested cases, where the direction of what is morally right is being decided, that immanent-transcendent processes come into their own as collective learning processes. It is here that the excluded middle must be opened up with no certainty of outcome. Thus, rival modal projections will be tested in the light both of deontological standards and their consequences, a process that in fundamental cases may well extend over a long time, indeed seem also permanently at issue, as in the examples of labour, race, gender, and ethnicity. In his account of abduction, Peirce argued that Kant too starkly separated the epistemic status of feelings from reasons (Peirce, 1931, 1.35). It is precisely here, where epistemically relevant feelings open up the structure of knowledge, that transcendental engagement is most manifest. Even established reasons rest on feelings, but many reasons are disputed, and even in cases where they may be de facto accepted contain a dimension of differentiated feelings, as in different motives for supporting a reason. Establishing normative innovation, or even understanding the depth structure of disagreement, entails 'sensing' possibilities beyond what currently exists and turning them into potentials, even actuals. Habermas's detranscendentalizing logic tends to obscure the generative implications of such uncertainty and the associated potential for transcendentally guided collective learning.

Unless democracy is thought of as potentially epistemically comprehensive in the capacity to know and control this human-induced external world at which agency is directed, these external or 'externalized' worlds in infinite ways confront some or all human agents as determining contexts over which they may have little or no control. The nature of such worlds is theoretically and methodologically at the core of the social sciences. From a universalist, participatory democratic point of view, such as that of discourse ethics, the goal is to reduce as far as possible, within the counterfactual, limit concept of its unachievable complete elimination, the contingency and lawlessness of the power of these external forces. In any foreseeable world, many such contexts will nonetheless retain distance from prescriptive democratic control, something which in many instances can be defended as a necessary condition of freedom and progressive collective learning, as in others operating as contexts of domination. These human-generated contexts of knowledge, the object worlds of the social sciences, will as much depend on

## 36 *Habermas, Communicative Reason, and the Social Sciences*

immanent-transcendent learning processes as does knowledge of external nature. There is no absolute immanent certainty as to how to normatively intervene in human forms of life. In this sense, the gap between theoretical and practical reason cannot be too wide as moral, legal, and ethical judgements are bound up with one another and with their functional implications, and all take place in situations of interpretation and critique. Analogously, Apel, in his theory of co-responsibility, followed Hans Jonas to argue that in the light of planetary endangerment, Kant's understanding of 'foreseeable consequences' could not be retained in the face of the consequences of enhanced complexity in society-nature relations (Apel, 1987; 1990). This indicates how the results of theoretical reason, which alone could provide the necessary factual knowledge, must be considered in practical reason. It also indicates how constraints imposed by lack of knowledge in conditions of risk must constrain normative judgement, where the lack of knowledge is itself to be scientifically explicated. This does not mean that the consequences of moral commitments derived from moral learning processes cannot constrain contexts of action. This is after all the very essence of democracy. It means, though, that moral innovation is both conditioned by a multiplicity of collective learning processes taking place in all social spheres, not just those formally designated as democratic, and is first explored in the unconditioned context that extends beyond all extant norms. These remarks in brief suggest that the architecture of theoretical and practical reasons bearing on human-made worlds is formally similar and that they are closely interpenetrated. Thus, Habermas's account of detranscendentalization in practical matters goes too far in effectively specifying theoretical reason as immanent-transcendent and practical reason as strictly immanent, even if they have at the same time quite different purposes and procedures of realization. The normative standpoints are not given nor simply worked up in democratic procedures but derive also from the observations of the social sciences, including the observation of interaction. In turn, as will be argued throughout this text, the logic of inquiry of these social sciences can neither escape transcendental operations nor deny they have normative commitments. Thus, even if ultimately chosen by practically situated actors and inserted into practical discourses, validity claims at societal levels of complexity depend on the social and natural sciences – or frequently rather badly do without them.

### The Social Ontology of Communicative Reason

Recently, there has been a turn back towards ontological thinking in the social sciences. In one sense, a certain privilege of ontology over epistemology has always been a hallmark of much mainstream social science with the emphasis on structures that unintentionally emerge through the actions of agents that in turn condition their further actions. A sustained appropriation of phenomenology in the late 20th-century sociology offered one route away from this kind of naturalistic ontology. Such a sociological phenomenology emphasizes constructive operations and, in many but not all cases, subjectivities dialectically embedded in social structures but allowing the power of agency in given situations. This admittedly rather ambivalent opening of epistemological horizons in sociology, often given the name 'the agential turn', involved a turn towards consideration of how agents actively process reality. This emphasis on mental processing, individual or collective, was not only of epistemological but also of ontological significance in that the human carriers became of interest as objective embodiments of social structures as much as subjective processors of meaning. The interpenetration of epistemology and ontology is well-captured in Bourdieu's account of the habitus, where it is presented as both objectively structured and yet capable as a structuring structure of shaping symbolic relations in concrete situations (Bourdieu, 1984). Another important indicator of this modern combination has been the focus on the symbolic 'representation' of reality; representations are taken to be the symbolic depiction by agents of the state of play of a world external to them but influenced nonetheless by the sense they make of it.

In *TCA*, Habermas makes new ontological proposals for understanding social reality. Here, he says that the 'rationality of worldviews is not measured in terms of logical and semantic properties but in terms of the formal-pragmatic basic concepts they place at the disposal of individuals for interpreting their world.' (Habermas, 1984, 45). He also claims later in this passage that one could speak of the 'ontologies' of worldviews, provided that the word is not confined in the classical philosophical sense to the objective world but also to the social and subjective worlds. The formal pragmatics underlying communicative action are intrinsic to the rationalization of worldviews in the lifeworld. Hence, it may be submitted that the threefold formal pragmatic structuration of communicative action and the lifeworld is of both an epistemological, active processing of meaning, and ontological, cultural structural, nature. Indeed, in line with Piaget as well as Bourdieu, formal pragmatics may itself be conceived as a type of quasi-transcendental structure specializing in spectra of validity, variously, truth, rightness, and sincerity. This structure extends the reach of ontology, beyond the traditional semantic idea of the 'whatness' of the objective world towards abstract cultural pragmatic structures that are context-independent and yet formally coordinate the achievement of meaning in communication.

In a commentary on Habermas's 'ontological radicalization', Strydom sets Habermas's ontological account within the broader linguistic turn (Strydom, 2013). In particular, he claims that Habermas's approach marks a step beyond the truth-conditional semantics extending from Frege to the early Wittgenstein and then to Davidson and Dummett. As Habermas himself puts it, with this ontological turn, truth-conditional semantics itself marks a shift away from a nominalist designation of objects. In truth-conditional semantics,

> The meaning of sentences, and the understanding of sentence meanings, cannot be separated from language's inherent relation to the validity of statements. Speakers and hearers understand the meaning of a sentence when they know under what conditions it is true.
>
> (Habermas, 2003, 276).

Habermas then successively claims that speech acts, and, finally, his own formal pragmatics further radicalizes this ontological turn beyond truth-conditional semantics.

## 38   *Habermas, Communicative Reason, and the Social Sciences*

The movement to speech acts involves a shift away from the representational function, the sole concern of truth-conditional semantics, to a wider range of illocutionary forces. Speech acts theory itself remains focussed on individual intentionality, whereas the account of formal pragmatics is intersubjective and hence has a wider and more complete range of what Habermas calls 'ontological presuppositions' (Habermas, 2003, 278), that is to say validity claims and corresponding worlds. The ontological presuppositions of TCA are therefore expressed in its range of interrelated validity claims structured by the cultural lifeworld that provide both distinctive and interpenetrating contexts for these validity claims. The lifeworld encapsulates the results of these validity operations, on one side, as symbolic habits bearing on settled contexts and, on the other, serves as a base for discursive problematization through communicative action.

The distinction in the immediate above between habitual reproduction and problematizing innovation captures a critical feature of Habermas's ontological perspective. It mirrors the distinction between actuality and potentiality that goes back to Hegel, through Marx, and then Peirce. The lifeworld is a horizon of potentiation as well as being a base of action-orienting habits. Human agents are always in it and yet can think beyond it. Hence, ontology should not be thought of as agents semantically representing an actual world that is external to them, as it has done in much sociological thought over the last century and more, but to do with agents always already immersed in the worlds they seek to make sense of but who are capable of thinking beyond this immersion. Potentiality always offers a route beyond actuality, and therefore the immanent-transcendent, formal pragmatic structure of that potentiality is also ontological, a characteristic of the being of worlds that have agents intrinsically within them. For Peirce, this characteristic of potentiality is metaphysical in the sense of a world-constructing reality in which metaphysics, the space of thirdness, may be understood as analogous to a phenomenologically shaped ontology that, like Habermas, is not individualist but collective in its form and communicative rather than monadic.

Returning to the point about Bourdieu's account of habitus, the phenomenological turn in the human sciences entails a quite different, dynamic interrelation of the structured world and structuring agency than that of the classic separation of ontology and epistemology. Hence, for the object domain of the social sciences, this relationship has become more reciprocally responsive. The culturally structured lifeworld forms an ontological context for the epistemic processes of communicative action. Moreover, the interpenetration of validity claims in communicative action fluidizes and makes socially immanent these ontological contexts. Moreover, the specification of the intersubjective construction of the lifeworld by means of the processing of validity claims equally from the three worlds means an extension of ontological considerations from the objective world to the social and subjective worlds.

In conclusion, I would like to raise one further matter regarding Habermas's ontological position that emerges more strongly in his later work, *Truth and Justification* (Habermas, 2003). This corresponds to what has already been observed in relation to his transformed relationship to the category of truth, which, as outlined, moves away from rightness to emphasize truth as a transcendent

*Habermas, Communicative Reason, and the Social Sciences*  39

standard that is different from the immanent and deontological standard of rightness. The ontological implications result in Habermas using terms such as 'the ontological primacy of a nominalistically conceived external world' and opposing it to the epistemological primacy of the lifeworld that should not consume the former's ontological primacy (Habermas, 2003, 33). What is clear here is that, unlike Peirce, Habermas is prepared to specify two separate kinds of epistemology/ontology relation.[9] The first, as already documented above, entails the nominalist strategy of being guided by an orientation to truth to make sense of external, natural objects. The second, which comes with an epistemic emphasis, is directed at the reproduction or transformation of the social world. The identification of these two strategies, which Habermas respectively associates with the natural and the social sciences, is used to show both separate procedures of knowledge generation but also their possible overlap. The overlap gives rise, on one side, to his account of weak naturalism a naturalism that is weaker than a presumed causal determination of the world by underlying natural processes, but it is still strong enough to include these natural processes in evolutionary and socio-historical theories that can bridge the difference between objective and subjective mind. The considerations arising with weak naturalism, notably the genetic primacy of nature over culture, explain why Habermas feels he must countenance such 'bipolar' nominalistic and social phenomenological epistemological/ontological strategies. On the other side, he advances a conceptual realism regarding the social world that emphasizes that it is a product of its construction by 'us' through the operations of extended social mind. This does not mean that such a social world is fully under 'our' control, just that its basic forms are a product of human cognitive activity in the widest sense. This distinction is basically sound, though, as above, Habermas overextends it when he denies rightness an immanent-transcendent form like truth.[10]

### Critique and Elaboration

In these concluding remarks, I will not further expand on Habermas's achievements, for example, the formal pragmatic account of validity, the ontology of potentiality, the extension of the range of validity claims to the social and subjective as well as the objective worlds, the theory of a 'detranscendentalized' cultural embodiment of reason, the social phenomenological account of the lifeworld, and, above all, the delineation of the significance of communicative reason in all of the above. Nor do I plan to return at this point to consider the present trajectory of the social sciences in relation to the fuller development of the theory of communicative reason, which will unfold further as the book progresses. Rather, I am going to take these formidable achievements as given and to lay out some key critical dimensions that point not against the theory as a whole but to ways in which it needs to be revised and further developed. These dimensions serve as indices for the challenges that need to be addressed to extend the theory and make it more sociologically fruitful, especially in the sense of advancing a critical theoretical sociology. I will deal first with some problems in the theory's commitment to consensus, then with issues

## 40 *Habermas, Communicative Reason, and the Social Sciences*

arising in the account of argumentation, then with the relation between semantics and pragmatics in the theory, and then with its bearing on historically arising social change.

### The Consensual Nature of the Theory

The claim that the Habermas's theory has been over-consensual is a repeated one. In certain instances, the critique has merit, but whether and how much depends on how consensus is construed, where the often-asserted view that it should be excluded entirely in order to make way only for dissent and conflict is unacceptable. The latter view, literally executed, is incompatible with a commitment to democracy, which depends on certain universal presuppositions, such as, normatively, certain constitutional norms, and, cognitively, the crucial orienting meta-principles that must guide argument, thought, and action in democratic contexts. The consensual quality derives from the 'good faith' emphasis of discourse ethics, which Habermas then sets into his formal pragmatic theory of validity claims in communicative action. Communicative action is a distinctive form of action that is separated from, precedes, and enables, respectively, the moral orientation of practical reason, the axiological search for values, and the teleological orientation to success of instrumental action. To accommodate this, the lifeworld is turned into an ideal structure that is a product of communicative action and in turn underpins the latter's further operations.

This architecture assumes a high degree of consensus, encompassing both the lifeworld and the reflexive form of communicative action that enables its problematization. The first provides an 'acritical' context of action in its 'normal' operations, while the latter contains the supposition that the intersubjective discourse addressing validity claims must yield a consensual outcome. This double idealization, of the background lifeworld and of communicative action, obscures insight into pathologies of the lifeworld itself, as distinct from reification pathologies imposed upon it by social systems. Viewing the lifeworld as a structure of acritical, implicit dispositions set Habermas off in the direction of a type of reconstructive critique. Such a reconstructive critique is intended as a critique of available but denied competences analogous to Honneth's account of social pathology. It is ultimately derived from the validity standards of an ideal order, specified ideals associated with specified competences for their realization. The lifeworld is the habitualization, the making implicit, of such ideal competences. Yet, its process of coming about and its susceptibility to change and transformation are never adequately demonstrated. We need to know exactly how the lifeworld is constituted out of the process of communicative interaction, including not only its justified but also its pathological forms. It is not the identification of an order of ideals that presents the problem, but the double problem of not showing the generative process of its coming to be and the possibility of ideals that may not be fully agreed upon but still contribute to the moral level of social integration. It could be said that this is where Honneth's attempt to add 'concretion' to ideal theories comes into play, where he specifies validity standards for different institutional spheres that are more empirically applicable (Honneth, 2014). Nonetheless, though different from Habermas in this respect, Honneth neglects the social epistemological processes that at least potentially could lead to genesis and variation within the ideal order (Renault, 2020). The point at issue here is that while reconstructive critique is intrinsic to critical theory the *construction* of its validity standards *in practice* must be demonstrated rather than asserted. Even if the social epistemological dimension in Habermas is path-breaking, it does not demonstrate how communicative interaction and the life-world shape one another over time. To do so would necessarily lead to radical changes in the societal ontology that underpins the theory, changes that would take on board the structure-forming implications of conflict and of what Miller calls 'coordinated dissent' (Miller, 1986; 1992). Some steps in this direction are proposed in later chapters of this text.

A noticeable change in Habermas's mode of theorizing was inaugurated with the theory of communicative action. Once the emphasis on communicatively achieved validity became truly central, later supplemented by the democratic turn, the concern for negative critique as a vital part of his suite of critiques was diminished. Some of the more radical orientation of the theory, arising from the neo-Marxist earlier frame was replaced by a liberal turn. This changed orientation, compared, for example, to his book *Legitimation Crisis* (Habermas, 1975), can be at least partly traced to its idealist philosophical roots in Kant and Hegel and how such roots influenced the strains of classical and neoclassical sociological thought from Durkheim, through Weber, to Parsons from which he extensively drew in *TCA*. A variation of Marxist critique of reification could also be retained, but the transformative society-altering influence of Marxism began to lose ground in this approach. With this, there is an increasingly lack of concern with the relationship between social and political change of the kind that was prominent in *Legitimation Crisis*.

While much of this shift is defensible given Habermas's important prioritization of the question of democracy from the late 1980s onwards, it came at a high cost. Negative critique of injustice, like the public in the core-periphery model, began to be moved more to the periphery of the architectonic. The re-balancing of the theory from an emphasis on negativity to a reconstructive emphasis on rational potentialities tended to exclude the collective learning that arises from injustice and suffering. Such learning processes may, for a long time, be embedded in conflict, where the new struggles to be born, and, accordingly, rational potentialities need to be teased out of vague possibilities. As vague, such critical orientation does not initially meet the threshold of fully rational argument; in this phase, it operates more as a set of dispositions that oppose instituted ideals and norms. It could be argued that the deliberative democratic and public-sphere architecture proposed can discern the necessary discourse to be transacted. Yet, how truly can such a comprehensive democratic architecture be envisaged, if not through pressure for transformed procedures to address various problem complexes, not to mention the substantive, and far from consensual, cultural shifts that are also required for democratic change no matter what the democratic architecture is to be?

## 42  *Habermas, Communicative Reason, and the Social Sciences*

Habermas's approach tends to exclude the specific, intrinsic pathologies of communicative reason, such as those identified by Miller (2002). In both the collective learning theories of Miller and Eder, and in the Cork tradition of critical cognitive sociology, collective 'progressive' learning and associated social change are regarded as a long-term outcome of initial conflictual processes in and beyond the public sphere (Eder, 1985; 1999; Miller, 1986; 1992; O'Mahony, 2013; Strydom, 1987; 2009). In the Cork tradition of Strydom and O'Mahony specifically, an attempt is made to demonstrate the existence of higher-level cultural structures in the form of fundamental human capacities, collective immanent-transcendent cognitive principles, and immanent cultural models of various kinds. Such higher-level cultural structures do not eschew the possibility – and the partial necessity – of consensus, but neither do they exclude rational dissensus – ongoing disagreement but with reciprocal acceptance of others' standpoints – as both a learning mode and even an institutional form. These structures lie above the situated give and take of validity claims in the type of co-present communicative interaction that Habermas emphasizes. Without further structural elaboration to allow for conflict, dissensus, and associated collective learning processes, Habermas's approach tends to move in a one-sidedly consensual direction, to the detriment of understanding how communicative reason operates in the actual conditions of society, including its utopian possibilities. Later in this text, these critical remarks will be further extended to address how the account of communicative reason must take the direction of a normative theory that does justice to negative critique and reasoning pathologies within its socio-democratic frame.

### The Structure of Argumentation

A theory as ambitious as the theory of communicative action has exacting requirements for its respective employment in societal diagnosis and normative redirection within an appropriate logic of inquiry. A key problem in Habermas is the absence of a logical account of how communicative action operates as intersubjective *reasoning* that would incorporate the twin processes of the genesis of innovation and the context of application. What is absent is a theory of *inferential* reasoning, which, in different ways, is present in the very different pragmatisms of Peirce and Brandom (Peirce, 1931; Brandom, 2000). Such an inferential account in the Peirce tradition is built on the general sign of *argument.* This means that what Habermas understands as the background context of the lifeworld is to be understood as a cultural schema built up from inferential communicative processes capable of providing the foundation for further communicative elaboration. At a given point of time, the lifeworld would then represent the action-orienting cultural templates that have come to be agreed upon through long-run inferential reasoning processes or by the indubitability of certain experiences. In contrast to such an inferential approach, which with Peirce leads to collective orders of meaning, Habermas's depends too much on speech-act theory, which is too individualist in its approach to adequately deal with generality. Further, it is not designed to show how logical reasoning operates and how, viewed normatively, either good or bad outcomes could emerge. While the elements are there in Habermas's account with the formal pragmatic validity claims, the background context of the lifeworld, and the problematizing frame of communicative action, it is not shown how these elements could be interwoven to variously demonstrate the genesis of the new or the generation of rationalized outcomes that become stored in the lifeworld. In addition, as many have found, it is hard to identify empirical variation over time and space by means of this theoretical structure.

In the absence of an adequately developed account of inferential reasoning, it is hard to satisfactorily distinguish communicative reason – to be left to the subjects themselves in Habermas – from the theory of specialized discursive reason conducted by third parties that he also accepts as essential. The theory of inference in the Peirce tradition spans the logical capacities that make inference possible, explicates intersubjectively deployed inferential reasoning, and presents a fallible account of truthbearing on the applicability of reasoning outcomes. Such a theory does not therefore have to proceed at the pace of all-involved but can proceed unevenly adding the benefits of theoretically generated knowledge as much as practical deliberation, even if the latter must in the end have the final say in democratic contexts.

The challenge is especially exacting in that it is not just a question of developing a general theory of inferential reasoning, as does, for example, Brandom, but also, beyond Brandom, of showing how such forms of reasoning take effect in different contexts (Brandom, 2000). When one moves beyond the activity of co-present intersubjective coordination of validity claims, as is necessary from a sociological perspective, the issue of the wider resonance of what is communicated comes to the fore, extending, as Strydom emphasizes, from the double contingent perspective of communication between I and Thou favoured by Habermas to the triple contingent perspective of the always virtually present general public (Strydom, 1999). This triadic structure, I, Thou, and the third point of view, is of significance in that it also corresponds to Peirce's idea of thirdness, which, in his account of interpretants, goes beyond the raising and assessing of validity claims between two parties emphasized by Habermas towards the general cultural order which structures the space between them. The core point here is that while Habermas in a certain sense has the components, the lifeworld and communicative action, his deployment of the theory of speech acts does not allow for a *dynamic* relationship between the 'actualized' cultural order and its communicative transformation. Here, too, arises the issue of how to understand communication on those matters that are undecidable in the here and now for a multitude of possible reasons, and that therefore inevitably extend beyond the temporal horizons of co-present interaction, for example, uncertainties generated either by factual lack of knowledge (on all sides) or deep-lying value differences. For all of this, core treatment of the inferential logic of inquiry and its refraction for different contexts of use is required. This is one of the areas where the revisiting of Peirce can help.

## 44 *Habermas, Communicative Reason, and the Social Sciences*

### *The Separation of Semantics and Pragmatics*

The import of Habermas's revised theory of truth, which, as Strydom shows (see above) has its own problems, is that it nonetheless demonstrates the importance of semantics to any normative account of reason (Habermas, 2003). Recapitulating the revised theory of truth, Habermas acknowledges that it is not just the coordination of validity claims that counts, as if agreement on that level could obviate the need to take account of what is the case in the objective world, and then he also denies that this applies to the socio-moral world that is ideally constructed by morally competent subjects. This theoretical settlement accordingly involves a distinction between the respective domains, where only truth is justification-transcendent because the object is not created by us, whereas rightness is justification-immanent because the object is fully constructed by us. Thus, while truth has an ontological relation to the external world, rightness has no such ontological relation to the human-made world. This allows rightness to be immanently constructed according to the precepts of Habermas's normatively inclusive discourse theory through the intersubjective deployment of formal pragmatic validity claims. From this vantage point, the social world appears to lie fully within our power. Habermas knows as well as anybody that it also, so to speak, gets away from us. What he postulates could only be true if we could both fully comprehend the social world in all its contingencies and then fully democratically coordinate it. Rather, the intricate, superabundant complexity and contradictions of the social world, driven on by so many forces over which any given individual or collective subject has, at least initially, little control, means we must know it before we can meaningfully speak of pragmatically coordinating it by democratic means. This is why Habermas's separation of pragmatics and semantics pertaining to the social world is not satisfactory. The normative pragmatics elides the contingency generating complexity and referential objectivity of that social world, which often presents itself as a contingent or at least uncontrollable source of factual compulsion. This idealized formulation of rightness actually occludes cognitive variability and contestation over the interpretation of ideals (Wiener, 2007) and cuts the theory off from the social sciences,[11] while it also encourages over-consensualism.

Starting the other way round, the social world is also the outcome of bad reasoning, misplaced, inappropriate, or even destructive feelings, manipulative strategic action, and much else. It would only be true that the social world is fully morally determined in those circumstances that Habermas himself sketches, that is, where the lifeworld is the 'positive' normative complementation of communicative action. Leaving aside the semantics of the actual social world, which must apply as much to rightness as to objective truth, the neglect of semantics also arises in the immanent-transcendent context of communicative action. In effect, the already extreme separation of locution from illocution in Habermas's *TCA* account leads to the neglect of content and the role of substantive reasons. Detailed, extended analysis of how validity is intersubjectively constructed would show how the validity of semantic constructs underlies the pragmatic coordination of validity. A vast spectrum of semantic validity claims to do with what Peirce calls secondness enter into illocutionary habits and procedures, viz., the grounds of the claim to sincerity of persons set against previous known behavioural history, the claims to efficacy of practical norms, claims about the degree of fairness of the distribution of income in a society according to the Gini coefficient, the state of legal norms pertinent to a given situation, and so on. These short examples serve to illustrate the interdependence of semantics and pragmatics. It is therefore not just the capacity to raise validity claims that is at issue, as vital as that is, but what kinds of validity claims are raised, on what meaning constructs do they rest, and how are they reasoned about given fallible knowledge and different perspectives?

Habermas is committed to his project of detranscendentalization to better integrate transcendental and empirical concerns. Yet, the immanent deontological account of rightness in *Truth and Justification* appears to satisfy neither concern. Such a position inhibits empirical assessment of the factually revealed world. Later, I will try to show how this requires, consistent with remarks above, a better integration of communication action – and, its offshoot, deliberation – into a logical theory that can satisfy the integration of transcendental and immanent concerns and thus the necessary integration of pragmatic and semantic dimensions. This will help to open the way to a clearer role for the social sciences within the theory, and it resonates with a recurrent theme, the necessary interrelation of the substantive and the formal, of history and evolution, of immanent and transcendent.

### The Static Ahistorical Quality of the Theory

Habermas's thinking is set in the co-present, interactional, double contingent context of illocution and presents an evolutionist reading of modernity. As such, it cannot do sufficient justice to the constitutive, dynamic agents of social change, those movements that over and over again advance or deny claims to injustice, subjective experimentation, and the need to unlearn pathological modes of societal integration (O'Mahony, 2021). The great movements of modernity get screened out, a product in part of the neglect of the substantive. If the core of modernity is a type of evolutionary instantiation of communicative action, whose pragmatic basic structure is distanced from how people, morally, evaluatively, and emotionally, orient themselves in social life, then it is not surprising that the theory exhibits this static, ahistorical quality. It is not enough to say that actors must coordinate themselves in the relevant communication community by means of fully operating communicative reason. For how they are societally oriented in doing so is fundamental, bearing in mind that such orientation currently can only be partly derived from communicative reason and the public sphere, and that part is mostly implicit, or achieved indirectly through representatives. Frequently, communicative norms lie beyond the active grasp of democratic participants, and in some cases, insight is consciously denied to them by others. Insofar as both the actual operation of such norms and their denial lie beyond the capacity of the actors themselves to see them, sociological imagination and an associated logic of inquiry are required to enable the necessary insight (Mills, 2000). Thus, theoretical reason becomes intrinsic to practical reason.

## 46 *Habermas, Communicative Reason, and the Social Sciences*

Touraine's theory, in one sense, is an instructive contrast to that of Habermas, while in another sense it is complementary (Touraine, 1977). Touraine's concern for the historicity of society, not on an evolutionist Parsonian model but because of movements vying for control of this historicity, imparts a constitutive dynamism to the coordination of society at given times and places. Touraine also places the future of the subject at the heart of history, mindful that the subject is more than the individual. It has a collective expression as the carrier of ideas that give direction to movements. In this respect also, we can say that Touraine is more phenomenologically aware of the centrality of consciousness, of the power of feelings congealing into identities to give form to reasoning. In these emphases, he is different from Habermas, and more in line with Peirce. However, Habermas's detailed account of communicative action and the logic of coordination of validity claims offer a 'horizontal' complement to Touraine's 'vertical' theory of collective action. Touraine, to be sure, has one of his own with his account of cultural models, and the societal stakes that constitute these models, but, when suitably elaborated and structurally extended, Habermas's account is a critical and necessary complementation of Touraine's theory on the horizontal, synchronic level. This proposal for complementarity is not just critical of Habermas's static, evolutionist model in *TCA*. It also draws attention to a crisis in the modern theory of society. For the macro-sociological direction in which Habermas was heading in *TCA*, a direction that could incorporate a multi-level sociology was right in many respects. The challenge is to build on it.

### Notes

1 This is a rather sweeping shorthand comment, which hides many variations and combinations ranging from feminist identity theory to Bourdieu's habitus theory, to Luhmann's shifting of the transcendental phenomenological perspective from egos to systems, and much else. It arises in combination with other basic orientations, such as those of structuralism and hermeneutics.

2 The concept of detranscendentalization has applied to Habermas creates much uncertainty as to how exactly it should be conceived. What is intended here is the assumption that Habermas moves the Kantian inheritance in an immanent-transcendent direction for which formal pragmatics is the expression. The term quasi-transcendental is sometimes used to capture the self-understood distinction between this position and a stronger Kantian transcendentalism.

3 It can reasonably be argued that the early Habermas, for example, in *Knowledge and Human Interests,* was indeed concerned with intra-psychic phenomena, common in critical theory as the first generation gradually ceded way to the second (Habermas, 1968). It is not clear, though, how the paradigm of consciousness and the subject, including the intra-psychic, fits into Habermas's later work, or later critical theory more generally, after the radicalization of the linguistic turn from *TCA* onwards.

4 See Chapters 2, 3, and 4.

5 See Chapter 8.

6 Illustrations of this communicative turn and its relation to reason will be given in later chapters, for example, through accounts of Luhmann, Munch, and interpretive sociology generally.

*Habermas, Communicative Reason, and the Social Sciences*   47

7  In Habermas's book chapter, 'Peirce and Communication', he describes the distinction within Peirce between the acritical following of habit and argumentatively tested knowledge (Habermas, 1995).
8  On this point, see Strydom on the relationship between the principles of truth and rightness in Habermas, which he, contra Habermas, sees as 'architectonically' analogous.
9  He criticises Peirce in 'Peirce and Communication' (Habermas, 1995) for his failure to consistently attend to the intersubjectivity, though he also thinks it is latently intrinsic to Peirce's conception of communication.
10  One of the challenges of taking these ideas forward occurs in very recent work, where Habermas takes on the task of extending Peirce's truth-centred logic to the domain of rightness, a challenge that this book also faces (Habermas, 2019).
11  This also has implications for addressing the vexed question of how to relate theoretical and practical reason in the critical tradition from Kant onwards.

## References

Apel, K-O (1987) The Problem of a Macroethic of Responsibility to the Future in the Crisis of Technological Civilization: An attempt to come to terms with Hans Jonas's "Principle of Responsibility". *Man and World*. 20(1): 3–40.
Apel, K-O (1990) *Diskurs und Verantwortung: das Problem des Übergangs zur postkonventionellen Moral*. Frankfurt: Suhrkamp.
Apel K-O (1998) *From a Transcendental-Semiotic Point of View*. Manchester: Manchester University Press.
Apel K-O (2001) Regarding the Relationship of Morality, Law and Democracy: On Habermas's Philosophy of Law (1992) from a Transcendental-Pragmatic Point of View. In: Aboulafia MBM and Kemp C (eds) *Habermas and Pragmatism*. London: Routledge.
Bourdieu P (1984) *Distinction: A Social Critique of the Judgement of Taste*. Cambridge, MA: Harvard University Press.
Brandom R (2000) *Articulating Reasons: An Introduction to Inferentialism*. Cambridge, MA: Harvard University Press.
Eder, K (1985) *Geschichte als Lernprozeß? zur Pathogenese politischer Modernität in Deutschland*. Frankfurt: Suhrkamp.
Eder, K (1999) Societies Learn and Yet the World is Hard to Change. *European Journal of Social Theory*. 2(2): 195–225.
Forst R (2015) *Normativität Und Macht: Zur Analyse Sozialer Rechtfertigungsordnungen*. Frankfurt: Suhrkamp.
Habermas, J (1968) *Knowledge and Human Interests*. Boston: Beacon.
Habermas, J (1975) *Legitimation Crisis*. Boston: Beacon.
Habermas, J (1984) *The Theory of Communicative Action, Volume 1. Reason and the Rationalization of Society*. Boston: Beacon.
Habermas, J (1987 *The Theory of Communicative Action, Volume 2. Lifeworld and System: A Critique of Functionalist Reason*. Boston: Beacon.
Habermas, J (1995) Peirce and Communication. In: Ketner, RL (ed) *Philosophical Inquiries: Peirce and Contemporary Thought*. New York: Fordham University Press.
Habermas J (1996) *Between Facts and Norms: Contributions to a Discourse Theory of Law and Democracy*. Cambridge, MA: MIT Press.
Habermas J (2003) *Truth and Justification*. Cambridge, MA: MIT Press.
Habermas J (2008) *Between Naturalism and Religion: Philosophical Essays*. Cambridge, MA: Polity Press.
Habermas J (2018) *Philosophical Introductions: Five Approaches to Communicative Reason*. New York: John Wiley & Sons.
Habermas J (2019) *Auch eine Geschichte der Philosophie*. Frankfurt: Suhrkamp.

## 48 Habermas, Communicative Reason, and the Social Sciences

Honneth A (2011) Verwilderungen des Sozialen Konflikts: Anerkennungskämpfe zu Beginn des 21. Jahrhunderts. Report: MPIfG working paper. Max Planck Institute for the Study of Societies. Cologne.

Honneth A (2014) *Freedom's Right: The Social Foundations of Democratic Life.* New York: Columbia University Press.

Horkheimer M (1974 (1947)) *Eclipse of Reason.* London: Bloomsbury.

Joas H (1988) The Unhappy Marriage of Hermeneutics and Functionalism. *Praxis International* 8(1): 34–51.

Joas H (1997) *GH Mead: A Contemporary Re-Examination of His Thought.* Cambridge, MA: MIT Press.

Miller, M (1986) *Kollektive Lernprozesse: Studien zur Grundlegung einer soziologischen Lerntheorie.* Frankfurt: Suhrkamp.

Miller, M (1992) Rationaler Dissens. Zur gesellschaftlichen Funktion sozialer Konflikte. In: Giegel, HJ (ed) *Kommunikation und Konsens in modernen Gesellschaften.* Frankfurt: Suhrkamp.

Miller M (2002) Some Theoretical Aspects of Systemic Learning. *Sozialersinn* 3: 379–421.

Mills CW (2000) *The Sociological Imagination.* Oxford: Oxford University Press.

O'Mahony, P (2013) *The Contemporary Theory of the Public Sphere.* Oxford: Peter Lang.

O'Mahony P (2021) Habermas and the Public Sphere: Rethinking a Key Theoretical Concept. *European Journal of Social Theory* 24(4): 485–506.

Peirce CS (1931) *Collected Papers of Charles Sanders Peirce.* Cambridge, MA: Harvard University Press.

Renault E (2020) Critical Theory, Social Critique and Knowledge. *Critical Horizons* 21(3): 189–204.

Strydom, P (1987) Collective Learning: Habermas's concessions and their Theoretical Implications. *Philosophy and Social Criticism* 13(3): 265–281.

Strydom P (1999) Triple Contingency: The Theoretical Problem of the Public in Communication Society. *Philosophy & Social Criticism* 25(2): 1–25.

Strydom, P (2009) New Horizons of Critical Theory: Collective Learning and Triple Contingency. New Delhi: Shipra Publications.

Strydom P (2013) The Cognitive Order of Society: Radicalizing the Ontological Turn in Critical Theory *Unpublished MS, University College Cork.* 1–17.

Strydom P (2015) The Latent Cognitive Sociology in Habermas: Extrapolated from between Facts and Norms. *Philosophy & Social Criticism* 41(3): 273–291.

Strydom P (2019) On Habermas's Differentiation of Rightness from Truth: Can an Achievement Concept Do without a Validity Concept? *Philosophy and Social Criticism* 45(5): 555–574.

Touraine A (1977) *The Self-Production of Society.* Chicago: University of Chicago Press.

Wellmer, A (1991) *The Persistence of Modernity: Essays on Aesthetics, Ethics, and Postmodernism.* Cambridge, MA: MIT.

West DE (2017) Virtual Habit as Episode-Builder in the Inferencing Process. *Cognitive Semiotics* 10(1): 55–75.

Wiener A (2007) Contested Meanings of Norms: A Research Framework. *Comparative European Politics* 5(1): 1–17.

# 2 Sociology and Reason

## General Considerations

Reason has recently once again become a theme in sociology, but in a disguised form. Despite this, there has never truly been an extended, explicit sociology of reason, even if consideration of reason has been latently present throughout the history of the discipline. Presently, the concern with 'reason' generally follows two principal paths that at times and places overlap. The first is a type of tentative rise in the sociology of reflexivity, which addresses aspects of the category of reason, but usually without addressing the theoretical history of reason. It operates, as will be explored below, as a type of sui generis account that has its own provenance and discursive structure. The second is more widespread and is mostly only about reason ex negativo, manifesting itself powerfully as a full-blown suspicion of reason or even, a totalizing critique of reason (Apel, 1993). A distinction must nonetheless be retained between the critique of reason in many strands of critical scholarship and the phenomenological hermeneutic tendency, enhanced in postmodernism, to dismiss reason altogether.

The path of taking up the question of reflexivity appears unavoidable due to a widespread perception both of a growth in educated reasoning competences and the manifest range of perspectives arising from societal plurality. In a very general sense, it also speaks to the post-empiricist situation of the social sciences, where law-like, recursively operating structures are no longer assumed to determine much of social behaviour. The path of the suspicion of reason aligns itself closely with the dominant contemporary form of the critique of power as a critique of hegemonic conceptualizations. Here, reason is taken to be no more than a dissembling ideology legitimating domination.

The finely threaded complexity of these paths in relation to the genealogy of reason in sociology will be further addressed in the next chapter. It is not an easy task due to its inherent intellectual complexity, made more difficult by the long-standing hesitation of sociology to take up an explicit discourse of reason. As already indicated, this does not mean that the idea of reason has not affected sociology. It is simply that this history must be reconstructed in part from outside sociology, above all in philosophy, and the implications of these developments for sociology must then be properly considered. And the account of paths would be far from complete if the above were regarded as the only paths. For there remains the

DOI: 10.4324/9780429060571-3

50    *Sociology and Reason*

heritage of critical theory that still mostly builds its claims on a defence of reason, an affirmation of the possible manifestation of reason in society without denying its pathological forms. More than merely an affirmation of reason, it is also an assertion of its explanatory necessity in making sense of the modern condition. Yet, throughout its various eras, critical theory has also been opposed to reason of another kind in the form of subjective reason imposing itself instrumentally or strategically and directing practical reason in a particular controlling direction (Horkheimer, 1974 (1947)). In so doing, it has a similar object of critique to many other critical currents in the social sciences, which doesn't stop it from being criticized for its association with reason in general. Nevertheless, this third path is promising, as it entails both a critique of a particular form of reason and, later with Apel and Habermas, an attempt to rehabilitate a positive concept, that of communicative reason. The part concerned with the critique of reason is, with Horkheimer, a critique of subjective reason, masquerading as reason as a whole, which in his account leads to a positivist, empirical-analytical path of a detached theory, viewing reason as manifested in the external law-like development of society, for which the epistemological standard was explanation, and the practical standard was successful intervention (ibid).

What seems little in doubt on all sides is that as modernity has progressed, the idea of reason has escalated in significance, not only in scholarship but also in multiple kinds of practice. Mostly, it is not explicitly asked why this might be so or whether society has an increasing need for reason of some kind. The period after the enlightenment in the 19th century was characterized by a widespread sense that the employment of reason in all its facets was required to coordinate public and even private affairs. The age of authority and dogmatic metaphysics was giving way to the age of science and democracy. In the interstices of this transition, simplified here for clarity, were to be found multiple struggles: liberal versus revolutionary enlightenment, deep-lying conservative hostility versus revolutionary egalitarian enthusiasm, old and more innovative forms of governing through established hegemony versus democracy and human rights (Israel, 2001). Beyond these rather starkly drawn polarities lie a myriad of variations. From all of this, it can still be concluded that the idea of reason has emerged strongly over the last 250 years. This is not to proclaim its triumph, merely to assert that, rightly or wrongly, the idea of it, or the various ideas of it, have strode on to the stage of history in a manner that cannot be circumvented either in theory or in practice, whatever one thinks about it and perhaps even whatever one makes of it.

One striking general characteristic of sociological responses to reason, notwithstanding the rise of text and discourse analysis in its many forms, is the lack of precise and detailed attention to the relation between reason and the normative. While the respective poles of this relation both require extensive further conceptual attention, the challenge of doing so is increased by the lack of sustained attention to how reason operates, a task that should be the home ground of the human and social sciences. This lack of attention to how reason operates applies not just to the few who, beyond philosophy, try to defend an explicit idea of a normatively significant reason but also to the many who are critical of reason. Some suggestive ideas for

*Sociology and Reason* 51

this situation may be traced back to rival enlightenment and post-enlightenment traditions and, not least, to counter-enlightenment traditions. These traditions have played a powerful, though often subterranean, role in shaping how reason is understood in the social sciences. In key respects, reason remains such a politicized concept that demonstrating its operations and effects struggles to get past first base.

Briefly schematized, several key currents in the history of the concept of reason may be related to the development of the social sciences. In the first instance, the scientific revolution, after a radical period in the early history of Puritanism in which science was taken to entail a transformative, emancipatory pedagogy, eventually assumed its characteristic modern Baconian form as neutral, dispassionate knowledge of the external world (Merton, 1936). For this task, in a way that later became characteristic of the emerging and maturing social sciences in the 19th century, the 'moderate' Enlightenment emphasized the secondary significance of reason. Knowledge for Hume was produced by the senses, and reason was accorded a secondary role as a supplement to the senses by making associations either of an empirical or moral kind. Sentiment, not reason, was the source of distinguishing good from bad in a moral register. The experience felt through the senses was paramount, and human behaviour accordingly followed sentiment guided by the direct 'passions', that is, feelings, emotions, and desires. In the empiricist tradition generally, habit played an important role, which it also did for Peirce. However, in the latter, habit, actively related to cognition, is built upon the reality of universals – general concepts on the trans-individual level – and hence must incorporate the power of reason, while this reality is denied in empiricism. Experiences lead to empirical associations rather than anything more general. The empirical-analytical translation of empiricist ideas in sociology, while taking many forms in various traditions, nonetheless generally concurred with empiricism in denying the abstract, general significance of cognition as reasoning, and operated with an understanding of mind, and hence reason, as the building of associations through experience about what is real in the external world.

A second current emerged in the critical enlightenment, of whom Kant is today the exemplary figure with his doctrine of critique but which was also characterized by a series of thinkers and a logic of practice that pushed in a radical democratic and egalitarian direction, such as Spinoza, Diderot, and Helvetius. These figures explicitly supporting democracy went in fact beyond Kant, according to Israel, even if the seeds of democratic transformation were also present in Kant's ideas (Israel, 2001). All of these figures held the view that reality is made by the mind through its capacity for reason, a view that carries on to Hegel and the left-Hegelians of the 19th century. According to Habermas, both the empiricist and rationalist enlightenment traditions moved in a post-metaphysical direction, one in which religious faith and divine ordinance were not regarded as lying behind knowledge (Habermas, 2019). This entailed the replacement of the objective view of reason that understood itself as a metaphysics already transcendentally permeating the human world and whose latent form was already there waiting to be discovered. The widely influential enlightenment idea that only the mediating epistemic potential of reason was in any sense transcendent opposed a subjective to

## 52 Sociology and Reason

such an objective conception. Immanent justification was a condition of the validity of knowledge for both theoretical and practical reasons. Such justification was a cornerstone of the idea of critique with, at its core, the idea that nothing should be shielded from critical illumination and evaluation. In the sense to which it is the heir of the critical enlightenment, ambivalently to be sure, critical currents in social thought are animated by the sense that there is something wrong in the world that must be righted and by the sense that a path can be found to correct such wrongs. However, the aura of enlightenment has diminished significantly over the 20th century, and even though Hegel is far less often singled out for critique than Kant – whose transcendentalism and formalism are widely employed targets –, it is the construct associated with him of the immanent potential for the realization of reason that has become most contentious in social scientific critique. In this context, claims to the legitimacy of reason are variously accorded Eurocentric, patriarchal, politically elitist, and other negative connotations. In multiple, indirect ways, reason is both employed and denied in much negative critique, and where it is employed it is paradoxically often through the frame of the critique of reason, seen as operating in the service of power, by means of ideology critique. Returning to the above-sketched intellectual paths adopted with respect to reason, it might be added here that the dominant forms of critique in the social sciences, as reluctant heirs of the critical enlightenment, currently lie in an awkward constellation with respect to the various other paths. Critical social science, as distinct from critical theory, inclines towards a modest, inexplicit rehabilitation of the idea of reason through exploring the idea of critical reflexivity. Yet, it frequently still implicitly draws from the nominalist subject-object framework of the empiricist tradition while claiming to oppose its root and branch. It also frequently incorporates elements of the totalizing critique of reason that is characteristic of philosophical hermeneutics in the Heideggerian tradition.

This reference to philosophical hermeneutics brings us to the third current connecting philosophy to sociology within the frame of reason, the current of critique of reason. This current has many carriers, ranging from Nietzsche, Dilthey, Heidegger, and Gadamer, among others. Its focus, widely influential beyond its primarily conservative home terrain, is on linguistic world disclosure of the history of being. Language and conceptual schemes make possible access to the full reality of being as the a priori of the historically contingent lifeworld. Such a reality, embodying a past-oriented historicism, emphasizes the ontological conditioning of the innerworldly lives of subjects within the already-formed horizons of the lifeworlds that they inhabit. The operations of a critical reason are blocked by the fact that meaning is understood as always relative to the deepest foundation of this lifeworld standard, a conception reinforced by Heidegger's idea of the primordiality of being at home. This primordial quality attests to an 'eternal' ontological form that is nonetheless also unavoidably differentiated into distinctive cultural lifeworlds. Being enmeshed in the world of Dasein through 'care' or 'belonging' takes precedence over any rational self-positing of the ego (self-consciousness) and also before any capacity for understanding between self and other (hetero-consciousness) (Apel, 1993). Taking this forward to the social sciences, if the empiricist tradition postulated naturalized understanding as an a priori and the rational tradition with Kant postulated transcendental subjectivity as an a priori, then the philosophical hermeneutical tradition postulated an ontology of being as another kind of a priori. Sociology developed an influential interpretive tradition in the 20th century that, following the lead of philosophical hermeneutics, was mostly happy to deny the possibility of critically operating validity in intersubjective contexts in favour of the disclosed validity of cultural-historically formed tradition. The potential of rational judgement through reason is de-emphasized in favour of the goal of clarification through hermeneutic understanding, in which the uniqueness of the other is the ontologically recessed standard. Reflexivity is seen as both ubiquitous and banal, and it is denied that it has the force of critique, or at least that such force imposes inappropriate standards on contingent subjectivities and contexts of life (Lynch, 2000). In much sociology, this ontological grounding impulse emphasizes the background-shaping context of the 'social historical' and the tendency to glide by epistemological issues, either those of scholarship or arising in everyday life itself. This tendency frequently ends up in what Apel calls the critique of logos, such as, for example, Derrida's critique of logocentrism (Apel, 1993).

Since the reason-embracing critical theoretical tradition is at the core of this book and will be addressed extensively, I will not comment on it further here. Dealing just with the immediate above traditions, what is striking in describing them is the neglect of cognitive-epistemological structures and processes. For the most part, sociology never developed an adequate epistemology of the operation of social forms in general, and certainly never one that matches the sometimes generality of its scope. This applies even more to its limited treatment of reason, whether in the form of reflexivity or otherwise. It cannot but be said that, to some considerable extent, it never saw the need to do so, since concern with ontology has tended to predominate. In some parts, investigative methodologies have taken up the slack, yet these either remain ontologically oriented and constrained, like critical discourse analysis or, in another way, positivistic approaches, or operate with a resolute micro-level, situated focus, like conversation analysis. For most of its history, the discipline has never *explicitly* taken on board the radical shift from ontology to epistemology in the critical enlightenment, and still less the rethinking and de-differentiation of the relationship between ontology and epistemology after the late 19th-century linguistic turn and beyond. This is manifested in, for example, the inability of Parsonian functionalism to address dynamic mechanisms of individuation or in the general inability to take forward and re-elaborate *TCA*.

More recently, after constructivist, cognitivist, and agential turns, there is a greater willingness to embrace such considerations. Nonetheless, the general sense is of a discipline that, forced with the need to extend its tentative epistemology does so by overwhelmingly moving in a micro-theoretical direction often accompanied by a dismissal of 'grand theory'. The overarching importance of the left-Hegelian tradition of reason *in society*, the goal of building a reasonable society, of rediscovering a plausible kind of complementary objective reason, is no longer addressed, outside of a few traditions, and notably that of critical theory in its social philosophical moment, even if not even widespread even there. Apart from

## 54  *Sociology and Reason*

the lack of interest in exploring the sociological potential of Habermas's pragmatic theory of communication, in which sociological theories were already extensively reviewed and assimilated, another feasible project that has excited no attention would be to develop in a sociological manner Rawls's ideal theory, which is generally dismissed as a type of unjustified idealization of social relations of no relevance to sociology. While it cannot be denied that the form of Rawls's theory is more consistent with Parsons than it is with modern sociology, there is at least within it the desire to address what a normative theory of (political) society should consist of. Even if not any kind of blueprint for a modern theory of society with normative intentions, Rawls's theory really should have more resonance, if reason, especially democratic, public reason, is to feature prominently within critical scholarship (O'Mahony, 2013).[1]

While after these above-mentioned 'turns', there has been a veritable sea-change in the sociological landscape in the form of theories that emphasize construction over determination – conflict theories, neo-Wittgensteinian theories, neo-institutionalism, discourse theory, social movement theory – the general 'space of reason' understood in anything other than a negative, often dismissive, sense remains unaddressed. That it *should be* addressed is of course implied here but not yet justified, something that will be attempted in the next section and in the book generally. In the place of reason, social theories today often emphasize the dialectical interplay of hegemony and disagreement, with the latter ascribed a type of orienting value, an index of some kind of potential societal health, or at least the capacity for resistance and change. The rise of a focus on disagreement is itself an index of an actual rise in societal plurality, animated by the will and capacity to resist. However, the appearance of disagreement, or the study of multiple episodes of disagreement, in itself offers no clarity on good or bad outcomes of disagreement on the normative plane. Still more fundamentally, it does not clarify the reasoning processes, embedded in orienting cultural structures, by means of which any kind of outcome is at all produced, and especially what might be regarded as a 'good' outcome. The immediate question of much modern scholarship, even much modern life, is to immediately respond to such an invocation of 'good' by the further question of 'who's good?'. It is a legitimate question, and the importance of attending to disagreement generally is equally so, but it cannot be at the cost of denying that some possible agreement is presupposed or possible to achieve, for example, on matters that Rawls calls 'constitutional essentials', even if only in the long run and possibly only through extensive social change. If this is a type of normative, or even moral, presupposition of any kind of good faith exchange, even and perhaps especially adversarial good faith exchange, then it rests on an even deeper set of presuppositions. By what means could such exchanges be negotiated, or more fundamentally still, how are they possible at all? This last question brings us to the heart of the issue of the societal-political form and significance of reason.

It is certainly not contentious to claim that the question of reason is complicated, traversing many scholarly disciplines and perspectives. So much so, it might be concluded that it is impossible to address without some kind of delimitation. Before that can properly begin, given that the delimitation is primarily

*Sociology and Reason*   55

sociological, what is first needed is some allusion to the question of why a sociology of reason, and especially why a sociology of communicative reason? This appears even more essential given the way a widespread discomfort with reason characterizes the sociological enterprise. The first steps to an answer to this question are taken in the brief general remarks in the next sections and in the following one, where a schematic framework is offered that seeks to embed the sociological enterprise in reason.

## Communicative Reason and the Left-Hegelian Linguistic Turn

The idea of reason and the practices of reasoning have suffered because of the inattention and hostility of sociology. Following the left-Hegelian Peirce, with Frege one of the two principal figures of the linguistic turn, logic, and hence reason, is to be understood as a social form. Peirce emphasizes a particular category of mind, social mind, as the locus of reason, but he also showed how it was connected both to sense perception and the world of objects. How he did so, clarifying many of the questions about the status of reason that came before him and the as many that survived after him – given that his work remained little known for a long time – is a subject for some later explication here and for other texts. However, the significance of understanding reason as a social form is that it entails moving beyond the subject/object consciousness of post-Cartesian philosophy that predominated even in Kant and the Enlightenment with Hegel as a partial but pivotal exception. It also moves beyond the ontological-epistemological frame of much of sociology, such as the structure/agency orientation, with rare sociologists standing beyond the frame – for example, critical theorists and, in a quite different way, Luhmann. The decisive aspect of Peirce's innovation was to have conceived of what he called 'thirdness', social mind, as the place of logical cognitive principles, rules, and habits that mediate between the subjective and objective worlds, respectively, characterized by subjective and objective mind. Thirdness is an operation of mind, that of extended, *social* mind, that is indispensable to agents in actively making sense of the world. It is, therefore, both cognitive in expressing the social form of reasoning and pragmatic in the sense of knowing how to appropriately use such reasoning. It should not be confused with any kind of structural semantics in which repositories of meaning are to be found, such as identity-securing beliefs or institutional norms. These belong at another level in the Peirceian scheme, that of secondness, the symbolic knowing of something 'in the world' associated with objective mind, including self-observation of the historically formed 'me'.

Bringing reason to the fore, then, following Peirce and emphasized also in another way by Wittgenstein, requires a dynamic, constructive account of cognition within and beyond the individual. Reasoning requires the use of socially generated capacities and forms, and reason in a more emphatic sense – still cognitive and not normative – involves the selection of ideals that recursively organize the validity of inferences. Deductively coordinated by such ideals, thirdness mediates between the perceiving subject and the apprehended object. Peirce further regarded transcendent cognitive universals as real (Friedman, 1995), and this led him to build

56  *Sociology and Reason*

from scholastic realism, while also drawing inspiration in different ways from the world-constituting idealism of Kant and Hegel.[2]

This indicates already where the answer to the question of why a sociology of reason lies? If reason is composed of sociality-constituting social forms, processes, and capacities, and if these elements are intrinsic to human social life and, in an even greater measure, modern social life, then it should be intrinsic to sociological analysis. Perhaps one cause of the non-recognition of reason in sociology is the indifference amounting almost to antipathy between some kinds of philosophy and some kinds of sociology, though paradoxically, these disciplines share a lot. If a philosophy from which they sought distance was taken as the locus of reason, then sociologists had one more powerful reason not to go there, that of disciplinary differentiation. However, the problem lies deeper than just disciplinary relations. Along with certain other currents of thought in the 20th century and beyond, the category of reason after the linguistic turn implied a transformation of philosophy too (Apel, 1980).

The answer to the question of why specifically a communicative reason follows from the above. Reason as logic is not just regarded as a social form by Peirce, but social forms are constituted through signs. Signs constitute humans and humans constitute signs; humans interminably add more information to signs and these signs correspondingly extend the reach of mind, the complementary formation of mind and meaning. Communication is therefore both internal to subjects and shared between them. Though the term semiosis, the study of the use of signs, has technical advantages in this light, the term semiotic reason is scarcely known, while Habermas has already done much to put communicative reason on the agenda. The latter is therefore generally favoured here. One important exception bears on the distinction between reasoning and disclosing. The term semiosis in this context indicates more clearly than that of communication that inference, whether it is conscious or unconscious, is essential to both. It is one further reason to be suspicious of the tendency, coming from Heidegger, to insist on an antagonism between disclosure through language and critical reasoning. Peirce's phenomenology of meaning does not insist on the separation of feelings and logos but on their inextricable combination, to be examined further in Chapter 5.

### Sociology and Communicative Reason: Towards a Social Ontological Framework

Having emphasized how the sociological and wider social scientific tendency to ignore reason is not justified, what follows here is the first attempt to provide a social ontological framework for communicative reason. It is the first of several attempts, each progressively gaining in depth of perspective, and it distils the main elements in this text to date. It will provide criteria of relevance to guide the survey of sociological literature on reason and reflexivity in the next chapter. It seeks to advance the core elements of a cognitive critical theory that would embrace, albeit critically, rather than reject the category of reason. Given that the sociological literature, overall, does not manifestly speak to this kind of frame, it is best to be explicit about what lies behind the review of sociological accounts of reason and reflexivity in the next chapter. It is also intended as a first synthetic introduction to a semiotic sociology of reason consistent with critical theory. The framework will not be *systematically* used in the review of literature per se, though it will be so used in evaluating outcomes of that review in Chapter 4. Effectively then, the framework, first offered explicitly here as an introduction to the review of theory and in Chapter 4 as the basis of a synthesis of findings, is further developed in the remainder of the book.

The general objective is to delimit a space for the introduction of a sociological contribution to a revised theory of communicative reason that, as will gradually emerge in the later text, is intended to have more than a sociological value. The sociological component is ultimately part of a wider transdisciplinary specification of how reason operates in modern societies. Any mature theoretical sociology must work from an inner conviction that it offers the best option for continuing the discipline in its wider interdisciplinary setting, and this is no different. Of course, it must also regard itself as fallible. The approach outlined here is set within the general context of critical theory, which partly explains why certain terms, not common in contemporary sociology, come to the fore. However, sociology is by now a long-established discipline, and some of these terms below were more prominent at other times in its history in analogous ways to how they are used here.

The first element of the proposed approach is that it follows the concept of *immanent transcendence*, a core concern of critical theory that was already presaged in Adorno's often misunderstood idea of immanent critique and has been further developed by, among others, Habermas and Honneth and, within a sociological frame, by Strydom. In both Habermas and Strydom, especially in the former's recent book, Auch Eine Geschichte, it is associated with Peirce (Strydom, 2011; Habermas, 2019). Immanent transcendence can be understood as transcendence from within, the idea that humans, though immersed in a familiar normative world, have a capacity for insight that reaches beyond that familiar world. They do this by projecting an idea – with Peirce, one can speak of 'idea potentiality' – into the future in such a way that it reflexively moves beyond the knowledge contained in the familiar, 'known' starting point. While this can happen by chance or by 'trial and error', recent insistence on the encompassing contingency of learning does not do the projection of idea potentiality full justice. For, beyond a rudderless idea of a fully contingent process, potential knowledge, extending from what is presently known but reaching beyond it, is organized in relation to what may be called continua, drawing from Peirce's characterization of continuity (Peirce, 1892). Such continua, which offer a situation-transcending orientation and an a priori of action, mediate and structure the infinity of possible ideas into general ideas or limit concepts. More can always be learned through engaging with these continua as thought reaches beyond the existing application of concepts. They operate as presuppositions of thinking and communicating with others. They provide orientations in the form of a 'surplus' of meaning. The organization of these orientations into immanently operating 'language games' or cultural models generates relevance and coherence for what would otherwise be a chaotic melange of incoherent particulars.

## 58 Sociology and Reason

For Peirce, this quasi-transcendent structure of continua acquires temporal significance in that it is through continua, though they are 'rooted' in the past, that humans can take a conjecturally grounded relation to the future in infinitesimal moments of present consciousness. By this means, thought and argumentation can anticipate the possible realization of potentials. The thought figure of 'reaching beyond' on a continuum is at its base a cognitive one. It chimes with the general usage of the word reflexivity to indicate a permanent capacity to go beyond what is normatively established.

The second element to be highlighted in the sociology of reason is that it should have a thoroughly *cognitive nature*. The reference to 'thoroughly' attests that the term 'cognitive' should be understood more widely than its dominant understanding as cognitive-instrumental, where it is frequently set in counterpoint to the 'affective'. Peirce identified three interrelated cognitively relevant processes. These were associated with the 'firstness' of sensation and perception that fed into logical conjectures or abductions, the 'secondness' associated with the implications of apprehending or experiencing the object associated with inductive reasoning, and the 'thirdness' of conceptually guided interpretation, the real locus of integrative cognitive operations. Peirce's triadic formulation of these cognitively relevant processes break with the by now conventional distinction between the cognitive as being about formal-logical exploration of truth as opposed to the affective as the domain of feeling. For Peirce, feeling was a quality of perception that was itself an unconscious but cognitively relevant process (firstness) that made possible and orientated another cognitive process, the conscious inferential process of reasoning (thirdness). However, both thirdness and firstness were 'about something', 'objects' in the world, whether social, technical, natural, or of mixed form, and this required another cognitive process, that of secondness, the mode in which sentient beings take an action-orienting, 'definite' relation to such objects. I introduce these categories here – to be developed later – to situate the idea of cognition as something much more expansive and pervasive to all forms of thinking and communication than its characteristic restriction to purposive-rational thinking.

The alternative conception of the cognitive at work here identifies mental capacities of different kinds that are intrinsic to all activities of making sense in the world and, beyond that, in actively making the actual social world. Strydom identifies various cognitive structures that are distinctively yet interrelatedly transcendent and immanent (Strydom, 2011; 2012). On the transcendent level, there are evolutionarily formed, meta-cultural, enabling cognitive structures essential to social life. These transcendentally anchored, enabling structures, meta-concepts, or principles give form to all cognitive activities – such as memorizing, classification, perceiving, interpreting, judging, and learning – located in specific 'domains' or 'universes of discourse' on the immanent level. The meta-cultural or transcendent level operates virtually through cultural structures of which agents are not consciously aware. Their presence is apparent in the difference they make in enabling multiple kinds of cognition. Further, beyond the narrowly epistemic understanding of the cognitive, the operational capacity to reach beyond what is known is bound up both with feelings logically transposed in abduction into rational, that is, cognizable, projections that animate and receive form from formal, transcendentally anchored capacities of mind. Thus, to speak of reason as a cognitive universal is to locate it on this meta-cultural level. It is a universal because all humans have it at their disposal. It is a product of cultural evolution, the set of presuppositions and orientations that humans have developed to achieve their many purposes.

This understanding of cognition as immanent-transcendent is an important point of emphasis for sociology in that its critique of reason is generally directed at reason's assumed transcendental and normative qualities, while for the critics, the employment of normative judgement is taken to be directly derived from the transcendent – a core element of the critique of ideal theory. In this sense, the immanent-transcendent framework described above comes into play; the use of reason entails the use of evolutionarily formed meta-cognitive capacities that operate on a level beyond specific normative or symbolic constructions, though such constructions, building from these cognitive universals, are applied and reformulated on the immanent plane. Thus, to accept the reality of reason requires acknowledgement of its cognitive forms, and these encapsulate certain basic normative orientations, without which any form of organized social relations would not be possible. Such cognitive orientations, which are characterized by a weak normative telos, for example, ideas of truth, rightness, or beauty, can be reinterpreted, contested, and hence take many 'strong' normative forms in actual worlds. In my view, Habermas's formal pragmatics is best understood in this way.

The third element of an account of reason is that it should be understood as *critical-reflexive* and enabling of learning on both individual and collective levels. For this reason, consistent with the above, the cultural plane should be taken to consist of two reason-relevant horizons: one, social-historically and immanently, operating with the arrow of time through the building of orienting cultural models of various kinds, and the other, against the arrow of time, operating by means of evolutionarily selected principles that enable learning on the meta-cultural transcendent level (Strydom, 2017). The critical-reflexive process involves the positing of a schema first developed in the imagination and then worked out through abductive conjecture formation and its further logical elaboration through modal projection. Following Habermas, this process is not only confined to testing the truth of propositions but also to justifying claims of rightness and authenticity. The reference to logical elaboration refers to cognitive processes in society in which the individual is but one operator and medium.

The critical-reflexive moment in reason is an intrinsic feature of humanity, a characteristic of the human form of life since at least the 'human revolution' of 60,000 years ago. Its centrality to reason is characterized by Kant's Copernican turn emphasizing the power of the mind. The human form of life is constructed through operations of mind, whose possibility emerges from socio-biologically formed natural endowments. These operations occur within natural substrate conditions that, in spite of progressively greater interventionist capacities, mostly lie beyond human powers, excepting, of course, the all too evident contemporary power to destroy. Critical capacity is perhaps most clearly illustrated by Peirce's account of inferential reasoning capacities, the interrelated capacities to discover (learning), to reason

## 60  *Sociology and Reason*

according to principles, and to test the validity of the joint operations of discovery and principle-based reasoning. Boltanski and Thevenot's sociology of critical capacity also contains assumptions about the inability not to engage in critical learning activities, though it is on a different level, located strictly on the immanent plane compared with Peirce's employment of evolutionary, meta-cultural categories (Boltanski and Thévenot, 1999). Nonetheless, potentially they are complementary. Two further points of elucidation are relevant here. In the first instance, critical reflexive capacity is not to be equated simply with critique according to a normative standard, part of the methodology so opposed by interpretivists and systems theorists. It is rather ineluctably at the very core of advanced – but still understood as universally available – cognitive activities. In the second instance, it is important to note that while the capacities for critical reflexive learning are transcendently anchored, these capacities are intrinsic to every dimension of social life. In this sense, reason is intrinsically the capacity for critical reflexive learning, and various cognitive competences are what make it manifest in social life.

The critical reflexive moment is not only confined to self-critique but also to other or hetero-critique and, more generally, to trans-critique or the critique of social arrangements. Through all levels of critique, as used within a critical logic of inquiry, it is necessary to address the nature of reasoning pathologies that result, inter alia, in self-deception, manipulation, reified practices, and self, other, or general societal alienation. Before further elaboration of what this might consist of, something fundamental about the status of reason must be introduced. In much of contemporary sociology, reason is presented as something that is only problematically present in social life, as something that could – almost – be discarded. It is certainly not represented as a capacity that, though permanently needing self-critique, remains fundamental if fully justified normative arrangements are to be conceptualized, let alone attained. For Peirce and second-generation critical theory both thought and language entail reason. Reason is a capacity both to convey ideas but also to add generality, to coordinate actions, and to solve problems; in short, to utilize the entire panoply of competences that bear on symbol-using cognition and communication. As understood in this sense, reason is plural in its manifestations because it underpins the sense of what is relevant for humanity and offers the required cognitive processes to make it socially manifest. Because it is framed here in this way, that is, as a social resource that can be variably appropriated, it cannot be assumed – as in certain epistemologies it is – that each new time an agent or agents begins to reason anew as if no history of reasoning precedes them. The structuring of reason is described in multiple ways: as institutions, as lifeworld, as cultural models, as schemata, and, though order needs to be brought to such conceptual plurality, they all attest to the desire to capture the cultural embodiment of reason, the transposition of multiple acts of reasoning into more enduring and action-orienting cultural forms.

While it is mistaken to represent reason in its entirety as a pathology, it is perfectly correct to identify pathologies of reason, or even pathologies associated with the repressive hegemony of one over other kinds of reason, as, for example, the domination of subjective reason. From Kant onwards, the fallibility of reason was stressed by the recognition of its constant need for self-critique. So, if reasoning is distinguished from reason, with the latter understood as the principles and ideals that derive from reasoning in the long run, and which reciprocally form its quasi-transcendent, core, cognitive orientation, then reasoning, the use of reason, can be wrong, pathological, misleading, or unjust in a multitude of ways. The cognitive core of reason cannot be pathological since it consists of those principles that are intrinsic to human purposes and do not preclude multiple ways of realizing them. However, it can be insufficient in not developing needed principles such as, for example, the ideal of ecological responsibility that is slowly becoming a presupposition of thinking and arguing. Reasoning, as distinct from reason, takes on pathological forms while remaining a universal capacity in that, without its use, human social life could not continue. It is employed in accordance with, in the sequence of reasoning, exploratory, normative, and discursive logics, all of which jointly and severally can and routinely do generate pathological, that is, unreasonable outcomes. Reverting to the relation between reason and embodiment, reasoning also occurs in the context of elementary basic social forms of human behaviour, which have also been lodged in the organism by evolutionary processes as basic drives, such as cooperation, competition, alliance formation, learning, conflict, rivalry, and others, as Durkheim originally identified (Strydom, 2017). These elementary social forms as aspects of first nature routinely influence the operations of a second nature conditioned by reason; in fact, the second nature of reason is built from them, but, as emphasized by Kant, it does not remain subservient to them. Kant distinguished between inclination and the normative authority derived from practical reason; inclinations hence must be educated for appropriate social use, and reason is the reflexive educator. These remarks on reason as reflexive educator lead to the normative element of reason, yet to be discussed here, in that normativity depends on how the cognitive core of reason, which conditions but does not determine, is transposed into normative forms through immanent social processes. Once again, to invoke Kant via Habermas, the selection of normative principles is a critical-reflexive competence to justify what is appropriate through the use of reason within a rational communicative process (Habermas, 2019).

A fourth element of a sociology of reason is that the disjunction between reason and embodiment should be recognized and yet overcome by addressing the relationship between *subjective processes*, including latent consciousness, and reason. Such a statement appears controversial in the present intellectual climate and could be taken to enthrone the rule of reason to follow only those principles of reasoning set down by the powerful. There is considerable point in this criticism, whether it applies to the excessive rationalism of late enlightenment deductive logic or how the accumulated inductively generated rationalities of empiricism were used to buttress an existing hierarchy of goods, or indeed to 'objectively' specify new hierarchies. Western liberalism has found a way to combine these dispositions by, for example, combining the importance attributed to the rule of law with the assumption of the uncontrollable autonomy of techno-economic processes. However, once again, following Peirce, the interdependence between feeling and reason should be stressed because feeling is intrinsic to the possibility of reason. In its indirect way,

62  *Sociology and Reason*

sociology increasingly recognizes this in various places, for example, in habitus theory, Touraine's account of the subject, and in the many discourses of feminism. However, even in these instances, the account of reasoning is incomplete in that the necessity of translating between what Kant separated as sensibility and understanding is insufficiently recognized. If the interrelation of these elements was properly acknowledged and if reason was understood to be capable of revising the norms that its operations previously produced, it could be shown to be also responsive to the implications of perceptual shifts related to embodied being. At least it could in the right circumstances. Reason would be seen to be animated by feelings, and yet, necessarily, to make them available on discursive terms, to move them to the point where such 'congeries of feelings' could in turn be seen to move the world. Even if there is much to be concerned about with regard to the negative influence of an autonomous instrumental reason, the distinction between reason and emotion, between the so-called cognitive and affective, while a valuable clarion call from the romantics onwards against reason used in the service of domination, taken to extreme it cannot but in the end tend towards irrationalism, the de-socialization of the subject, and the erosion of actual and potential solidarity. Simply standing on the side of feelings against reason is not a good sociological option, while extending feeling into reasoning and reasoning back into feeling indeed is.

The fifth element in a sociological theory of reason is the way the *actualization of reason* is to be understood as intrinsic to social coordination. The concept of validity, present in neo-Kantian sociology, and significantly advanced by Habermas in *TCA*, is fundamental. According to Habermas, subjects in interaction raise various kinds of validity claims in their speech acts. Strydom further develops the theory of validity in the light of the immanent transcendent framework by distinguishing between what he calls validity concepts that are unconditioned and located on the transcendent plane from achievement (goal-oriented validity) concepts that apply to the conditioned, immanent plane (Strydom, 2019). Taking this idea further, O'Mahony has identified various levels of validity on the immanent plane that are attached to levels and modes of communicative coordination (O'Mahony, 2013; 2016; Kaczynski, 2021). These will be elaborated on later in the book.

The key underlying idea is that of social coordination by means of generals. The cognitive order principles, the ideas of reason (Kant), above located on the transcendent plane, are to be understood as generals or real universals'. They operate as cognitive universals, rather than normative universals, as is frequently assumed, and stand as open presuppositions of discourse. They are open in the sense that only the weak normative assumption that they are relevant – and implicitly – important in social life needs to be accepted. The weak normative assumption of relevance must allow for the fact that these cognitive universals have been selected over a very long period as in some way essential for social coordination and for helping to realize many possible forms of human fulfilment. Their preponderantly cognitive form is contained in the assumption that many normative interpretations, or, one might say, derivations of these principles are not alone possible, but they occur. A cognitive universal or validity principle, like that of legitimacy, is open to very restricted or quite radical *normative* application in that an action may be regarded as legitimate if, on the one hand, it can be reasonably assumed to meet 'general' societal agreement or if, on the other hand, it requires the actual approval of all in a comprehensive procedure. It is also true that legitimacy, or any other cognitive universal, may be blocked on the normative plane. This does not necessarily mean that it ceases to normatively operate – though it could mean that, wholly or partially – but that it is no longer possible to sustain critical-reflexive learning in this register, at least generally and publicly, because of closure wrought by the material or symbolic effects of power. Nor is such blockage an abnormal case; in most societies, even those that understand themselves as democratic in some meaningful sense of the word, cognitive universals such as legitimacy and others may be at least partially blocked, such as, for example, the concept of cosmopolitanism in the post-2016 Brexit debate in Britain (O'Mahony, 2016).

The sociological concern with the actualization of reason combines with a suspicion of the teleological constructs of reason operating as a philosophy of history. As Brunkhorst notes, sociology 'deconstructs' Hegel's teleology of history step by step (Brunkhorst, 2014). Care must be taken, though often it is not, that antagonism to a teleology of reason should not be at the expense of addressing the rational potentialities present in social arrangements, or thinkable beyond existing arrangements, even at the limit where this extends to utopian projections, as in, for example, the ideal of socialism in Marx. This kind of thinking does require fallible teleological projection. For, after Hegel, once the possibility of concretely specifying the precise and permanent social form arising from the realization of reason has been given up, it nonetheless remains critical to relate the transformative operations of reason to the impact, actual and possible, of reason in society. The effects of reason are inescapably present in society, whether its social realization is good or bad from a normative perspective. Further, commitment to let us say a domination-free society does require a normative theory and projection of that theory. Such a projection, operating as a society-spanning normative one, must indicate what an equivalent state of society should be, and this takes the form of a teleological construction against the backdrop of resistant social arrangements. However, such a teleology would have to be fallibly articulated with an end-state that is driven by as much a negative sense of what to avoid as a positive sense of what should be. All major social transformations, including the recent neoliberal one as well as the previous welfarist one, require both the articulation of a normative philosophy and its teleological projection as a prelude to possible implementation. However, following discourse ethics and Rainer Forst here, only in cases that can be fully democratically justified can such a projection be defended. Later, I will discuss discourse ethics within the context of social theory from this perspective.

The process of collective normative learning and its societal projection may be explicated further by following the ontological-epistemological implications of Peirce's three categories. In the first instance, something that is existent – in society or its natural environment – excites awareness, which could potentially be an immediate experience of a novel kind. Such awareness reacts against the existing habitus of the individual or group in question, including their normative commitments where normative innovation is at issue, and in so doing leads to perception

## 64   *Sociology and Reason*

and associated will formation, where this will could be of many kinds given the nature of the context and the obtaining universe of discourse. Such an orientation must *logically* locate itself in general contexts of relevance in order to generate meaning and, in so doing, counterfactually encounter principles of reason. The principles of reason – the cognitive principles discussed earlier – are expressions of human purposes. These purposes orient every possible human end, lofty or mundane. In an encounter with such principles, either the insight of the will takes the form of an operative habit, or a habit change indicates potential learning. If the latter, it remains only potential until tested for societal relevance, bearing in mind that it frequently goes beyond whether some claim to validity arising from the perceptual form, now logically transposed into an abduction, is valid or not in the here and now. In those cases of going beyond, it becomes a matter of whether it could become valid in some possible future. In more complicated cases of extended collective learning, many validity claims, frequently contradicting one another, must be taken into consideration over an extended time span. In this way, reasoning is to be understood as an experimental process in which learning with societal implications is possible but far from assured.

The final sociological element of reason relates to the *democratic conditions of the use of reason* within a rational communicative process. There are several pivotal dimensions to this element. The first is that rational cognition, the cognition of thought, of language, of other sign systems, is sign-mediated. Internally within individuals, intersubjectively between them, and trans-subjectively 'above' them, rational cognition is a product of reflexively utilized cultural forms. As sign-mediated, it entails a communicative theory of rational mind, applying both to subjective, objective, and extended social mind. The second is that what is rational is a particular kind of social construct. It is the capacity to form logically compelling chains of reasoning, or in another word, arguments. However, to say that an argument is rational, or reasonable, for that matter, does not mean it is true, right, or good. It merely means that it makes sense in a given universe of discourse and that it performs an appropriate action within this domain. The question of whether it is in accord with a more encompassing standard of reason is not something that attaches to it in its own immediate context. It can only be understood as fully rational within the temporally extended, long-run process of coming to, always revisable, conclusions in an actual communication community operating within the idealized standard of the unlimited communication community (Apel, 1995). In this latter sense, rational can be spoken of differently, as an outcome of a fully justified process. For rational or reasonable in this sense, there are various modalities of stabilization of the reasoning process: habits, norms, schemata, and cultural models, on which I will further elaborate later. The third and final dimension is that what is rational is not necessarily real in the above-instituted sense. Claims, world views, and ideas generally may be potentially rational, even if at a given state in their communicative diffusion they hold little or no traction in the instituted order (O'Mahony, 2010). Claims in this sense may also be implicit; they may, in fact, be no more than unarticulated, perhaps even unelaborated, feelings, as in one sense of Peirce's quali-sign as an unembodied possibility (Friedman, 1995). However, even

Sociology and Reason 65

such claims present an implicit claim, or possibility of a claim, that may have the potential to be fully justified in the long run, since they contain the germ of a new practical or theoretical standard. The rationality of feelings in this sense is usually only discernible after the fact or through being identified by outside contemporary observers since they have not reached the point of full articulation by their carriers. They exist as latent rational possibilities.

Habermas stresses the manner in which Peirce de-transcendentalizes reason by showing how, through its idealizing force, its operations reach beyond the world as it is while still remaining an event in the world (Habermas, 2019). It can thus bring out rational potentialities present in society through this idealizing force beyond any supra-mundane, transcendental a priori assumed to exist as a timeless universal. By contrast, transcendental in the sense intended here, following Habermas, involves the distillation of capacities on multiple levels, natural, sociocultural, and individual. Discourse ethics developed its immanent-transcendent framework based on Peirce's account of communication communities, real and unlimited. A state of full agreement ideally projected for the unlimited communication community – in the long run – creates an idealizing standard for orienting validity standards in the real communication community of the here and now. The standard of performative consistency – or, its opposite, performative contradiction – to capture the impossibility, without loss of orientation, of denying the validity of certain standards of inquiry, such as the pursuit of truth in theoretical discourse (Apel, 1995). Claiming not to follow such a standard, which is essential for rational argumentation, entails a lapse into performative contradiction. It also, possibly, indicates a disrespect for rational argumentation in the first place, for example, denying the status of the other as a participant to be respected or the substitution of strategic for rational communicative goals. Discourse ethics draws its normative standards of full inclusion and full autonomy in the operation of both theoretical and practical reason from this idea of a communication community. In extreme shorthand, from the critical enlightenment onwards, and especially since Kant, the use of reason involves the supposition of autonomous rational subjectivity – being bound by the laws one gives oneself or communities of autonomous individuals give themselves. It therefore separates itself from the Humean idea of reason as a hierarchy of goods and commits to reason requiring a rational orientation towards getting ever closer to unconditionally valid norms. Implied in this are a whole host of further presuppositions about the operations of law, legitimacy, and much else, but its most basic premise is the moral one of equal respect for all subjects (Forst, 2013).

If the degree of diffusion of the presuppositions of respect, together with others such as equality and esteem, is fully considered, it becomes apparent that modern life is saturated with them, as critical theorists such as Forst and Honneth have shown in their different ways. Of course, this is not meant to suggest they possess unquestioned hegemony in actual forms of life, as the ongoing critique of the pathologies of reason and the continuous presence of unreason amply shows. Nonetheless, the denial or non-recognition of their presence is also a manifestation of a performative contradiction, when in fact these standards operate implicitly as presuppositions in the kinds of perspectives that animate argumentation in the

## 66   *Sociology and Reason*

social and human sciences. Critical sociology to some degree manifests this kind of performative contradiction. It is clear in the main that it seeks to defend certain of these standards in its arguments, but it tends to deny that they already have a hold in modern life. This is to claim that modernity in some spheres, and to some degree, manifests the outcomes of the justified operations of reason and also manifests unrealized rational potentialities immanent in as yet non-institutionalized or only partly institutionalized learning processes. It is true that this kind of performative contradiction does not seek to deny the validity of the standards themselves, but it does do so indirectly in the supposition that no possible world may be envisaged in which their validity could be realized. This both makes contradictory the intention of the intervention, given the apparent hopelessness, and it also leaves out of consideration that the sociologist – and presumably some of her audience – must have certain cognitive, normative, and material resources to engage in it in the first place, begging the concomitant question of from where they might have derived.

While it is true to say that the perspective of discourse ethics has within its core aspects of the moral foundations of modernity – the autonomy of the subject, universal inclusion, the right and duty to justify, the need for performative consistency in argumentation – and that at least the first two of these are tacit presuppositions of critical sociology, it is also true to say that these by themselves do not have sufficient normative amplitude for a comprehensive normative perspective of sociology. To briefly develop this, let us go back to the distinction drawn above, following Strydom, between validity concepts and achievement (goal-oriented validity) concepts. If this is placed within a logic of time, it will be seen that the temporal perspective of discourse ethics is rationally motivated agreement *in the long run*. This raises two related questions. What happens in the shorter run? And how do we adjust to the fact that we cannot be sure what is in the long run, given the unpredictability of the future and the conditions of detrancendentalized, processual operations of reasoning? From a sociological perspective concerned with the dialectical interplay between reason, its societalization, and the potential for transformation, it may be concluded that more is needed than such long-run temporal horizons and the standard of full agreement or consensus. What is also needed are standards of rational dissensus since, in the domain of practical reason in conditions of pluralism, full agreement may never be forthcoming, and, even where it is, something 'lesser' like rational dissensus, the respectful agreement to differ, may subsist for a long time (O'Mahony, 2013). I will not go further into this sixth, normative, element of reason here – It is already by far the longest – beyond saying that there are further and significant normative implications that follow from a detranscendentalized operation of reason related to different kinds of goal-oriented validity. In other words, individuals and groups may believe in different concepts of justice and, even where they agree on these, may differ on how they might be realized and over what time span. Even with the strong counterfactual example of good-willed people, perhaps in Rawls's sense committed to a more just future guided by certain basic principles, that future will remain significantly open-ended. Notwithstanding this open-ended quality, sociology should not turn away from its responsibility to generate normatively relevant knowledge

*Sociology and Reason*   67

that would realize rational potentialities and avoid the inevitable consequences of their absence. These should involve the types of commitments made by discourse ethics, and one might add the theory of justification to the normatively necessary operating conditions of reason. However, it should also, following Peirce's idea of concrete reasonableness, Rawls's concrete utopia, and Honneth's theory of recognition, show what should be the tasks of reason so enabled to bring about a better world. Even then, sociology cannot be satisfied with what is worked out philosophically, even if this latter orientation is indispensable. Instead, it has to translate such an orientation into its own discourse and, through this, help to shape the general direction of theorising across disciplines. It will not want to leave, as philosophical projects more readily can, the actual discourse of agents or the feelings, manifest or suppressed, embodied and unembodied, that are potential harbingers of discursively achieved normative innovation.

The above account of these various sociological elements of reason fulfils a variety of purposes that are far from fully in harmony. It offers a type of introduction to a particular kind of critical cognitive sociology, the one followed in this volume. It offers a brief commentary on some dimensions of reason as used more generally in sociology. It relates sociology to other disciplinary considerations, principally and inescapably, that of philosophy. Overall, it begins with consideration of certain issues that will recur and that were only roughly indicated in the above, given their complexity and magnitude. The above considerations are only intended to provide insight into background assumptions. In the next two chapters, I will bring the above elements explicitly into play in addressing the sociology of reason, so often articulated as a concern with reflexivity.

### Notes

1  Such a call will appear as ideal-theoretical heresy to some, but can an interdisciplinary normative political theory, properly developing the sociological inheritance, really be developed without reference to Rawls? For an extended account, see my attempt to integrate Rawls and other political philosophies in a sociological framework (O'Mahony, 2013).
2  More extended treatment will be given to generals in Chapter 5 and subsequent chapters. The comments here work on the distinction between transcendent cognitive universals and immanent ideals. Friedman's analysis is insightful and productive on this issue, taking a distinctive position in affirming Peirce's transcendentalism but from a perspective that has affinities with what is here described as immanent-transcendent within the frame of critical theory.

### References

Apel, K-O (1995) *Charles Peirce: From Pragmatism to Pragmaticism.* New York: Prometheus.
Apel K-O (1980) *Towards a Transformation of Philosophy.* Milwaukee: Marquette University Press.
Apel K-O (1993) Challenge of a Totalizing Critique of Reason and the Program of a Philosophical Theory of Rationality Types. In: Freundlieb D and Hudson W (eds) *Reason and Its Other: Rationality in Modern German Philosophy.* Oxford: Berg.

## 68   *Sociology and Reason*

Boltanski L and Thévenot L (1999) The Sociology of Critical Capacity. *European Journal of Social Theory* 2(3): 359–377.

Brunkhorst H (2014) *Critical Theory of Legal Revolutions: Evolutionary Perspectives*. London: Bloomsbury.

Forst R (2013) *Toleration in Conflict: Past and Present*. Cambridge: Cambridge University Press.

Friedman L (1995) CS Peirce's Transcendental and Immanent Realism. *Transactions of the Charles S. Peirce Society* 31(2): 374–392.

Habermas J (2019) *Auch Eine Geschichte der Philosophie*. Frankfurt: Suhrkamp.

Horkheimer M (1974 (1947)) *Eclipse of Reason*. London: Bloomsbury.

Israel JI (2001) *Radical Enlightenment: Philosophy and the Making of Modernity, 1650–1750*. Oxford: Oxford University Press.

Kaczynski R (2021) *The Societal Capacity for Democratic Justification: A Social Theory of the Reasonable Society*. Doctoral Dissertation, Johann Wolfgang Goethe-Universität Frankfurt am Main.

Lynch M (2000) Against Reflexivity as an Academic Virtue and Source of Privileged Knowledge. *Theory, Culture & Society* 17(3): 26–54.

Merton RK (1936) Puritanism, Pietism, and Science. *The Sociological Review* 28(1): 1–30.

O'Mahony P (2010) Habermas and Communicative Power. *Journal of Power* 3(1): 53–73.

O'Mahony P (2013) *The Contemporary Theory of the Public Sphere*. Oxford: Peter Lang.

O'Mahony P (2016) Reason, Reasoning, and Critical Theory. *Unpublished MS, University College Cork.*

Peirce CS (1892) The Law of Mind. *The Monist* 2(4): 533–559.

Strydom P (2011) *Contemporary Critical Theory and Methodology*. London: Routledge.

Strydom P (2012) Cosmopolitanism, the Cognitive Order of Modernity, and Conflicting Models of World Openness: On the Prospects of Collective Learning. In: Giri A (ed) *Cosmopolitanism and Beyond: Towards a Multiverse of Transformations*. India: Duwamish Books.

Strydom P (2017) Infinity, Infinite Processes and Limit Concepts: Recovering a Neglected Background of Social and Critical Theory. *Philosophy and Social Criticism* 43(8): 793–811.

Strydom P (2019) On Habermas's Differentiation of Rightness from Truth: Can an Achievement Concept Do without a Validity Concept? *Philosophy and Social Criticism* 45(5): 555–574.

# 3 Reason and the Reflexive Turn in Sociology

Reflexivity has become such a pivotal and widespread concept in sociology that it presents quite a challenge to grasp its significance in the history and contemporary state of the discipline. Sociologists certainly appear more comfortable talking about reflexivity than they do when talking about reason. As a specific concept, reason as opposed to reflexivity or rationality tends not to be regarded as a native concept of the discipline, as is also the case in the human and social sciences more generally. In many areas of the social sciences in recent times, reflexivity has acquired greater centrality than rationality, which owes much to the history of the concept of rationality in the discipline, as it also owes much to the positioning of the concept of reason outside the discipline.

Accordingly, there has been a noticeable tendency to turn to the use of the term reflexivity over the last half-century in the social sciences. It coincides with what is sometimes called the agential turn. Many books and articles from the most prominent sociologists, ranging from Gouldner to Bourdieu, to Archer, take reflexivity as a core idea, a situation that did not obtain in the preceding half-century (Gouldner, 1971; Bourdieu, 1990; Archer, 2010). As a first attempt to explain this, the transformation of the discipline in related post-empiricist, interpretive, and critical directions in the second half of the 20th century is obvious, even if also essential. Well before this, even if the term reflexivity was not in widespread use, something akin to it was alive in the discipline, variously in Marx's account of praxis, Weber's rationality theory and verstehen methodology, in a symbolic interactionism influenced by pragmatism, in Schutz's social phenomenology, and even in the early Parsons's voluntaristic theory of action. At least the idea of reflexivity, then, had a life in the discipline avant la lettre. This gives some insight into how it has been, implicitly or explicitly, intrinsic to major currents in sociology. The discipline became comparatively slowly institutionalized in the late 19th and early 20th centuries, when the world at large was being transformed by great waves of democratization, industrialization, urbanization, and secularization. Though this is an encompassing statement inviting qualification, it is scarcely to be doubted that in most parts of the world, the situation of the human being was being transformed. In 'most parts', because even if these dramatically accelerating complexes belonged more to the so-called 'developed' part of

DOI: 10.4324/9780429060571-4

## 70 *Reason and the Reflexive Turn in Sociology*

the world, they had immense, often negative, repercussions for other parts. In the first half of the last century at least they could not stop, indeed in their unbalanced and unjust implications induced, other powerful forces from generating unparalleled levels of destruction.

I dwell on this here to emphasize in a simple, hardly-to-be-denied manner that whatever nuance may be brought to the interpretation, whatever process-oriented depth interpretation of events is offered, it is not to be doubted that many human beings became in the period of the development of sociology equipped with quite different competences to those of their forebears. The more fortunate were equipped with competences to read and to write; they acquired a range of civil, political, and social rights; through the development of publicity, they acquired political and symbolic influence; and through the expanded economy and public administration, a wider range of possible careers were made possible. While sociology was far from blind to the downside of these developments, with Marx the exploitative and alienating domination of capital, with Weber the 'iron cage', and with Durkheim anomie, it did not amount to a denial of Hegel's insight that modern civil society at least held the potential for an encompassing freedom of a kind not seen before. Such freedom had no other foundations in the context of modern civil society than in autonomy, both public and private (Habermas, 1996). The idea of autonomy ineluctably generates the need for collectivities and individuals to understand that they do or could have it and raises the possibility of how they might use it to further assert and protect their freedom. Even where modern sociology identified forces that led to its practical denial, autonomy still stood as a regulative ideal of the kinds of freedom and associated competences that humans should possess. The largely implicit concern for autonomy in contemporary sociology is bound up with the assumption of the reflexivity of agents, calling forth in turn the need for a reflexive sociology. The combination of reflexivity and autonomy is close to the province of reason, but as explored this is a concept that sociology is wont to exclude.

It is reflexivity in its more explicit, later flowering that is of chief interest in this chapter, understood as both a component and entry point to how sociology understands reason. I will first examine some key aspects of the concept as it has appeared in various branches of sociology in, more or less, the second half of the 20th century. My interest is not in a sociology of reflexivity per se but in the relevance of a reformulated communicative reason for the discipline and for wider scholarship. Nonetheless, the way reason has become associated with or, more accurately, channelled into reflexivity in the discipline is of fundamental importance for assessing the potential for its incorporation of, and contribution to, communicative reason. So, the first step in the chapter is to provide a highly selective review of sociology and reflexivity. This review will be impelled by, as far as possible, the need to identify general features. Following on from this in the next chapter, I will seek to isolate specifically what dimensions of the sociology of reason adumbrated in the last chapter resonate with the general sociological treatment of reflexivity outlined in this one. A factor that has to be kept in mind is that reflexivity is often advanced in sociology as a critique of elitist forms of reason, assumed in many cases by such critics to be the essence of reason. Thus, sociological constructivism in the last

*Reason and the Reflexive Turn in Sociology*  71

sixty or so years can be interpreted in part as a revolt against the assumed denial of reflexivity in accounts of reason.

A useful starting point for taking up the theme of reflexivity in sociology is the debate between Parsons and Schutz in the early 1940s (Buxton, 1994). While admittedly here the term was not explicitly used, it was effectively at issue and served as a prelude to new developments in sociology over the following half-century or more. In any case, Parsons's theory of the normatively regulated voluntarism of action is a type of reflexive position, even if many would hold that it was the break with Parsonian functionalism that really inaugurated a reflexive turn in the discipline (Gouldner, 1971). Parsons did himself hold a reflexive position of a certain kind in that he advanced a normative sociology with reflexive epistemic commitments. At least for the early Parsons, the ultimate ends or values that underlay that position depended on a conception of reflexivity that, elitist to be sure, advanced the idea that this system of quasi-transcendental ultimate ends was constituted and maintained by professional strata, including academics (Parsons, 1990; Buxton, 1994). The parallels with Rawls's account of public reason are striking (Rawls, 1993; O'Mahony, 2013). Nevertheless, though elitist, this position is quite rightly described by Buxton as reflexive in that the outcome was a product of willed and motivated action, striving for nothing less than comprehensive means of social control. As the debate with Schutz made clear, Parsons viewed the specification of values as a matter of theory, not practice, in which academics played a pivotal role; it serves as a type of theoretical or scholarly reflexivity.

Even if Parsons conservative type of liberalism viewed theoretical reflexivity in one light, others could develop it differently, as, for example, Bourdieu. In a matter not entirely removed from how the sociology of critique of Boltanski and Thevenot criticized Bourdieu for his choices, Schutz criticized Parsons (Bourdieu and Wacquant, 1992; Bourdieu, 2004; Boltanski, 2011). For Schutz, meaning constructs manifested themselves in the everyday lifeworld as the product of common sense (Schutz, 1932). Cultural forms of the lifeworld are dialectically bound up with symbolic action. In Schutz's view, Parsons foists theoretical constructs onto lay audiences, and there are no reliable means to demonstrate that they have any traction there (Schutz and Parsons, 1978). This debate between the empirical-analytical, Parsons, and the Weberian-hermeneuticist, Schutz, also has resonance for the critical position. In critical theory, while the emphasis is on the inclusion of all in reflexive practice, it nonetheless also utilizes a type of explanatory critique based on theoretical – also called scholarly or external – reflexivity. Such a type of reflexivity asserts that those affected by injustices and pathologies may not be aware that this is the case because of ideological screening or recessed pathological processes. In order to avoid the potential contradiction between theoretical and popular reflexivity, it argues that the social world is not fully transparent to itself, and that complexity of all kinds requires multi-level interventions. Accordingly, theoretical explanatory interventions are needed to assist lay subjects to themselves overcome deficits of reflexivity.

Conceiving reflexivity in this latter critical sense is contested by Michael Lynch (Lynch, 2000). Lynch takes up the tradition opened by Schutz by emphasizing

## 72   *Reason and the Reflexive Turn in Sociology*

reflexivity as a linguistic achievement manifested in the practices of everyday life. Reflexivity in this sense is not a matter of virtue, the idea that reflexivity is in some sense a societal good. As he puts it, reflexivity depends on who does it and, by implication, not on some distinction between non-reflexive communications based on automatic or mechanical considerations as opposed to critical reflexivity. He holds further to the idea, developing this point, that reflexivity is a universal attribute, intrinsic to 'the street' rather than the preserve of reflexive virtuosi, who alone might be able to practice it correctly. Its universality is, in this sense, not normative but cognitive. The cognitive grounding of reflexivity was canonically developed by Cicourel as another type of critique of Parsons (Cicourel, 1981). Cicourel asked how Parsons could account for the genesis of universally binding values in modern circumstances of interpretive openness. For Cicourel, attention must shift to the interactive competences manifested in normative accounting practices that actors use to justify the validity of their claims to knowledge, where these accounting practices in turn depend on socio-cognitive processes of thought, socially organized memory, selective attention, and sensory modalities (O'Mahony, 2013). Lynch and Cicourel together indicate the chasm opened with Parsons by contemporary interpretive sociology. Reflexivity for them is emphatically a lay accomplishment, or, following Cicourel, when done by professionals requiring a distinctive kind of 'abductive' creative reasoning, a term he took over from Peirce (Cicourel, 2011). Such a perspective has, with remarkable speed, opened a methodological perspective that emphasizes the situated nature of constructing knowledge and the progressive dethronement of the observer role, including the role of external critique.

Reflexivity, as advanced by Lynch and as extensively used in the methodological literature of, inter alia, some forms of feminism, in science studies, and generally many constructivist approaches, is associated with a focus on the micro-level of social action/interaction. The way the concept of reflexivity is employed is geared towards this micro-level orientation, as by choice it does without the macro-normative connotations regarded as attaching to the concept of reason, even to the more mundane and methodologically oriented analysis of 'reasoning'. In line with this, much modern social thought evinces a quite widespread urge to distance itself from macro-normative commitments. There are several discernible reasons, not least the assumption that the complexity and pluralism of modern societies make some kind of relativism inevitable. On the intellectual level, this sense of the necessity of relativism goes back to the early formation of the discipline and was carried into much of the interpretive tradition, narrowly understood to distinguish it from the wider interpretive transformation of knowledge in the linguistic turn. Narrowly understood then as the province of a certain kind of sociology, this tradition is opposed to the critical social scientific practice of generalized normative judgement. Such practice is viewed as foisting a scholarly viewpoint on lay actors and denying them their own capacity for reflexivity. In the sociology of knowledge tradition following Mannheim, the reflexive relation is taken to lie between carriers of worldviews, generations, and social groups and their associated ideologies, where the word ideology is understood neutrally rather than critically (Mannheim, 2012). The evaluative position

*Reason and the Reflexive Turn in Sociology*   73

of the social scientist is strictly screened out and denied as relevant. The absence of a normative reference is precisely what came under attack by critical theorists. Nonetheless, a certain interpretation of reflexivity has become widespread, stemming from interpretivism, narrowly understood, and accentuated by the relativistic stance of postmodernism.

Reflexivity from this point of view is a type of 'individual' reflection on relevant background factors that affect the academic interpreter, though the 'Individual' might also be a collective actor in Mannheim's sense. This might be called the first dimension of interpretive reflexivity, where the second is that the academic interpreter has no special status in her capacity for reflexivity since all subjects can equally well do it. From these dimensions, it can be inferred that any additional value coming from academic reflexivity merely derives from its role as a medium of translation between conversations going on generally in society, perhaps best understood through the idea of providing clarification of societal communication but having no other directive or critical force.

The above briefly lays out two positions, Parsons and interpretivism, often regarded as in direct competition, but there was also a tendency to fuse them in various ways as the 20th century wore on. Frequently, if not always, the interpretive tradition narrowly understood had more conservative leanings, certainly in terms of its historical genesis, yet its theoretical-methodological influence grew in almost all branches of sociology. In various ways, wider interpretive-type positions that bear on the linguistic turn and an associated highly ambivalent and inexplicit relation to German idealism are employed in critical thinking in the social sciences. The pure Parsonian type receded in importance, with his most prominent system theoretical successor, Luhmann, grounding his work on a communicative system phenomenology. With Parsons and the associated general current of thought, macro-sociology also began to lose traction despite attempts to revitalize it towards the end of the century by an attempted fusion of micro and macro theorizing (Alexander et al, 1987). Overall, reflexivity in many social theories tended to combine elements of theoretical reflexivity, derived from the empirical-analytic tradition, and lay or popular reflexivity from the interpretive tradition. Beyond these, there was also further development of a type of critical reflexivity, whose origins go back to Kant's emphasis on the need for reason's self-critique. Critical reflexivity in the modern post-Kantian format used in critical theory breaks with individualism, both as the isolated observer of theoretical reflexivity and as the situated individual reflection of interpretivism. In critical theory, at least, wider contextual and context-transcending elements are incorporated in the sense of the immanent and transcendent justification previously outlined. There is a basic difference, though, in that while the concept of reflexivity can be imputed to certain kinds of empirical-analytical theory, it is not an explicit or 'native' concept there, while it is so in the other two traditions. The concepts of reflexivity in these other traditions have different origins, and partly also different accounts of similar origins; critical reflexivity derives from a critical reading of the idealist heritage, especially Kantian and left-Hegelian, and the interpretive concept springs from the hermeneutic tradition filtered through various 20th-century forms of interactionism.

## 74 *Reason and the Reflexive Turn in Sociology*

Reflexivity is a key concept for grasping how modern social theory relates to the heritage of reason, given that explicit consideration of the concept of reason is rare across all approaches. A noticeable feature of both critical and post-Parsonian traditions, for example, neo-functionalism, is its frequent reliance on a concept of interpretation at least partly derived from premises of the interpretative tradition, though substantially emended. Such an approach, including its emphasis on binaries, takes the place of what I emphasize here, reliance on an alternative source and kind of interpretation in the form of the pragmatist semiotic tradition. In critical scholarship, such a pragmatist semiotics is mainly associated in social theory with critical theory and critical realism. At least in the former case, it allows the possible articulation of a comprehensive concept of communicative reason that can meet the needs of the social sciences.

In the following reviews of relevant social theoretical dimensions of reflexivity, my concern will be with the post-Parsonian and critical traditions. The Parsonian tradition still offers the most suggestive ways to continue to develop macro-sociology, though its relation to the rise of interpretivism is ambivalent and not systematically pursued directly within the tradition. The critical tradition is my main object of interest, following the recent provenance of the concept of communicative reason in Habermas. This tradition relies on all three kinds of reflexivity, but as indicated above, it has its own account of the linguistic turn and the significance of interpretation. The reviews below will accordingly mainly concentrate on post-Parsonian and critical sociological approaches, as these are most germane to building a theory of communicative reason within the critical theoretical tradition. Such a theory is designed to facilitate the emergence of a new impetus in the critical theory of society that, while mediated across different levels from macro through meso, to micro, would not neglect the significance of the macro moment. The interpretive tradition for the multiple kinds of reason already offered has become embedded in the other traditions of reflexive thinking, but it has tended to neglect the macro-sociological moment that is of great concern here. I will accordingly begin the reviews with three theorists who have been historically regarded as updating Parsons: Alexander, Munch, and Luhmann, though the former has moved a considerable distance from his earlier neo-functionalist contributions. That will be followed by two accounts of critical sociology in the structure-agency paradigm, before concluding with some remarks on two third-generation critical theory contributions, Honneth and Forst, the latter subject to a critique by McNay, as they bear on the relationship between reason, normativity, and the social sciences. The wider implications of these reviews on the critical cognitive-sociological approach outlined in Chapter 2 will be addressed in the next chapter, Chapter 4.

### Alexander

Alexander's most focused account of the issue of reason and reflexivity is in *Fin De Siecle Social Theory: Relativism, Reduction and the Problem of Reason* (Alexander, 1995). The focus of the book is anticipated in the first pages, even in the first short paragraph, where the author identifies a dilemma arising from the decline of the

*Reason and the Reflexive Turn in Sociology* 75

pre-eminence of reason in the 20th century by contrast with the growing importance attached to the ability to be reasonable. The ability to be reasonable depends on culturally ordered, interactive capacities that can mediate between general aspirations and particular circumstances Such mediation is achieved by means of symbolic codes and grand narratives rooted in traditions. Philosophical hermeneutics, especially an account of Gadamer, is employed to defend this mediated position. Gadamer is also said to be important for grounding universalism against extreme contextualism, for which Rorty and postmodernism are represented as exemplars. Evincing a type of weak communitarian position, Alexander follows Gadamer in the view that strong social bonds are needed to make universalism possible, making requisite communities of normatively aligned members.

Alexander emphasizes the importance of a culture of civility based, following Durkheim, on the distinction between sacred and profane, which shows faith in liberal democracy. The latter is presented as pivotal to collective solidarity, embodying what is civil and standing opposed to the uncivil. Alexander sets out his position as at variance with two others. It is opposed to a relativistic standpoint that dismisses reason as a facade for repression and violence and advances an 'anything goes' tolerant orientation as an antidote. It is also opposed to a reductionist, materialist position that reduces reason to a method of inquiry rather than a cultural pattern or substantive goal. To generalize, the first position would be roughly equated with postmodernism and the second with the kind of subjective, formal reason already criticized by Adorno and Horkheimer. This general mapping of the field of reason is correlated with Alexander's gradual self-distancing from his previous neo-functionalist position, which sought to mediate material and ideal factors, in the direction of a greater emphasis on the ideal pole. Such an ideal pole is characterized by a view of culture as supporting autonomous reasoning by agents, leading to what he calls 'cultural pragmatics' (Alexander, 2004). The history of neo-functional theory had gradually internally evolved from a concern with functionally identifiable cultural imperatives, to taking account of the plans and strategies of agents who tried with varying success to shape functional logics, to finally arriving at a type of self-dissolution of this line of functional thinking in cultural pragmatics.

In the light of this shift, Alexander began in the 1990s to pursue the idea of social coordination through culture. Culture is understood in two complementary senses. The micro-cultural order of individual autonomy is, in the first instance, strongly emphasized. The capacity to autonomously stand apart from social structures is regarded as fateful for the prospects of a better world, while also crucial to the preservation of what is currently good, as actuality or potentiality. In this respect, Alexander's position is consistent with Archer's account of reflexivity (see below) in emphasizing the autonomous capacity of individuals. They are similar too in seeking distance from structural determinism, which in both cases includes a critique of Bourdieu. The second sense in which Alexander understands culture is that of a macro-societal order of meaning, taking form in symbolic codes and grand narratives. The manner, in which these codes are ordered, consistent from the 1995 text to his mammoth

## 76  *Reason and the Reflexive Turn in Sociology*

work on civil society, is that of sacred and profane. In this respect, he claims that American society over several centuries has been consistently structured by discourses of civil and uncivil (Alexander and Smith, 1993). The first element of this binary structure emphasizes the idea of the reasonable, which is advanced as one of the two great possibilities of the cultural order, with uncivility as its opposing moment.

The book, *Fin De Siecle Social Theory*, is written in what feels like a paradoxical appreciation of the zeitgeist. On the one hand, we are told of the apocalypse of reason in the 20th century, in which reason in the form of instrumental rationality overreached itself and contributed to a cataclysm, not once but several times over. On the other hand, the book was written in the 1990s with intimations of the triumph of liberal democracy, but a liberal democracy that would have to rein in its ambitions regarding social justice given the normative climate that was then emerging. In this latter sense, Alexander did prove quite right, at least as regards the empirical trend. Overall, the sense of threat overcomes the spirit of optimism and the possibility of radical change, inducing a perceived need to recognize customary bounds of democracy. In this way, Alexander's account is redolent of the conclusions, if not the reasoning, of quite a number of democratic theorists, including Sartori, Bobbio, and Heller, who wrote in the last decades of the 20th century (O'Mahony, 2011). All these diagnose and predict inclement times for democracy and express the need to defend a formal, liberal democratic core for fear of worse. It is a conserving vision, even if not in the strict sense of a conservative one; though, in blocking potentials for change, it could become so. This would be the case if it became associated with a democratic centrism that cannot learn from societal peripheries and instead takes on the air of resignation to ineluctable normative constraints on 'progressive' action, a worldview that has typified western social democracy in the last three decades.

By and large, in *Fin De Siecle Social Theory*, Alexander distances himself from Rawls in a manner that is consistent with, perhaps even anticipates, the general sociological distancing over the last two or three decades. In one respect, Rawls would seem to be somewhat in line with Alexander's basic template of the endurance of liberal democracy in given political cultures over time, for example, as expressed in the former's account of a 'sense of justice' (Rawls, 1999). Such a sense of justice encapsulates the commitments to justice that arise within a particular 'people' and endure over time. However, Rawls is imbued with too much rationalist optimism for Alexander. He notes that while Rawls and also Habermas have developed a type of critical alternative to technocratic social engineering, nonetheless it is a view from which he takes distance due to its rationally grounded optimism (Alexander, 1995, 79). He notes by contrast that Walzer and other 'internalist' critics – internalist means an emphasis on the immanent, eschewing the transcendent – of this position argue that justice cannot be 'understood in terms of abstract criteria and transcendental positions....but must be theorised from within the cultural practices of particular spheres of life' (ibid). He then goes on to say that social movements that ignore 'these structures encourage the domination and violence that has characterised the degenerate line of twentieth century life' (ibid).

*Reason and the Reflexive Turn in Sociology* 77

The inferential moves in Alexander's argument at this point are rather tendentious, but they are also perhaps meant to be. The argument progresses from the critique of a certain kind of rationalism – whose references, Habermas and Rawls, in any case, show both similarities and considerable differences –, to the assertion of the importance of Walzer's idea of spheres of life, to the warning to social movements that step outside of this framework. Ironically, somewhat akin to the implications of Rawls's sense of justice, how can a justice framework, that itself had serious limitations at its origin, somehow be assumed to continue over centuries without radical transformation? How are the impacts of issues of race, globalization, gender, nature, and dignity, to name but a few, to be grasped? And hence, what does the unspecific warning to social movements to work within established cultural structures connote?

This uncertainty, extending to what Alexander ultimately understands by reason, is compounded by the apparent stability of the symbolic codes and grand narratives of tradition, which underpin the reflexive capacities of individuals. It is not at all clear why individuals, or groups, with such reflexive capacities should not generate a depth of collective learning that would bring about transformation of the cultural structures traditionally established at any given time. Perhaps the rather ironic answer is that such reflexive capacities are regarded by him as animated by the non-rational, which is said to be the necessary mode of theorization of social change. We must theorize not only the past but the present and the future too. This can only be done in a non-rational way so as to not only accommodate what we know but also what we believe, hope, and fear. Perhaps it is this non-rational fundament, that he says exists in a narrative form that will carry 'us' forward, that will challenge us to be reasonable but also indicate in what directions being reasonable tends? In this sense, perhaps Alexander is suggesting that it might be some kind of 'other of reason', presently beyond reason, that might be the kind of social change that requires theorizing. If this is so, it appears to be at considerable variance with the idea of the encompassing stability of tradition and its defence of moral universals. It is more likely that Alexander believes more in the contrast between what he envisages as a rationalistic, perfectionist, and hence unattainable enlightenment idea of reason and the non-rational in the form of the emotional substrate of human life. This emotional substrate and reason can never be reconciled and will remain permanently in tension; hence, overemphasis on either end of the polarity creates a threat to the survival of civility through excess emotional resonance or formal rationality. Either it will bring about a pervasive relativism that can give no orientation, or it will lead to a technocratic rationalism that generated alienation and emotional privation in the 20th century.

At no point through Alexander's book on reason is there a satisfactory elaboration of what he understands by reason and how it does or could relate to actual or possible worlds. Only one side of the enlightenment is emphasized, the Humean tradition, which is found wanting, with the critical enlightenment scarcely mentioned. Correspondingly, the emphasis placed by Kant on the affinity between reason and critique is not developed. While great, if rather paradoxical, emphasis is attached to the individual capacity for reflexive freedom, there is no account of

# 78  *Reason and the Reflexive Turn in Sociology*

the modalities of reasoning and the relationship between reason, reasoning, normativity, and world creation. If any account of reason is at all discernible, it lies in an unusual amalgam of empiricism and interpretivism. The empiricist dimension stresses the customary, or traditional, quality of reason as a kind of established common sense. The incorporated emphasis on sensibility is given effect, with a twist, by attending to emotions and the non-rational. The complementary interpretive dimension derives from a communitarian type emphasis on the societal community.

In general, the emphasis on being reasonable makes space for reflexivity, though it is not explicitly a central concept for Alexander, and the later combination of social performance theory and cultural pragmatics could be imagined providing a theoretical-methodological ground for its operation. The emphasis on social performance, with its Goffmanian heritage of dramaturgical action, is aligned with Durkheim's emphasis on ritual order (Alexander, 2004). Ritually produced order, whose determining power is waning in modern society, nonetheless remains an important aspect of the background culture. Social performance, grasped by means of cultural pragmatics, allows a more dynamic relationship between this background culture and human activities to emerge. Accordingly, some dimensions of the approach I am advancing arise from the common desire to examine the relationship between cultural structures and situationally located cognition. Nonetheless, as the current book proceeds, it will become apparent that the placement of the elements, the aesthetic, cultural codes, order, reason, and the introduction of quite different elements, inference, immanent transcendence, and others, indicate in the end a quite different approach.

## Richard Munch

Munch offers another post-Parsonian account that, in some respects, is compatible with Alexander (Münch, 2010). Both accounts attach considerable ongoing importance to the intellectual legacy of Durkheim. This is especially so in relation to the account of the voluntaristic theory of action and the communal account of solidarity. If Alexander's problem focus was to be translated into Munch's terms, it would be one of how to theorize both the obligatory communal nature of values and the radical voluntarism of individual reflexivity. While Munch stresses that Durkheim did not solve this problem, nonetheless, beyond other intellectual traditions, including neo-Weberian scholarship, he did crucially emphasize the affective foundations of action. This is consistent with Alexander's idea of the critical interplay between non-rational and rational dimensions of social order; in this view, order always rests ultimately on its affective foundations. However, Durkheim cannot actually show how such affective foundations arise because his theory of reflexive individuation, the theory of solidarity, lacks the necessary critical-reflexive capacity.

This problem is endemic in modern social theory. Through Munch, one can point via Durkheim to the necessary affective foundations of normative complexes, the idea that individuals and groups must be attached to them so that they acquire obligatory traction. Munch uses this point to criticize the various accounts

Reason and the Reflexive Turn in Sociology 79

of Weber, Parsons, and Habermas. Though Durkheim can identify the necessity, his theory is unable to adequately show how the micro-foundations of affectivity operate. Various modern theories emphasizing discourse, performativity, emotions, rational choice, or narrative, in many ways and sometimes in combination have turned attention to this challenge. They typically today offer an extensive but one-sided account aimed at the individual and/or the interactive levels of coordination, but they leave the question of societal rationality in abeyance. What is frequently emphasized in these accounts is the irrational bases of individual agency, often positioned against the imputed or specified domination of modern rationality, itself often interpreted in the way of Alexander as an excess of purposive rationality. By contrast, Munch, who is anxious to retain something of Durkheim's assumption of potential positive synergy between the two poles, emphasizes that the non-rational need not be irrational; it could also be a candidate for later rationalization. Such a view raises important issues regarding the status of the irrational, which Munch tends to interpret in terms of what elsewhere is called the pre-rational, as coming before rationality. He also describes rationality in formal terms as an 'empty category', whose orientation must ultimately come from an irrational but not non-rational – perhaps this could be translated into pre-rational – affectivity. He notes that:

We cannot call into question the standards of rationality without deserting rationality itself. Any other form of order has a similar non-rational basis, the rational questioning of which would destroy the order.

(Münch, 2010).

At one level, this position may be defended as the drawing of attention to the cognitive, desiring, and willing, as what comes before and conditions the kinds of logical reasoning that give rise to rational conduct. The position, at the same time, still suffers from what Durkheim was unable to demonstrate: how affective foundations consistent with any kind of rationality could be shown to have come about rather than simply being objectively postulated. In the end, though, even if the mechanisms of the path from affectivity to reasoning have not been shown from this theoretical standpoint, and, going back to Schutz's criticisms of Parsons it can generally be said they have not been, the attention to this problem is important. It was part of a general theme in sociological theory in the 1980s and contributed to the structure-agency paradigm that has defined a considerable amount of recent theoretical work. While there has been diffuse consideration of the normative implications of this link between affectivity and narrativity within the post-Parsonian theoretical tradition – Alexander's account of narrativity and performativity being one example –, very little has been taken on board from the critical tradition, even if that critical tradition is understood in a very general way as originating with the critical enlightenment. Hence, questions of how to distinguish between good and bad affectivity or good and bad reasoning, to put the issues in a simplified way, have not been obviously attempted and certainly not with sustained and productive attention. It is precisely here that the link between

## 80  *Reason and the Reflexive Turn in Sociology*

feeling (affectivity) and reasoning first arises in Peirce's semiotic theory, taken up in later chapters.

The general emphasis of the post-Parsonian neo-modernization movement has been to stress modern society, even modern western society, as a project to be affirmed. This position involves a hybrid of communal solidarity and voluntaristic action, as we have already seen with Alexander, which is intrinsic to the Parsonian tradition. Of great importance to this tradition, taken as a whole and even in this respect extending to Habermas, is Weber's rationalization theory, which, at least in principle, allows insight into what a flexible link between macro-social order and micro-level processes could look like. Though the cognitive mechanisms of how rationalization takes place have not been systematically addressed, Weber's encyclopaedic knowledge has allowed insight into important social processes. Even if the precise import of such social processes, as in the Protestant Ethic thesis, cannot be agreed upon, Weber still offers essential pointers to the development of an encompassing rationality theory. In this *Theory of Action,* Munch actually combines Weber's theory of the hegemony of means-end rationality in modern society and Durkheim's solidarity theory to indicate what is normatively needed in modern societies that could not operate, as he claims, on the basis of consensus alone (Münch, 2010). To do so would impede the capacity to cope with scarcity, to reach political decisions, and to deepen knowledge. Accordingly, if consensus were really carried through as a societal goal, the level of rationality in society would decrease to below the level a modern society requires.

What Munch proposes instead is the reconciliation of antinomies across the value spheres of politics, economy and knowledge creation and diffusion. Two further types of rationality would follow from the initial specification of a goal within political rationality. They would respectively be the choice of means (economic rationality) and, associated with fiduciary or professional rationality, the problem of situation definition involved in 'transferring symbolic definitions of situations from senders to receivers' (Münch, 2010, 61). This latter sphere, especially interesting in the light of communicative reason, is further differentiated according to what he calls the modes of symbolic articulation, the cognitive sphere of the sciences, the aesthetic sphere of the arts, the normative sphere of ethics, and the meaning-constituting sphere of religion and the interpretation of the world.

These spheres are spheres of rationalization and Munch's explores the sequence of their operationalization. He also attaches great theoretical importance to interpenetration between these spheres, using Durkheim's distinction between mechanical and organic solidarity. Mechanical solidarity has to do with the establishment of an ethics of fair compromise between group loyalties in the context of the whole of society. He suggests that one of Parsons's four interactive media, influence, is developed for the purpose of mediating individual conflicts of interest in this sense. As Durkheim emphasizes, organic solidarity only comes to the fore in modern societies and requires the use of all four interactive media. These media regulate interchange between systems of outputs specific to them. This is coupled with the reciprocal restriction of the inner laws of the various sub-systems as they penetrate each other. Advancing this theory, the theory of interpenetration, on the basis of

*Reason and the Reflexive Turn in Sociology* 81

a theory of media shows how a societal logic could emerge that would transcend the isolated social spheres of Weber's kinds of rationalization, goal-rational, affective, traditional, and value-rational. The progress of rationalization in each of these spheres, therefore, has to be converted into an overarching kind of solidarity. Such general solidarity entails appropriate equilibrium between the (action) spheres, each with its own irreducible domain of efficacy. Following a deductive, functional line of argument, rationality in each of these spheres is as such not examined with regard to its genesis and specific operational modality but by its necessity to the abstract model of society that has already been postulated.[1] Munch nonetheless can evade much of what comprizes the standard critique of functional arguments, that they cannot deal with conflict or ongoing disorder, by advancing the idea of uncertainty and conflict, resulting in contingency within and between the spheres. Such an account of conflict, however, is, in line with Parsons, not determining. It is commitment to generalized values that normatively transcend utilitarian motives that is decisive. However, even if these utilitarian motives are transcended, they remain present in action schemata in conjunction with values. In the Kantian lineage, nonetheless, the order of priority from utility to norm is reversed. In an earlier, important text by Munch, Parsons is represented squarely within this Kantian lineage (Munch, 1981). In this text and in Parsons's own late text on institutionalism, Parsons can be clearly interpreted as following an immanent-transcendent strategy of a kind in his account of 'rational transcendentalism' (Parsons, 1990).

Munch also adds a cognitive fluidity to the model by suggesting that communication taking place within a common affectively grounded lifeworld is intrinsic to socialization through values. More generally, communication is referenced in various ways through the 2010, originally 1987, book and is the central focus of the – in real time – later book on the emergence of a communication society (Münch, 1991). While it is plausible to believe that the work of interpenetration between the spheres and even rationalization within them must depend on communication, nonetheless, no grounding account is given of the forms of that communication and the implications of those forms for the various spheres of society. He simply advances the 'externalist' idea that as modern society develops, communication becomes more and more essential to the interchange between the generalized symbolic media (Munch, 1991). We are left no wiser as to how communication *processes* drive on rationalization or interpenetration. That it occurs through symbolically generalized media of communication is clear, but these are already quite 'down the line' in terms of the communication process. This is the neglected space of reason and reasoning beyond rationality.

Munch's theory also suffers the objectivist fate of theories springing from structural functionalism; the societal concepts and their relationships appear to be fully identifiable through the objectivating gaze of the scientist. This is accentuated by the underlying affirmation of an idealized state of society, with little or no attention given at the most abstract level to critique of pathologies, mis-developments, and injustices. In a certain sense, it is the mirror opposite of theories predominantly or exclusively oriented by negative critique. Nonetheless, the idea of symbolically generalized media of communication and its relation both to rationalization of the

## 82 Reason and the Reflexive Turn in Sociology

spheres and the overall rationality of society have an important place in a sociological account of reason. The fundamental question, though, is whether the cognitive-communicative processes that make it possible are essential to its explanation? In line with previous observations, the answer to this question is in the affirmative. This is, as I later hope to show, precisely where inferential theories of reasoning and learning must come into play.

In conclusion, both the strengths and the weaknesses of the objectivist theory of society offered by Munch arise from some important remarks he makes on the relationship between the system of values and the institutionalization of norms. He claims that particular norms must be subsumable under the common, general system of values. This common, general system of values is rooted in collective solidarity, which, as explained above, amounts to appropriate interpenetrating equilibration between the steering media of the various societal systems. One pivotal condition for the institutionalization of norms from such a value system, supposing it to have been achieved and to be sufficiently solidaristic, is the nature of interpretation. This is taken to include the types of interpreters responsible for both the general system of values and the normative specifications of it. It also depends on the manner of integration of these interpreters into societal spheres and groups, and whether the system of values is a superordinate, society-wide one or specific to a group. Such a specification of the relationship between societal values and norms identifies relevant conditions and mechanisms for movement between the two complexes, though always deductively from values to norms. The focus on interpreter and interpretation emphasizes that interpreters are responsible for the general system of values and the norms that are specifications of it. This is in line with Munch's communication theoretic position. What is not shown is how such interpretation processes might operate. Further, they are described as interpretation processes, but what are they to interpret? In other words, how did the values and the norms derived from them arise in the first place? If this cannot be elucidated, how can the direction of change be ascertained? These observations show the limits of an objectivist theory of society, even where its basic architectonic remains highly suggestive for further theoretical developments in this direction.

### Luhmann

Luhmann aims to redeploy the idea of rationality from individuals and other social agents to social systems. This shift in perspective is given substance by four problems he identifies with contemporary sociological thinking; that concrete individuals compose society; that society is integrated by consensus about values and interests shared by these individuals; that territorial boundaries differentiate societies; and that societies can be observed from outside their own boundaries (Luhmann, 1999, 24–25). This problem identification asserts the non-identity between agents and the social order. Amongst contemporary sociologists, Luhmann takes this to the extreme and removes agents altogether from the theory of society. Furthermore, there is no longer any privileged vantage point from which society may be observed. With the advent of functional differentiation, replacing

*Reason and the Reflexive Turn in Sociology* 83

segmentary and stratificatory differentiation, a multiplicity of perspectives opens up on the observation of society. Against the assumption of an encompassing normative structure of society that could integrate such perspectives, Luhmann instead envisages endlessly increasing cognitive diversity, only susceptible to being ordered by the integrative capacity of overarching social systems.

Luhmann adopts a radical constructivist 'anti-ontological' approach. At the extreme end of the modern – since the late enlightenment – prioritization of epistemology over ontology, Luhmann breaks with the classical Aristotelian understanding of the world based on the distinction between being and non-being. In the 'mirror' epistemology of this Aristotelian way of thinking, a formal logical epistemology acquires a special place within being. Such a position delineates the space of reflection, but such reflection merely operates as an extension of being, consistent with the Humean empiricist standpoint. In other words, the implications of the knowledge gained through the senses are logically explicated, but not fundamentally altered. Such a position, according to Luhmann, made sense only in a stratified society. Effectively, the standpoint of the privileged elite became the overarching perspective, the locus of truth, and the carrier of rationality within the social order. Luhmann believes, unlike Bourdieu, for example, whose position still has much in common with the stratified standpoint, that this type of differentiation is on the way to being fully replaced by a functionally differentiated society. Characteristically, systems theory emphasizes this process as a shift from normative to cognitive expectations, that is, in their understanding, from expectations relating to politics, law, and morality to those centred on economy, science, and technology. It is not asked within the theory as to what part the cognitive construction of normative expectations, for example, the construction of the principle of freedom, has played in the advent of the multi-perspectivalism that Luhmann associates with the assumed advent of dominant functional differentiation.

Notwithstanding Luhmann's dismissal of reason as an Old European idea, he does identify the advent of a post-metaphysical construct of reason in the later enlightenment as a staging post to a fully modern functionally differentiated society (Luhmann, 1998). In general, the later enlightenment distinguishes between the strictly other-directed reflection of the classical episteme and self-related reflection achieved through categories of thinking. On the positive side, here to some degree following Hegel in a way not often appreciated, Luhmann saw in the post-classical, late enlightenment account of reason the distinction between self- and other-relations, together with the defining third position associated with Hegelian dialectics, what he was to term the unity-in-the-difference. Negatively, however, he understood enlightenment reason as outmoded in its focus on the subject's capacity for transcending the given state of knowledge. For Luhmann, the evolutionary long disjuncture between individual and society has in modern societies reached the point where the subject is unable to act overall because it cannot grasp the whole. Nevertheless, like the left-Hegelians, Marx, and Peirce, Luhmann follows Hegel in turning to a third mediating logic beyond subject and object, a second-order observation of a higher-level self-reference beyond the first-order observations of self-reference and other reference. Second-order observation offers a third point

## 84 *Reason and the Reflexive Turn in Sociology*

of view that can itself be overtaken by a further reflection of the same kind on the same infinite continuum of meaning. Human agents, who are locked in psychic systems, come to know these continua when they transgress their semantic structures, for example, by bringing moral perspectives into the legal system. At that point, the legal system will reject their moral standpoint, and they have to cope with 'disappointment' (Bora, 1999). In this way, systems maintain their autonomy by rejecting the intrusion of 'foreign bodies'.

From the vantage point of the development of sociology, Luhmann's formulation is both enabling and disabling. It opens core dimensions of a truly modern cognitive epistemology, but it does so in terms of, at least in Luhmann's intention, stripping sociology of any 'traditional' ontological component, an ontological component that was once more prominent and, even with the powerful growth of constructivist influences, remains prominent, for example in the use of the concept of capitalism in subject-centred theories. While Luhmann rhetorically maintains his opposition to ontological theorizing, it is another matter as to whether there are not latent ontological elements in his own theory? This observation is not meant to tie Luhmann back into a pre-modern understanding of ontology as the 'true' observation of the external world, but, taking account of the modern epistemological revolution, it asks whether a different kind of ontology is compatible with modern constructivist epistemologies. A modern ontology in the light of constructivism is 'behind' epistemological constructions that have the task of making sense in a future tense, where meaning is cognitively projected into the future, guided but not determined by past outcomes. Such outcomes then may be understood as both the symbolic-material outcomes of completed reality-constructing processes that now become ontological presuppositions of new epistemic operations and as the concatenation of the necessary epistemic structures, biological, cognitive, cultural, and social, that make possible such epistemic operations. Some of these structures and outcomes operate on the evolutionary plane, some on the ontogenetic plane of individual biographies, and some on the socio-genetic plane of the historicity of societies. These outcomes and structures constitute what is possible to understand as social ontology in the context of modern constructivism. Beyond the ontology of the social world remains the ontology of nature itself, which, even if it can only be known by 'us' through our constructions of it, nevertheless is a reality that exists beyond those constructions, as Latour and Habermas emphasize in their different ways (Habermas, 2003; Latour, 2004).

Luhmann's explicit denial of ontology, therefore, while necessarily employing theoretically self-limited ontological constructs, elucidates both his own account of rationality and the status of reason in sociology more generally. Modern ontological theorizing denies the primacy of the classical ontological approach of positing an external world about which we seek to gain knowledge through the senses. After the epistemological turn and the subsequent linguistic turn, the most basic sense of ontology is associated with those evolutionarily developed cognitive structures that make complex world constructions possible. These constructions are based on the primary modalities of the senses but can add inestimable further levels of meaning to 'naive' sensory experience. The logicians of

*Reason and the Reflexive Turn in Sociology* 85

the 19th century who had 'carried' the linguistic turn, Frege and Peirce, were alike hostile to the confusion of psychology with cognitive logical powers. It was the latter that were these logicians' focus of interest, those generalized reasoning capacities of the human species as they had come to be through evolution. For Peirce, what it had come to be was the question that animated the 'transcendental' or 'metaphysical' evolutionary focus of the general science of logic, leaving what could be done based on these capacities to those special sciences like psychology and sociology, among many others. In the last half-century, sociology has turned against evolutionary theorizing, mainly and correctly against evolutionary modernization theory, but also and deeply problematically against the evolutionary cognitive foundations of logical theorizing. Mainly, it has turned towards the socio-historical, understanding it as in opposition both to the evolutionary in social matters and to the supra-historical logical foundations of reason assumed to be associated with such theory. All the latter has increasingly come to be understood by sociology as either a social project of the privileged in the critical version or, in the interpretive tradition, as an over-elaborate theorization of naive competences that can be studied by the human sciences without the help of any transcending scientific frame, least of all an evolutionary one.

One of the reasons why Luhmann's theory is not widely entertained beyond the core band of theorists that make up the tradition of systems theory properly derives from the fact that he is an evolutionary theorist. Luhmann understands social theory formation on three levels: the level of evolutionary theory; differentiation theory; and communication theory. Regarding evolutionary theory, Luhmann is a universalist. Homo sapiens consists of one species with the same cognitive capacities, even if these may be differentially realized due to variations in social conditions. According to Stichweh, Luhmann often uses evolutionary theory to show how social systems manage to build social structures – differentiation – by making use of accidental events – that create variation (Stichweh, 2007). For Luhmann, communication is an evolutionary invention that, at higher levels, only happens in a few species. His account of communication proceeds from the chance evolution of social structures in a manner compatible with the ultimate formation of systemic media of communication. As human society evolves, there is also a progressive and ultimately radical differentiation between sociocultural evolution at the species level of social systems and biological and psychic evolution at other levels, Luhmann's version of the non-identity of individual and society.

Two critical social ontological features of Luhmann's theory then follow from this evolutionary perspective: that structural differentiation determines communication forms and that psychic communication is decoupled entirely from social communication. With the advent of worldwide processes of functional differentiation, implicitly characterized in a move akin to Hegel as the necessary telos of world history, there is no longer any need to trace back the structural consequences of social communication onto social structures. In general, Luhmann is notably silent on this point. In a sense, this view entails that, ontologically, functional differentiation is as timelessly decisive for understanding society as the differentiation

## 86 *Reason and the Reflexive Turn in Sociology*

between social and psychic structures. Only through these acts of radical separation can he advance the idea that his theory has no ontological implications. This is like orthodox Marxist theory asserting the thesis of the timeless – at least until the socialist revolution – causal significance of the forces of production. In the end, albeit with a different architecture, Luhmann – implicitly – follows Hegel in postulating how reason teleologically embeds itself in social structures. Luhmann's reason is understood not in the Hegelian form of inescapable normative structures of modern society that historically result from but now undergird cognitive operations. Instead, it is in the evolving rationalities of various social systems. The rationality of these systems is that each is characterized by a distinctive, binary-structured medium of communication. However, where will the 'improbable' outcomes of such mediated communication go but to the furtherance of the functional differentiation, ontologically posited in the first place?

I conclude from this that Luhmann has ontological commitments, but highly restrictive ones. Reference to the external world is, in an idealist sense, restricted to the only admitted social reality behind the systemic mind of society, functional differentiation. By means of the lens of the second-order observation of systems, the limitations of the first-order observation of objects become transcended. The chance variation at the heart of this functional differentiation replaces the evolutionary 'logic' of mind in idealism. In addition, though Luhmann refers to the power of the 'imagination' in Observing Modernity, concerned with 'understanding that we do not understand what we do not understand' (Luhmann, 1998, 42–43), such imagination is not assumed to enter into intentional reasoning processes with societal implications. Such imagination effectively can only become societally actual through the 'disburdening' realization by agents of the limits of their understanding, faced with the distinction-drawing powers of systems that are situated on a third level above self- and other-reference. By simply leaving out any kind of cognitive praxis done by humans on this third level, except derivatively as doomed attempts at negations of expectations (Bora, 1999), both the distinctive apprehension of the external world and the variation of subject positions are disregarded. For this reason, Luhmann stands far from the generally understood contemporary sense of reflexivity in wide swathes of social theory. This sense of reflexivity is agent-led in one way or another, whether the agency is that of the intellectual observer or the lay actor, and whether animated by narrow or broader perspectival reflection. By contrast, in Luhmann, any possible reflection can only operate as reflexivity, learning the limits of systems by adapting communication and action to the general and constraining logic of autopoietic system coding (Luhmann and Schorr, 1999).

Luhmann's concept of expectations does much work for him, both cognitive and normative. Expectations are differentiated from the concept of 'norm' by being shorn of any voluntaristic quality of agreeing with norms deemed justified. Expectations are instead general success-oriented guidelines on what rules should be followed, deviations from which will not be punished by sanctions but by cognitive failure for infractions of system logics, that is, learning through 'disappointment'. Peirce distinguishes expectations from judgements by their lack

*Reason and the Reflexive Turn in Sociology* 87

of a conditional character (Peirce, 1931–1958, 5.486). It may be inferred that in Luhmann's account of expectations, judgements have already taken place, but on another level, that of second-order observation from system perspectives. Hence, nothing equivalent to justification in the Kantian tradition is assumed to take place, or at least not the kind of voluntaristic reasoning that would have implications for social organization, including normative rules. Deviant reasoning that produces judgements out of line with expectations will be corrected by their failure. Luhmann's account of expectation-expectations refers to the structure of expectations that are built up in social systems through the operation of their specific symbolically generalized media. Expectations in this 'higher' systemic sense condition expectations in the 'lower' sense of publics, including interpretations of public needs carried by politicians. This neo-Hegelian infrastructure envisages such structures as transcendent, meta-cultural, cognitive structures that, operating as cognitive generals, guide communication processes. He turns away from any creative openness that could follow from such a scheme to envisage these structures in decision-oriented terms as manifest, immanent forms of guiding reality by experts equipped with the requisite disillusioned competences. In the end, since any kind of will-driven situated reasoning is paradoxically only going to lead to disillusionment, then truly the old European idea of reason can be dispensed with.

Temporally, Luhmann emphasizes the improbability of communication. Improbability, associated with the autonomous self-generating power of communication, indicates cognitive operations not bound to past arrangements but instead capable of making their own future. It is a limited kind of creative freedom because these cognitive operations are permanently embedded in already established binary codes. Anything beyond that is merely described as 'noise', with the semantic core of distinctions taking the form of codes of established social systems. Luhmann's emphasis on distinctions is like that of Foucault on the 'dispersion' of objects; both convey a centrifugal property that denies any possibility of normative generalization. Both are opposed to enlightenment humanism and its concerns with freedom and responsibility – however selectively applied these may have been. Both challenge the value of enlightenment individualism with its goal of autonomy as self-control, asking the disillusioning question of what emanated from such aspirations. Though both these starting points and their methodologies of inquiry have much in common, with Foucault, the suspicion persists that there is much ambivalence in his critique of enlightenment, even regarding its treatment of reason. This suspicion is supported by the background sense that humanism is not just the classifying operations of a semiological functionalism but is also a project of social power by an emerging group aimed at both the construction and domination of other groups. The undertones of Marx here can scarcely be denied. Revealing the genealogy of this social form of power enables critique. As Honneth observes, Foucault wavers between this orientation, that is, towards social struggle, and a semiological functionalism (Honneth, 1991). However, his semiological functionalism may too be read as an attempt to move away from dogmatic certainties associated with the unmasking of social projects and their replacement with a 'better' one by

## 88 *Reason and the Reflexive Turn in Sociology*

showing that the construction and operation of worlds is infinitely more complex and plural than such a view assumes. The late emphasis on the redemptive quality of the ethos of enlightenment gives further support to this reading (Foucault, 1984).

With Luhmann, there is no such ambivalence. Any possibility of reason, even to the extent of identifying a background social project of domination, is stripped away. Like Foucault, Luhmann concentrates on the positive, the 'is' of the actual, even if in his case the selection context embraces potentiality (Luhmann, 1999). Both convert the 'is' into regimes of functional power. However, Foucault's power concept accepts some role for social power, admittedly indistinctly, and for the me-diating thirdness of discourse. Both in his concept of power and in his description of worlds, Foucault account is less absolute than Luhmann's and less ontological in one sense of the word. A limitation of Luhmann is, by contrast, the relentless binary order of the world, which leaves no room for reflection, even reflection directed at a strategy of domination. Fuhrmann well outlines the consequences of this for any possibility of reflective critical thinking (Fuhrmann, 2019, 12). He claims that with the discovery of Spencer-Brown's laws of form, systems theory loses any possibil-ity of adding an operation – reflective thirdness – beyond the two-sided form. In the binary form, every subsequent operation – of drawing a further distinction – can only be understood as a negation. The law of excluded middle in classical episte-mology is thereby sustained. Fuhrmann claims further that systems theory thereby loses the opportunity to take on a critical form in which meaning loses its totalizing quality and becomes *operational* as a medium of reflexion. To this might be added that meaning would thereby acquire a critical-reflective and inferential form, which it does not have at all in Luhmann and only indirectly, implicitly, and ambivalently in Foucault. This reflective and inferential form holds the key to any kind of norma-tive generality. In agreement with Fuhrmann, if systems theory is to lose its hyper-observational, 'neutral' stance it must recognize that one indispensable component of sociological analysis is that society is composed of pathologies and injustices.

What Luhmann offers beyond Foucault is an explicit distinction between poten-tiality and actuality, that is, that which is improbably realized in actual social forms (Luhmann, 2012). However, this remains a variation on the 'is' in that no conscious cognitive operation is envisaged that could generate the social variation required to realize achievable potentiality. No set of inferential operations of reasoning are countenanced that could turn potentials into actuals – or indeed reject them on vari-ous grounds. Luhmann claims that meaning is the gap between potentiality and ac-tuality, but this gap is not only a socially available semantic code but one requiring transformation through the inferential operations of mind. Luhmann places con-siderable emphasis on media of communication but misses the most fundamental, at least for humans, inferential operations of critical common sense. For all their creativity in grasping the regularities of human social forms, both Foucault and Luhmann in the end are encumbered by an empiricist hostility to reasoning. They rightly seek to correct the world by describing strategies of the social sciences in the light of the linguistic turn, but they also reinforce one of the most problematic aspects, the denial of the necessity for critical reasoning in human forms of life.

## Archer

Margaret Archer has advanced an account of reflexivity within the well-established tradition of critical realism, a tradition first crystallized in the philosophy of Roy Bhaskar. Archer has been its leading social theoretical representative. Along with many others who, like Bourdieu and Giddens, are not critical realists, her approach is built upon the structure-agency paradigm dominant in sociology since the 1980s. Structure-agency theory takes seriously both the previously dominant idea of structure in sociology – society as a regular, structurally determined form – but added to it the insights arising from cultural and agential turns in the social sciences, given considerable impetus by the dramatic social transformation emerging within and beyond the 1960s. In this latter dimension, the paradigm also encapsulates the renewed importance of micro-sociology in a context in which, from the last decades of the 20th century, micro-level theories have become much more influential, whether used on their own or as part of an attempt to build linkages between micro- and macro-social 'levels' (Alexander, 1987). The emphasis on the micro-macro linkages, indicative of the structure-agency paradigm more generally, kept alive the intention to offer critique of issues of societal importance, even if generally the macro-sociological critique of society has languished.

Archer's specific approach, in line with her commitment to critical realism, re-emphasizes ontology. An ontological starting point has been central to Marxism for a long time, and, in a different way, it has also been central to the Heideg-gerian and communitarian wings of hermeneutics. Other receptions of semiotics and hermeneutics, including the linguistic-semiotic and critical-hermeneutical turns spanning a variety of disciplinary and sub-disciplinary spaces, have brought cultur-ally conditioned agency to the forefront. The renewed emphasis on agency – in Luhmann, it is the agency of systems – in its many forms has in turn brought epis-temological concerns to the centre of the social sciences. These concerns remain distant from the reason-based epistemology stemming from the enlightenment, and accordingly from modern democratic proceduralism. The epistemological shift has rather offered a post-Wittgensteinian and semiological account of the significance of language, often influenced by postmodern themes of contingency, chance, and relativism. Most theoretical traditions in sociology have felt themselves forced to grapple with this version of the linguistic turn in one way or another, with only a few standing out against it.

This far-reaching shift does not mean that ontology, the question of the nature of reality, the 'what' of sociological investigation, simply disappears. However, the old emphasis on the determining force of an external natural or objective, law-like social world is waning. The reflexivity debate must be understood in the light of the altered theoretical alignment. The exploration of reflexivity may therefore be seen as the incorporation of epistemological concerns into the social sciences in a manner previ-ously filled by a theory of rationality, whose dominant purposive-rational and method-ological objectivist form had always been subject to critique from phenomenological, hermeneutical, functionalist, and critical sources. This critique could not displace it from the centre of the social sciences until the post-empiricist and cultural turn

## 90   *Reason and the Reflexive Turn in Sociology*

commencing in the 1950s in a variety of disciplines. Often, the renewed emphasis on epistemology in contemporary social science has been expressed in methodological terms as a turn towards reflexive qualitative methodologies that would both recognize the fallibility of the standpoint of the theorist and affirm the voice of the subject.

Archer's emphasis on ontology should be understood in the above context. She does not seek to pursue an ontological project that hearkens back to the autonomy of the empiricist focus on the primacy of the external world. Her concomitant emphasis on reflexivity indicates a shift from naive realist ontologies of this kind, including the classical positivism that dominated official sociology for a long time and lives on surreptitiously but powerfully (Archer, 2009). The most basic aspect of her ontological position is the primacy of the human being over the social being. This has features in common with the philosophical-hermeneutical emphasis on the historical process of the revealing of being. Archer's human being is anchored both in natural and spiritual worlds. Immersion in these worlds is part of the telos of their being that underpins their capacity for reflexivity in both dimensions.

One ontological 'node' in Archer's theory is accordingly the individual human being, while the other is expressed in the form of societal structures that take two forms: materially embedded social structures and the cultural system (Archer, 1984). Each of the two structural levels and the agential level of the individual are taken to be endowed with distinctive properties and emergent causal powers; they enjoy a high degree of autonomy from one another and can independently exert causal force. Because of the degree of autonomy, and hence distinctiveness, Archer supposed to exist between individuals and societal structures, her theory can reasonably be described as dualist (Piiroinen, 2014). Nonetheless, she also assumes a 'bind' between these poles through processes of co-development. The external work is internalized and reflexively processed through an internal conversation. Such a reflexive process allows individuals to situate themselves in the external world in the course of which cultural and social structures become internalized in personal acts (Elder-Vass and Archer, 2012). Yet Archer says the reflexive process is autonomous from such structures and that the latter is 'mediated' through the form of internal conversations (Archer, 2007).

The most fundamental impulse to co-development, interacting with supra-individual structures, is the human capacity to imagine alternative social forms. Archer perceives this as an individual capacity that is irreducible to these social forms but impacts on them, while, in line with the theory, the social forms also partly independently evolve and act in reverse on individuals. In her account, emphasizing the underlying version of mind-independent realism, social change has brought about conditions that, in her terms, favour morphogenesis, the proclivity towards change, over morphostasis, the proclivity towards order. However, morphogenesis is partly also driven by the reflexive qualities of human beings initiating change as they respond to conditions that, so to speak, structurally come to them. In morphostatic conditions, the power to operate reflexively is reduced, but in morphogenetic conditions, it comes into its own. Reflexivity is an epistemological capacity derived from ontologically accumulated properties – where accumulated can be understood

*Reason and the Reflexive Turn in Sociology* 91

in my view as a product of social evolution, though for others including Archer, it may also be a property to be understood in terms of a religious metaphysics. Regarding the latter, important for her account, in a 1990 essay, she refers to the sociological neglect of 'Weberian "non-social" relations to both the phenomenal and noumenal worlds' (Archer, 1990, 97). In general, the combination of ontological properties, both embodied and spiritual, along with epistemological capacities at the level of the agent is Archer's contribution to the social scientific need to envisage ontology and epistemology anew as interrelated ideas. Reflexivity at the epistemological end is core to such interrelation.

Archer's understanding of the process of societal development as a shift from a dominant morphostasis to a dominant morphogenesis is a sociological reading of the modern condition, including the condition of being human. She aligns this with Peirce's distinction between the 'me' and the 'I', made famous through G. H. Mead, though Archer dissents from Mead's account, even if some aspects of Mead, for example, the internalization of the social world and the inner conversation, appear to be analogous to Peirce. She understands the 'I' of Peirce as being distinct from the social and hence to evince an irreducible individual and human quality (Archer, 2010). Much turns on this, for Archer accuses others such as Bourdieu and Giddens of a type of 'conflation' of structure and agency that elides the autonomous, and hence creative, cogitative powers of individuals. She also regards Mead as allowing the social to dominate the individual.

Her account of Peirce, at the core of her theory of reflexivity, where she seeks to distinguish him from Mead and those others whom she regards as overestimating the power of structures over the mentation of agents, is not entirely convincing in all respects. Where she is on good ground is her emphasis on that aspect of being that Peirce captures by means of the category of firstness, which for him makes possible but is still distinct from the conjectural mode of abduction as the first step in logical reasoning. It is also true that such firstness, the realm of immediate consciousness in Peirce, involves a type of mediation between the object and the world of reasoning, which has affinities with how Archer understands the mediating role of the individual reflexive process. However, there are significant differences. First of all, in her 2010 paper, Archer argues against the excessive dependence of some sociologists, Bourdieu, for example, on the concept of habit over that of reflexivity (Archer, 2010). She suggests – in an account similar to Durkheim's idea of the secular shift from the dominance of criminal to civil law – that reflexivity has grown in modern life and, as it has done so, the morphostatic conditions that are conductive to the hegemony of habit and the suppression of reflexivity have declined. Reflexivity has substantially replaced habit, and more societies are therefore predominantly reflexively coordinated. However, to the contrary, it is clear from Peirce's doubt-belief model that he was against the idea of radical doubt that such a view of reflexivity entails (Peirce, 1998). Patterns of beliefs are socially sustained precisely by habits, which Peirce understands as mental operations that could potentially range from low complexity to very high complexity. In the latter sense, habits for Peirce could precisely embody what Archer understands by reflexivity, since the mere repetition of a high-level, perhaps unusual, mental

## 92  *Reason and the Reflexive Turn in Sociology*

capacity does not render it routine. In the end, whether habits are merely routine or represent learning processes that are not widely diffused, hence innovative, is a question of social judgement and social research. In Peirce, it is true that there is also a more profound kind of reflexivity, the reflexivity that arises when we have cause to question our existing beliefs – we experience doubts about those beliefs – and this leads us to habit change (West and Anderson, 2016). However, the possibility of this should not distract from the essential role he identified for what he understood to be cognitive habits or habits of reasoning. Such habits lay at the heart of the rapidly changing American society in which Peirce lived as much as they do in contemporary societies. The point is that habits for Peirce are universally present in cognition across time and space.

The second point that gives cause for question in Archer's account of Peirce is the claim that his concept of the 'I' can be understood as an individual capacity separate from the social world. Though, to my knowledge, Archer does not refer to Peirce's categories, some support for her claim may be found there, even if it is rather tenuous and excludes other relevant issues that point in the other direction. The supportive dimension would lie in Peirce's account of pure phenomenological firstness, the perception of that which is irrespective of everything else. This pure perspective allows unconscious imaginative scope to be exercised, beginning the process of construction of social or natural objects. On one level, such a perspective carried through immediate feelings expresses the most recessed capacity of an individual subject to see the world in a distinctive way. Here, Archer's position is loosely consistent with Touraine's emphasis on the subject and, in a diffuse sense, the phenomenological inheritance. However, even this unconscious, phenomenological 'I' is not asocial for Peirce, even if it may be beyond what has been recognized to be social up to that point. His synechism and account of continua mean that the subject in this qualitative activity is engaging in extending understanding of the world or, more prosaically, in everyday life, responding to the social or natural world in a particular way.

This 'I', which Mead also understands as the creative part of the self, is just the unconscious beginning of perception, the first expression of the 'I' that must yet reach the stage of a perceptual judgement and the beginning of conscious inferential operations of thought. Through all of this, this 'I' is interacting with the orienting power that is retaining in the history of the self, the repository of both a unique biography and yet the effects of social structuration for which Bourdieu's habitus theory offers a powerful model. Further, this 'I' to 'me' relation as it moves towards conscious thought begins to take on the deliberative competence that Archer associates with reflexivity. For Peirce, by contrast, gains in deliberative capacity arise through learned conscious control and are thoroughly social. As he put it, 'there is no faculty of introspection', only the introjection of external signs. As Habermas points out, Peirce's account of reasoning is to be understood as an intersubjective process, always the case virtually but actually as well in real social exchanges (Habermas, 2019). The individual is reasoning in relation to a virtual world of possible interlocutors – a process Mead called a 'parliament of selves' and this means all inner conversations have anchorage in the social world (Mead, 1934). In this

*Reason and the Reflexive Turn in Sociology* 93

sense, contrary to Archer, both Mead and Peirce are exactly in alignment, not distinguished as she claims into respectively a social theory and an individual theory of reflexivity. Hence, what Archer highlights as central to the 'inner conversation' and a preserve of the individual, the activity of *deliberate* reflexivity, is precisely to the contrary a social activity in Peirce, though partly taking place inside individual minds and always in some way mediated through them.

Finally, the structure-agency perspective used by Archer and others does not do adequate justice to Peirce's category of thirdness, the cognitive processes of extended mind, incorporating also the conscious cognitive operations of individual minds in the manner described above. While Archer's theory has been mainly interpreted in terms of the social structure/agency relation, equally important for her in the theory's architecture has been the distinction between cultural structure and social structure. She distinguishes within the cultural order between the cultural system and what she calls sociocultural interaction, as in the realm of 'the social' similarly, she distinguishes between social structure and social interaction. These distinctions, since they are not really tenable as applied to actual practice, are described as *analytic* distinctions in line with long-run usage in functionalist theories. They are analytic in the sense that they can be identified by the theories but also because they are taken to have a social presence that only social theorists can perceive. Hence, the cultural system is produced and reproduced through the transsubjective outcomes of sociocultural interaction and social structures through the mostly unintended consequences of social interaction. The identification of 'analyticity' in both the theoretical world and in the actual world to which it is applied is because it must be supposed that what is analytically distinguished is somehow at work in the world, but mostly not consciously perceived. So, what the theorist sees 'analytically' is also occurring behind the backs of agents. Reflexivity, then, in this light, becomes the capacity of both theorists and 'ordinary' agents to see further into the mechanisms that condition the agents' situations and the situation of theorizing itself.

But this kind of analytic separation of social structure and cultural system, with corresponding kinds of interaction, is different from Peirce's account of mind, here only making two short points bearing on Archer. The first is that, in Peirce's account, what Archer calls culture would be present in all interactions. For Peirce, culture as thirdness mediates between the immediate quality of firstness and the reaction to firstness that is secondness. The category of thirdness is a means of building relations, where these relations bear on the humanly constructed understanding of objects in the world, including all aspects of human cognitive structuration, for example, humans, institutions, milieus, and so on. Thirdness is therefore not equivalent to Archer's cultural system but to the cognitive capacities, individual and collective, that make knowledge possible since they are used in building it. Thirdness therefore contains cognitive properties that humans use to cognize all aspects of natural and social worlds. The second is that, as above, thirdness is through and through a set of socio-cognitive forms, to be sure impelled by feelings, but in charge so to speak of the deliberative quality of reasoning that Archer sees as central to reflexivity. From these two points, it may be concluded that Archer's

## 94   *Reason and the Reflexive Turn in Sociology*

account of reflexivity, requiring deliberative capacities as it does, cannot fully rest on Peirce's architectonic. It also means that the kind of analytic separation of structure and action that Archer espouses would make no sense in relation to Peirce's idea of the construction of worlds through minds, whose capacities in turn make reasoning – and interaction – possible in the first place. There is simply no equivalent to mind in that sense in Peirce. What emerges is that the society-defining kind of mediation for Peirce is not individual consciousness in the sense of Archer but the distributed collective mind of society that consists of thirdness. She thus has one moment of the Peirceian reflexion right, the creative phenomenological powers of firstness, but the second aspect, the relation to thirdness, is absent. For a theory of reasoning, thirdness in this sense is intrinsic, and thus Archer's account, reflecting the dominant dualist tendency of sociology, advances reflexivity in a way that unsatisfactorily precludes the explicit, social forms of reasoning that Peirce's inferential logic emphasizes.

### Bourdieu

Bourdieu's account of reflexivity is central to his theory, yet there remains some general puzzlement as to how he could have a strong theory of habit and a strong theory of reflexivity. Some, like Archer indeed, conclude that his account of reflexivity is so much in thrall to his account of habit that it must be a weak and, for her, insufficient one (Archer, 2010). Yet, in following the critique of Archer's account of Peirce above, it will be shown that Bourdieu has both strong accounts of habit and of reflexivity. In so doing, it can be shown more generally that his account of reflexivity and of reason – he is one of the few recent sociologists who addresses reason explicitly – is an important contribution towards understanding the cognitively mediated relationship between reason and normativity.

Beginning with the idea of 'cognitively mediated', Lizardo understands Bourdieu as out and out a cognitive theorist (Lizardo, 2004). He notes that this central feature of Bourdieu is not widely discussed, partly because this aspect of the theory, even if intrinsic, is not very clear. Lizardo claims that the habitus is a socially produced cognitive structure 'composed of systems of bodily operations that generate practical action in the world' (id, 293–294). Bourdieu's theory sought to clarify how objective macro-level social structures mediated through socialization lead to a system of practical correspondences in embodied social structures or habituses. The latter generate practices in tune with the social structures in which they are embedded and accordingly 'reproduce and transform' these social structures over time. In Bourdieu, the social structures are embedded in social fields, and habitus relations are set within these fields. These habituses in turn generate reproductive or transformative practices that react back on the social structures, hence potentially altering the social fields

According to Lizardo, the cognitive dimension in Bourdieu arises from his emphasis on the historical development of schemata regarded as responsible for macro-structural reproduction and change. The concept of schema may be traced back to Kant, and Bourdieu's account, influenced by Piaget, is of a post-Kantian

*Reason and the Reflexive Turn in Sociology* 95

neo-structuralist kind. It is also to be differentiated from a Wittgensteinian neo-pragmatist kind. The influence of Piaget on Bourdieu lies in his account of cognitive structures. These structures, as they operate through learning processes, both transform and are transformed by their environments. Lizardo follows Piaget in claiming that knowledge primarily consists of cognitive structures and that it is 'always social, practical, and grounded in action and never individualistic and purely cognitive in an exclusively representational-symbolic sense' (id, 383). Further, Piaget identifies three kinds of cognitive processes: perceptions, schematization, and action-generating scripts, which has affinities with Peirce's emphasis on feelings, reasoning, and facts to be explored later in the book.

Just as Bourdieu distinguishes his account of taste from Kant by emphasizing the social plurality of standards of taste rather than the universalism of the Kantian position, Lizardo claims he differentiates himself from Piaget in a similar manner. The external reality confronted by an agent is, for Bourdieu, not a single abstract environment but is instead a range of socially distributed environments composed of 'interconnected and differently valued material, cultural and symbolic resources' (Lizardo, 2004, 16–17). This emphasis on differentiated cognitive regimes provides his theory with cognitive micro-foundations that do not succumb to the sociological proclivity to stress shared representations and ideological domination. Finally, in an associated way, fields as the carriers of structural orders and differentiated habituses as carriers of cognitive structures are not hierarchically related to one another but are perceived as mutually constitutive on the same meso-level. This implies that patterns of domination cannot simply be read off structural levels of society but must be deciphered in the flux of culture and situation.

These observations provide a foundation for understanding Bourdieu's account of reflexivity. He is against the widely practiced idea of reflexivity as 'bringing oneself into the research process', with the connotation – often not even explicitly drawn but implied – that this should incorporate the self-reflections of researchers on their social positions. Such an account of reflexivity is merely conventional, and Bourdieu describes it as 'narcissistic'. The specific problem with such narcissistic reflexivity is that the perspective of the scholar does not change; in fact, the apparent exercise of conventionally consulting oneself simply confirms the perspective. Consequently, scholars see what they want to see. What they want to see are the 'pre-constructed' objects that fit with their worldview, in other words, 'comfortable' objects that have already been constructed by them (Bourdieu, 1988). What they instead need to do is to examine their own position much more radically in relation to their positions in social fields, to historicize themselves as inquiring subjects, to recognize what positions they stand for, and what are the probable consequences for their belief systems and commitments of being 'in' such positions? Though to my knowledge Bourdieu has never used these terms, such an account of reflexivity fits in well with the distinction between conventional and post-conventional as used in development psychology and taken up in discourse ethics (Apel, 1978), where conventional entails the closure of thinking in line with assumed predictable consequences and post-conventional involves the openness of thinking guided by principles and relatively indifferent to consequences, for example, Kohlberg's

## 96  *Reason and the Reflexive Turn in Sociology*

illustration of the Heinz dilemma learning on whether Heinz should break the law by stealing to feed his family. It is also in line, as will be examined later, with Peirce's accounts of critical common sense and abduction.

Bourdieu's theory of practice also allows for understanding action as powerfully shaped by unconscious forces, ranging from the effects of a collective unconscious carried through socialization to the making of a practice unconscious by forgetting the cognitive processes entailed in its initial creation. Reflexivity, as understanding one's social position in the fullest sense, thus also requires an interrogation of the unconscious structures that lock oneself into such a position. This hold, both conscious but not reflected upon and unconscious, is what Bourdieu styles as the doxic modality, and reflexivity is the cognitive activity of breaking with it. Another parallel with discourse ethics is at least partly appropriate here in the idea of performative contradiction; avoiding performative contradiction in theoretically guided argumentation is reflexivity properly at work (Apel, 2001).

Not much remarked upon in the account of his scholarship, Bourdieu reaches for a quasi-transcendental argument in indicating the necessity for this kind of deep reflexivity, when he identifies as 'the hidden' within the 'transcendental unconscious' (Bourdieu, 2004, 86). The hidden in this sense is that which is hidden from the gaze of the scientist, who is 'pre-reconstructed' not to notice it but is still profoundly affected by it. The only possible solution to this is 'to historicise the subject of historicisation, to objectivate the subject of the objectivation, that is, the historical transcendental, the objectivisation of which is the precondition for the access of science to self-awareness, in other words to knowledge of its historical presuppositions' (ibid). Two important points are being raised here. The first is that objectivation in some form is critical to science, and the second is that this objectivation depends on becoming aware of transcendental presuppositions. One can conclude from this that the acquisition of reflexive capacity for Bourdieu cannot be of a relativistic form, the act, so to speak, of individual scholars examining their own consciences, but must instead be of a kind that presses towards the transcendental presuppositions that must be observed within the logic of inquiry. The paramount transcendental presupposition of objectivation, bearing in mind all that Bourdieu has said against the excesses of universalism, must be through encounters between different perspectives articulated in historical times. The result of examining transcendental presuppositions therefore reaches towards the point of what Strydom describes as a convergent limit concept (Strydom, 2017), the identification of an ideal that should be obtained in the light of the many different interpretations that can be offered within the 'space' of the ideal. It may also be understood as the idealized horizon of rational dissensus (Miller, 1992), arguing in the light of an ideal where the inevitably of difference about that ideal is known and, in the final analysis, has to be respected in some meaningful sense.

While Archer utilizes Peirce explicitly, she rather contradictorily, in the light of this, condemns Giddens for pursuing a semiotic approach, assuming that such an approach is antagonistic to the ontological realism she espouses (Archer, 2010). Above, I have already sought to show that I do not regard her approach to reflexivity as fully consistent with that of Peirce, indeed exhibiting one crucial contradiction

*Reason and the Reflexive Turn in Sociology* 97

relating to Peirce's account of reflection as a social operation, as opposed to her own denial of this. By contrast, though Bourdieu does not often reference Peirce, his approach is more consistent with the Peirceian framework. This may well be influenced by the mediating effect of Piaget. In some important respects, similar to Peirce, Piaget distinguishes between figurative and operative aspects of thought, where the operative dimension is primary in involving transformation of the preexisting state (Piaget, 1972). In this sense, Bourdieu's theory of cognition may be understood as potentially making possible transformations through 'post-conventional' reflexivity that, in turn, at least potentially, transform habits. Reproduction is also possible in which mental operations merely confirm the habits. Against Piaget, however, both Bourdieu and Peirce do not seek to isolate cognitive structures – analytic capacities, necessary thought – from empirical observation (Otte, 1998), but seek to understand abstraction through the medium of reflexive operations that always contain the import of the object. This is prevalent in Peirce's critique of Kant – and of Hegel – and in Bourdieu's own critique of Kant. The basic problem they both perceive in Kant – though Peirce holds as fundamental Kant's epistemological breakthrough – is the isolation of formal cognitive operations – necessary reason – from synthetic cognitive operations, both of qualitative feeling and of reactions to encounters with existents, that is, actual objects of cognition.

A critical category for both Peirce and Bourdieu is that of habit, which, because of their assumption of the interpenetration of analytic and synthetic judgements, is assumed to always be responsive to the world. In the continuous flow of cognitive operations, habits are continuously confirmed or challenged. The parallel with Piaget lies in the assumption that it is transformative cognitive operations – in Peirce hypostatic abstraction and in Bourdieu reflexivity – that are fundamental. Habit in Peirce, or the habitus in Bourdieu, is a symbolic outcome of this kind of higher cognitive operation. It results in another interlinked cognitive operation, that of reliably relating to the world of objects. Peirce says that

> signs which should be merely parts of an endless viaduct for the transmission of idea-potentiality, without any conveyance of it into anything but symbols, namely into action or habit of action, would not be signs at all.
> (Peirce, 1998, 388).

If Peirce is followed and Bourdieu interpreted accordingly, reflexivity should be associated with reflective cognitive operations and consciously brought about habitus change (habits) viewed as the outcome. It does not therefore depend on an empiricist reading of ontological states of the world, which has been dominant in sociology for a long time and still lives on in changing times. Habituses will forever exist, perhaps in ever more plural forms, because of the different possibilities of stabilization of reflexive cognitive operations as well as the increased variability associated with these operations in the first place, a point similar in emphasis to Archer's morphogenesis but with a dynamic understanding of the role of habits.

Habermas associates Peirce's doubt-belief model, analogous to Bourdieu's reflexivity-habitus relation, with the idea of social integration (Habermas, 2019).

## 98 *Reason and the Reflexive Turn in Sociology*

Bourdieu's account of social integration ultimately depends on his concept of field, which is a more articulated sociological account of objectified social relations in which a range of relevant habituses is embedded. Most of Peirce's examples show human constructions of natural objects, while Bourdieu's account of field is based on complexes of socially objectified relations. However, the intellectual model is remarkably similar, built up from what Peirce calls the logic of relatives – to be addressed in more detail later – and what Bourdieu calls the space of relations. He says that directly visible beings

> 'exist and subsist through difference'; that is, they occupy relative positions in a space of relations, which though invisible and always difficult to show empirically, is the most real reality (the ens realissimum, as scholasticism would say) and the real principle of the behaviour of individuals and groups.
> (Bourdieu, 1998, 31).

Bourdieu goes on to assert, like Peirce and against any Aristotelian idea of substance, that it is such relations of difference that 'construct' individuals and groups. The principles of difference vary significantly from society to society – he understands fields as variable social spaces that are responsible for these differences – and the theorist must 'reengender theoretically the empirically observed social space' to identify orders of social classification such as classes (id, 32). Based on this, it may then be inferred that the specification of any given habitus may be theoretically constructed from the structure of fields, but this theoretical construct also describes something that is real, the relational ordering of actors' habituses constructed from the range of distinctions they are able to draw. Such distinctions, when viewed in the light of the operations of the field, lead to generalized relations of difference. On the basis of these relations of differences, relations of symbolic power are in turn made possible. The corollary of this is that the habitus is animated by the power of practical reason to carry out social-logical operations of relational classification in conditions of difference.

Such an invocation of the concept of 'reason' in the last sentence above might appear strange in view of what frequently amounts to sociological antipathy to it. However, Bourdieu offers more than a sociologically inspired opposition to reason. In *Science of Science and Reflexivity*, Bourdieu sets out to 'save' the idea of reason. He does this, quite beyond the mainstream of contemporary sociology, by invoking a type of immanent-transcendent position (Bourdieu, 2004). For example, he favourably opposes a type of grammatical reading of Wittgenstein, which depends on laws of thought that supra-conventionally express the essence of the human mind, to the sociological conventionalist reading of Bloor, for whom rationality, objectivity, and truth are local sociocultural norms (id, 81). Hence, the opposition to 'the transcendental' as such in the classical Kantian sense, which is often ascribed to his position on art and religion, is correct, but not if it is taken to mean he has no commitment to a realm of thought beyond the empirical. He says explicitly that he sets out to save reason without the Kantian type of transcendentalism but not without a transcendental perspective (Bourdieu, 2004, 81).

*Reason and the Reflexive Turn in Sociology* 99

He explicitly invokes Habermas – while questioning the historicizing value of his universal pragmatics – on the necessity of the force of the better argument that must in the end prevail in science (id, 82). Habermas's position was originally taken from Peirce's account of the logic of inquiry and has been recently revisited (Habermas, 2019). As Bourdieu goes on, the affinity with Peirce becomes increasingly apparent. He speaks of truth accumulating because of the cooperative competition of scientists in scientific universes and gives this an intersubjectivist twist, saying that it goes beyond Kantian intersubjectivity to reveal its underlying social conditions and that 'objectivity is an intersubjective product of the scientific field grounded within the presuppositions shared within this field' (id, 83). Here, the field is seen in a manner entirely analogous to Peirce, Apel, and Habermas as a community of cooperating interpreters. Thus, Bourdieu's field is more than a space of forces and struggles between forces; it is also a space of struggle between ideas.

In the book *Practical Reason*, not alone is there a suggestive title, even if what follows is not a sustained treatment of it; there is also an incisive treatment of the logic of universalization (Bourdieu, 1998). This logic, Bourdieu proffers, attaches a profit to the appearance of universality. The powerful in any field, even the field of art, can claim to be acting universally and to develop a rationale that only appears as universal while serving specific interests. Bourdieu doesn't leave the claim to the universal merely like that. Such a claim puts those in positions of power in a potentially vulnerable position because they can be criticized for merely using the facade of universalism while carrying on the project of domination. Bourdieu says that the dominated can also use reason to oppose their own domination, including domination through science. This creates a new challenge for sociology that must more than ever confront the effect of rationalized domination by laying bare its mechanisms. Instead of offering rational instruments in the service of domination, it must rationally analyze domination and especially the contribution that rational knowledge can make to that domination. It must therefore, speaking from another place, offer a counter-reason that reinvigorates reason. If Kant understood reason as necessitating its own far-reaching critique to discover its errors and excesses, Bourdieu suggests that the sociological self-critique of reason cannot assume a recurrent triumph of the universal, for society is in ceaseless conflict and is never fully coordinated, even temporarily, by a just logic of reason. Bourdieu is mindful that any regulative idea must respect what Peirce called the 'outward clash', the play of differences whose conditions of possibility nonetheless paradoxically depend on a prior ideal that can be contested. At least this is the case, where anything like respectful relations can be found amid the differences. So, also with Habermas here, the emphasis is placed not on the form of the ideal, which is only an illusory, would-be timeless universal taken by itself, but on the capacities, processes, and mechanisms whereby it is socially instantiated. In a very general sense, for all these thinkers, these dynamics are discursive, but they are always mindful that discursivity itself is encrusted in power. It might be said with Rainer Forst that the truth lies not with the ideal but with the adequacy of the processes whereby it might be reciprocally and generally justified (Forst, 2007).

100   *Reason and the Reflexive Turn in Sociology*

Finally, isolating one final similarity between Bourdieu and Peirce, both identify a close relationship between perceptual experience and habitual dispositions. As is well known, disposition is a key feature of Bourdieu's account of the habitus. Peirce uses precisely the same word in relation to possible modulation of habit:

> By a habit I mean any modification of a person's disposition or tendency, when actuated by certain desires, to respond to perceptual conditions by conduct of a certain kind, such modification resulting from previous external experience and from certain previous voluntary actions of effort on the part of the same person.

> (Peirce, Ms. 318, 1907, 285)

Peirce's account in this respect is analogous to that of Bourdieu. What it reveals is that habit is the expression of learning. Habits then allow certain recurrent responses to be selected in given perceptual conditions. More than mechanical in nature, they also allow the transferability of the habitual template to broadly analogous, though in some respects different, perceptual conditions. Piaget may be invoked to illustrate this point. Within a given arrangement of cognitive structures, competences evolve that in turn facilitate certain perceptions, but, for higher competences, and thus perceptual judgements, to be attained, a new arrangement of cognitive structures is needed, in other words, in developmental psychological terms, a stage shift.

For Bourdieu, reflexivity, habit, and perception continuously interact with one another, where perception is taken to embrace objects of all kinds, social, natural, and technical. Reflexivity in this relationship becomes the means of modifying habits or beliefs that sustain habits. Reflexive operations are animated by doubts as to the sufficiency of existing habits and lead to personal – it could also be collective – self-analysis. As pointed out above regarding Archer, existing habits may also be understood as self-analyzing, such as a 'good' habit of exposing in one's practices a tendency to follow 'bad' habits. Reading Bourdieu closely indicates that what might be called radical reflexivity begins to operate when habit change is envisaged. In Bourdieu's terms, this could, for example, consist of a particular group ceasing to perceive an object as they want to see it in favour of seeing it in relation to its actual, or envisaged, potential form. These remarks suggest that those who see reflexivity rather than habitus as Bourdieu's key concept are therefore broadly correct, at least in the sense of the genesis as opposed to reproduction of worlds. Yet, the concepts are mutually dependent, and, in line with Peirce's doubt/belief model, reflexivity requires habitus for its initiation and its completion.

In conclusion, I want to emphasize Bourdieu's idea of the realpolitik of reason (Bourdieu, 1998, 138–139). He is anxious to avoid what he considers to be a type of Platonic idealization he takes to be at the heart of the concept of reason. Such an idealization represents it as a 'faculty' or a type of nature of human beings transcendently superordinate to historically located practice. Bourdieu identifies various manifestations of such idealization, including Habermas's idea of rational discourse. The danger he perceives is that of erecting a timeless idea of reason

*Reason and the Reflexive Turn in Sociology* 101

rather than a reason that is the product of specific struggles in fields at given times. Reason then becomes converted into a historically relative standard, for Bourdieu also recognizes that these struggles should not be transposed by means of a timeless empiricism into a permanent struggle over interests. Rather, pathological motivations, some of which spring from excessive pursuit of interest, need to be converted into *logical* ones. When this happens, something akin to what Peirce calls concrete reasonableness begins to manifest itself in certain fields, the intellectual field par excellence. The organization of such a field should never be represented as something beyond history; it rather has a dialectical form – though Bourdieu does not develop this – where a type of justified synthesis emerged from difference and its relatively temporary resolution. Reason, operating through logic, leads to those norms that are here and now 'agreed upon' because of a struggle between different normative conceptions that are also anchored in interests. Such 'agreement' in Bourdieu is the outcome of classification struggles waged in the currency of symbolic power (Bourdieu, 1984). Social positions underlying such struggles depend on an implicit sense of relational positions in social fields. Bourdieu tends not to emphasize any consensual potential for the outcome of these classification struggles, instead stressing mainly hegemonic outcomes. His account of such struggles is very valuable for conceptualizing basic problems in understanding social integration when processes such as classification struggles and symbolic power are given their due prominence. It opens up a social theoretical architectonic that is, in many respects, highly compatible with that outlined in the previous chapter. There are two noticeable absences, though. The first is the lack of concern for demonstrating actual or potential democratic mediation of such struggles. The second is the related lack of a thorough account of the discursive and logical currency by means of which any kind of mediation could proceed, where, by currency, is intended the medium of signs. Bourdieu's account has had a significant influence on the theory developed in this book. However, it is the purpose of the book to also address the issues bequeathed by the above-listed absences.

**Honneth**

Along with Habermas, Axel Honneth is the 'philosophical' critical theorist of recent times who has made the most concerted attempt to work with the original intentions of critical theory in aligning philosophy and the social sciences. His elaboration and reconstruction of the significance of Hegel's heritage for critical theory align with certain elements in classical and neoclassical sociology with the left-Hegelianism of Marx in the background. His principal orientation in this respect is towards the solidarity theory of Durkheim and the institutional role theory of Parsons. What attracts him to these theorists is the macro-sociological vision they advance, with their emphasis on generalized values, legitimate norms, and reciprocal role orientations within institutional spheres. This theoretical architecture chimes well with his Hegel-inspired theory of recognition. He even shows in a 2011 paper how Parsons explicitly developed a recognition theory, both 'negatively' conceived as the fear felt by modern individuals of loss of respect for others

## 102 *Reason and the Reflexive Turn in Sociology*

and 'positively' as their embracing of reciprocal relations of recognition through appropriate taking up of role obligations (Honneth, 2011).

Honneth's normative orientation is both consensual and dissensual. It is consensual in the foundational idea of a society necessarily built on agreement, whose basic direction is founded on a defensible process of the realization of reason. For him, following Hegel, there is potential symmetry between the rationality potentials that a given era generates and the type of institutions it could develop on their basis. It is also dissensual in that appropriate relations of recognition don't just happen by themselves. They are rather to be regarded both as drivers and outcomes of social struggles. In this latter respect, Honneth has a pronounced scepticism about the 'ideal-theoretical' tendency in the Kantian tradition to emphasize the reasonably conducted exchange of reasons in law and in the wider public domain. Rather, beyond this, he emphasizes the multi-modal logic of struggle and negation that he regards as fundamental to bringing about social change. This latter emphasis also allows him to bring strongly into play the subject in the wider supra-individual sense, as also understood by Touraine (Touraine, 2005). In turn, this requires attention to be given to pre-reflexive orientations in the form of feelings of injury or suffering that may, through a relational social logic, give rise to revived or new claims to recognition.

A particular account of reason is at the heart of Honneth's project. First of all, he affirms the profound importance of a critical theory of the Left-Hegelian idea of the actualization of reason in society (Honneth, 2011). In this account, the criterion for both the form of outcome and degree of attainment of reason lies in its societal actualization. In his later work, Honneth distinguished three fundamental kinds of freedom, which, in his view, is the most basic normative category of modern societies (Honneth, 2014). He distinguishes between the 'classical' liberal form of negative freedom, the form of reflexive freedom in the ability to rationally consider options, and, most intrinsically, the form of social freedom, the freedom that fully accounts for and potentially removes blockages to the societal capacities for freedom possible at that time. The degree of attainment of the form of social freedom is always relative to the rational potentialities of society at that time, and the gap between the two is to be explained by learning blockages, mis-developments, and social pathologies. In line with the pragmatist tradition, Honneth is clear that the realization of reason in society is to be found not in individual beliefs, though these of course could be rational, but in the spanning context of institutionally regulated social relations of recognition. The reflexive freedom of the public sphere and the negative freedom conferred by private rights, including the right not to opt into certain social arrangements, are vital, but social freedom defining the necessary space of social cooperation remains critical to both their operations. Negative freedom must not be such for any sphere or for any privileged group that it impedes the possibility of just cooperation. The conditions for the full exercise of reflexive freedom thus depend on the degree to which social freedom has been realized.

Social freedom is therefore understood as derived from the society-directing values generated in history that Honneth regards as decisive for social cooperation (Honneth, 2014). Here, a choice is made between the substantive and the

*Reason and the Reflexive Turn in Sociology* 103

formal, with Honneth putting emphasis on the former. The formal, procedural emphasis of Habermas's version of communicative reason, together with other theories of a similar orientation, will be found wanting by this criterion. Honneth does not base his prognosis simply on realizing those formal conditions that their proponents optimistically claim would allow a fully democratic and reasonable society to come about. More fundamental in his view is the necessity of indicating the direction of travel that such a coming about would necessarily mean through specifying the values guiding social institutions. He therefore stands squarely in the left-Hegelian tradition of Marx and, in certain respects, also in the younger Habermas's historically grounded theory of the public sphere, in advocating a vision of what is societal-historically possible (Trenz, 2023). Equipped with the diagnostic power of such an anticipatory vision of a better society, not down to its precise parts of course but in broad outline, Honneth identifies problems with the functioning of the public sphere that reach beyond the diagnosis of deliberative approaches. It is the under-development of social freedom that impinges on the capacity of the public sphere to properly fulfil its function, a lack of capacity that takes the form of social rationality deficits (Honneth, 2014). Such rationality or reflexivity deficits may be traced back among other realization problems of social freedom to the multiple absences of class transcending communication spaces, constitutionally differentiated media, and widely participatory, differentially mobilized, and solidaristic publics. Furthermore, for the realization of these absent conditions for effective and legitimate publicity, a new adumbration of the constitutional state in post-national conditions will be required.

A principal feature of Honneth's account of reason is his emphasis on immanent transcendence, or quasi-transcendental analysis, one of the defining approaches of contemporary critical theory (Fraser and Honneth, 2003, 45). This approach implies that normative principles cannot be positioned beyond social life as determining principles. Rather, it must be shown how they arise within it. With Lukacs, Honneth clarifies this in relation to capitalism (Honneth, 1995). The form of capitalism contains potentialities for its just organizational transformation but they are blocked by existing social relations. For Hegel, the transformative power of reason expresses itself through speculative reason that enables insight into the movement of history. For Honneth, the sequence of this process of seeing beyond occurs, firstly as diffuse, embryonic pre-reflexive feelings animated by perceptions of denied recognition and then, secondly, as the focused identification of desirable general values or ideals, before, thirdly, incorporation of these values into general norms and reciprocal role obligations. The parallels with the account of Munch supplied earlier are striking. Apart from Honneth's insistence on the role of conflict and his equal insistence on the blocking of potentials, there is in this formulation of the status of values as ideals a distinct consistency with classical and neoclassical sociology. Yet there is in Honneth's general approach, say in Freedom's Right, a manner of considering the social implications of general ideals that is far from that kind of sociology. Honneth emphasizes the immanent-transcendent transformative power of reason, which, in the right conditions, has the capacity to redirect societal development. It is therefore a mistake in interpreting Honneth to reduce his account

104  *Reason and the Reflexive Turn in Sociology*

down to a quasi-communitarian account of values and/or a strict affinity with the societal account of Parsonian sociology.

There are, nonetheless, some limitations in Honneth's account that induce interpreters to see him narrowly in the above light. Given the distinction he draws between invariant linguistic orientations and those ideals that guide rationalization processes, it is not clear how those ideals could have arisen in the first place and what relation they might have with communicative rationality? Habermas took the step towards emphasizing formal pragmatic and communicative universals to non-arbitrarily advance validity standards for societal development. He perceived that to identify specific carriers of universalization in the historical process, such as the role imputed to the bourgeoisie in the advent of the constitutional state in his own earlier work, led to problems of perspectival selectivity and excessive historical concreteness. His turn to linguistic communication was accordingly a processual turn that would show under what conditions the evolutionary-formed cognitive capacity to develop and agree on basic orientations to the world could be realized. What Habermas neglected, and what remains a major problem for critical theory, is how such orientations could be actualized in social life, both in the factual sense of how they have been and in the projective normative sense of how they could be ideally envisaged. Honneth does not deny the value of Habermas's post-idealist differentiation of reality, which equates to putting the question of validity over that of values. However, as much as Habermas is not able to demonstrate the relation between social freedom and deliberation, Honneth is not able to show how reasoning processes bring about and underpin social freedom in the first place. In other words, he is not able to provide a genetic account of social freedom from the viewpoint of demonstrable democratic reasoning. Without such an account, there is the danger, manifested by Hegel himself, of viewing reason as susceptible to theoretical reflexive specification by the scientific observer without sufficiently considering how it has also to be manifested and shaped by its public use. It is not just a question of recognizing its public use but of concretely demonstrating it.

Theoretical or academic reflexivity is a necessary hallmark of critical scholarship. Such scholarship cannot confine itself to departing merely from the current state of the public use of reason, not least because the current use of reason will, understood in terms of projected normative ideals, always represent a highly differentiated spectrum. Beyond that, the task of the critical scholar will be to advance the diffuse, pre-reflexive feelings of certain kinds of radical learning and to fill out the implications in cooperation with those social actors who initiate this process. The problem in Honneth's account arises from the fact that the specification of the range of institution-guiding ideals is fixed in advance by the theorist, and even their modified specification in *Freedom's Right* is mainly in line with the original account of Hegel. To this end, the cognitive processes and associated collective learning that must underpin the multiple possible ideals that could orient social change are not adequately explored as a process of contingent becoming. This is only possible on the supposition that Hegel was right in his designation of the value spheres of modernity. Not alone is this contested, indeed serving as a recurrent critique of Honneth, but, even if it were correct, it would still leave unaddressed the

*Reason and the Reflexive Turn in Sociology* 105

complex problems of rationalization and interpenetration of symbolic media across spheres, explored earlier in the Munch section. The proper consideration of culturally conditioned, discursively organized, learning processes, together with their institutional outcomes, is indeed complex, but only by demonstrating the genesis of ideals, good and bad, their interpenetration in discourse and action, and their institutional outcomes can a macro-sociological account of society be developed. Contemporary sociology has lost its way in these matters, which is undoubtedly one reason why Honneth reverts to classical and neoclassical sociological sources. Nonetheless, these remarks draw attention to the absence of an appropriately developed and differentiated social ontology in Honneth that would clarify such genetic processes and their reciprocal structure-forming implications through the deployment of concepts such as ideals, conflict, learning, positioning, reasoning, institutions, and even pathology (Renault, 2020). For this and other problems, his heavy reliance on classical and neoclassical sociology is problematic, even though it is understandable given the common ambitions for macro-social analysis and normative diagnosis. Hence, the problem emerges of how opens understanding macro-sociological and critical normative intentions can be accomplished in the new social and epistemological conditions of modern sociological scholarship.

Honneth, like Bourdieu, offers a rich and productive architectonic for assisting with this task. Nevertheless, in line with the above social-ontological critique, Honneth's account of reason too strongly focuses on convergent limit concepts as outlined in the previous chapter, diametrically different from the opposite problem in Kant-inspired scholarship with its strong transcendentalism. This kind of Hegelian approach is rightly concerned with the potentials contained in the actual but neglects those that are extra-institutional and latent. It also neglects the vast *cognitive* membrane of thirdness, including its immanent-transcendent cognitive structuring, that makes transformative learning possible, and hence any kind of translation between identifiable potentials and their long-term institutionalization. However, the problem is, in a way, even deeper. As will be explored later, the possibilities of reasoning thirdness depend on its relation to phenomenological firstness and factual secondness. Seen in this light, Honneth attempts to add a more realist and phenomenological dimension to thirdness in the left-Hegelian tradition moves in the right direction, but for various reasons it is incomplete. Above all, it is not enough to indicate the existence of deficits of reflexivity as a suite of social pathologies. It is necessary to go deeper into the multiple semiotic processes that bring about and consolidate these pathologies.

## Forst and McNay

In this concluding section on 'sociological' accounts of reflexivity, I broaden out the consideration to address a critique of a political philosopher and critical theorist, Rainer Forst, by a political theorist, Lois McNay (McNay, 2020). I should say at the outset that my concern, at least in the first instance, lies less with outlining Forst's extensive and stimulating contribution to the debate on recent critical theory, not least on the question of reason, than drawing attention to what McNay

# 106    *Reason and the Reflexive Turn in Sociology*

finds objectionable in this account. McNay's critique opens a wide span of considerations that highlight important aspects of the relationship between the social sciences, critical theory, and reflexivity/reason. The exchange between McNay and Forst reveals much of the space that sociological critical theory needs to address, to be elaborated on in later chapters.

At its core, McNay finds Forst's context-transcending account of justification unacceptable, claiming it is excessively detached from the immanent world. She acknowledges that Forst differentiates himself from pre-democratic and prescriptive tendencies of ideal theory; justification must take on a disclosing and critical-reflexive form that is sensitive to questions of power and hierarchy. However, she argues that 'Forst's paradigm is less radical than claimed in so far as it fails to establish an immanent connection between the role of justification as a transcendental principle and as a tool of disclosing, reflexive critique' (id, 27). She also notes that critique is only politically effective when it is guided not by transcendental principles but by existing values and norms embedded within the practices and struggles of a given age. The task of critique is to identify these 'endogenous normative resources', reconstructing them in such a way as to establish the evaluative emancipatory perspective from which it diagnoses a particular social order (id, 27).

Partly for reasons already stated in the last chapter on the significance of the idea of immanent transcendence, I do not find this a satisfactory account of the status of critique in critical theory (see also Chapters 11 and 12). At one point, for example, McNay intimates that there could be a satisfactory relation between transcendence and immanence (id, 43) but also claims that Forst's approach is too transcendental to be able to locate it. It is certainly an interesting and appropriate line of inquiry and does address the same theme of lack of concreteness identified by Honneth and by social scientific critics of ideal theory generally. But this is said in passing, and in any case, it contradicts the general emphasis on immanence of the remainder of the text. No reference is made to the characteristic immanent transcendence of such other major critical theoretical figures as Honneth and Habermas. Her own position parallels the search for emancipatory normative standards in a wide swathe of contemporary scholarship. These standards are assumed to already exist as 'endogenous normative resources' in immanent cultural orders. They thus need to be argued for in an immanent critical-reflexive way and, on this basis, have their prospects for realization enhanced. From a sociological point of view, this viewpoint limits how we can think about the issue. There are a multitude of different views, even within what might loosely be called labour or feminist movements, on how to pursue equality. Equality, to stretch a metaphor, is only one note on the piano, and perhaps it is better even to think of it as one note in one key. What about all the other notes on the other keys? How, for example, do we think about equality when we bring environmental responsibility into play in a relationship that remains poorly developed? Each cultural element, such as equality and responsibility, requires that its genesis, evolution, contestation, and institutionalization be examined as an extended process in which collective learning is manifest. Moreover, the same element will have general cognitive, ideal, contestatory, and normative moments, variously dispersed across populations. Beyond the context of innovation,

Reason and the Reflexive Turn in Sociology 107

complex 'selection' processes, involving contestation, power, and another kind of collective learning, attend to the process of stabilization, bearing in mind that as Klaus Eder once put it 'societies learn and yet the world is hard to change' (Eder, 1999). Thus, to grasp the full extent of a normative commitment is highly complicated and calls for a dynamic processual category such as justification in an immanent-transcendent register.

McNay's approach is consistent with the approach of much of modern social science. There is a clear interest in normative transformation generated by social movements read in a wide, society-constituting sense. Its precondition is conceived as learning within the situated context of appropriate reflection endowing, phenomenologically accessed experience. The subjective quality of imagination is therefore privileged over what is called fixed 'categorization' based on 'standardised norms', a position she attributes to Forst (id, 40). On the contrary of Forst, she cites Fricker (Fricker, 2007) on the importance of 'epistemic responsibility' that would involve combating 'the inherited cognitive and discursive habits that sustain the hermeneutically marginalizing effects of the supposedly impartial perspective' (ibid). This would in turn lead to 'renunciation of fixed principles of interpretation, willingness to render oneself vulnerable to others, embracing rather than smoothing over experiential disruption and complexity and the use of imagination and sympathy in interactions with others rather than fixed categorisations' (id, 40). She also follows Azmanova (Azmanova, 2011) in claiming that the exploration of imagination and sympathy should 'be grounded in personal experience and the narration of how one has come to one's view and reasons that prompted one to form it' (id, 40).

In advancing a micro-level theory of justification in this manner, McNay valuably condenses an important strand in the contemporary approach to reflexivity. Overall, reflexivity is differentiated from reason, which is often represented as a kind of macro-level ideology in the control of the privileged who espouse 'impartial' norms, which, as Bourdieu might say, are only impartial if we ignore the ethos that seeks to make appear impartial what is in fact arbitrary. This is an important approach, though it is also limiting. It is important to draw attention to the transformative power of subjectivity within the logic of normative innovation, a position that McNay repeatedly references with the idea of disclosing injustice. Transformative personal learning involves understanding oneself as a suffering being, also as one who could inflict suffering, and hence gaining the impetus to transform social arrangements more generally. This dimension of subjective transformation is pivotal to the entire tradition of critique in the Frankfurt tradition. Recently, it has acquired new impetus with the advent of new social movements animated by a sense of the suffering subject whose story must be told and listened to as a vital step in the emancipatory process. The limitation of such an approach is that it cannot offer a theory of social change as a whole, only one vital component, which suffers from its isolation from relevant contexts, including what Forst – as well as Adorno and Habermas, among others – stresses, the 'context beyond', the imperative to learn in the process of justification, and the need, emphasized in this text, to go beyond existing knowledge by using mediating meta-contextual cognitive structures. This is precisely where a dialectically affirmative account of reason is required. Accordingly, justification must consist of more than reflexive self-justification or justification with or against immediate proponents or opponents. It must *generally* relate to law, morality, the ethos of forms of life, and the building of social structures and related practices.

In a different kind of critique of Forst, Benhabib alludes to the construction of a general space of morality that comes from cumulative reflection on moral innovation in various social struggles, feminist, anti-slavery, workers, anti-colonial, and so on (Benhabib et al., 2015). This general moral resource, captured in various kinds of rights and moral sentiments, is never fixed and unchangeable, but it is a general cultural structure that offers a base for further innovation. It is not just the preserve of the privileged but a surplus of moral potentials that can be drawn upon in social struggle. While this is entirely correct, it leaves open the cognitive-communicative question of how further innovation based on this normative structure takes place. Once again, it raises the issue of how 'seeing beyond' existing normative structures, even counter-institutional ones, might eventuate.

The above raises the question of how such a normative structure might be described? Forst himself gives a clue to the answer. Moral justification is a particular kind of justification, whereas other social spheres have other kinds, viz., ethical, legal, political, and others. From early on in his work, he describes these as contexts of justification (Forst, 2002). Hence, what McNay describes is the micro context of ethical justification, where ethics is understood as the ethos of an individual but within a group frame. This by no means implies that, as an ethical context of justification, it is without moral content. Moral content is an intrinsic part of ethics and, indeed, all forms of justification. Ethical disclosing critique of the kind McNay instances intrinsically contains moral content. However, it is only moral justification, or perhaps in this sense one should say *full* moral justification, if it becomes something that social and political institutions and citizens have a moral responsibility to uphold so that, in Forst's sense, it meets the standard of being general and reciprocal. These distinctions echo the issue of interpenetration following Munch above and continued in the account of Honneth. Here, it is not meant in exactly the sense of Parsons and Munch, but in the sense of the interpenetration of contexts of justification and their respective discourses. The relation between forms of discourse, and the variable cognitive principles and ideals they contain, is always complex, more complex than any analysis of this phenomenon of which I am aware. However, such relations cannot only be conceived as confined to micro- and meso-level contexts of action/interaction. They are also intrinsically macro-level in form, which includes universal moral validity in many important instances. What is critical is to understand how such universal moral validity could be generated, rather than simply be assumed to have happened, or a type of de-contextualized assertion that certain moral claims should be preferred. Much of the effort in the second part of this book is directed at how such a process should be conceptualized. In part, it expands on a theory of justification, developed as a theory of reasoning, but it also seeks to integrate this with the existing normative culture as described

*Reason and the Reflexive Turn in Sociology* 109

by Benhabib and with the phenomenological conditions for imaginative leaps that McNay highlights.

McNay's article also addresses Forst's concept of noumenal power. This concept generates significant bewilderment in the social sciences, mainly because of its transcendental associations with Kant's philosophy. The idea of something regarded as beyond the world being influential within it meets downright resistance. McNay objects to such a concept of power both as an illustration of Forst's inability to mediate immanence and transcendence as well as impeding insight into the material bases of power. McNay asks how could a concept of power that claims to be both transcendent and immanent address the real and variable grounds for critique? How could its presumed permanent form, what she calls the universal constant of justification, address these variable grounds? By extension, how could such an idealist account make sense of material formations? These are indeed penetrating questions. It is true that in his basic architectonic that Forst denies himself some important intellectual perspectives to address such objections, such as evolutionary theorizing and an associated genetic theory of the formation of the human logical mind, as well as an encompassing social ontology in which power relations could be inset and that would follow from his concern with a fully justified basic structure. However, it is also true that McNay, in keeping with the more general tendency of the social sciences today, in one part, does not at all address and would probably reject, the idea of evolutionary formed capacities of individual or extended mind, and, in another, assumes that 'material power' requires no embedding in higher-order cultural constellations, including those that can bring about an 'affirmative' actualization of reason in historical, normative, and collective learning processes.

It might be concluded from the above short remarks that there is an epistemological and ontological abyss that separates McNay from Forst in a way that is symptomatic of how ideal and non-ideal theoretical currents coexist in tension within critical theory. This remark also overlaps a certain tension between normative philosophy in the Kantian tradition and general, critical sociology. McNay's critique puts on the table certain basic issues to do with agency, embodiment, and power that cannot be side-stepped but, at the same time, do not have to be articulated against a Kantian theory of justification, or, at least, to such an extent against it. However, this also depends on how we understand the form of a democratic theory of justification today, including any radical modifications that may be needed to Kant's original paradigm to realize it.

When Forst speaks of a basic structure of justification or justification relations, he is adverting to what might be understood as a cognitive structure that lies above substantive social and political relations (Strydom, 2015). At one level, such a transcendent structure identifies the universalistic properties that attach to all human beings; at another, it is the cognitive membrane of which humans can avail themselves to reflexively criticize existing states of affairs. Both levels can be understood as evolutionary achievements. As cognitive, they do not depend on historical learning processes in norms and values. They can go beyond such instituted normative orders. Though their interpretation is conditioned to some degree by these instituted orders, the meta-cognitive capacities they enable are not confined

110 *Reason and the Reflexive Turn in Sociology*

by them. In this latter sense, we can with Kant describe them as unconditioned (Kant, 1998). In this sense, when Benhabib and McNay seek to emphasize historically accumulated normative insight, there is a risk that the formal structure of cognitive relations may be obscured. To speak with Peirce here, who radically modified Kant, the reason why accumulated learning is possible in the first place depends on the effects of learning through abduction, the imaginative generation of new ideas, and its wider justification. This process, moving through abduction and other forms of inference, requires collective capacities and structures to reflexively achieve collective learning. As Strydom suggests, movement in this direction follows from Forst's idea of *relations* of justification (Strydom, 2015). Such a structure is critical to understanding the context-independent capacity for reflexivity, a capacity that is triggered in situations – the conditioned – but is independently graspable beyond these situations – the unconditioned. This requires showing not just ontogenetic capacities of individuals but also collective phylogenetic capacities of groups up to the level of the species. Both vitally depend on natural, natural-social, and cultural evolution.

This account of this exchange between Forst and McNay completes these short reviews of how reason and reflexivity are addressed in sociology and the broader social sciences. In the next chapter, I will not return in any depth to the individual reviews. For these reviews are ultimately meant to assist in delineating the general contours of the societal ontology that must be adressed to develop a sociological account of reason. The next chapter will examine what the social scientific state of knowledge as outlined here intellectually enables and where it needs further development in the light of the ontological framework outlined in Chapter 2.

### Note

1 Wolfgang Welsch also considered the interrelation between rationality spheres but, unlike Munch, places a transversal concept of reason at the general level (Welsch 2008).

### References

Alexander JC, Giesen B, Munch R, Smelser NJ(eds) (1987) *The Micro-Macro Link*. Oakland, CA: University of California Press.

Alexander JC (1995) *Fin De Siècle Social Theory: Relativism, Reduction, and the Problem of Reason*. New York: Verso.

Alexander JC (2004) Cultural Pragmatics: Social Performance between Ritual and Strategy. *Sociological theory* 22(4): 527–573.

Alexander JC and Smith P (1993) The Discourse of American Civil Society: A New Proposal for Cultural Studies. *Theory and Society* 22(2): 151–207.

Apel K-O (1978) The Conflicts of Our Times and the Problem of Political Ethics. In: Dallmayr FR (ed) From Contract to Community. Political Theory at the Crossroads. New York, NY: Marcel Dekker.

Apel K-O (2001) *The Response of Discourse Ethics*. Leuven: Peeters.

Archer M (1984) *Culture and Agency: The Place of Culture in Social Theory*. Cambridge: Cambridge University Press.

*Reason and the Reflexive Turn in Sociology* 111

Archer, M (1990) Theory, culture and post-industrial society. *Theory, Culture and Society.* 7(2-3): 97–119.

Archer MS (2007) *Making Our Way through the World: Human Reflexivity and Social Mobility.* Cambridge: Cambridge University Press.

Archer MS (2009) *Conversations about Reflexivity.* London: Routledge.

Archer MS (2010) Routine, Reflexivity, and Realism. *Sociological Theory* 28(3): 272–303.

Azmanova A (2011) *The Scandal of Reason: A Theory of Critical Political Judgment.* New York, NY: Columbia University Press.

Benhabib S, Flynn J, Fritsch M, and Forst, R (2015) The Right to Justification by Rainer Forst. *Political Theory* 43(6): 777–837.

Boltanski L (2011) *On Critique: A Sociology of Emancipation.* Cambridge: Polity.

Bora A (1999) Discourse Formations and Constellations of Conflict. In: O'Mahony P (ed) *Nature, Risk, and Responsibility: Discourses of Biotechnology.* London: Macmillan.

Bourdieu P (1984) *Distinction: A Social Critique of the Judgement of Taste.* Cambridge, MA: Harvard University Press.

Bourdieu P (1988) *Homo Academicus.* Redwood: Stanford University Press.

Bourdieu P (1990) *Essays towards a Reflexive Sociology.* Cambridge: Blackwell.

Bourdieu P (1998) *Practical Reason: On the Theory of Action.* Redwood:Stanford University Press.

Bourdieu P (2004) *Science of Science and Reflexivity.* Cambridge: Polity.

Bourdieu P and Wacquant L (1992) *An Invitation to Reflexive Sociology.* Chicago, IL: University of Chicago Press.

Buxton WJ (1994) Academic Dispute or Clash of Commitments?: The Schutz-Parsons Exchange Reconsidered. *Human Studies* 17: 267–275.

Cicourel AV (1981) Notes on the Integration of Micro- and Macro-Levels of Analysis. In: Knorr KK and Cicourel AV (eds) *Advances in Social Theory and Methodology: Toward an Integration of Micro and Macro Sociologies.* Boston, MA: Routledge and Kegan Paul.

Cicourel AV (2011) Evidence and Inference in Macro-Level and Micro-Level Healthcare Studies. In: Candlin CN and Sarangi S (eds) *Handbook of Communication in Organisations and Professions.* Berlin:De Gruyter, pp. 61–82.

Eder K (1999) Societies Learn and Yet the World Is Hard to Change. *European Journal of Social Theory* 2(2): 195–215.

Elder-Vass D and Archer MS (2012) Cultural System or Norm Circles? An Exchange. *European Journal of Social Theory* 15(1): 93–115.

Forst R (2002) *Contexts of Justice: Political Philosophy beyond Liberalism and Communitarianism.* Los Angeles, CA: University of California Press.

Forst R (2007) First Things First: Redistribution, Recognition, and Justification. *European Journal of Political Theory* 6(3): 291–304.

Foucault M (1984) What Is Enlightenment? In: Paul R (ed) *The Foucault Reader* Harmondsworth: Penguin.

Fricker M (2007) *Epistemic Injustice: Power and the Ethics of Knowing.* Oxford: Oxford University Press.

Fuhrmann, JT (2019) *Postfundamentale Systemtheorie.* Vienna: Passagen.

Gouldner AW (1971) *The Coming Crisis of Western Sociology.* New York, NY: Avon.

Habermas J (1996) *Between Facts and Norms: Contributions to a Discourse Theory of Law and Democracy.* Cambridge, MA: MIT Press.

Habermas J (2003) *Truth and Justification.* Cambridge, MA: MIT Press.

Habermas J (2019) *Auch eine Geschichte der Philosophie.* Frankfurt: Suhrkamp.

Honneth A (1991) *The Critique of Power: Reflective Stages in a Critical Social Theory.* Cambridge MA: MIT Press.

Honneth A (1995) *The Fragmented World of the Social: Essays in Social and Political Philosophy.* New York, NY: SUNY Press.

## 112  Reason and the Reflexive Turn in Sociology

Honneth A (2011) Verwilderungen des Sozialen Konflikts: Anerkennungskämpfe zu Beginn des 21. Jahrhunderts. Report: MPIfG working paper. Max Planck Institute for the Study of Societies. Cologne.

Honneth A (2014) *Freedom's Right: The Social Foundations of Democratic Life*. New York, NY: Columbia University Press.

Kant I (1998) *Critique of Pure Reason*, Trans. Paul Guyer and Allen W. Wood. Cambridge: Cambridge University Press.

Latour B (2004) *Politics of Nature*. Cambridge, MA: Harvard University Press.

Lizardo O (2004) The Cognitive Origins of Bourdieu's Habitus. *Journal for the Theory of Social Behaviour* 34(4): 375–401.

Luhmann N (1998) *Observations on Modernity*. Palo Alto, CA: Stanford University Press.

Luhmann N (1999) *Die Gesellschaft der Gesellschaft*. Frankfurt: Suhrkamp.

Luhmann N (2012) *Theory of Society, Volume 1*. Redwood, CA: Stanford University Press.

Luhmann N and Schorr K-E (1999) *Reflexionsprobleme im Erziehungssystem*. Frankfurt: Suhrkamp.

Lynch M (2000) Against Reflexivity as an Academic Virtue and Source of Privileged Knowledge. *Theory, Culture and Society* 17(3): 26–54.

Mannheim K (2012) *Essays on the Sociology of Culture*. London: Routledge.

McNay L (2020) The Limits of Justification: Critique, Disclosure and Reflexivity. *European Journal of Political Theory* 19(1): 26–46.

Mead GH (1934) *Mind, Self and Society from the Standpoint of a Social Behaviourist*. Chicago, IL: University of Chicago Press.

Miller M (1992) Rationaler Dissens. Zur Gesellschaftlichen Funktion Sozialer Konflikte. In: Giegel HJ (ed) *Rationaler Dissens. Zur Gesellschaftlichen Funktion Sozialer Konflikte*. Frankfurt: Suhrkamp.

Munch R (1981) Talcott Parsons and the Theory of Action. I. The Structure of the Kantian Core. *American Journal of Sociology* 86(4): 709–739.

Munch R (1991) The Law as a Medium of Communication. *Cardozo L. Rev.* 13: 1655.

Münch R (1991) *Dialektik der Kommunikationsgesellschaft*. Frankfurt: Suhrkamp.

Münch R (2010) *Theory of Action (Routledge Revivals): Towards a New Synthesis Going Beyond Parsons*. London: Routledge.

O'Mahony P (2011) Democracy, Complexity and Participation. *Irish Journal of Public Policy*. 3(1): 11–30.

O'Mahony P (2013) *The Contemporary Theory of the Public Sphere*. Oxford: Peter Lang.

Otte M (1998) Limits of Constructivism: Kant, Piaget and Peirce. *Science & Education* 7(5): 425–450.

Parsons T (1990) Prolegomena to a Theory of Social Institutions. *American Sociological Review* 55(3): 319–333.

Peirce CS (1931–1958) *Collected Papers of Charles Sanders Peirce*. In: Hartshorne C, Weiss P, and Burks PW (eds). Cambridge, MA: Harvard University Press.

Peirce CS (1998) The Fixation of Belief (1877). In: Hauser N and Kloesel, C (eds) *The Essential Peirce: Selected Philosophical Writings, Volume 1 (1867–1893)*. Indiana University Press.

Piaget J (1972) *The Principles of Genetic Epistemology*. London: Routledge and Kegan Paul.

Piiroinen TJSt (2014) For "Central Conflation" a Critique of Archerian Dualism. *Sociological Theory* 32(2): 79–99.

Rawls J (1993) *Political Liberalism*. New York, NY: Columbia University Press.

Rawls J (1999) *The Law of Peoples*. Cambridge, MA: Harvard University Press.

Renault E (2020) Critical Theory, Social Critique and Knowledge. *Critical Horizons* 21(3): 189–204.

Schutz A (1932) *The Phenomenology of the Social World*. Chicago, IL: Northwestern University Press.

Schutz A and Parsons T (1978) Parson's Theory of Social Action: A Critical Review. 8–60.

Stichweh R (2007) Evolutionary Theory and the Theory of World Society. *Soziale Systeme* 13(1-2): 528–542.

Strydom P (2015) Critical Theory of Justice: On Forst's' Basic Structure of Justification' from a Cognitive-Sociological Perspective. *Philosophical Inquiry* 39(2): 110–133.

Strydom P (2017) Infinity, Infinite Processes and Limit Concepts: Recovering a Neglected Background of Social and Critical Theory. *Philosophy and Social Criticism* 43(8): 793–811.

Touraine A (2005) The Subject Is Coming Back. *International Journal of Politics, Culture, and Society* 18(3–4): 199–209.

Trenz H-J (2023) The Theory of the Public Sphere as a Cognitive Theory of Modern Society. *Philosophy & Social Criticism* 50(1): 125–140. 01914537231203905.

Welsch W (2008) *Unsere Postmoderne Moderne*. Berlin: Akademie Verlag.

West DE and Anderson M (2016) *Consensus on Peirce's Concept of Habit: Before and Beyond Consciousness*. New York, NY: Springer.

# 4    The State of Reason in Sociology

## Introduction

The preceding chapters have outlined, firstly, in chapter 2, a general perspective on the requirements of a sociological account of reason. Then, secondly, in chapter 3, some sociological – mainly – theories have been assessed from this general standpoint. This second step was done 'weakly', in that it was apparent that the overall account would not be richly productive if I followed each theory step by step for each of the identified elements of the general standpoint. Rather, the intention was to produce an account of reason, or, where perceived to be different, reflexivity, mainly in terms of how the theories themselves saw it. As already observed, what emerged was mainly not so much an account of reason in the strict sense but an account of reflexivity as a component or surrogate of reason. As a component of reason, reflexivity could be represented as the capacity to engage in something like reasoning in something like an 'appropriate' way, a sense of appropriateness that varied with the theory. Mostly, reflexivity was not addressed as a component of reason at all but as a kind of replacement for it, generally with no reference at all to the canonical literature on reason. The theories were, of course, not exhaustive. They were a survey of approaches in sociology that are explicit about reflexivity, as almost no sociological text deals with reason head-on. Most are a kind of oblique critique of a perceived kind of reason, for example, patriarchal reason, post-colonial reason, ideal theoretical reason, and communicative reason. This review of texts provides the raw materials for the present chapter, a type of assessment of what the state of reason is in sociology in the light of the general framework and of the review of texts. The question could be posed that given that reason is rarely explicitly mentioned in sociological texts is it not easy to simply dismiss the sociological contribution? This, in fact, would be premature in that sociology could, and in certain respects does, contribute to the understanding of reason, and its contribution could be even more significant in the future. Such a future, further, would be unlikely to emerge in any positive way at all, if it was not already the case that certain themes were present in the discipline, either historical or contemporary, and certain latent themes, inchoately emerging, have gone unobserved.

The present chapter therefore attempts the challenging task of assessing the actual contribution of sociology to understanding the nature of reason in

DOI: 10.4324/9780429060571-5

contemporary society, viewed from the standpoint of the general space of reason outlined in Chapter 2. At the same time, it seeks to anticipate how the immense and relevant theoretical resources of sociology could be significantly further developed to advance the critical and reconstructive dialectic of reason.

## Immanent transcendence, Convergence-divergence

It is not so surprising in view of the relentless emphasis on immanence in contemporary theorizing, that, beyond critical theory proper, there are few intimations, let alone developed accounts of immanent transcendence, in the recent sociological literature. Even within critical theory, as illustrated by McNay, the idea of a non-, or in some hands, anti-transcendental immanent critique has gained considerable ground, by virtue of a widespread account of immanent critique, an account that differs from Adorno's assumption that immanent critique incorporates a transcendent moment (Adorno, 2003). Immanent transcendence identifies that feature of human learning in which humans who find themselves in a situation are yet to be able to see beyond it to further possibilities that as yet do not exist but can conditionally be anticipated. This cognitive – in the widest sense – quality suffuses human social and self-relations. Like the other dimensions regarded as critical to a theory of reason under discussion here, it is treated as a necessary quality of human cognition and social world-making. As indicated previously, the very idea of a transcendent capacity of this kind inspires a negative reaction in contemporary sociology, which often satisfies itself with reference to the imagination, as in the widely used term of social imaginaries (Castoriadis, 1998), without reference to what hold imaginative acts might have on a possible future reality beyond initiating the first intimation of it.

Yet, the classical origins of sociology tell another story, one in which variations on immanent transcendence were present. Durkheim replaced God with society: 'since society is the transcendental precondition of the possibility of that [moral] experience, it must be demonstrable how it makes experience possible' (cited in Rose, 1981, 17). Society is thus the transcendental precondition for the use of the conditioned categories. Through evolution, the societal core acquires an a priori status, not built up inductively from experience. This is what allows 'objective' grounds of validity to be attached to moral experience. Like Kant and Hegel, therefore, Durkheim views the mind as having a quality of transcending what is directly given to it in experience. Through the idea of collective mental capacities whose precondition is society, Durkheim approaches a meta-cognitive structure whose transcendental quality is an outcome of cultural evolution. In the functionalist tradition with which Durkheim is most associated, something of this quality of immanent-transcendence is retained, for example, in Luhmann with the construct of expectation expectations (Luhmann, 1990, 46), and in Parsons with his account of transcendental ends (Parsons, 1990).

Weber, too, like Durkheim, also identifies an immanent-transcendent quality when he says: 'The transcendental presupposition of every cultural science is ... that we are cultural beings endowed with the capacity and will to take a deliberate

116   *The State of Reason in Sociology*

attitude towards the world and lend it significance' (Weber, 1949, 96). Like Durkheim, the nature of mind is emphasized as that which can transcend given experiences, the capability to be able to attach additional connotative significance to objects of experience. While Durkheim's focus was on objective, universal validity, Weber's was on differentiated values whose priority could not be rationally decided upon, leading to his emphasis on an ethic of responsibility guiding the decision of the actor. Weber's emphasis on values was taken up by Parsons in the idea of ultimate religious values, the telic system, from which integrative norms can be derived.

Among the theorists reviewed in the previous chapter, even if not generally in applied sociological discourse, 'transcendence' does feature in some way, though only Bourdieu, and, as one would expect, Forst and Honneth, really develop a position that could be said to be immanent transcendent in any clear sense. Perhaps, though, it could also be argued that it applies to Luhmann with his emphasis on systems constructivism, and to Archer's position in its relation to Bhaskar's transcendental ontology, taking the place of Kant's transcendental subjectivity. Ultimately, Archer relates this transcendental ontology to the ultimate incognizable, the idea of God (Archer et al., 2013). This transcendence is reflected in the differentiation of beliefs among agents, who manifest Weber's value relation in their self-understanding. Such agents feel the transcendent working in upon them and influencing their actions, though this process cannot be explicitly justified or explained. In this respect, the ontological transcendent escapes epistemic processes but is still to be regarded as shaping the lives of individuals. McNay, at one point in her essay, also makes positive reference to the need to integrate immanence and transcendence, but this is never subsequently developed in her version of immanent critique, and she mainly offers a critique of Forst's Kantian transcendentalism. From an overall standpoint, the impression created is that nowhere is the figure of immanent transcendence made into a key component of theoretically guided social scientific research strategies. Even in the case of Forst's critical theoretical transcendentalism, from the other side, as it were, the relation to the immanent is not extensively developed, at least in such a way as could support the nuance and dynamism of a fully developed logic of inquiry within the tradition.

Following Peirce, Kant, and modern mathematical theory, the difference between divergence and convergence is a key element in Strydom's understanding of immanent transcendence (Kant, 1972; Peirce, 1998; Strydom, 2017, 82). Combining Peirce with Strydom, at the apex of human meaning systems are to be found generals, those crystallizations of multiple, related constructs of meaning that give orientation to human forms of life. These are ultimate 'Ends' of inquiry, such as truth, right, and beauty. They can be grasped with Kant, as explicated by Strydom, as two kinds of world orientation, that to divergent 'limit concepts', ideas of reason or the paths that Ends could somehow follow, and to convergent limit concepts, general 'cognitive' ideals that provide immanent orientation. These limit concepts hence guide the process of forming meaning within an unlimited range of possibilities. They represent those intimations of the infinite spectrum of possible meaning that humans can grasp and potentially make actual. They therefore represent systems of orientation derived from the more fundamental purposes of human life. For Strydom, there is a close articulation between convergent and divergent limit concepts. Divergent limit concepts are those general meta-concepts that are attached to the flow of meaning so that, in this or that respect, an aspect of meaning should be considered and find its relevance. These are true cognitive constructs in that no one can determine exactly how they should be used – on this meta-level – but without them, any form of cooperative life in the broadest sense would not be possible. They form presuppositions or idealizations of what is necessarily relevant in human affairs. Ideals are, on the other hand, those entities, derived from such meta-cognitive presuppositions, that serve as value goals at the highest immanent level. Strydom distinguishes between the two as follows (ibid). Divergent limit concepts, on the one hand, are to be understood as validity concepts, that is, they indicate in what spectrum of relevance some meaning construct may be cognitively elaborated. Convergent limit concepts, on the other hand, are to be thought of as general ideals that have been established in society over time and that are manifestly recognized as such. Such convergent ideals are highly general goals towards which a society agrees to orientate and, accordingly, they have general cognitive powers of normative orientation.

The distinction between divergent and convergent is vital to understanding immanent transcendence. The transcendent divergent dimension gains its force in the capacity to go beyond, to recalibrate relations of meaning within and between cognitively general ideas of reason such as truth, rightness, and beauty, and to fundamentally learn. The immanent convergent dimension gains its force in the specification of general regulative ideals that more rapidly shift over time, as, for example, the ideal of equality that, at minimum, manifestly means that no person should have no chance of achieving those minimum goods and competences for 'human flourishing'. Of course, this is not always, perhaps even mostly, realized, but you will struggle to find a politician in a democratic system who will explicitly say they do not support such a value. Many more examples might be given, but I will leave more detail on the specification of this and other related levels until later, specifically where I will address Peirce's idea of logical interpretants.

It is a presupposition of this book that only very rarely outside of critical theory is there any elaboration of immanent transcendence, although, as illustrated in the review, Bourdieu is something of an exception, even though he does not make extensive use of the concept. A considerable part of Hegel's enduring appeal in sociology, whether recognized or not, lies in this combination of transcendental speculation with immanent ideals. However, at least in its explicit self-understanding, sociology at most tends to concentrate on the level of convergent ideals; for example, beyond the figures here one could also add Boltanski and Thevenot's justification types. I say 'at most' because a whole series of contemporary sociological movements attack the presumed normative universalism of ideals and are ever eager to demonstrate that theoretical claims to universalism practically falsify themselves in making the universal the deceiving outcome of the hidden particularism of interested actors. While Bourdieu criticizes such a position quite strongly – the Platonic illusion of the universal –, it is nonetheless possible to discern how the cognitive architecture of his theory could allow for the possibility of general

## 118    *The State of Reason in Sociology*

ideals to become manifest. However, his theory of practice was more oriented to revealing false ideals than in any kind of affirmation of justifiable ideals, even if the revealing of false ideals, such as in the supposed impartiality of the legal system, ultimately depended on the non-distorted and hence 'objective' validity standards that must guide the logic of inquiry, the avoidance of performative contradiction in Apel's sense or of the affirmative dialectic in Badiou's. As Bourdieu began to understand the logic of inquiry in a progressively more 'Peircean' way in his late career, albeit not explicitly, this objectivity in the production of 'starting points', that is, basic validity orientations, became more the outcome of intersubjective and, in the end, collective processes. Nonetheless, convergent ideals that could be identified and affirmed by some kind of reconstructive logic never became intrinsic to his work.

Honneth's work is manifestly a variation on immanent transcendence, a position he explicitly defends (Honneth, 2007, 63–79). His work on social freedom, along with Forst's on tolerance, is among the most sustained treatments of a convergent ideal in the contemporary literature, creating an interdisciplinary space between sociology and philosophy (Forst, 2013; Honneth, 2014). In the present context, surveying the specific sociological literature, Munch's elaboration of Parsons is of considerable interest. Munch understands ideals as generalized values rooted in solidarity that, in various ways, gave form to the social system, all the way down to level of group support or opposition to them. While respect must be accorded to the thoroughness of the neo-Parsonian account he offers, it does suffer in the present context from two limitations. The first is the limitation of not demonstrating how these generalized values might themselves have been produced, a deficiency at the processual, epistemic level. The second is the tendency to regard them as having unqualified affirmative implications, which is constraining for any kind of critical sociological analysis given that it is without adequate consideration of how they can alternately become embroiled in constellations of power and deception.

Combining Bourdieu and Munch and viewing them both from the vantage point of critical theory, general ideals can only be affirmatively asserted when they can also withstand the test of social critique as to their possible illusory quality. The lesson of the fate of reason in the 20th century applies here. Ideals as an expression of reason are not self-standing the way they can be socially instituted may contradict the good intentions that may lie at their heart. It may well be in those circumstances that the good ideal turns out to be means to worsen societal domination and bad faith; for example, the manner in which some libertarian ideas of freedom are dogmatically applied. As against this, it should not be assumed either that ideals always facilitate domination by the permanent inversion of their good intentions in practice. The regulative force of ideals is intrinsic to the possibility of normatively defensible and enabling practices, even to the possibility of many forms of critique. Without the force of ideals, the possibility of social change cannot be envisaged, just as without the force of transcendental ideas of reason, radical social change cannot be thought of or argued for. In the main, sociology has never quite fully incorporated these lessons from the history of reason, partly, as Horkheimer and Adorno respectively make abundantly clear, because of the dominant form of subjective, formal reason in modernity that underpinned sociological positivism and moved it towards merely categorial schemes of social facts (Adorno, 2019 (1964); Horkheimer, 1974 (1947)).

## The Cognitive Dimension

While a cognitive approach to sociology manifests itself from many standpoints within the discipline, scientistic, interpretive, critical, and variations of two or three of these, what unites these approaches is the measure of autonomy granted to actual cognitive activity. Though similarities between the various approaches cannot be exaggerated, the cognitive 'turn' emphasizes how agents at many levels and of many kinds play a critical role both in understanding and ordering the worlds they inhabit. This is so even where these agents are assumed to operate with quite different epistemic rationalities. This is quite different from the symbolic understanding emphasizing shared values that has been dominant in sociology for much of the last century in one form or another. It entails moving from the semantic representation of a world already assumed to be there towards the active construction of schemata that make sense of the world in potentially variable ways. In this sense, sociology is still catching up with Kant's originating epistemic turn, even though it is equipped with a remarkable history of Kant interpretation of its own. Little acknowledged in this move within the discipline of sociology – speaking in a broad sense of the general self-understanding of the discipline and how it explicates its key ideas – is that this approach builds upon and recapitulates the post-metaphysical turn of the late enlightenment and its 19th-century successors. There is therefore an ineluctable relationship between the cognitive turn in sociology and the enlightenment history of reason, even if this relationship is mired in controversy. This is partly revealed in the extent to which Kant and Hegel play a shaping role of one kind or another in many of the theories addressed in the previous chapter, directly or indirectly, and this can arise even where disagreement with these figures is asserted. It is therefore impossible to think of the cognitive turn without, in some way, being in the frame of what Habermas describes as post-metaphysical thinking, where such thinking contains the idea of breaking with a fixed understanding of the world as composed of unchanging metaphysical essences that unfold in our lives behind our backs and beyond our powers of comprehension (Habermas, 1992).

Regarding the sociological figures surveyed in the last chapter, this cognitive turn is manifested in a variety of ways. In the interpretive tradition at its most intrinsic, it is the phenomenon of interpretation itself that is at issue, as illustrated by Lynch. This suggests a mundane cognitive form that incessantly creates variation and specificity, due to the creative possibilities of language as a medium of communication and the uniqueness of situations. Cicourel's idea of normative 'accounting practices' that underpin the gestation of values is an explicit cognitive move that attends to how such accounting practices bear on normative outcomes and the ongoing varied reception of these outcomes. One clear line of development in cognitive sociology involves the critique of Parsons's 'normativism', manifested as early as

120    *The State of Reason in Sociology*

Schutz and taken further by Cicourel and the interpretive turn generally (Cicourel, 1974). Normativism in this sense is criticized because of its symbolic status that, in Parsons's case, has a transcendent quasi-ontological quality. Therefore, accounting practices in Cicourel's sense emphasize interpretation as a cognitively grounded practice of justification in a manner that would be later systematically developed by Boltanski and Thevenot (Boltanski and Thévenot, 2006).

The previous chapter addressed the cognitive foundations of Bourdieu's theory. Insofar as this theory is bound up with Bourdieu's objectivist account of theoretical reflexivity, as in theoretical reflexive practices, it begins to take on an ambivalent quality with regard to the relationship between cognitive practices and reason. This ambivalence, in some part, explains why Boltanski and Thevenot, originally part of the Bourdieu circle, eventually broke with it. Their commitment lay in moving beyond theoretical reflexivity towards ordinary reflexivity and hence to an understanding of the cognitive as operating in everyday settings guided by the interpretive accomplishments of the agents themselves. The late Bourdieu did make significant strides towards at least indicating how his understanding of the cognitive, just like Cicourel, viewed the cognitive as underpinning the normative. In this sense, generally, it can also be asserted that they both stand in at least the spirit of the later enlightenment in associating the cognitive as basic, hence involving the freedom to fashion those norms to which we agree to be bound, lying at the very core of the idea of reason. This is at the very heart of what Habermas, among others, understands by the post-metaphysical (Habermas, 2019). Luhmann's account of the cognitive shift is rather different, in that it construes the normative powers of agents negatively and as likely to lead to disappointment because the 'mental' operations associated with cognition are directly performed not by humans but by systems. He adds to this the idea that society is embroiled in a long-run evolutionary shift from the preponderance of normative to cognitive expectations.

By contrast to the above, those thinkers that have historically been associated in one form or another with structural sociology, Archer, Alexander, and Munch do not give direct attention to the cognitive in the sense understood here. Aspects of their theorizing do give voice to something akin to the cognitive construction of reality, whether it be in Archer's internal conversation, Alexander's cultural pragmatics, or Munch's account of the communication society. In the latter two cases, the symbolic remains primary, given the emphasis on fixed codes in Alexander and on generalized values in Munch. Though they remain within the symbolic paradigm in the main, they are alive to the fact that this paradigm has become contested. In Archer's case, the emphasis on the inner conversation leads to a type of nominalist fragmentation of perspectives that is consistent with many theories that identify themselves, unlike hers, as micro-level theories. These theories emphasize the pluralism of perspectives and the uniqueness of individuals' world constructions (Turner, 2010). These cases of more modest cognitive influence attest to the varied ways and degrees with which the cognitive paradigm is received in sociology. What remains as a task for later in this book is to clarify how sociology can understand itself within a cognitive paradigm that would also be immanent-transcendent. Indeed, it is its contention that this can be done with no

The State of Reason in Sociology    121

loss to its concern for the felt, the cognizable, and the normative in contexts both of justifiable societal rationalization and of domination and injustice.

## Critical-reflexive, Mediation, Critique

In relation to the third dimension of the presumed necessary components of a sociological account of reason, outlined in Chapter 3, lies the question of reflexive practices. Reflexivity in this sense can be understood, according to Lynch, as radical reflexivity, that is, reflexivity that encodes the basic capacity to reflect beyond the given situation and to imagine a new situation. I understand this as critical reflexivity in the sense of Peirce's doubt-belief model, that is, for any reason, the epistemological questioning of a belief through the advent of doubt (Peirce, 1998; Habermas, 2019). In various ways, most of the specific accounts of reflexivity in the previous chapter do not doubt the existence of critical reflexivity in this sense whatever they might call it, except for Luhmann, who has a quasi-naturalistic account of adaptation to systems that are, in the long run, indifferent to the cognitive practices of human subjects.

The cognitive turn implies that beliefs, norms, values, and dispositions have a constructed quality, that they emanate from reflexive practices of some kind, even agent-induced system reflexivity in Luhmann. Different theories have different accounts of what constitutes the medium of these reflexive practices. Such practices link the immediacy of perception to a world that can be known in its *relative* stability, even where this knowing relates to processes of contingent becoming whose outcome is unclear. It is this triadic process, whose operations are hyper-complex to fully grasp, that is the medial correlate to theories of the cognitive. In these circumstances, there is a profound relationship between cognition and medium, both biologically and socioculturally, in that the cognitive apparatus must orchestrate with the medium and vice versa. Peirce's account of sign mediation substantially taken over from Hegel but 'linguistified', interpretant signs mediating between articulated signs and their objects, is the most productive available concept of mediation. It provides the necessary understanding of how perceptual judgement grounded in bodily experience can lead through mediating inferential reasoning processes to adequate – in all the senses of good, true, and right – world relations.

Applied more generally, this triadic schema leads to a double concept of mediation within human sense-making. Firstly, a theory of mediation must show how it can generate reliable knowledge and also new knowledge. Secondly, a theory of mediation must show, to the contrary, how knowledge with merely the appearance of truth, rightness, and authenticity can be produced, where this appearance may either be the result of deliberate intention or of error in its construction. With the first, I associate a general 'positive' theory of mediation, incorporating critical-reflexive learning, and with the second, I associate critique, but also, intrinsic to critique, identifying those reasoning processes that underpin either deliberate subterfuge or genuine error.

Three of the sociological approaches described in the previous chapter involve strong accounts of mediation: Bourdieu, Luhmann, and Munch. The combination

## 122 *The State of Reason in Sociology*

of Bourdieu's reflexivity and habitus concepts covers the dimensions of dispositional quality, sphere of relevance, and world reference. The reflexivity dimension, not fully developed in this sense by Bourdieu, can be extended to explain the connotative accretions of meaning that lead to change or potential transformation of the habitus. This would also entail 'liberating' the habitus concept from the over-determining context of field in Bourdieu. Munch uses Parsons's media theory of the four generalized symbolic steering media: money, power, value commitments, and influence. In Parsons's system of codes developed late in his career in 1977, he shows how Durkheim's distinction between forms of solidarity can be used to differentiate the integrative codes of influence – justification, organic solidarity –, and value commitments – rights, mechanical solidarity (Parsons, 1977). Finally, Luhmann's media theory is, as outlined in the last chapter, based on systemic media of communication that operate through including and excluding codes. This theory is confined to systemic 'interpretants', the systems that interpret signs, and accords no social role for human cognitive operations in the semiotic coordination of society. Luhmann thus offers an extreme variation on the linguistic turn that sought to separate psychology from logic, which, in Peirce, for example, was regarded as a strictly social form. Whereas in Peirce the human mental apparatus is the ultimate medium, in Luhmann, human cognition is separated out from the social and treated differently as psychic systems. There is some parallel here with Archer's idea of the autonomous reasoning capacity of individuals, who are taken to have properties that lie beyond their social contexts. In both Luhmann and Archer, what is screened out is intersubjective agreement – based on the reconciliation of interpretants – between subjects on the meaning of something and its implications. In the critical realist context, this indicates what Bertillson, speaking of Bhashar, describes as the absence of thirdness, the mediating power of reasoning, in the dominant subject-object framework of critical realism (Bertilsson, 2009).

One of the perennial manifestations of the use of 'reason' is to postulate that reason engages only in 'positive' mediation and that deformations in the use of reason lie somewhere else than in reason itself. This inspires much of the resistance to the idea of reason. I put reason between commas above to indicate that this affirmative idea of reason involves the close coupling of reason and the normative, also understood affirmatively. The coupling is so close in fact that they come to be identical. Reason itself is not so much directly theorized, as it is regarded as something that can be used to specify the appropriate societal codes and values, and by derivation, norms. What is prevalent here is the implicit deployment of reason without a demonstrated justification or adequate consideration of the subject positions that might support it. In various ways, the Parsonian tradition manifests this danger, as reflected in Munch and Alexander above, notwithstanding that the tradition specifies a medium of generalized justification, influence, and a medium of generalized norms and value commitments. Even though such media are specified, there is no examination of the contestation that lurks within them. It could be countered that Alexander's specification of a bifurcated societal code, civil and uncivil, performs this role. The problem lies in the fact that this code is attributed such long-run historical valency, spanning hundreds of years with more or less the same form,

The State of Reason in Sociology    123

that no realistic analysis is plausible of the mechanisms of its constitution and maintenance and the particular ideological functions it might facilitate (Alexander and Smith, 1993). Generalized judgements of this kind about media that are not examined through their public use or codes that are assumed to take only a single decisive form over time open the door to reason being seen as a project of the dominant. If the normative well-being of society can be objectively prescribed, and if something like the history of liberal democracy is regarded as its carrier, the question ineluctably forces itself forward regarding the fate of those whose interests were sacrificed along the way? The latter judgement, for example, stands as a critique of assumptions about the stability of the culture of civil society over time (Alexander) or 'a sense of justice' (Rawls) that are taken to be of originating significance for establishing the boundaries of the reasonable. In this account, the deviations from reason, or incapacities to reason, of the public recurrently appear as the problem, not the material and cultural conditions in which these supposed deviations and incapacities do or might occur.

Ultimately, the problem in the above lies in the way in which an objectivist position entails that the symbolically pre-decided normative constellation colonizes the cognitive operations of mediation. In other words, what Wiener describes as a logic of contestedness that intrinsically allows for conflict and critique has to be directly incorporated as a component of mediation (Wiener, 2007). Working out the relational threads of mediation to discover their implications is a complex process, one of the most complex and least examined in the social sciences. It is, nonetheless, at the core of the left-Hegelian tradition in both the lineage of pragmatism and of Marx. Honneth, also standing in the left-Hegelian tradition, offers a more extended account of how critique logically operates as a process of mediation, that is, as critique of a pathological or unjust deviation from the rationality of ideals. However, his work does not extend to the detailed explication of the logical-semiotic dimensions of the process. This should necessarily include the ontological presentation of the theory of society, not on Hegelian lines with the absolutization of a transcendent reason, but on fallibilist semiotic lines guided by cognitive universals and generals, the interpenetrating logic of validity and achievement concepts playing out over time.

In Peirce's account of the role of the normative sciences within the logic of inquiry, they should set ends that guide logical processes. On the contrary, the outcomes of logical processes may lead to changes in the nature of the guiding ends. Peirce understood such normatively set ends as the effects of the will. So, on the one hand, the will directs logical operations and, on the other, is changed by them. From a sociological view, especially in the case of modern society, the retroactive effect of logical processes on normative ends – and the factual relations that inform them – grows ever quicker. This is in part why a fixed account of normative ends in relation to the factually comprehended organization of society seems ever less satisfactory, and indeed why questions of reflexivity have come so much to the fore. The critical sociological default position is to treat reflexivity, understood as positive and structurally anchored agencies of certain kinds, with a negative sign. In this latter sense, such agencies could include manifestations of patriarchal,

124   *The State of Reason in Sociology*

racial, or capitalist domination. Yet, without demonstrating how such agencies are relationally constructed from processes of cognitive mediation, it is not possible to determine sensitively how social change is proceeding and how contradictory manifestations of power, subjectivation, and norm-building play out. It is a mistake to set reflexivity only as positive against such negative structural constellations, for, even supposing they exist in the way ascribed, their carriers will also use reflexive logical operations to further their ends. In a general way, sociology has developed an intimation of how reflexivity and the building of a wide range of relational structures proceed, but it is far from demonstrating the mechanisms. This is perhaps even being too gentle; sociology has a radically incomplete sense of the kind of semiotic account of society that is needed, and, without it, it will fly blind. In some contrast, but only programmatically, certain critical theorists such as Honneth, with his account of pathologies of reason, and Forst, with his account of bad justification, do indicate how reasoning can have negative consequences (Honneth, 2004; Forst, 2007). The task remains to work out how processes producing such outcomes, and the recurrent mechanisms they generate, could be more generally embedded in a semiotic theory of society as a prelude to being employed in social research.

## Subjectivation

In the human and social sciences, the concept of embodiment has become progressively more important over the last century. Its greater salience is in part derived from the widespread idea that the way reason has historically operated has been used to bring about multiple kinds of hegemony. It is assumed that such hegemony utilizes the claim to possession of the universal achieved by means of an impartial claim to have reason on one's side, the voice from nowhere and yet everywhere. Bourdieu's account of the differentiation of the habitus employs this kind of embodied critique against alleged false universalism. His critique of Kant's aesthetic theory, for example, is that taste is irreversibly socially differentiated; there are no universal criteria for deciding between its different expressions (Bourdieu, 1984). Bourdieu's vantage point is that different experiences of life are felt through the body; phenomenological judgements take root there, creating the possibility of distinctions that emphasize either superiority or inferiority. The subjugated body holds itself in a certain way, moves in a certain way, and feels social situations in a certain way, and, accordingly, these feelings of subjugation are not accidental. They are the product of the power of a habitus that has acquired and continuously enacted a social practice of *relational* superiority or subjugation in each field. Such relations of hierarchy are not set in stone, as Bourdieu claims that the subjugated nonetheless possess a type of cognitive freedom, are able to practice their own kind of reflexivity, and thus seek to mitigate the power of others.

Bourdieu's is a compelling account of the interplay of social and symbolic power. Social power can also be sustained by material means, though Bourdieu's phenomenological inheritance is too strong for him to simply assume that the material means are free of human will. However, his position is less well-designed, and

The State of Reason in Sociology   125

Archer has a point here, to show how a new kind of contesting subject begins to emerge, one who could make an assault on the citadel of existing dominant reason. In modern sociology, it is perhaps Touraine who has come closest to developing the contours of this kind of radical subjectivation, the subject who, akin to Adorno, is by some possible means capable of breaking the circuit of rationalization and subjectivation, who does not remain a prisoner of externally imposed technologies of the self (Touraine, 2021). In sociological and social-historical accounts from Marx to E.P. Thompson, the monumental shift in consciousness required by labouring people to contend with combined material and cultural fetters is compellingly documented (Thompson, 1963). The story is told repeatedly across a multitude of anti-discriminatory social movements. The story can also be told in reverse in the form of movements, like the new white nativism, that strive to enact a new (old) hegemonic proto subject and a subjugated other.

The general tendency of those who speak from a radical perspective in terms of embodied freedom is to set that project against reason tout court. It is a mistaken strategy that leads to a cul-de-sac. The immense effort that is often so carefully documented to generate an emancipatory subject should only set itself against a certain kind of unbalanced or unjust use of reason, not the potential of reason. It is in this sense that left Hegelianism speaks of rationality potentials, potentials for a new kind of reason that would incorporate the new subject position in the relational fields of social relations. Such a transformation is brought about by, using Lynch's term, lay reflexivity, but it is, against his account, also a virtue reflexivity in that it is driven by what Honneth calls moral injury arising from the denial of due recognition (Honneth, 1996). The sense of denied recognition is constructed out of relevant feelings. Feelings when they fall on fertile symbolic ground crystallize the desires of the will and animate reasoning, or, in this case, counter-reasoning. Eventually, such counter-reasoning has normative implications, at least potentially, in that the reason/norm complex is disturbed and reconfigured.

In considering the various texts examined in the previous chapter in the above light, Bourdieu is highly relevant, if limited in relation to contestation as described above. McNay develops aspects of the critique of hegemonic reason in its neglect of the subject, drawing from the feminist register of disclosing critique. She extends her critique of reason to incorporate Forst's ideal theoretical transcendentalism and accuses him of being insufficiently sensitive to the voice of the relatively less powerful. Archer has a variation of this in her critique of the dispassionate reason she associates with Kantian proceduralism. Munch emphasizes the pre-rational basis to social order that is not amenable to questioning. Alexander emphasizes the role of emotion and the non-rational. Overall, the sense remains of the deep predilection of sociology and cognate areas of scholarship with the question of the subject and also with the particular variation of it that is the 'other of reason'. This gives a strong, though highly differentiated, sense of what forms of reason might exclude – the non-rational in the sense of the prerogative of negative freedom in private affairs, the voice and criteria of taste of the less powerful or non-recognized, the role of emotions, the power of the unconscious, among others. However, it does not really take the debate on, indicative of sociology generally, to address what is

126   *The State of Reason in Sociology*

essential in reason and its relation to the normative. In this, the status of feelings is immensely significant. In one way, sociology, taking inspiration from phenomenology, is rightly concerned with the neglect of the subject, but, in another, it does not sufficiently contribute, as a discipline with its analytical pedigree, to the codependence of feelings and reasoning, good and bad. For this reason, the danger of what Bourdieu calls 'narcissistic reflexivity' is ever present, a type of reflexivity that runs the risk of dogmatism and that contributes little to the theorization of how a generally reasonable society might be brought about.

## The Relation to Actuality

From a sociological perspective, Hegel plays an ambivalent role in the relationship between reason and the existent world (Strydom, 2011). On the one side, what he called the Idea was postulated as already present in the world, hence opening the vista of rationalization. On the other, the close association of transcendence and immanence, in which rationalization is assumed to happen through the self-movement of the Idea neglected the role of agents and forces in this process. Peirce offers an insight that goes some way to correcting this neglect while maintaining Hegel's Idea in a new form in his own account of thirdness. The objects of cognition have independent existence, but they are cognitively constructed by available or possible human capacity for making sense of them. There are two related dimensions to this construction. The ontological moment arises from their perception, the epistemological moment in reasoning about objects oriented by a judgement arising from perception and opening towards logical abduction. Perception, which potentially adds to our understanding of what exists, remains to be confirmed by reasoning. It is only through reasoning that knowledge is acquired that is anything other than a particular perspective, which is not to say that a given perspective might not in the end prove to be right. The process of building knowledge through reasoning is not only one of confirming what already exists in the world but also a generative one of contributing to the gestation of new knowledge.

The power to intervene in the world also implies the power to construct quasi-external social worlds, that is, to build sociocultural forms such as institutions, networks, associations, movements, orders of knowledge, discursive forums, socialized selves, milieus, and the vast panoply of other social relations. Reasoning processes make these worlds possible, and they necessarily become regularized into forms guided by habits, expectations, and reciprocal role obligations as one set of outcomes, but also into contradictions, contingencies, and unpredictable events and patterns as another set. These worlds acquire a force that operates through factually recognizable constraints. Hence, if firstness is the capacity to feel and see the world in a different way, no matter how minimal the difference, then secondness is the ontological constraint of fact on the imagination of firstness, a constraint that can also be loosened by the impetus to world reconstruction that emanates from firstness and proceeds to the world through reasoning (thirdness). By conceiving of ontology, epistemology (reasoning) relations on these basic Peircean categories, the Hegelian insight can be properly grasped that reason is always already

*The State of Reason in Sociology*    127

operative in the world, though not necessarily the full potential of reason. It replaces the epistemological excess of Hegel's Idea with the sobering insight of a world that resists at many points, including through the plural perspectives arising from agents' ontological constructions.

The reference texts indicate that the concerns of sociology do not adequately extend to the relationship between reasoning and world construction, not even in Habermas, who made extensive use of Weber's rationalization thesis in his account of the lifeworld. What is missing in most cases are the actual reasoning processes and in almost all cases demonstration of mechanisms and outcomes that would be associated with such processes. This is also a methodological challenge. While there has been an explosion in the range and number of text analysis approaches in the discipline that have contributed much, these neglect the study of the cumulative effects of reasoning and its outcomes. The actualization of reason in the world does not here mean any positive normative evaluation of its impact. If Habermas's account of selective rationalization in relation to Weber, the multiple accounts of reification, the account of alienation in Marxism and critical theory, the type of generalized critique of reason as technical rationality, and much more are considered, then evaluation of the historical process as amounting to a gain in reasonableness has to be advanced with proper caution and highly selectively. Beyond any judgement on its 'progressive' quality, to understand rationalization it is necessary to first proceed from patterns of reasoning in the light of orienting general cognitive principles and ideals. The proper understanding of reasoning in turn cannot neglect its dependence on ontological sensibility.

The reference texts in the review chapter – Chapter 3 – say very little about the above question, the *dynamics* of rationalization. Along with a vast range of other sociological texts, they do provide orientations and partial descriptions of relevant concepts, such as systems, habitus, fields, institutions, action, change, and others. As demonstrated, there are also accounts of symbolic power (Bourdieu) and material power – briefly in McNay and generally regaining momentum with the 'new materialism' –, but for a range of reasons, the role of reasoning as constitutive is neglected both in relation to power and to general formation of social structures. Rather instructively, though one of the most resonant concepts in the history of sociology, Weber's rationalization thesis, though brilliant in its pathbreaking implications, suffered from one basic limitation. In operating with a phenomenological but not communicative theory, he remained bound to the horizons of the individual consciousness at the cognitive core of action. In this way, a problem that extended to Parsons after him was that he could show neither the mechanisms of rationalization in given spheres nor the interrelationship between the different kinds of rationalization. Following Munch, Parsons did add to Weber an account of the interpenetration of the different value spheres. Even if productive in its conceptualization, this took the problem even further away from the dialectic of reason and rationalization, in that interpenetration loses the connection to reasoning that the theory of rationalization could still claim. Without the necessary interconnecting communicative theory that would have allowed him to connect the theory of rationalization across societal spheres, Weber, as Habermas shows, ended up with a selective theory of rationalization that also ended up as one-sided, in both the sense

128 *The State of Reason in Sociology*

that it was expressed as a purposive-rational ethic of responsibility and because it left out the explicit general public construction of reason. For reasons already indicated, Parsons did not satisfactorily address the latter issue either, though his action theory was wider in its range than that of Weber. In the end, while both Weber's theory of rationalization and Parsons's theory of interpenetration were breakthroughs in sociological conceptualization, there has been little further development of Habermas's attempt to deepen their foundations by means of a theory of communication.

**Normative Perspectives**

Reasoning is guided by normative ends, and part of the output of reasoning is potential change to such ends. This is particularly important in the sphere of practical reason in which those normative ends most pertinent to sociology are to be found. From an evolutionary perspective, the human capacity to understand the world has been built up from unconscious perceptual operations and conscious cognitive ones. Available graspable or usable, culture emerges from the totality of human unconscious and conscious operations of drawing distinctions and adding further connotations to the understanding of objects, including social objects like relations, memory, sense of the self and others, and so on. The building of connotations in these dimensions is in effect the building of meaning because of progressive elaboration through mediating, general, cognitive principles. Such mediating principles were addressed above as ideas and ideals of reason, in other words, both those grounding quasi-transcendental cognitive orientations and immanent, recursively operating ideals. In the basic idea of Peirce, such mediating transcendentally anchored cognitive principles and immanent ideals permanently interpose between feelings and facts, including factually operating normative prescriptions.

The transcendental cognitive principles are principles of reason. As cognitive principles of this kind, they cannot be automatically equated with normative ends, though normative considerations proved important in their evolutionary selection and refinement. They are inescapable general ideas of human association without which, though they can be actualized in many normative forms, the human form of life would not be possible. A basic distinction is between the core categories, firstness associated with feelings, thirdness with reasons, and secondness with facts, and the limitless number of ways these categories can be used in the kinds of inferential chaining that generate schemata of various kinds, all the way from transcendent principles to actions. The understanding of the external world, including the constructed external social world, on which we can now consciously draw, has been built up over time. By means of inferential chaining, external objects 'out there' have been made objects 'for us', that is, objects subject to semiotic understanding and action. These schemata inform us about the world of objects, including the human 'objects' with which we must deal, one of which is our own historically formed self. While everything is potentially knowable, there are significant practical limits to the knowledge of any one individual or even group. Some of it has been built by others in distant places and times; some of it has been built

The State of Reason in Sociology   129

by specialists; and some of it we have ourselves contributed to building but don't know quite why or how.

A general normative standpoint of the kind that is to be found in social and political theory involves, firstly, a certain degree of closing down of reflexive, inferential processes. The closure could be brief and experimental, such as, for example, adopting a norm to test it, or it could represent a longer run closure in the form of an enduring normative philosophy integrating many related norms and embedded in a practical life context. This more enduring kind of normative constellation will exhibit a persistent way of 'seeing' the world, made possible by instituted habits of action and volition. Such habits are a secondary utilization of the basic cognitive capacity for inferential reasoning, a socially guided selection from it. Such habits might be judged by others at the time or by the proponents at a later stage as right or wrong, good or bad. Either way, in appropriate conditions, they conduce to a consistent social position, which could also be described as building a milieu effect. Further, enduring feature of the sociological normative position-taking is that it frequently tries to deny its status as a social position that must ultimately be justified. When it does, it evinces a significant degree of schematic closure, though it continues to project itself as fallibilistically open to change. These 'hardened' or 'calcified' theoretical-methodological standpoints tend to invariably find normative boundaries beyond which they do not stray. At this point, I am not interested in the relative merits of the different normative perspectives themselves. I am only suggesting that each must understand itself in a fallibilist manner in that it cannot, without reverting to dogmatic metaphysics, refuse to consider its own justification and be willing to learn through this process. At the same time, subject to the willingness to learn, such normative positions may legitimately exhibit some degree of normative closure in the sense that the cognitive implications of reasoning consistently point – for each of them – in the same direction as is the nature of a social theory.

I will defer to later detailed explication of the most interesting implication following from the above, the need to explicate the inferential forms of reasoning that sustain normative standpoints. It is at that point that the idea underlying this whole enterprize will become fully manifest, that of demonstrating the ineluctable dependence of sociological theorizing on reasoning with general implications. I will also seek to show at that point how the discipline's partly self-imposed limitations in this respect prevents it from making the kind of contribution its potentials suggest. There are multiple fault lines in normative theorizing in the discipline; normative theorizing that suffers, on the one hand, due to its fragmentation and lack of true exchange between positions, such as those covered in the last chapter. On the other hand, it is beset by a general lack of attention to the post-metaphysical dependence of normative theory on reason and the implications this has for adopting normative positions of both logical force and subtlety that should characterize consciously pursued, intersubjective argumentation.

Following from the immediate above, the general features that bear on the relation between reason and normative theorizing in the various reference texts are as follows; objectivism without intersubjectivism (Munch, Bourdieu, and Alexander),

130　*The State of Reason in Sociology*

self-conversing without general reasoning (Archer), positional critique without generals and immanence without transcendence (McNay), lay reflexivity without critique (Lynch), symbolicity without cognitive elaboration (Alexander), and mediation without subjectivation and critical learning (Luhmann). These come together with a variety of normatively guided positions on mediation (Bourdieu, Munch, and Luhmann), the hermeneutical everyday grounding and accounting strategies of ethnomethodology (Lynch), the embodied critical sensibility of McNay, the emphasis on general ideals by a variety of thinkers, and suggestions of immanent transcendence in the later Bourdieu that are explicated in the different critical theoretical stances of Forst and Honneth.

Overall, a serious limitation of this work from a normative standpoint is the lack of attention to democratic public communication. The modern focus on communication in various ways does generally permeate the sociological imagination. However, the sociological version of the linguistic turn remains only half carried through at most. Habermas's attempt to systematize it in the 1980s has not found extensive resonance. Luhmann's alternative account has gained a wide audience, but democratic communication is far from its concerns, notwithstanding Teubner's attempt to develop it as the voice of civil society (Teubner, 1996).

Further to this democratic lacuna, it is striking that critical sociology offers no 'positive' normative vision, however counterfactually hedged. Indeed, even for non-critical sociology, the neo-Parsonian model has not enjoyed favour for some time, and the era of texts such as that of Munch is passing, if undeservedly. Yet, nothing offering a critical but affirmative vision has replaced them, at least on the level of macro-social theory. There is accordingly extremely little in these texts, representing the discipline more widely, that amounts to a vision for the future of democracy. As a discipline, sociology is overall remarkably past-oriented where general, and only future-orientated by dint of a nominalist focus on particulars. In the interstices of these temporal boundaries, critical sociology uneasily lives.

More generally still, a shift in emphasis can be discerned from the formerly dominant neo-Durkheimian synergy between the assumption of a rationalized general ethos supported by common affective foundations of familiar modes of life towards, presently, a variously Marxist or Weberian influence – occasionally both – tilting towards contested ethics and counter-reason. On the whole, the emphasis on counter-reason per se is less strong than that on contested ethics. The idea of counter-reason, explicitly or implicitly, belongs to the relative margins of the discipline in the form of social movement theories to some degree and among a sociologically informed political philosopher like Nancy Fraser, from whom, along with Negt and Kluge, I originally took the term (Fraser, 1992; Negt and Kluge, 1993; O'Mahony, 2013). In Fraser's case, counter-reason could be complemented with an equivalent institutional transformation towards another concept of hers, 'participatory parity' (Fraser and Honneth, 2003). Of course, in critical theory and beyond, counter-reason is associated with ideology critique. Again, ideology critique was associated in Marx with a vision of universalist social transformation, a critique of dominant reasoning that would seek to institutionalize a new socialist form of societal organization.

*The State of Reason in Sociology* 131

Hence, in sociology, the partial transition to a more dynamic and conflictual model can be discerned in varied ways. The Weberian way points to a permanent conflict over values that cannot be discursively resolved by any formation of a political will, only by a constant political struggle for Herrschaft or domination and to control the space of decision. It is a liberal vision of the political process and a form of democratic elitist theory. In the Marxist tradition, after Marx, conflict is associated with a kind of negative critique that eschews any kind of productive reconciliation of the contending forces. Many modern thought traditions in sociology emphasize the impossibility of consensus, motifs deriving from post-structuralism, post-colonialism, and philosophical hermeneutic currents, as well as from the reception of Marx and Weber. From this vantage point, it can be seen why, with the assumption that reason is inextricably bound to consensus, either Kantian moral consensus or Hegelian value consensus, there is such a strong inclination towards its near total rejection. Yet, paradoxically, it is seen as a strong adversary in that its selective rationalization in the spheres of bureaucracy, capitalism, and science is assumed to enforce consensus by means of a narrow political hegemony based on mass apathy. In this way, the scene has been set within a great deal of sociology, with a focus on the assumed conflict between subjective creativity and instrumental rationalization. There appears to be no end in sight in this epistemic conflict between ever-new variations on the creative subject, encouraged by the penetration of hermeneutical concepts into the discipline, and ever-more encompassing means of its suppression through direction repression, symbolic hegemony, or incorporation. It contains a kind of partial truth, but it ultimately reflects too neatly the sociological penchant to consider the relation between subject and object and to forget the immense challenge of understanding their relations through forms of mediation, for with mediation comes reason, and that is assumed to have been substantially discredited. Also, with mediation comes the kind of critical cognitive sociology that this book is concerned to elaborate on.

The legacy of functionalism embodies these constraints and opportunities fulsomely, here in the respective forms of Munch and Luhmann. Munch's text reflects the great problems the discipline has encountered with the Parsonian legacy. In terms of depth and range regarding the theory of society, nothing in the sociological repository matches it. However, it is characterized by an objectivist and elitist kind of reflexivity that fails to satisfy the admittedly not very coherent requirements of linguistic and phenomenological turns in sociology. After the 1960s and the pointed critiques it then received, it was also perceived as normatively problematic in being too institutionally affirming of liberal democracy. Yet, while the limitations of the Parsonian tradition make it quite insufficient for grounding a theory of communicative reason, it still more than any other sociological tradition draws attention to basic concepts – emphasizing important relationships between them – developed in the sociological traditions of Durkheim and Weber and, later, system theoretical developments in the mid-20th century. This is what made it, in some respects, attractive to the Habermas of *Communicative Action*. One challenge it poses is how can a communicative theory of society avail itself of the remarkable range of concepts and forces mustered in that sociological tradition? A further

## 132   *The State of Reason in Sociology*

challenge is how the balance between descriptive and normative dimensions of theories can be met, given that the post-empiricist climate has long ago demonstrated that claims to be only descriptive manifest hidden normative commitments? Sociology has spent a great deal of time since the description of how justification operates, mostly called something else, for example, 'discourse', that can obscure the task, and, for this, reflexivity in some forms serves as a primary concept. The challenge remains as to whether sociology will ever commit itself to an explicit normative justification of its arguments or whether it will continue to generate an ever more detailed description of normativity in operation, with implied normative standpoints lying behind them.

These remarks lead into a final brief reference to Luhmann, whose position on the futility of advancing a general normative position in the 'old European' way, one associated with reason, has already been addressed. Such a position involves a sustained attack on the role of the state, envisaged as the discredited and disappearing moral-legal centre of society, a centredness that assumes relentless social change towards a society organized by pluralistic systems. Luhmann's stance does capture one of the primary tendencies of modern societies, ever-growing pluralism and an increasingly polycentric architecture. Further, his transformation of Parsons's steering media – applying in Parsons to 'merely' the AGIL range of subsystems –, into a wider range of binary-coded symbolically generalized media for a potentially unlimited range of social systems offers rich theoretical insight. This theoretical architecture can be productive for understanding the communicative construction of mechanisms of social coordination. Yet, the problem remains that it evacuates any kind of conscious normative societal ordering, at least anything of a 'positive' kind. While much of sociology rages at forces dominating everyday life, Luhmann simply recommends resignation before them. Not fighting back will somehow produce better outcomes than attempting to do so and becoming disappointed. Nothing in sociology today could sum up the Weberian thesis of disenchantment leading to the iron cage better, and nothing can illustrate better the sense of helplessness induced by a world prognosis that excludes agents availing themselves of will and consciousness in any way.

In one way, this last formulation of Luhmann's 'refusal' illustrates well the dilemma of a discipline like sociology living in a world that denies reason, castigating it as irrelevant and overbearing, but also implicitly using it in the many oblique ways it advocates responsible social cooperation. The dilemma goes to the very heart of much of its epistemic practices, which tend to take some facets of reason as comprising the whole in combining the world mastering dimension of instrumental reason inspired by Weber's theory of rationality and ethic of responsibility with the post-Marxist critique of subjective reason. The central idea of Habermas has been to correct this unnecessary and unproductive self-limitation. Nonetheless, it is rooted deep in the heart of a discipline whose goal has always been to derive its normative lessons from the most complete description of relevant worlds. When this goal of complete description of the world is mostly pessimistically construed as the triumph of instrumentalism, requiring either resignation or rage as a response, then the abdication of the normative implications of practical reason in favour of the employment or critique of functional reason is more understandable but normatively disabling in its consequences.

## References

Adorno T (2003) *Negative Dialectics*. London: Routledge.
Adorno TW (2019 (1964)) *Philosophical Elements of a Theory of Society*. Cambridge: Polity.
Alexander JC and Smith P (1993) The Discourse of American Civil Society: A New Proposal for Cultural Studies. *Theory and Society* 22(2): 151–207.
Archer MS, Collier A and Porpora DV (2013) *Transcendence: Critical Realism and God*. London: Routledge.
Bertilsson TM (2009) *Peirce's Theory of Inquiry and Beyond*. Frankfurt: Peter Lang.
Boltanski L and Thévenot L (2006) *On Justification: Economies of Worth*. Princeton, NJ: Princeton University Press.
Bourdieu P (1984) *Distinction: A Social Critique of the Judgement of Taste*. Cambridge, MA: Harvard University Press.
Castoriadis C (1998) *The Imaginary Institution of Society*. Cambridge, MA: MIT Press.
Cicourel AV (1974) *Cognitive Sociology. Language and Meaning in Social Interaction*. New York, NY: Free Press.
Forst R (2007) First Things First: Redistribution, Recognition, and Justification. *European Journal of Political Theory* 6(3): 291–304.
Forst R (2013) *Toleration in Conflict: Past and Present*. Cambridge: Cambridge University Press.
Fraser N (1992) Rethinking the Public Sphere: A Contribution to the Critique of Actually Existing Democracy. In: Calhoun C (ed) *Habermas and the Public Sphere*. Cambridge, MA: MIT Press.
Fraser N and Honneth A (2003) *Redistribution or Recognition?: A Political-philosophical Exchange*. London: Verso.
Habermas J (1992) *Postmetaphysical Thinking: Philosophical Essays*. Cambridge, MA: MIT Press.
Habermas J (2019) *Auch eine Geschichte der Philosophie*. Frankfurt: Suhrkamp.
Honneth A (1996) *The Struggle for Recognition: The Moral Grammar of Social Conflicts*. Cambridge, MA: MIT Press.
Honneth A (2004) A Social Pathology of Reason: On the Intellectual Legacy of Critical Theory. In: Rush FL (ed) *The Cambridge Companion to Critical Theory*. Cambridge: Cambridge University Press.
Honneth A (2007) *Disrespect: The Normative Foundations of Critical Theory*. Cambridge: Polity.
Honneth A (2014) *Freedom's Right: The Social Foundations of Democratic Life*. New York, NY: Columbia University Press.
Horkheimer M (1974 (1947)) *Eclipse of Reason*. London: Bloomsbury.
Kant, I (1972) *Critique of Judgement*. New York, NY: Hafner
Luhmann N (1990) *Essays on Self-reference*. New York, NY: Columbia University Press.
Negt O and Kluge A (1993) *Public Sphere and Experience*. Minneapolis, MN: University of Minnesota Press.
O'Mahony P (2013) *The Contemporary Theory of the Public Sphere*. Oxford: Peter Lang.
Parsons T (1977) *Social Systems and the Evolution of Action Theory*. New York, NY: Free Press.
Parsons T (1990) Prolegomena to a Theory of Social Institutions. *American Sociological Review* 55(3): 319–333.

134 *The State of Reason in Sociology*

Peirce CS (1998) The Fixation of Belief (1877). In: Hauser N and Kloesel C (eds) *The Essential Peirce: Selected Philosophical Writings (1867–1893)*. Bloomington: Indiana University Press.

Rose G (1981) *Hegel contra Sociology*. London: Verso.

Strydom P (2011) *Contemporary Critical Theory and Methodology*. London: Routledge.

Strydom, P (2017) Infinity, infinite processes and limit concepts: Recovering a neglected background of social and critical theory. *Philosophy and Social Criticism*. 43(8): 793–811.

Teubner G (1996) Globale Bukowina. Zur Emergenz eines transnationalen Rechtspluralismus. *Rechtshistorisches Journal* (15): 255–290.

Thompson EP (1963) *The Making of the Working Class*. New York, NY: Vintage.

Touraine A (2021) *La société de Communication et ses Acteurs*. Paris: Seuil.

Turner SP (2010) *Explaining the Normative*. Cambridge: Polity Press.

Weber, M (1949) *The Methodology of the Social Sciences*. Glencoe, Ill: The Free Press.

Wiener A (2007) Contested Meanings of Norms: A Research Framework. *Comparative European Politics* 5(1): 1–17.

# 5 Peirce, Reason, and Signification

Habermas and Peirce together stand in marked contrast to the present development of sociology and the broader social sciences. This is so, even allowing that in certain respects, over the course of the 20th century, at least some of the philosophical orientation of the social sciences came more into line with Peirce's basic framework. The latter development is captured in certain now-established presuppositions of the social sciences, such as a general concern with the phenomenological and the relational. While Peirce was by no means a critical scholar in the way of Marx, he did broadly stand in the left-Hegelian tradition –at least in terms of his logic of inquiry – with his logical socialism (Wartenberg, 1971). Hence, his theoretical-methodological 'politics' so to speak in some ways chimed with the renewal of critical sociology in the last third of the 20th century, whose critical-normative emphasis extended well beyond the established neo-Marxist formulation. There has been, in part related to the latter, a new emphasis on the power of agency. A concern with nature, both outer and inner, is also on the rise for many reasons. So, terms that permeated Peirce's texts, such as habit, discourse, feeling, reflexivity, signification, discourse, cognition, relationality (relatives), nature, and others, are in general use. Peirce may thus be seen as in line with these new emphases, though potentially still adding from behind as it were unthought-of variations and greater systematic intent. By contrast, some elements fundamental to Peirce, such as the immanent-transcendent form of reason itself, mediating thirdness beyond dyadic subject-object relations, evolution, learning, and general purposiveness, are not much evident in sociology and the social sciences and, beyond them, even in more normatively oriented disciplines. While Peirce offers many additional insights, even some that are in a general sense profoundly reorienting in relation to the above concepts in contemporary use, it is noticeable that what is most absent is the consideration of those cognitive activities he captured through thirdness in relation to the other categories. Some of these activities have already been addressed in earlier chapters, reason, evolution, mediation, learning, generality, limit, infinity, continuity, and some others may be added, intellectual discourse, growth, concrete reasonableness, and vagueness. The fate of these ideas is similar in important respects to the fate of related concepts of Habermas, but perhaps the differences that Peirce manifests, properly understood, might address at least some of the more obvious reception

DOI: 10.4324/9780429060571-6

136 *Peirce, Reason, and Signification*

problems of the social sciences regarding Habermas and form something of a bridge between the ideas of communicative reason and them.

The above remarks bear on considerations to do with reason and the social sciences that have been taken up in earlier chapters. At this point, I will not offer anything further of a programmatic nature to them, though I will return to them at the conclusion of this chapter. To do so now would create the difficulty of placing Peirce systematically in that context, rather than following those considerations that arise directly from his work on its own terms. Perhaps needless to add, the considerations already outlined about reason do still bear heavily on my account of Peirce, because in substantial part they already derive from him and his broader temporal positioning in intellectual life, including both those preceding and succeeding. Neither is the following a systematic and chronological account of Peirce's work. Others have done remarkable work in this regard, especially in recent decades where there has been a tremendous expansion in scholarship. If anything, it is based more on Peirce's later writings, for example, taking profit from the logic of relatives that became ever stronger in his writing from the 1870s onwards and the revised sign system after 1900. However, there is no claim to original exegesis of his thinking here; it is simply an attempt to put this thinking in the service of theory-building in critical theory, especially with a view to establishing semiotic foundations for a renewed critical theory of society (O'Mahony, 2023a; 2023b). I should point out that the following only tries to supply as much of Peirce's basic architecture as is pertinent to the task at hand: that reason is an indispensable basic category for modern social science and that the reception of Peirce should be indispensable to critical theory's account of it.

## Signs and Categories

At the core of Peirce's theory is his account of signs, which are developed by means of three foundational categories of firstness, secondness, and thirdness. The theory of signs evolved from this first attempt in the 1860s that made use of three basic sign types – symbol, index, and icon – to his later, more elaborated account, especially after 1900. The latter took mature form in 1903 where, instead of three single signs that corresponded to the thirdness of the symbol, secondness of the index, and firstness of the icon, he elaborated three sets of triads (Peirce, 1998; Short, 2007). These were composed of three sub-categories of thirdness, three of secondness, and three of firstness, where thirdness, secondness, and firstness are the essential categories of knowing, classifying, and sensing, respectively, reasons, facts, and feelings. Meaning is made possible using these categories, including the process of ascribing validity to meaning. In various ways, the categories process signs, where signs are taken as indispensable for mediating mind and world.

The interpretation of Peirce will accordingly be based on the 1903 account, rather than from the earlier account that Habermas still mainly uses (Atkin, 2010; Habermas, 2019) or from later accounts where, towards the very end of his career, Peirce developed a 28 and 66 sign system as opposed to the more restricted sign system of the 1903 account.[1] A basic description of the content of the signs is offered below, a description that will be amplified in the remainder of the book, where, building on Peirce's commitment to the scientific logic of inquiry, the sign-system will be elaborated for societal analysis. Utilization of the sign types for such analysis is the main purpose lying behind this account of Peirce, where societal analysis both means the development of a communicative societal ontology and the application of that ontology in a theoretical-methodological fashion.

In the 1903 account, each of the three categories, that is, firstness, secondness, and thirdness, is comprised of three sub-categories. For signs of firstness, the intrinsic sign of firstness, the firstness of firstness, is a sign of a specific *quality* occasioned by an object in the environment, without actual explicit awareness of that object and without clarity at this point, the very advent of signification, on any rationally intended assertion that could be made about it. It is simply and only the unexpressed possibility of one or more of the innumerable qualities that could pertain to the object, or objects present in the situation. This is termed the quali-sign. Still within firstness, this is followed by the secondness of firstness, an experience of action and reaction expressed in an emerging sign as the qualities present in the immediacy and limitlessness of the quali-sign encounter the resistance of the world. This action and reaction process leads to the formation of a percept, a possible something in the world that could have a quality or qualities attached to it. In his writings, Peirce provided multiple examples, for example, the resistance of a door to the attempt to open it, an unexpected blow from a passing ladder, which shows we cannot make of the world what we will, but neither is the world as it is fully resistant in all respects to what we think of it. The reflexive capacity becomes more insistent when the objects are those that humans themselves make. Percepts emerge within the space between the qualities that could become attached to objects and the resistance of the objects to these qualities. They thus combine subjective qualities with the objective environment with which the communicative intervention must reckon. In the final general element of firstness, the thirdness of firstness, are to be found the signs of 'law' in which the emerging percepts acquire general elements. For Peirce, signs could not signify recognizable objects were it not for general relevance they could command. The singular reference of the percept only becomes 'usable' by a community by the incorporation of that which has general relevance. This also indicates his decisive break with nominalism; generals are not aggregations of singulars to which a name is attached but are themselves real. Overall, the signs of firstness can be understood as the firstness of firstness, the quali-sign, the secondness of firstness, the sinsign, and the thirdness of firstness, the legisign. For each of the other categories, secondness and thirdness, it is also the case that they will have sub-categories of a similar kind deriving from the other categories.

In the 1903 account, signs of secondness take on the terminology previously encompassing the entire range of Peirce's account of signs, respectively symbol, index, and icon. In the previous account, dating from his early work in the 1860s, a symbol represented all that belonged to thirdness, an index similarly represented all that belonged to secondness, and similarly, an icon represented all that belonged to firstness. Now these sign types have become distinctive stages of secondness,

138    *Peirce, Reason, and Signification*

though they retain a relationship to their original categories, thirdness and firstness, respectively. Secondness pertains to our beliefs about objective entities arising from what we believe is or will be the case. To have such a belief, we must also be committed to its standing as a valid conception before being applied to particular things. The symbolic sign, the thirdness of secondness, contains general conceptions of valid ways of indicating objects. Their validity is determined by the outcomes of thirdness, the communicative process of deciding such validity, based on which they represent definite, widely shared conceptions that have institutional significance, descriptively, prescriptively, and evaluatively, even though such claims to validity are often far from universally accepted. For now, it is easier to go no further than to say that they are institutionally filtered, commonly held conceptions of objects of experience.

The index, the secondness of secondness, is the intrinsic sign of secondness. It refers to what is taken to exist, whether simply that it exists or whether it is regarded as good or right. To refer to 'that dog', for example, is an indexical expression. Such an indexical expression rests on the meaning provided by a symbol, a commonly held conception, for example, basic features of what is generally taken to be a dog as distinct from a kangaroo or any other non-canine animal. In Peirce's relational conception, such sign usage must be distinguished from characterizations of dogs that start with any idea of the fixed substance of the dog. Observation and reasoning about dogs enable new relational forms of being a dog, symbols, to emerge, and, on top of any behaviour of actual dogs, there are the multiple meanings that can be ascribed to dogs, such as common assumptions of the emotions of dogs that come to be believed whether dogs actually have the assumed emotional properties. The index is thus the sign that enables reference to specific objects based on relational conceptions of these objects.[2] Thought about in this way, dogs are complex symbolic forms that ordinarily admit of a wide variety of characterizations, and these characterizations are ultimately infinite in possibility. As commonly held conceptions, recognized properties of dogs can be identified, assumed to be regular, and accordingly indicated as actual objects. Such objects in general are thus accorded here and now actuality, as existing. Nonetheless, they are also to be regarded as permanently subject to change through a range of forces operating with different and often opposing temporalities.

Beyond the symbol, the thirdness of secondness, to which can be ascribed a manifest rationality of some kind, and the index of what is or foreseeably will be the case, secondness also comprises a particular kind of firstness, the firstness of secondness, represented in the icon. Firstness is a matter of feeling, of what appears in the mind in response to a stimulus of some kind or those latent possibilities that could be applied. Icons are the carriers of the distinctive kind of feelings that belong to secondness, feelings attaching to indexes of objects. Such indexes, as explored, refer to objects identifiable by a 'validated' or 'regularized' symbol. Icons, then, the firstness of secondness, provide the ground for grasping indexes. A particular dog could have no status for us if we cannot produce a mental image of what a dog is and does. Before a symbol can emerge, there must be not just a stabilization of a set of mental relations, nor only the stabilization of propositional forms deemed to be true, right, or good, but also the stabilization of mental imagery. To speak of a dog as playful requires collateral information on what a playful dog could possibly be, derived from experiences of actual dogs being playful. To speak of any kind of regularity of such images, it must be supposed that they are widespread in possibility if singular in use. The dog some person deems to be playful must also elicit similar imagery from another, though the other, confronted with the dog, may in fact believe that particular dog does not conform to the image of 'playfulness' of dogs in general that she has in her mind. Nonetheless, to grasp secondness, it must be assumed that there is compatibility between symbols, indexes, and images *in principle* so that some kind of stabilization of worlds of reference is made possible.

Thirdness is the sphere of thought mediating between signs and the objects they signify. It contains the general resources required for different kinds of signifying activity. The signs of thirdness are therefore signs that enable other kinds of signs, those of firstness and secondness, to forge meaningful relations. Firstness generates variation; thirdness explicates the possibilities wrought by this variation; and secondness applies outcomes of the combined operations of firstness and thirdness. Thirdness is the sphere of conscious activity that operates by means of generals. Generals are categorial forms in which the various kinds of particulars of firstness and secondness are oriented. Thirdness is therefore order-bestowing in the sense of imposing cognitive forms on the contingencies of worlds, an ordering that potentially allows the formation of rational relations in these worlds. Thirdness can thus be understood as learning, as reasoning, as growth, as intelligence, and as evolution. This does not decide the question of what better kinds of rationality are to respond to normative ends but shows how operations of rationality can be brought to bear in the first place. Thirdness differs from what was earlier described as the thirdness of secondness, the symbol, in that thirdness in itself does not operate with settled meaning but examines the potential validity of meanings as a stream of 'validity candidates' emerging from firstness. These validity candidates are possibilities that, even before they have a rational conjectural form, exist as feelings striving for expression. When they enter logical thirdness through abduction, they serve as what Habermas calls validity claims, though that is only the beginning of the journey that may end in a form of accepted validity. As with Habermas, validity claims can exist in any of the three domains of truth, rightness, or goodness. Thirdness is the journey of generals to various kinds of validity destinations, evolutionary transcendentally anchored concepts, immanent goals, universal symbolic conventions, normative standards, and claims to goodness. All but the first of these destinations are forms of the thirdness of secondness, symbols, and this makes the first, the operation of transcendentally anchored concepts, intrinsic to thirdness as thirdness, as the modality of change and development in all its possible facets. This is also what gives the signs of thirdness the property of esse in futuro, potentialities that must continue to be, may be, or should be.

The three signs of thirdness are like the signs of firstness and secondness, composed of one intrinsic sign and two other kinds of signs, the thirdness of secondness and thirdness of firstness. As in the account of secondness, I will begin with the intrinsic sign of thirdness that Peirce understood as 'mind strictly' or 'argument'.

140    *Peirce, Reason, and Signification*

I will stick with the latter term, though the former contains the important truth that the signs of thirdness are ultimately signs of mind and hence contain a theory of mind. It is ultimately a theory of collective mind in line with the significance accorded to generals. The significance of generals means that the traditional order of logic from terms to propositions to arguments is instead turned the other way round. Arguments come first, and propositions and terms are located within this frame. This does not mean that the other categorical orders do not have their own powers that come to influence logical argument or reasoning, the firstness of unconscious creativity, and the secondness of the sobering influence of existing forces. However, it is the mental infrastructure of thinking, thinking with generals, that defines – especially but not only – the human form of life. Reasoning, or the sign of argument, is the sign that carries general thinking of this kind. This is where Peirce's logical theory is located, with the initiating and creative logical form of abduction at the genesis of sense-making processes.

With the reversal of logical priorities putting argument at the head, the other signs of thirdness are ultimately meaningful because of the general form of the sign of argument. These other signs, the dicent, or the form of propositions, and the rhema, the form of feelings, do not intrinsically reckon directly with mental evaluations, but only do so in conjunction with argument. Propositions, as dicents, have a standard subject-object form, 'that is a dog', but the predicate 'dog' depends on the outcomes of its extended logical construction in argument. Argument is, on the one hand, contextual, in acting as a repository of the continuous growth of meaning that can be expressed through propositions, and, on the other hand, supra-contextual, in its dependence on the natural, social, and cultural evolutionary growth of the capacities of extended mind. Ultimately, this means that the validity of propositions depends on their wider inferential relations. Only in this way, can complex arguments be grasped; the significance of their individual elements must be understood through what grants cohesion and coherence to the whole.

Regarding the signs of thirdness beyond the sign of argument, the rhematic sign, the sign of feeling is, following Atkin, an unsaturated predicate, for example, – loves –, or – gives – to –, whereas the dicent is a saturated predicate as in 'the dog loves the cat' (Atkin, 2010). What is at issue in these examples is the form of the verb, which, in the rhematic sign or rhema, conveys a diffuse kind of meaning not accompanied by actual predicates. These signs of feeling are elementary terms, or qualities, for example, loving or giving, that could be associated with a possible object. As signs of feeling, rhemas show qualities that can be potentially attached to propositions and arguments. The dimension of thirdness arises in that, though a given quality stands by itself without relation to anything else, it has, in its form as thirdness, the inherent possibility of being communicated in certain ways in certain situations. The validity of such signs is simply in the claim that they represent appropriate responses to situations in the form of feelings.

The sign of argument is the most fundamental for understanding human communication. This is where the multiple processes of critical interpretation and justification are located. As alluded, sociology and the social sciences nonetheless make very scarce use of it as an explicit construct, though implicitly they inevitably make use of it in their various operations. The sense of its scholarly – as well as general – importance may be growing from a low base, but perception of its societal significance remains largely descriptive rather than normative. It is not possible to understand the nature of argumentation – or reasoning, as more generally used in this book – without understanding its interdependency with other sign types. This is manifest in that the sign in question is constituted by three kinds of reasoning: abduction, which builds from firstness; deduction, with its affinity with thirdness; and induction, with its relation to secondness. It is also manifest in that this sign is the culmination of a process of signification that begins with signs of firstness, continues with signs of secondness, before leading into signs of thirdness. Signs thus must be grasped as interconnected across the three categories.

Signs of firstness take their possible form from the firstness of thirdness, the rhema and their content from secondness, and their creative distinctiveness from firstness. The same applies to signs of firstness, form from thirdness, content from secondness, and expression from firstness. Signs of firstness, in this expanded sense, are signs of possibility, signs of secondness are signs of facts, and, finally, the sign of argument, the thirdness of thirdness, are signs of reason. This latter sign is the logical space of reasoning. It can interrogate and change outputs of the other sign types and find a set of qualities uninspiring and a set of apparent facts misleading. However, it cannot stand beyond these other signs, on which it fundamentally depends for orientation and content. Yet, it is through reasoning within the sign of reason that the validity of meaning possibilities becomes settled. These meaning possibilities emerge from firstness, are subjected to validation in the sign of reason in a process of inextricability concerned with implications for states of the world, and become applied as validated factual orders through instituted signs of secondness.

## Signification and Potentiality

Peirce's architectonic, where feeling, freedom, and spontaneity balance the rationalizing effects of reason, bears on an acute contemporary issue in the social sciences. The now widespread rejection of reason arises from the view that reason is a type of epistemological imperialism that discounts real differences in social relations, where such differences are assumed to be ontologically recognizable in domination-serving and phenomenally experienced social structures. The imperialism of reason is also assumed to discount the status of the subject, whether embedded unknowingly in such structures or relatively independent of them in 'counter-structural' performative practices. Those social and cultural sciences concerned with the hegemony of reason have the strong point that certain concepts of reason tend to exclude 'the empirical', understood both as the grounds of domination and the expression of new forms of consciousness of all possible kinds. Such is Bourdieu's critique of Kant, where in *Distinction* he opposes Kant's 'universalism' for erecting an elite canon of 'pure taste' that ignores the multiple kinds of socially differentiated taste that contradict the canon. Peirce's approach overcomes the problem of the assumption of 'transcending purity'. By attaching reasoning to

## 142  *Peirce, Reason, and Signification*

phenomenal consciousness of the external world – including the objectified self – Peirce granted a distinct ontological ground to reasoning. Moreover, through the interaction of the categories, feeling and reasoning were understood by him to be permanently present in one another's operations.

But Peirce also explicitly built from idealism, while reconstructing it, and did not reject it as with many contemporary critiques of reason. Analogous to Hegel, who was a vital influence, he developed a tripartite phenomenology that has already been encountered above in the categories of firstness, secondness, and thirdness. The phenomenological status of firstness accounts for the perception of an object, a perception that might, through the development of the resulting sign, contribute something new or different to the general understanding of the object. In Peirce, therefore, the object has an independent existence but is nonetheless subject to construction. This construction takes the form of the immediate object captured through the sign, or, alternatively put, the manner in which this object influences the sign of feeling within firstness. Phenomenological firstness is therefore the way objects are first of all associated with certain qualities, and, as the process of perception evolves, they are further shaped by the indexical and volitive signs of secondness and the signs of interpretation (interpretants) of thirdness. Firstness is the starting point of ontological construction. Interpretant signs, as signs of thirdness, are the carriers of epistemic processes, the imposition of interpretive form through signs of reason that determine the implication of the sign. Secondness, as signs of fact related to the actual world, is of primary methodological significance, serving both as the ground of ontological construction and the outcome of reasoning and other cognitive processes. In its ontological-phenomenological role, firstness therefore anticipates the constructivist impulse of the 20th century and beyond, within the overall complexity and, in the broadest sense of the term, the ontological structure of Peirce's overall sign theory.

Firstness, in its role of sensing, experiencing, and feeling the world, is at the origin of ideas of any kind. It contains what Peirce called idea-potentiality, a potentiality that might become anchored in the world if the potential of the sign is ultimately realized (Peirce, 1992, 387). The three dimensions of firstness entail the sensing of a quality of the object (quali-sign), forming a first relation to it by making sense of the experience that animates the process of developing the idea (sinsign), and establishing it as a sign of feeling pertinent to a particular medium of communication (legisign). However, as subjects move along these dimensions with the astonishing speed of fast processing (Kahneman, 2011), they activate the various kinds of interpretants in the sequence described above. As they activate these interpretants, the signs that emerge also incorporate the signs of secondness. The initial quali-sign, a simple sense of something pertinent, for example, a colour or a sense of emotion, becomes 'entangled' with the range of interpretant concepts held in the quasi-mind of the rhematic interpretant, the one not saturated with predicates. However, in the sign of experience, the sinsign becomes developed, not monadically as with the quali-sign but dyadically in relation to the preliminary conception of the object achieved through secondness. In this process arises the first stirring of volition, guiding the direction of development of the sign. This movement in turn activates the propositional predicate-attaching form of the second interpretant, which activates further possible forms of predication of relevant predicate forms. Volition is present at this second stage. If someone wishes to say, 'Did you see this?', they are utilizing the iconic, indexical, and symbolic resources of secondness. They are engaged in a willed selection of what is relevant, indicating what is the particular object, or even range of objects, about which they are asking the question. Incorporated in this is already the basic concept that is entailed in the use of the verb 'to see'. The verb has a form that serves the index, meaning to see this particular, physical thing, but also, metaphorically, it can connote much more, as in the wide implications of 'social' perception on the iconic plane of secondness.

Finally, in the case of the logical interpretant, a vast range of possibilities opens up. Bear in mind that the apparently simple interrogative sign, 'Did you see this?', is an amalgam of signs. By the time the sign's construction reaches the legisign a vast range of possible connotations have emerged. The logical interpretant, or the sign of argument, will incorporate all the connotative possibilities that have already been historically constructed, providing a menu of options for completing the sign. At this moment, movement along firstness has progressed from the diffuse feeling of a quality of something in the world, the quali-sign, to the volitional and reference-selecting sinsign, to now reach the legisign, which the later Peirce would describe as a sign of the generality of feeling, habits of feeling. Since the legisign is the concluding sign dimension of firstness, as a sign of feeling, it summates what the process has been about, constructing a relevant habit of feeling that serves as an impulse for explicit reasoning in the logical process of thirdness. The relations between the sign types of firstness are much more complex in Peirce's account – and that of his interpreters – than I have been able to describe here. The upshot is that in the legisign elements of generality enter in and the feeling matures as its orientation becomes clearer. It has now acquired a quality arising from pure phenomenal firstness, a volitional dimension associated with the experience of the object and is on its way to becoming a feeling that influences the process of thinking. It is important to remember that with the legisign and the clarification of the feeling involved, unconscious inferences are beginning to give way to the conscious inferences that first emerge in perceptual judgement. At this stage, the move has commenced from the unconscious generation of a feeling towards the expression of that feeling in a proposition that will undergo further elaboration and justification before allowing the sentence 'Did you see this?' to be articulated. I will not follow the story of how the logical interpretant, the locus of reasoning, operates at this point, but I will take it up again in later chapters, beginning in the next chapter, where it will emerge as an indispensable social theoretical concept.

There is one last point to be brought out. With the arrival of the sign process animated by the legisign, there is, as immediately above, also the emergence of habits. There is more than one kind of habit emphasized by Peirce – in fact, there is one for each of the phenomenological categories, firstness, secondness, and thirdness. The habit that Peirce associated with the legisign is set within present consciousness, which is of remarkably short duration – perhaps a fraction of a

## 144  *Peirce, Reason, and Signification*

second –, and it involves the 'imposition' of the inner world on the outer world of which it is trying to make sense and with which it is dialectically engaged (Peirce, 1931–1958, 5.493). The outer world consists of everything that bears upon the immediate consciousness of firstness, and yet through this ephemeral consciousness, Peirce claims that individuals come to gain ontological orientation in the world and to sense what is surprising or new for them in it. Peirce emphasized objects of nature in most of his examples, but such examples can be expanded to include what he also included: the historical self, the 'me' that precedes the provisional phenomenological creativity of the emerging 'I' in firstness, and other similar stabilized symbolic orders such as institutions. These human-created orders are externalized signs, signs embedded in 'objects', much like the concept of capital as dead labour in Marx, but also analogous to Weber's account of rationalization. These references evoke a range of long-run themes of critical sociology, such as reification, alienation, colonization, and commodification, which were present in Weber too in another form. Latterly, Touraine has expressed this motif, one could say in summary form, in both pragmatist terms, the domination of the 'me' by social forces, and also in Freudian terms, domination of the ego by the super-ego, both resulting in a corresponding loss of individual freedom (Touraine, 2000). Touraine's concept of the subject eventually adopts a radicalized Sartrean idea of individual freedom as freedom from the social, whereas Honneth's Hegel-inspired account of social freedom balances such a conception of reflexive freedom with the social conditions in which meaningful social freedom could be actually realized (Touraine, 2005; Honneth, 2014). The externalization of signs into such quasi-objects as selves and institutions is not just problematic from a critical standpoint but intrinsic to human forms of life. They serve as a kind of actuality principle that conditions but do not fully determine ontological construction beginning in firstness.

Peirce's account of consciousness in firstness, which was in various consistent and inconsistent ways taken up by other pragmatists, sought both to assert the radical freedom of the subject. Yet, the spontaneity of these first moments of affective freedom was connected to generals in the legisign. As Dewey recognized, the consciousness of firstness is not to be understood as something consistent with stable states of consciousness, as identity is often understood to connote, but as a responsive and creative process of the organism in its environment, an environment that is itself constantly changing through independent 'transactional' processes. Dewey also distinguished between experience as undergoing and experience as doing (Leddy and Puolakka, 2006). It is the latter kind of experience that Peirce identified as the secondness of firstness, where he identifies a characteristic experience of firstness as surprise at something unexpected (Peirce, 1931–1958, 8.266). In the thirdness of firstness of the legisign, the development of the close interaction between individual perception and the social context of the community can be deciphered. In this way, Peirce shows the ineluctable relation between first consciousness and its later development in the expanded, explicit potential consciousness that would characterize reasoning with the logical interpretant in those cases where such reasoning was actually reached.

From Peirce onwards in pragmatism, there was recurrent, if not entirely consistent, critique of the Cartesian dualism of mind and nature and, in an associated manner, that of mind and feeling. Just as events in the objective world relentlessly 'happened', ceaselessly changing the dyadic relations between objects, firstness manifested unlimited possibility for distinctively perceiving these events in phenomenal consciousness. This unconscious consciousness underpinned the novelty of the knowledge claims that would be further worked out in the process of reasoning. Knowledge as the outcome of reasoning already incorporated feelings and the process of fixing knowledge through reason constantly must adjust to changes in perception. Idea potentiality first becomes apparent in firstness, where, in the legisign, a quality of perception tied to an experience becomes joined with general elements (Peirce, 1992, 387). In this way, the general and the particular co-evolve, what is known and what could be known become cross-articulated. The critique of the separation of affect and reason, which has taken many forms and has become highly insistent in modern social thought, therefore has it right where it appropriately criticizes a reason that claims autonomy from feelings, where duty is taken to suppress inclination without trace. Yet, this critique goes too far in the supposition that affect can replace reason or is entirely autonomous from reason, for inferential operations are present in all human thought and action. In the end, a mature understanding of the necessary interconnection, the dialectical codependence of feeling and reason, must be set within the framework of an adequate societal ontology that obviates one-sided emphases either of empiricism or of methodological holism.

**Extended Mind and Generals**

Peirce's theory of signs was far-reaching. It involves the interconnected development of a theory of social mind, mediation, subjective innovation, and effects of sign-based cognition on actual practice. As such, it amounts, in tendency, to a comprehensive account of cognition within a coherent, modern framework. It has the potential to be extended to underpin a communicative theory of society, including society-nature interaction. At its core lies the idea of logic as a social activity. Logic is understood as the capacity to engage in reasoning through the inferential use of signs. The distinctiveness of Peirce's approach – it reaches far beyond contemporary philosophical theories of joint intentionality – is that reasoning depends on collective cognitive capacities to learn through the use of signs, embodied in the idea of a communication community (Apel, 1995). At its centre lie signs of argument, but these could not function, indeed would have no sense, without embodied signs of feeling (firstness) or world-referencing signs of fact (secondness). The extended mind built from such collective capacities is the preserve not of individuals but of collectivities, with the collectivity par excellence being that of society, anticipating Dewey's account of publics (Dewey, 1927) and also Durkheim's conception of society as a secularization of Kant. Extended mind, in Peirce's sense, consists of those logically coordinated semiotic 'moves' that depart from and adapt inferential patterns of understanding.

146 *Peirce, Reason, and Signification*

The theory of extended or social mind, thirdness in Peirce, is a significant philosophical 'innovation'. In Peirce's case, such extended mind incorporated a dynamic account of reasoning. Reasoning occurs within innumerable process forms – discourses – that build extended relational patterns from inferences. These interlinked patterns of inference provide cultural templates in situations of all kinds, small and large-scale. The use of inference in Peirce is thus different from Brandom's localized pragmatics of linguistic coordination, which notwithstanding its remarkable technical quality, tends to exclude any possible consideration of sociologically relevant societal contexts, including possibilities as well as actualities (Brandom, 1998).[3] In extended processes of reasoning, generals are abstracted over time from concretely situated understanding, and gradually become meaning oriented presuppositions of further reasoning. Abstraction enriches generals as their connotations grow and they become applied in more and more situations. In a manner that will be explored more in-depth later, generals take the form of immanent societal ideals, where ideal here means recurrent principles of collective orientation without which nothing at all could be done of an enduring nature.

Ideals stand on the immanent plane. They can be consciously constructed, contested, and subject to directed change. Peirce's cosmological evolutionary metaphysics points to something above the immanent. This is the sphere of cognitive universals that serve as the directing force of meaning continua, that which gives such continua an identity that specifies what is within and without their form. Strydom interprets Peirce as operating with two limit concepts, one operating convergently through immanent ideals, as above, and the other operating divergently through evolutionarily stabilized limit concepts (Strydom, 2019). Though Peirce is mostly inexplicit on this point, and there is a lively polemical debate on the subject, it makes sense in terms of his mathematical understanding of infinity and the general mathematical foundations of his architectonic. It also brings the dimension of sociocultural evolution into play, notably genetic variation within it. To restate the idea of immanent transcendence, how do humans, from a position within the world, reach beyond established understanding to generate new possibilities of meaning? Or putting it in line with the above paragraphs, on what could rest the innovative quality of first feelings or quali-signs? The evolutionary transcendent element of cognitive universals that stand above cognized ideals appears a plausible answer. These cognitive universals are ideas of reason in Kant's sense. They specify directions of thinking with always infinitely possible new variations. They have never existed as supra-mundane, timeless transcendentals. They are instead generated from 'below', and through cultural evolution, they become abstracted and stabilized within the extended mind of society and thus come to operate from 'above' as necessary presuppositions and orientations of 'sociation' itself. They stand as cognitive in being conceptual directions of cognition and thus directions of validity or validity concepts (Strydom, 2019). They are in their nature implicit, addressing the question of the kind of universal human purposes that lie beyond any particular goals. They enable goal setting, whose highest immanent form is ideals, but do not prescribe what an ideal should be, only making possible arguments, thoughts, or actions in relevant directions. Though generated from it over

*Peirce, Reason, and Signification*   147

evolutionary time, they stand above experience on which they exert an inescapable structuring force. They are thus evolving constructs, without whose regularity social life would be chaotic and ultimately impossible, even if their presence does not guarantee forms of acceptable ordering, it only makes the thinking of it possible.

In Peirce's account of thirdness, generals mediate particulars. This means not that they fully determine particulars, but that generals and particulars mutually constitute one another; they move together. The manner of mediation is especially important for understanding the way Peirce took over Hegel's dialectic. The conjectural claims of each abductive moment potentially add to the connotative breadth of an abstracting general, conferring more interventionist powers on human agents, whether good or bad. However, these powers will always remain dependent on assumptions about particulars – of firstness, or secondness – that underpin them, and the actual 'behaviour' of these particulars may force revision of the generals. Cognitive universals are a particular kind of general, a transcendently grounded general that is largely impervious to change in the short run. However, ideals are another kind of immanent general in that their stability can shift relatively quickly, though the more enduring will last a long time. The difference is captured by the difference between the idea of legitimacy – a cognitive universal – and the fate of particular theories of legitimacy that are in practice opposed by other kinds. It is true that over time there can be a progression towards consensus on an ideal, and general agreement on important ideals often emerges. It is also true that ideals remain contested for a very long time and that different interpretation of ideals point to social arrangements and conduct of radically different kinds. Yet, sometimes, despite these differences, a kind of social integration with some degree of general justice is built on ideals. Generals in this sense of ideals are fundamental to the idea of society in a way that has affinities in different respects with Durkheim and Marx, with the latter, utterly contrary to a widely held view, having an emphatic sense of society's ideal self-constituting powers, viz., the ideal of socialism together with its ideological blocking. This ideal is ultimately built on the philosophical anthropology of Marx's deployment of relevant cognitive universals, for example, dignity, equality, critique, and so on.

With the idea of the relative autonomy of thirdness, the reality of generals including cognitive universals, Peirce took aim against both nominalism (Forster, 2011), which he equated with materialism, and strong idealism. Nominalism sought to confine itself to the merely individual, seeing no value in an independent ideal realm beyond the material. Nominalism rests on emotivism, whereas, for Peirce, even though perceptual judgements rest on habits of feeling, as habits they contain elements of generality. The realm of generals, which first becomes manifest in habits of feeling in the construction of objects, entails a general kind of reality that reaches beyond mere aggregated individuals. This critique of nominalism also applies to Saussure and his followers, in that they locate meaning in the conceptual system of language, and thus stand apart from the interpretive actions of situated actors in a way that does not make intersubjective space for reasoning. In this way of thinking, language can seem like a 'prison-house' and the concept-constituting and concept-employing power of semiotic agency as inferential reasoning is neglected. Idealism, as with Hegel's spirit or with Kantian transcendental

## 148  *Peirce, Reason, and Signification*

subjectivity, comes with the peril of detachment from the existent, of constructing universals within a supra-mundane realm and rendering them immune from societal elaboration and testing. This tendency of idealism becomes even more detached when, as with Plato and his heirs, it is tied into world-revealing standards that lie absolutely beyond the world. Peirce, therefore, neither stands in the realist nor idealist traditions as hitherto defined, yet he himself develops a version of idealist realism in supposing the independence from one another of the material and ideal worlds, yet their profound interrelation in human cognition, for which he assumes that humans, being part of nature, have a capacity to guess right about the objective world (Tiercelin, 1998). This account of cognition, when coupled with thirdness as the unlimited but in principle available template of evolving generals, provides a powerful means of conceptualizing the extended mind of society as a reality. It is this reality that 20th- and 21st-century thought has had so much difficulty in grasping, yet it holds the key to any concept of reason and the reasonable that remains pivotal to just social organization.

### Reasoning and Symbolization

The great importance of feeling in this theory did not lead Peirce to an emotivist theory of knowing that, in empiricist fashion, denied interpretation and trusted to the immediate judgement of the observer. Royce observed that Peirce extended philosophical consideration, including logic, beyond questions of perception and conception to those of interpretation (Royce, 1913). In Peirce's theory of signs, the consideration of feeling gives weight to the empiricist tradition, while the theory of reasoning that occurs within *argumentation* (thirdness of thirdness) incorporates and goes beyond, in its interpretive and critical quality, the existing rationalist tradition. As opposed to Kant, the logical operations that bring unity to sense impressions are not innately transcendent but semiotic, guided by principles that, in turn, emerge from these semiotic operations over time. The critical quality is not merely self-critique but critique by actual others within a communication community. Peirce's account of reasoning is within interlocking processes: subjective, intersubjective, and transubjective. The subjective or perspectival moment presents itself in logical operations through abductive inference; the intersubjective moment arises through other interpreters as one of the dimensions of inductive inference, and the transsubjective moment lies in the coordinating capacity of deductive inference guided by principles, ideals, and habits. These logical forms are coordinated and not discrete, forming a dynamic interacting process of critical sense-making.

Peirce's semiotics, in contrast with formal semantics, is strikingly open. The range of feelings associated with even the simple exemplar sentence – Did you see this? – opens very many possibilities, including those feelings that unconsciously entered the consciousness of the speaker but were not manifest in the final expression. In line with the theory of thirdness as mediation between a sign and object, feelings are transformed through logical operations and acquire conceptual status within universes of discourse. These logical operations have the entire, relevant universe of discourse, actual and possible, from which to draw to select appropriate paths of inference for expressions. This process is shaped by the feelings that have become attached to the emergent sign as it makes its way through firstness. When the emergent sign arrives at the process of 'interpretation' activated by the final stage of firstness, the legisign, therefore, has already gone through a situationally stimulated yet unconscious inferential selective process. In line with Peirce's critique of Kant, the role of feelings is not only present at the beginning of rational cognition but accompanies it throughout, giving subjective orientation to socially unfolding inferences. Reasoning is accordingly not a process that happens entirely after qualitative feeling has opened a direction but is something that is permanently accompanied by feelings that align with advanced reasons in reasoning processes, processes that follow or change interpretant-based schemata.[4]

A sign like the interrogative, 'Did you see this?', is an Interpretation both in the sense of a reflective internal exchange 'within' the producer of the sign as well as one that calls forth interpretation by another (Royce, 1913). In internal, reflective sign production, the sign is developed through logical operations that anticipate the response of another. Depending on the complexity of the potential reference of the 'this', complex connotations may be introduced that necessitate interpretation. For example, should someone be drawing the attention of a house owner to wastewater beyond her gate, the physical object is the wastewater, though that is only one, manifest aspect of the 'this', which would also contain some combination of relative force, technical, legal, ethical, moral, and other connotations. The connotations are part of the intersubjectivity of the exchange, bearing on both its semantics and pragmatics, and are anticipated in the question. Unless there had been a recent dispute about the issue, they would very likely at first lie more in the background as a diffuse sense of relevance. Such a diffuse sense of relevance indicates the directionality that implicit feelings bring to reasoning. At a general level, associated with the possibilities raised by the discourse, this intersubjective sense is shared, even if interlocutors have a different concrete sense of what aspects of the common background are more relevant.

This idea of the background understood in terms of Peirce has much in common with the respective accounts of Gadamer and Habermas. Peirce's approach, though, has greater potential to be 'analytically' elaborated and thus holds out the tantalizing possibility of being applied to actual discourses. It is tantalizing in that it has not yet been done in any sustained manner, at least for the kind of legal-political matters at issue here. If done, it could be used to show how cultural forms are generated and reproduced. Habermas's account in *TCA* has many of the parts, above all, the idea of problematizing aspects of the lifeworld in communicative reasoning, but they are not fully woven together. One of the benefits of Peirce's approach lies in the idea that particulars can only be identified through generals, whereas the latter are the cultural forms that allow such identification. The challenge is to account in various contexts of discourse for the evolution of such generals and the form they impose on particulars, exploring the interplay between relative stability, secondness, and relative dynamism, firstness. The various forms of generals, such as truth, legitimacy, control, and legality, to be explored in later chapters, are themselves dynamic in some degree, responding both to change

150    *Peirce, Reason, and Signification*

in particulars or to changed interpretations of them. Some generals, the cognitive principles, change only very slowly across evolutionary time, while others, the convergent ones, do so much more quickly within historical time. In later chapters, I will explore further the relationship between different kinds of generals, drawing a distinction between generals that are active in reasoning and those that have a relatively settled symbolic form.[5] This distinction is less than clear in social science, in which reasoning, the pivotal source of normative order, has been sidelined. This will also explore how the role of generals has been poorly addressed, where the legacies in this regard of Marx and Durkheim have mainly been considered in a highly restricted manner, and where, for a long time now, gain in insight in some respects through constructivist approaches has paradoxically led to greater obscurity about generals.

Peirce regarded reasoning as that which takes place under the influence of a leading principle, establishing logical consistency between premises and conclusion, and which is conscious and involves deliberate self-control. Reasoning in part rests on beliefs that one does not doubt, for example, that putting one's hand in a fire will cause pain or the power of unconsciously fixed associations. There are also indubitable beliefs of a general kind that are only indubitable because they have not been criticized. This latter draws attention to limits on the scope of reasoning in that some beliefs are granted validity because they have either not been tested or are held immune from testing by dint of power differentials. Not everything can be doubted at once. Some matters have been settled by prior reasoning, for example, specialized legal or scientific-technical reasoning, and their outcomes are simply granted validity in everyday life, even though they must, in democratic contexts, pass through various institutional checks and balances, even if it is often the case that these are imperfect and operate with a kind of truncated validity testing. This process can generate 'mediation' problems arising from the domination of certain kinds of elite or, at least, power-encrusted, reasoning.

Peirce distinguishes between secondness with its conceptions both of what is or has been the case and of 'certain' futures – temporally ascribing them 'has beens', 'is's', or predictable 'will be's' – and the 'would be's', 'can be's' and 'may be's' of thirdness influenced by the creativity of firstness. The latter kinds give rise to modal, future-oriented inference, whereas that of secondness – induction – seeks definiteness as a guide to action. Following Galileo, Peirce describes abduction as inspired by 'il lame naturale', a type of instinctive and, at least initially, vague sense of what might be correct in each situation (Peirce, 1931–1958, 1.80). Reason depends on this 'occult' power to form a conjecture, to move beyond given states of knowledge anchored in sighs of fact by means of abductive processes that are recondite and difficult, perhaps even impossible, to fully clarify (Peirce, 1931–1958, 5.291). This is, in some ways, analogous to what in modern sociology might be described as the power of the subject (Touraine, 1996).[6]

'Firstnesses' as idea-potentiality are, in Peirce's words, mere 'airy nothings' that must gain traction in the social world to acquire substance (Peirce, 1931–1958, 6.455). Most fail to reach the threshold of expression; some succeed, but whether they succeed or fail, they comprise a form of reality, or, in his term, a Universe of

Experience. This universe is about the genesis of possibilities, qualities that can be ascribed to objects in some possible world. It is also the case that this universe is the basis of freedom and plurality. The coordination of its implications must take place somewhere else, for it is not a controlled kind of thinking. The second Universe of Experience is the 'Brute Actuality' of things and facts, which furnish a kind of constraint on creative possibilities, in some part a necessary constraint in that relations to the objective world require reliable conceptions of it. This is secondness. To speak here of constraint should not be taken strictly 'negatively', for the constraints can also be the norms and values that oppose the possibility of mistaken or inappropriate interpretations. He describes the third Universe of Experience in words that cannot be improved upon as that

> whose Being consists of the power to establish connections between different objects, especially between objects in different Universes. Such is everything which is essentially a Sign – not the mere body of the Sign, but the Sign's Soul, which has its Being in its power of serving as intermediary between the Object and a Mind. Such, too, is a living consciousness, and such the life, the power of growth of a plant. Such is a living institution, – a daily newspaper, a great fortune, a social 'movement.'
>
> (Peirce, 1931–1958. 6.455).

This third universe of experience is thus crucially characterized by the power to make connections. For humans, this is made explicit by the power of inferential reasoning. This power to make connections, that is, establish relations, defines the very essence of thirdness as *argument*. Thirdness is a living, future-oriented type of power. The socio-cognitive capacities to make connections – and distinctions – are oriented on the one side by feelings arising from firstness and, on the other side, by self, other, and world conceptions located in secondness. Thirdness, and reasoning within it, is, therefore, a cognitive power; it is a suite of modalities for sense-making, for taking the potential discoveries arising from feelings and transposing them into collective social forms – the communication community. It thus operates as a vast virtual storehouse of ways of making connections and distinctions – produced by the logic of relatives – and of testing their applicability to actual worlds. As with Hegel's absolute spirit, it is constitutive. As a real communication community, it consists of everything that is actually known, if not universally shared, but as an unlimited communication community, it can infinitely expand. In the latter sense, thirdness is thus fundamentally about collective learning. For Peirce, a thought is general in its essential form; it circulates incessantly and is ever only provisionally finalized. The power of thought, therefore, in including all possible facts, exceeds all known facts. Possible facts lurk in the latent realm of feelings, diffuse and yet unrealized, with some entirely unknown – or in human practices not yet created – in the present but still possible through the kinds of leaps of learning that can be historically documented.

Modalities of construction in thirdness, as above, take three basic forms: modalities of generating feelings (syntactic), modalities of generating facts (semantic),

152  *Peirce, Reason, and Signification*

and modalities of generating thoughts (cognitive pragmatic). One rests upon the other, with the modalities of feelings at the base. The most elementary form is therefore not semantic reference to an external world, but a world-constructing phenomenology of feelings. These three kinds of cognitive form parallel Peirce's three kinds of normative science, aesthetics, ethics, and logic, with the same hierarchy. The 'higher' normative sciences of aesthetics, associated with firstness, and ethics, associated with secondness, define the ends to be pursued through the more dependent normative science of logic. Peirce's account of the normative sciences is complicated. It is also critical for understanding both reasoning and its outcomes in structures and actions. It captures the movement from ideals that are in principle general and open, to preferred normative commitments, to the logical means to determine whether the commitments within the ideals are justified.

This conception of the normative sciences may be elaborated by an account of the various kinds of limit concepts in Peirce. Earlier, following Strydom's lead, I presented the basic concepts held, among others, by Peirce of immanent transcendence and convergence-divergence that correspond to Kant's distinction and relation between transcendent ideas of reason and immanent regulative ideals. Ideas of reason are evolutionarily formed, universally shared human competences of both an individual and collective nature. They are presuppositions and anticipations that make possible human cognitive activity. All cognition proceeds from these encompassing cognitive principles. They are the orientations necessary for human kinds of meaning. They specify the possibilities of qualitative human perception in firstness – the quali-sign, qualitative immediacy – and are further semiotically elaborated from there. Regulative ideals on the immanent place, on the other hand, emerge from cognitive processes and are thus orientated. They are immanent generals in Peirce's sense. Without such generals taking effect in reflection supporting schemata, there could only be chaos and coordinated forms of life would not be possible, even as an aspiration. Yet not all ideals stand on the same level. Some are 'decontested', at least for a period, as, for example, shared constitutional ideals of democracy, while others are contested, such as the difference between certain contemporary visions of hierarchy and equality. The evaluation of ideals is closely bound up with the specification of normative standards of validity in ethical systems, of which, for critical theory, discourse ethics has been a dominant paradigm over the last half-century or so. I will be returning to this theme of ideals and validity standards more systematically in later chapters.

There is a significant divide in the scholarship on Peirce as to whether his philosophy had transcendental foundations. Peirce was not, or at least ceased to be over the course of his career, a transcendental thinker in the sense of Kant's transcendental subjectivity. Nonetheless, for Peirce, according to Deledalle, there were three ontologically derived 'Transcendentals', Beauty, Ethics, and Truth, which he held from as early as 1857 (Deledalle, 2001, 155–161). Many commentators ignore this transcendental suggestion as early error, later corrected.

Bergman offers a careful and knowledgeable account of his own misgivings, notably regarding the hierarchy that places aesthetics at the summit of the normative sciences. He is concerned that the famous reference to aesthetics as that which

*Peirce, Reason, and Signification* 153

could encompass the summum bonum, that which is admirable in itself, takes Peirce in a transcendental direction and away from immanent justification and from balanced consideration of the normative sciences (Bergman, 2014). Looking at it from the opposite standpoint of immanent transcendence, the aesthetic construction, appropriation, and reconstruction of 'ideals' in abduction draws from both the 'transcending' evolutionary-derived status of cognitive universals or ideas of reason, and from immanent regulative ideals. The aesthetic appropriation of the transcendental reflects their necessarily weak normative status; they point to normatively relevant discourses, but they themselves do not promote a normative standpoint, for this only happens immanently. This is why they can be described as *cognitive* principles, which are nonetheless weakly normative in specifying orientations towards desirable human purposes. Moreover, they are transcendental only in the sense of crystallizing for thought those hidden parts of continua, that is, those parts that are possible but not yet revealed. This is also the very essence of Peirce's idea of a general as that which reaches beyond multitude. Also, regulative ideals have a general status, but of another immanent kind.

Feelings are the primitives that both initially orient ideas – in their initial vague state – and remain intrinsic in connecting them to one another. They thus orientate proto ideas that potentially have a purchase in the future, either guided by existing cognitive generals or with the potential, in some cases, to contribute to new ones. In either case, they must pass through reasoning processes that convert their subjective form to a shared social one. In reasoning, they encounter other ideals derived from ethics and logic, by means of which Bergman's desideratum of the interrelation of the normative sciences is achieved (Bergman, 2009). The insights opened in abduction, instructed by the habits of feeling of the legisign, have the potential to achieve a gain in knowledge. Hence, radical and 'true' abduction reaches beyond even established orders of discourse guided by dominant ideals and their manifestation in habits of reasoning. In this eventuality, they trigger the overarching evolutionary-formed universal ideas of reason, resulting in episodes of radical learning. They could, however, also and more routinely trigger further learning within the framework of existing ideals. The more radical kind of learning may be associated with habits of habit change, while institutionally bounded learning takes place through the diffusion of already established habits.

Abduction begins the logical process and 'triggers' deductive habits of reasoning. Such habits establish ways of reasoning that 'solve' problems or are at least assumed to solve problems in particular universes of discourse. These kinds of habits can be broken into two kinds, on which, to my knowledge, Peirce is not explicit, though it seems to follow from his general account. Thus, they would either be, on the one hand, habits held by individuals or like-minded groups of individuals or, on the other hand, collectivities operating as the fully operating real communication community who, over time, come to agree on how to reason about some matter and, accordingly, routinely produce the same outcome through the same reasoning strategies. Reasoning habits, and the reasoning process generally, should serve truth. However, truth is not just aesthetically guided, in the manner understood above as the pursuit of general ideals, it must also serve ethical purposes.

## 154 *Peirce, Reason, and Signification*

This entails the involvement of the second of the normative sciences, that of ethics, understood as those normative standards that provide ends for reasoning. The aesthetic moment of abduction therefore reaches to a thoroughly general level, but only in a conjectural manner, whereas the normative ends are concretely specified as the goals of the inquiry. It then falls to logic as the third of the normative sciences to reason on the validity claims present in the conjectures in the light of the normative goals directing the inquiry.

The application of ethical ends only gives reasoning a normative orientation; it does not foreclose on that orientation being changed because of the reasoning. Morality, according to Peirce, is a matter of conceptions of right or wrong conduct. If Peirce's account of reasoning were to be transferred from his predominant interest in theoretical reason to matters of practical reason, as Habermas suggests is possible on the basis of the universalism of his theory, then from the vantage point of Peirce, two possible orientations to the latter might be envisaged (Habermas, 2019). The first, that reasoning should be used to settle moral matters, would not be consistent with the division between normativity and reasoning in the theory, where the former guides the latter. The second, which Peirce seems to assert should apply to what he calls practical matters, would be to separate moral norm formation from reasoning altogether. Morality, and other normative orientations, could enter into reasoning, but from somewhere external to it. Morality, in this view, would be constructed not through reasoning but through sentiment, understood as formed over time by communal practices that are not, or perhaps should not be, subject to radical reappraisal in reasoning. In this regard, Peirce often emphasized that individuals in practical matters frequently showed a greater capacity for being right through trusting instinctually given competences than through reasoning. Certainly, changes brought about by events or changes in perception over time due to accumulated experiences could, independently of reasoning, have a significant influence on moral commitments. Taking Peirce's demonstration of the relation between reasoning and conduct elsewhere in his theory, and his emphasis on how reasoning should produce a gain in self-control, what seems most likely is that he understood practical morality in both the above senses, that is, intuitively sentimental, on the one hand, or reason based as the rational pursuit of normative ends on the other. In any event, the distinction between the normative sciences rests on aesthetics as an orientation to ideals in the strongest sense, to ethics, that is, morality, as ideals grounded in actual conduct, and to reason as ideals of right and true reasoning.

As is well known, Peirce's account of the operation of inference within the logical interpretant was based on the interweaving of three kinds: abductive, deductive, and inductive. The sequence of inference moves from abduction that emerges from the thirdness of firstness, as outlined above, to deduction where the abductive conjecture is subject to analysis based on established forms of reasoning, and thence to induction, which is the final operation of reasoning in which the deductively elaborated abductive conjecture is tested for its fit with actual states of affairs, possibly calling forth action. While during matters discussed above, I have offered some remarks about abduction. I have said little about deduction and induction,

*Peirce, Reason, and Signification*    155

steering clear of technical logical terms or argumentation, rather using the modes of inference in a general sense as would be of value in analyzing social theoretical constructs of society generally and specific social situations by means of the Peirceian logic of inquiry. Yet, the whole point is that logic is indispensable as the carrier of reason and should not be evaded.

Peirce describes deduction as necessary reasoning, reasoning that encapsulates a logical chain of premises and conclusion where the conclusion is true if the premises are true. With the introduction of abduction, a mode of inference most associated with Peirce and most developed by him, deduction does not serve only as the conclusion of a known and valid chain of reasoning but as a means of clarifying on what grounds something may be valid in the light of a conjecture or hypothesis. The conjecture or hypothesis could encounter in deduction a ready-made argument that generated a definite and necessary corollary. Such deduction, the standard kind, Peirce called corollorial, and, from this, the task of induction would be to reason on whether the facts conformed to the presumption. However, abduction might also call forth uncertainty as to what deductive rules might apply, requiring a theoretical reorientation before induction could properly commence. This type of deduction Peirce called theorematic deduction (Peirce, 1992). In the manner described above, the first kind of deduction involves the employment of existing habits of reasoning; the second kind involves their modification to some degree. This is why Peirce changed his mind in his later career about whether reasoning could in fact generate new knowledge. Abduction is a conjecture or hypothesis derived from the generalization of epistemically relevant feelings, and he originally thought that new knowledge could only come from this source. With theorematic deduction, he speaks of the need to perform an 'ingenious experiment' on a deductive structure – Peirce mentions a diagram in this regard – so that, by further observation of the modified structure, the truth of the conclusion may be ascertained (Peirce, 1992, 291). In considering a conjecture, a hypothesis, or a modal projection, it is not clear in complex cases what deductive rule, or rules, should apply to it. Hence, deduction draws upon signs of secondness, symbols, indices, and icons, to clarify the relevant universe of discourse. This involves the insertion of semantic references into the cognitive form of deduction, leading to its further elaboration to gain soundness in the universe of discourse in question. It also enables deduction to mediate between abduction and induction, developing sufficient scope to cover the different challenges posed by these other modes of inference, which respectively carry the predominant powers of discovery and testing. Accordingly, deduction is the locus in which the ontological impulse coming from abduction and the methodological import of induction are epistemologically brought together.

Peirce says that an induction is a method of forming dicent symbols concerning a definite question (Peirce, 1992, 298), where dicent symbols are symbolic forms of the thirdness of secondness. Thus, generally, through induction, the ability or not to form dicent symbols is a means of confirming or disconfirming the deductively explicated conjecture or modal projection. However, beyond that, it is also a means of showing in what ways these conclusions or rules may be applied to multiple issues. It is a method of fixing the logic of arguments at the 'output' dyadic level

## 156 *Peirce, Reason, and Signification*

of symbolic conception and action. However, it is also a method for transposing the signs of this dyadic level back into the triadic logic of the sign of argument, for induction also plays a role in imaginative projection. For example, in this latter regard, the question might be asked: What does this pattern of events indicate about the comprehensiveness of a deductive rule, or what do they signify about the assumptions underpinning the inductive translation of the rule? Thus, induction lies within the foundational triadic exercise of building and using generals, but it also shows how, factually, these generals dyadically index universes of existence so that the definitiveness requisite for the application of thought – as knowledge – can be attained. Abduction sets the triadic capacities of thought in motion, deduction coordinates its general forms, and induction regulates its relation to the dyadic forms of actuality.

For Peirce, then, going back to an earlier point with emphasis, generals really exist. More than that, reasonable generals really exist. Reasonable generals are generals that recurrently produce justified, true outcomes. For Habermas, extending Peirce, rational generals, if he were to accept their reality, would produce justified right outcomes or justified ethical outcomes. The nature of these generals is contained in their articulation through forms of *argument*, abductive, deductive, and inductive, and if the arguments hold and gain traction, they give rise to dyadic forms. It is Luhmann's error to exclude reasoning thirdness, in other words, rational mind, from his account, but it is his insight to recognize the significance of its dyadic outcomes in the codes of systems, in other words, in symbolic coding of worlds of experience. Peirce distinguishes between cognitive habits, which are forms of thirdness, and expectations, which are forms of secondness (Peirce, 1931–1958, 5.486). Expectations contain no conditionality, hence no learning. The reality of generals is an infinite spectrum of conditional argumentative forms, some of which can be validly applied as knowledge and some of which exist only as potentials. In every act of thinking about the future, within habits or in learning beyond them, this spectrum is always engaged. Its outcome lies in creating new constructions of objects of all kinds, building through logical processes the dyadic relations of action/reaction achieved through secondness. Secondness is therefore a realm of expectations, where, borrowing from Luhmann, different kinds of binary distinctions organized as system codes, for example, true or false, just or unjust, congeal in agents' expectation structures, inducing them to behave according to 'appropriate' conduct rules. Secondness is itself, therefore, a vast, endless enterprise of semiotic indexing and iconizing of signs relating to pasts and expected futures. Only thirdness allows progression, learning, rational volition, and evolution. Thirdness orders secondness, but secondness will endlessly pick up on contingencies hitherto 'unresolved' in thirdness, resulting in doubt and a new learning cycle of some kind.

Peirce is clear that reasoning may serve or dissolve gains in self-control and knowledge, and scientific knowing – or any other complex, general kind of knowing – must progress through good reasoning or fail. If reasoning were fully excluded, it would not be just this or that enterprise of knowledge that would fail, but the possibility of any kind of rational order in human affairs the possibility of coordination in human forms of life desirable in the light of justified ideals. A good injunction for normative projection following from Peirce might then be to expand good reasoning of all kinds. The word 'good' is preferred instead of the more usual 'sound' in the anticipation of expanding reason to deal with questions of rightness and goodness as well as truth in line with Habermas (Cooke, 2006). Such an expansion of reasoning should take heed of its three branches: abduction should be alive to feelings in the service of new ideas or *discovery*, deduction should be alive to the truth – or rightness – conditions of the reasoning in different spheres in its *analysis*, and induction to its general appropriateness to situations in its *justifications*. These last remarks recall Habermas's validity claims, but they are inserted, in the first instance, into the sequential form of Peirce's modes of reasoning and hence radically extended in their social applicability. In later chapters, the question of validity understood in terms of Peirce's semiotic framework will be made central to the question of reason in society at the core of the book.

## Notes

1 I do not distinguish here in the 1903 account between 'signs' as the elements of the triad associated with each of the categories of firstness, secondness, and thirdness, and the specification of signs that arose from the combination of sub-categories. The number of the latter was 10 signs. A sign in this latter account began with a third, continued with a second, and ended with a first. The important aspect of this latter use of signs is to show how signs must be understood as spanning the three categories. Ongoing in the book, I will describe the three subcategories of the three categories, firstness, secondness, and thirdness as signs, as this is more amenable to general understanding. Peirce technically confined the term 'sign' to three signs of thirdness in the 1903 account. Some insights from the still later account – after 1906 – will also inform the analysis. Distinctions and qualifications will be used where necessary.

2 Later, more will be said about the basic idea of relations, for which Peirce's architectonic has many advantages. It is likely that it stands at the base of much 20th-century thinking on the relational, but mostly without knowledge of the original progenitor.

3 According to Descombes, who serves as one important exemplar of this point, Peirce inverts the traditional order of logic in which arguments are built from propositions that are in turn built from terms – or names – from a nominalist perspective. For Peirce, the starting point is argumentations that encapsulate propositions and terms, precluding the atomistic construction of arguments from 'below' (Descombes, 2014).

4 Schemata and their relation to interpretants will be addressed in more depth in later chapters.

5 Properly speaking, only the transcendent cognitive principles are 'true' generals. These principles can also be understood as cognitive universals. Such immanent entities as ideals and norms have degrees of generality. Sociology and the social sciences have frequently and mistakenly tended to confine claim to generality to these immanent entities. This problem is by no means confined only to the social sciences. The unfortunate consequence has been an abandonment of generality within theories, or, more accurately, its surreptitious and under-theorized presence.

6 Touraine in this text emphasizes the autonomy of the subject in her role as a perceiving, experiencing being, roughly the 'I", guided by the sense of rights held by her 'double', roughly the 'me'. In this respect, Touraine's theory has distinct analogies with that of Peirce.

158 *Peirce, Reason, and Signification*

## References

Apel K-O (1995) *Charles Peirce: From Pragmatism to Pragmaticism*. New York, NY: Prometheus.

Atkin A (2010) Peirce's Theory of Signs. In: Zalta EN (ed) *Stanford Encyclopedia of Philosophy*. Stanford, CA: Metaphysics Research Lab.

Bergman M (2009) *Peirce's Philosophy of Communication: The Rhetorical Underpinnings of the Theory of Signs*. London: Bloomsbury.

Bergman, M (2014) Gabriele Gava, Peirce's Account of Purposefulness: A Kantian Perspective. *European Journal of Pragmatism and American Philosophy*. 6: VI-2.

Brandom R (1998) *Making It Explicit: Reasoning, Representing, and Discursive Commitment*. Cambridge, MA: Harvard University Press.

Cooke M (2006) *Represesenting the Good Society*. Cambridge, MA: MIT Press.

Deledalle G (2001) *Charles S. Peirce's Philosophy of Signs: Essays in Comparative Semiotics*. Bloomington, IN: Indiana University Press.

Descombes V (2014) *The Institutions of Meaning*. Cambridge, MA: Harvard University Press.

Dewey J (1927) *The Public and Its Problems*. New York, NY: Holt.

Forster P (2011) *Peirce and the Threat of Nominalism*. Cambridge, MA: Cambridge University Press.

Fraser, N, Honneth, A (2003*) Redistribution or Recognition?: A Political-philosophical Exchange*. London: Verso.

Habermas J (2019) *Auch Eine Geschichte Der Philosophie*. Frankfurt: Suhrkamp.

Honneth A (2014) *Freedom's Right: The Social Foundations of Democratic Life*. New York, NY: Columbia University Press.

Kahneman D (2011) *Thinking, Fast and Slow*. London: Penguin.

Leddy T and Puolakka K (2006) Dewey's Aesthetics. *Stanford Encyclopedia of Philosophy*.

O'Mahony P (2023a) Critical Theory, Peirce and the Theory of Society. *European Journal of Social Theory* 26(2): 258–281.

O'Mahony P (2023b) Introduction to Special Issue: The Critical Theory of Society. *European Journal of Social Theory* 26(2): 121–135.

Peirce CS (1931–1958) *Collected Papers of Charles Sanders Peirce*. In: Hartshorne C, Weiss P, and Burks PW (eds). Cambridge, MA:Harvard University Press.

Peirce CS (1992) The Fixation of Belief (1877). In: *The Essential Peirce (Vol. 1): Selected Philosophical Writings (1867–1893)*. Bloomington, IN: Indiana University Press.

Peirce CS (1998) *The Essential Peirce (Vol. 2): Philosophical Writings (1893–1913)*. Bloomington, IN: Indiana University Press.

Royce J (1913) *The Problem of Christianity*. Washington: Catholic University of America Press.

Short TL (2007) *Peirce's Theory of Signs*. Cambridge, MA: Cambridge University Press.

Strydom P (2019) On Habermas's Differentiation of Rightness from Truth: Can an Achievement Concept Do without a Validity Concept? *Philosophy and Social Criticism* 45(5): 555–574.

Tiercelin C (1998) Peirce's Objective Idealism: A Defense. *Transactions of the Charles S. Peirce Society* 34(1): 1–28.

Touraine A (1996) A Sociology of the Subject. In: Clark J and Diani M (eds) *Alain Touraine*. London: Falmer Press, p. 291.

Touraine A (2000) *Can We Live Together?: Equality and Difference*. Stanford: Stanford University Press.

Touraine A (2005) The Subject Is Coming Back. *International Journal of Politics, Culture, and Society* 18(3–4): 199–209.

Wartenberg, G (1971) *Logischer Sozialismus: die Transformation der Kantschen Transzendentalphilosophie durch Ch. S. Peirce*. Frankfurt: Suhrkamp.

# 6 Reasoning and Schemata in a Societal Frame

A motif of this book is that contemporary sociology and the wider social sciences pay little explicit attention to reason, reasons, or reasoning.[1] Sociology and the other social sciences have almost gone out of their way to deny their importance. In those scarce places where it is claimed that they have been explicitly addressed, it is often represented that they serve as a form of ideology, for example, in the claim that Habermas's use of reason manifests a liberal or Eurocentric ideology, or represents a type of pathology, for example, the assumed hegemony of instrumental reason. Yet, sociology has always regarded itself as having a privileged vantage point on actuality, of being concerned in many ways with the observation, interpretation, and criticism of external worlds, frequently understood as characterized by extensive domination. The problem that arises is that if reasoning counts in society as an institutional order and is indeed, in key respects, productive of society in that sense, then a sociology attempting to operate without reason will miss this generative dimension, leaving a major gap in the understanding of processual dynamics. The proclivity to dismiss reason as an ideology of the dominant is particularly fateful for critical sociology, which has essential normative concerns. Without recourse to a concept of reason, the various bases of the discipline provide different answers as to how society is ordered, or put more strongly, integrated? Some answer on the implicit basis of finding the rationality – a type of indirect nod to reason – that is already inscribed in the world, arising both via natural laws and technologies of various kinds; others that there is no overarching integration, only localized mechanisms of generating partial meaning in spaces differentiated from the overall; others emphasize the domination through power that fragments and renders void normative goals; and others emphasize reflexivity, though as we have seen in a limited fashion.

Yet, from the vast storehouses of knowledge that resource the discipline, few theorists assert that society is ordered, integrated, or made coherent in some way or other through reasoning. This non-attention is perhaps surprising, as it was at least partly addressed in Weber's account of rationalization. This account has had immense instructive value in some respects, manifested, for example, in the amount of attention it receives in *TCA*. Yet, Weber's own account of rationalization is disconnected from in-depth analysis of forms of reasoning. Instead of analyzing the

DOI: 10.4324/9780429060571-7

## 160  *Reasoning and Schemata in a Societal Frame*

sign-based construction of meaning, Weber instead turns to the objective observation of the effects of different kinds of rationality on the social world. Moreover, as Habermas says, Weber's account of rationalization is selective, ultimately favouring purposive rationality while ambivalently condemning its corrosive effects on individuals and social relations. In any case, Weber was representative of multiple traditions in early sociology that took on board central theses of German idealism. These include figures normally set apart in the history of the disciplines like Durkheim, Simmel, Mead, and others (Shalin, 1990; Belvedere, 2023). The overlapping idealist figure of thought was centred on the idea of the self-creation of society, and transcendental epistemic categories undergirded objectively general cognitive capacities. Taking this further, it was an ineluctable conclusion of the post-metaphysical and post-empiricist thought of early sociology that the deepest reality encountered by humans was ultimately a product of the collective cognitive forms that made knowledge possible, in this sense breaking with the individualism of much of the idealist legacy. Such an idealist legacy would lead to a characteristic emphasis on generative processes as upstream of 'social facts', for example, manifested in the various ideas of the transcendental at work in the classical figures of sociology outlined in Chapter 4.

Less explicitly emphasized than Weber, the theme of reason was also present in Marx, strikingly in the theory of ideology, where ultimately ideological practices can be read as pathological deviations from the *justified* normative standard of socialism. Just like Weber, but more explicitly, Marx contributed to the specification of pathological forms that blocked justice and the reasonable, including, reification, alienation, estrangement, exploitation, and ideology itself. Very little has been done in the social sciences to turn these into communicative theses.[2] In critical sociology, stemming from Marx, the contrary idea persists that reason serves domination and the unreasonable, not just the dominant form of subjective reason in the first-generation Frankfurt texts but reason tout court. Partly this relates to the perceived role of degenerated or ideological forms of reasoning in dominating the very idea of reason, viewing reason as the exemplar of various 'conserving' philosophies of history, from pre-democratic conservatism to an increasingly dominant liberalism. Both the legacies of the old conservatism and the new liberalism are assumed to harness democracy for particular social interests, while effectively hollowing it out. It thus seems clear, from this vantage point, that for the goal of rescuing the idea of reason in critical thought, the pathologies of reasoning must be made manifest.

Identifying pathologies of reasoning cannot be done without addressing the other side contained in the question of validity, how can a communicatively reproduced, rational society be envisaged? With this emphasis on normative ends reached through communication as a necessary sociological task, I do not mean to suggest that the vast expenditure of normative effort in this direction in disciplines other than sociology has been in vain. Rather, I draw attention, as a very general claim to be sure, to another kind of objectivism in specifying normative precepts, one that, even when asserting normative positions, does not extensively address actual reasoning practices that underlie them and make them possible. The in-depth

*Reasoning and Schemata in a Societal Frame*   161

treatment of the latter is inescapable if the intrinsic role of communicative publics, actual and potential, in bringing closer to an appropriate democratic society is to be fully addressed. For this task, critique must be balanced with validity. Later, I will suggest how a re-positioned and further sociologically supplemented discourse ethics could at least begin to address this essential task, that of the communicative formation of publics, and its societal implications.

Themes of reasoning and rationality, taken together, do raise very complex problems, requiring a disciplinary division of labour that is extremely hard to bring about, notwithstanding the efforts of critical theorists and others. At the very heart of reasoning, there is always the insistent issue of how the local encounter where active reasoning happens, usually called interaction or conversation, relates to the forbiddingly broad and variegated terrain that lies beyond it. As already observed, when Habermas made some very promising beginnings to exploring communicative reasoning in its broader societal context, the discipline either could not or did not want to take it forwards. There are many reasons for sociology's lack of interest in the societal implications of reasoning. These variously include the temporal orientation to the future, the conditional modal form – could, may, would, or should be – rather than a narrowly factual orientation, and the normative implications. One reason perhaps surpasses all of these. It has not been demonstrated how sociology could simultaneously operate as both a special or positive science, concentrating on certain kinds of empirical domains, and a normative science concerned with evaluating what happens in these domains and, indeed, even more basically, *whether* it should operate in this stereoscopic manner. It is one of the implications of the critique of positivism and the general shift to post-empiricism from the 1950s onwards that the absolute nature of the fact/value distinction can no longer be sustained. This recognition gave significant impetus to a renaissance of critical sociology in the decades subsequently, even if it happened for other reasons too. In the main, sociology has characteristically stopped short of normative proposals for social change. They are not entirely absent, just highly implicit in the fore-grounded critical impulse. The question arises as to whether, through attention to normative argumentation within the world and within sociology, these implicit normative affirmations of certain ideals might not become explicit?

In what follows, not just in this chapter but in subsequent ones, the concept of validity will come more to the fore. Validity offers a means of addressing the question raised just above. To properly grasp the various levels and kinds of validity, it is first necessary to show how it requires an account of the reasoning process, and its structural inputs and outputs, within an appropriate overall architectonic. The architectonic, some of whose properties have already been advanced in earlier chapters in the accounts of Habermas, the critical cognitive sociology framework, and of Peirce, will first be further developed in this and the next chapter. A distinctive account of validity will be shown to emerge from its foundations. Two subsequent chapters then address discourse ethics-inspired account of the forms of validity, in turn, set within the Peirce-inspired account of the reasoning process. Understanding reasoning in this sense as the key to validity also allows the further claim that the communicative construction of validity is the key to understanding

162　*Reasoning and Schemata in a Societal Frame*

the role of reason, a construction that takes a distinctive form in democratic societies. Validity is not understood as merely a 'progressive' standard but also as a contested one that can take on pathological forms. Thus, a distinction energes between the ideal and de-facto validity of normative concepts. The question then arises, deferred for now, as to how to think of reason when validity is thought of as contested? This is precisely where critique comes into play, a critique that extends to the reconstruction of the validity standards themselves. For all of this, the forms of reasoning associated with various conceptions of reason must be demonstrated if progress is to be made towards demonstrating that a totalizing suspicion of reason is not justified, which indeed defeats the goals of critical thought.

## Reasoning, Inference, and Schema-building

A sociology that on the whole did not concern itself with reasoning progressively also felt free not to concern itself with ideals, – which, mostly, it understood as values –, and accordingly felt it could exclude transcendent, mediating, cognitive, and dynamic generals from its consideration, Such cognitive generals act as generative media and stand as real in their own right in their cognition shaping function, not simply as in nominalist theories generated from within the minds of individuals. Sociology traditionally had an interest in values – often operating as sociological surrogates for ideals – as indices of various kinds of commitment and as guides to action (Rose, 1981; Münch, 2010). Yet, the processes and mechanisms whereby these values were formed and sustained were never properly examined and could not be where the discourse leading to their emergence and change was excluded. If this were fully included, the architectonic would inevitably change.

In the 20th century, with the dominance of positivism, values, like other cultural components of the discipline, were predominantly elaborated by quantitative means as properties of individuals that could be aggregated. They were later seeded into the qualitative revival in the second half of the 20th century, but one that was never particularly concerned with their genesis, that is, those generative processes that made them possible in the first place. On the qualitative side too, the injunction to focus on immediate situations in its later incarnation practically precluded consideration of transcendentally anchored cognitive principles and immanent general ideals, quite different from its early pioneers, for example, Mead's generalized other, Weber's ideal types, Marx's associationism, and Durkheim's society. The idea of interpretation took on many forms, but mainly influenced by certain kinds of hermeneutics, it tended to be backward-looking and less than committed to the implications of interpretive practices for any kind of social transformation. Despite various attempts at mediation, for example, Ricouer's critical hermeneutics, interpretive sociology took its distance from what it understood as critique. This led to a permanent tension with various expressions of modern epistemology that, following Kant, took critique as indispensable to reason. It also stood in tension with critical neo-Marxist schools that advanced ontological readings of the modern condition, such as critical realism. The overall sense ranging across the latter manifestations of sociology as a discipline is one of fragmentation and partiality, where the attempt to displace transcendental, critical-normative, and generative powers does not seek a reconstructed reason and appropriate normative commitments as much as its final displacement. It is, of course, one thing to note the relative absence of the theory of reasoning in sociology, and quite another thing to try to introduce it to such a relatively empty landscape in this regard. It is for this reason that I believe the second-generation's embrace of Peirce is fully justified. The social and human sciences must build from a rational and processual immanent-transcendent architecture that does not shy away from explaining the genesis of the many kinds and levels of societal schemata. Nor can it stop just at a vaguely indicated genesis of such schemata, as in the contemporary tendency to emphasise social imaginaries, but it must also address the normative rationality of societal outcomes.

For Peirce, reasoning is the activity of attaching relations of inference to signs, where signs vary in their universes of discourse and function, their producer's meaning intention, the receiver's interpretation, and communal standards. Reasoning has an a priori quality, standing above particular experiences, that derives from the evolutionary formation of three categories of reasoning capacities: abductive, deductive, and inductive. It also has an a posteriori quality introduced by the conjectured revisions or transformations of received understandings in abduction, right up to the inductive formation of knowledge (Chevalier, 2016). Accordingly, if reasoning is based on relations between signs, then these sign relations must be relevant to their actualities, namely, natural objects, objectualized social beings, and socio-technical systems. As the relational turn in sociology makes clear, and Foucault, there are intrinsic relations between these objects, not just relations between mental signs that construct these objects. Yet, it is the relations between such mental signs, relation of final causation, that are decisive for semiotics, though such relations in Peirce's brand of semiotic realism also remain constructs of objects that form relational interdependencies on the material level of the objects themselves. In empirical-analytical sociology, by contrast, relations between sociological objects articulated as adaptation requirements were taken to be fundamental, and orders of meaning functionally followed from these relations. In other words, the second dimension of relationality was separated from the first, the genetic, socio-mental, and transcendentally enabled capacity to build ever-new relations. In interpretive and later constructivist sociology, the order of priority was put in reverse, and it was interpretation, though not reasoning, that was given primacy. What is required is the kind of mediated account that Bourdieu called for in reconciling subjective and objective sociologies, but which requires a more decisive articulation than either he supplied, or the wider structure/agency paradigm can supply.

Such an account cannot simply involve leaving assumptions about subjectivity and objectivity as they are. It must provide an elaborated architectonic in which communication is fundamental. Against the contemporary sociological tendency, it requires a communicative logic within an immanent-transcendent architecture. Therefore, I turn to Peirce's category of thirdness or mediation for its processual emphasis on forms of reasoning. Peirce's account of logic was modally projective in allowing for conceptions that were *possible* in exceeding everything that was already known to be actual. Accordingly, endless possibilities of variation,

## 164 *Reasoning and Schemata in a Societal Frame*

open-ended learning that reaches beyond what is currently known, lie at the very core of sign-mediation. This is captured by the distinction in his paper *Issues of Pragmaticism* between vagues and generals, where vagues are more or less dimly felt possibilities, something could be, while generals are conditional necessities, what would be if given conditions obtained (Peirce, 1992 346–359; Lane, 2007). Peirce held that possibilities could remain unactualized but nonetheless still be real. The idea of real vagues and real possibilities arose after the modal turn in the 1990s, which, in its conception of continuity, articulated the possibility embodied by the fact that any collection exceeded a definite multitude and that more could always be added to it (Lane, 2007; Forster, 2011). Possibilities could simply subsist as unactualized possibilities within the continuum of meaning, or they can be elaborated through generals – transcendent cognitive principles or regulative ideas – and bring about innovation in what is held to be knowledge. Such generals offer a means beyond what is already known in thought and argument. Something is provisionally conceived that either is projected to be the case or that could or should be the case, but it is vague, and a process of innovation is accordingly put underway that involves rethinking the relation between possibility and actuality. Potentiality, the elaboration of possibility to clarify potential relations to actuality, mediates between possibility and actuality. It involves the continuous further elaboration of meaning in a given direction towards a given object. Viewed from the standpoint of the socio-historical process, the elaboration of potentiality by mediation through *real* generals can bring about change in ideals, where ideals are that which is immanently graspable as a horizon, such as the ideal of equality, an ideal that has a cognitive-normative form. It is cognitive in remaining open to many interpretations, including opposing interpretations, but normative in defining a space of argumentation that corresponds to its sphere of relevance. An ideal, such as that of equality, is an 'actual general' in that it offers continuity on the immanent plane and can always accommodate new possibilities arising from learning within its discourse form. It is not fixed and stable in perpetuity, but over an extended period of time, it can provide a stable, ideal context for the settling of goals. The ideal circumscribes the space for the formation of such goals, but it does not decide their actual form. This is the result of wider political and social processes at lower levels.

Vagues and generals define the opposite ends of a given continuum, a continuum that continues to infinite possibility. In one way, a continuum associated, let us again say, with 'equality' may always have further interpretations added to it, further interpretations of what equality could mean that, culturally embodied through reasoning, will change both its meaning content and forms of validity. There is no absolute finite limit to this process because the basic substrate of the continuum is composed of feelings, which make up the content of consciousness, individual and collectively shared, and the possibility of new feelings is limitless. In another way, for Peirce, the mathematical concept of infinitesimals offers the key to understanding reflexive innovation. Infinitesimals are intercepts on a continuous line that can always be further subdivided and therefore do not equate to fixed points (Zalamea, 2001). The capacity to go 'further' within the continuum is underpinned by the continuous possibility of further infinitesimals. Translating between infinitesimals

*Reasoning and Schemata in a Societal Frame* 165

and feelings, new or changed feelings may reflexively inspire innovation within the given continuum, but the realization of such potentiality is far from automatically given. Just as it was immanently normatively generated as a potentiality, it must also be societally realized by immanent processes of actualization.

The above has major implications for the long-run sociological emphasis on the power of the actual as a structuring focus, the generalized empirical. This has widely endured across different theoretical-methodological traditions. Sometimes it is a base for direct theorization, sometimes it is the explanatory variable smuggled into analyses of situated interaction. The actual, in the sense of normative rules, is the product of discourse, as so signally demonstrated for the human and social sciences by Foucault (Foucault, 1972). Peirce did it too, but with a different kind of non-nominalist logic of inquiry. In Peirce's account, which is mirrored in a less complete way – in this respect – in Habermas, the actual may be rationally explained – even if it is irrational or contradictory in form – by the generalizing power of the continua of possibilities and necessities, or vagues and generals. The formation of the actual involves a rupture of the continuum through the logical process of reasoning. This amounts to an inductive selection of that which is granted factual status or, in contexts of practical reason, should be accorded a factual status. Knowledge of the actual depends on continuous cognitive processing, supported by the scaffolding of 'achieved' knowledge, that is, knowledge known to be, or at least thought to be, relevant and effective. Inductive inference is part of ampliative or non-deductive, synthetic inference, which also includes abductive inference. Abductive inference is the creative ability to envisage the potentialities that, across the spectrum, have a much better than random chance of being true, right, or good. Inductive inference is manifested in two ways: as a contribution to a conjecture or hypothesis, that is, as a contribution to abduction, and as the process of testing abductively projected and deductively elaborated potentials against actuality. The latter involves both testing the factual consonance of actuality with the posited logical relations of potentiality and the imposition on actuality of normatively selected, preferred relations. As will be developed later, inductive inference within the broader logical process must be intersubjectively completed to become socially manifest. This can happen in a vast variety of ways, including that of greatest relevance here, that of democratic discourse and its coordination forms.

Some of the preliminaries for understanding inductive inference were raised in the previous chapter regarding the bivalent format of cognitive order principles, their combination and transformation in immanent thirdness before their application to the world as the secondness of thirdness and the thirdness of secondness. Peirce describes this output of reason as taking the form of dicent symbols, where dicent is the secondness of thirdness and symbol is the thirdness of secondness (Peirce, 1903). Dicent symbols have the dyadic, p not p, form of secondness, but they have incorporated within them the triadic, justificatory form of thirdness. Dicent symbols are dyads presumed regular action/reaction patterns, but they emerge from triadic patterns of interpretation of natural or social objects. The dicent part has to do with the structural form of dyads – representations of facts that can only be valid or invalid – and the symbolic part, as the thirdness of secondness, has to

166    *Reasoning and Schemata in a Societal Frame*

do with the selective organization of these dyads to provide a stable pattern for organizing actuality.

In his 1902 application to the Cornegie Foundation, helpfully tabulated by Nööth, conception is the secondness of thirdness, the dicent, and representation, the symbol, is the thirdness of secondness. Conception thus refers to the propositional form of conceptions and the a priori capacities to advance them, while representation refers to those dicent symbols or dyads that emerge with the completion of thirdness and that take on coordinative powers in action contexts (Nööth, 2011). Nööth also tabulates the sign typology appearing a year later in Peirce's 1903 paper *Sundry Logical Conceptions*, where the secondness of thirdness is described as 'Signs of Secondness or Action, i.e., modes of conduct' and the thirdness of secondness is described as 'Facts of Thirdness, or Signs' (Peirce, 1998, 267–288). Putting these functionally similar typologies together, conceptions are associated with commitment to forms of conduct, and representations are the validated symbolic forms that show what acting out that conduct must concretely consist of. The conduct in question may be of many forms: ethical, moral, functional, defining, promising, committing, delegating, blaming, criticizing, and so on. The dicent provides the expressive rules that are substantively specified in the symbol. They are both enabled by the interpretation process accompanying the thirdness of thirdness, 'mind strictly' in the Carnegie application, part of whose function is to inductively generate valid propositions – or sets of interdependent propositions – whose manifest form is coordinative symbols or representation. Symbols are thus derived from their valid production. The symbols amount to regularized beliefs manifesting a valid social form, where once again it should be assumed that 'valid' does not necessarily mean 'just'.

The above provides the format of the scaffolding of actuality. According to Chevalier, Peirce shifted over the course of his career from an emphasis on thirdness as representation to thirdness as semiotization and inference (Chevalier, 2016). He may then be regarded as lying on, but also overcoming, the distinction drawn by Brandom between inferentialist and representational theories of mind (Brandom, 2000). In the end, he can accommodate both, with representation shifting over to the facts of secondness and with thirdness acquiring an inferential, modal form. The challenge for the social sciences and social philosophy is to put modality, not actuality, at the centre of their accounts while, of course, by no means neglecting the implications of those social and natural forces that come to structure actuality.

If 'mind strictly' or 'forms of thought' represent reasoning and open-ended possibility, then 'modes of conduct' represent rationalization in the Weberian tradition, which Habermas also uses for the encompassing idea of the rationalization of the lifeworld. The introduction of the concept of rationalization shows the material constraints that the stabilization of the social object world imposes on reasoning. Such a stabilization is vitally dependent on institutionalization as rationalization, in other words, the legitimacy and effectivity of the coordinating symbolic form. In modern terms, this process could be spoken about as creating path dependency that is frequently difficult to change, often with change only occurring over a

*Reasoning and Schemata in a Societal Frame* 167

significant period. This formulation is also applicable to Marx, for whom a self-defeating and unjust kind of capitalist rationalization was eminently crisis-prone, crisis-prone because the various kinds of rationalization, respectively in technological organization and social relations, are contradictory. Relevantly, Habermas also speaks in an analogous way of the rationalization of the lifeworld along the dimensions of culture, society, and personality. As expressed in the framework offered here, the rationalized lifeworld consists of regularized action competences along these dimensions. In Peirce's, and Bourdieu's, account, these competences would be stored as habits of action or instituted beliefs. The difference in levels between the triadic and cognitively open processes of thirdness and the relatively closed and dyadic forms of the thirdness of secondness also captures what Habermas means by the difference between reason and rationalization. In *TCA*, Habermas speaks of the problematization of the lifeworld, the cognitively active examination of previously background lifeworld 'certainties' in communicative action. Here, the equivalent in Peirce is more extensive, having to do with dynamic inferential relations within a sign typology that can accommodate a variety of rational phenomena such as beliefs, desires, intentions, meanings, perceptions, actions, and interactions. They are rational, as Habermas also saw, because they depend on attributed validity in the relevant dimensions, and in this sense understanding how this validity is attributed together with its reasonableness is essential to modal, normative, and social criticism.

One important facet of a theory of reasoning based on Peirce is that it can accommodate all levels of reasoning, internally reflective, intersubjective, and trans-subjective. His account of logic was not one based on terms (concepts), or propositions (judgements), even if these had their place, but one based on relations arising through inferential reasoning and argumentation. The foundation of this logic in the thirdness of thirdness rests on the encompassing quality of the sign of argument that shows how signs are connected in universes of meaning, in other words, on the systematic relations that extend between signs viewed as systems of meanings in a communication community. Hence, individuals can internally reason using inferential moves leading from sign to sign or sign to habit, whether reaching for a meaning beyond what exists – or what they as individuals believe exists – or reproducing validated facts. The same sequence of inferential moves that might be made internally by one individual could also be made between two interacting individuals. As individuals reason, individually or interactively, through the play of interpretants, they are building patterns of trans-subjective general validity that Peirce understands as the final logical interpretant, that which cognitively coordinates the interplay between actors. Such final interpretants are habits of interpretation that take on schematic forms at both subjective and intersubjective levels. Such forms coordinate validity, lending it coherence, but also, potentially pushing reasoning back into reconsideration of the underlying validity claims. In the architectonic being developed here, such interpretive habits, viewed intersubjectively, are ideals out of which goals are fashioned.

For Peirce, the interpretation process is guided by interpretants. An interpretant is a sign or habit that is determined by the textual context and preceding signs in

## 168 *Reasoning and Schemata in a Societal Frame*

the act of realizing many kinds of purposes. General meaning, meaning at the level of argument rather than at levels of propositions and terms, results in networks of meaning, or schemata. Some schemata are composed of interpretant relations or interpretant chaining of high probability, even sometimes certainty, which means that the 'interpretantation' process is logically 'secure' and likely to result in recurrent normative states, dispositions, and ultimately actions. Other emergent schemata, by contrast, are more tentative and give rise to ongoing doubt or contestation over the appropriate direction of thought and ultimately action. In these cases, the preferred direction of interpretants is not decided. The validity of claims rather than claims to validity defines the state of settled employment of interpretants, where claims to validity are what characterize states of uncertainty and/or disputation. There are different accounts of precisely how to understand the role of interpretants in Peirce's semiotic system. Here, bypassing an intriguing debate, I am going to use the convention of immediate, final, and dynamic interpretants. The immediate interpretant is a validity claim and accordingly has an affinity with abduction; the dynamic interpretant is an interpretation of the implications of a validity claim and has an affinity with induction; and the final interpretant is equivalent to a semiotically grasped regulative ideal that, in Peirce has, provides relevance criteria for reasoning and has an affinity with deduction.

The final logical interpretant following Peirce's example of what can be grasped by the phrase 'stormy day', both in terms of historically usage and possibilities (Peirce, 1931–1958, 8.314). It can be understood as all that can be agreed by interlocutors to bear on what valid interpretant paths should belong to the sign. As the issue is much more than logical cogency or linguistic coherence, it is the import of the sign in the widest sense of being (ibid). It operates therefore as a trans-subjective regulative ideal that serves as a kind of common denominator coordinating the play of meaning in dynamic interpretants, not unlike Brandom's scorekeeping, where dynamic interpretants are responses to propositions originally arising in the immediate interpretant. While, as is well known, not least from the interpretations of Apel and Habermas, Peirce also holds out the idea of 'finalization' of the state of knowledge on given issues in the long run, this by no means shows that, for him, consensus is the only necessary or even likely outcome. Indeed, the final interpretant may have a weak status characterized more by difference than agreement. The final interpretant therefore, in part, records the state of relations between different interpretations of a given object domain without any necessary presumption that there will or should be ultimate agreement between these interpretations. It further has the status of an idealization in the sense of progression towards a justifiable ideal, for example, factual truth or normative rightness.

This account of the final interpretant illustrates the essential triadic nature of Peirce's account of reasoning. In the later Peirce, the final interpretant did not necessarily mean final interpretation, though the ideal of final interpretation could be approximated. It could also mean the actual state of agreement on validity that could be realized at a given time within activities of cognitive thirdness, such as thinking, believing, accepting, agreeing, giving, and so on. While it is consistent with the idea of the fixation of belief to accept that belief cannot be endlessly

*Reasoning and Schemata in a Societal Frame*   169

indeterminate if a coordinated common life is to be achieved, there is nothing to say that such coordination cannot be achieved amidst plural viewpoints. Every interpretation of every sign within a universe of discourse adds or subtracts in some way from the level of agreement contained in the final interpretant. However, the emphasis on the play of differences and the dominance of distinctions should not be assumed so strongly as to distract from something equally fundamental. Social life must entail the capacity to coordinate differences within and between universes of discourse to induce some measure of agreement on what and how to think and act. The right kind of scholarship taken far enough can show that this does in fact happen, ultimately through recognition of the implications of transcendentally anchored cognitive principles and of ideals, the corresponding immanent generals. If this is recognized, and their power is demonstrated, it can be shown that these principles and ideals are not to be diminished, for they are among the most powerful forces in the universe.

Peirce resolutely opposed nominalism and its doctrine of common sense, especially the Cartesian assumption that doubt can be summoned at will. He set against it an account of reasoning that presumed 'real' origins of doubt arising from pre-existing beliefs coming under scrutiny. His philosophy of critical common-sensism went along with such actual foundations of doubting (Peirce, 1992, 109–123). Doubt leads to the questioning of belief in reasoning, thus establishing whether it is justified or not, and, if not, its replacement with a justified belief. However, this opening of the way, or the beginning of doubt, is not achieved by a process internal to reasoning but by surprising experience outside of reasoning that subsequently enters it as an abductive stimulus. The perceptual surprise of experience leading to new percepts is conditioned by existing 'unsurprising' beliefs – organized through secondness as habits of conduct of all kinds. Peirce makes clear that learning by surprising experience does not always result in reasoning; experience itself is an educator. Reasoning is a more extended, even elevated, practice that requires cognitive discipline and even special techniques, as, for example, in law, economics, or the various special sciences.

By contrast, he attributes the moral commitments of the public to sentiment rather than to reason. It was not his concern to truly explain what this sentiment consisted of. In this respect, it is not difficult to reflect on the fact that even in contemporary society many people hold moral positions that may be deemed to be justified according to some standard without the holders of the positions themselves being able to do so. The grounds of sentiment may be rational grounds, but the rationality so to speak is not directly achieved by the agents themselves. Rationality of whatever kind therefore must be understood as socially stored as well as directly achieved by involved agents. This in turn means that justified reasoning does not always have to be accomplished by agents who hold the commitments entailed by such reasoning. These commitments may instead arise from a sense of what is appropriate that derives from reasoning accomplished long before or, contemporaneously, by other agents, for example, in law, and stored in the organizing principles of society.

In *A Sketch of Logical Critics*, Peirce says that justification in reasoning is where one inference logically follows from another (Peirce, 1992, 451–462). Hence, it

## 170  *Reasoning and Schemata in a Societal Frame*

follows that an extended sequence of reasoning is justified when all inferences logically follow one another. The claim that inference is justified on such grounds does not mean that the reasoning clearly serves what is good or right for the interpreter, simply that it is logically sound. Even logically unsound reasoning, bad induction, for example, can appear justified, with corresponding social consequences, unless subject to criticism. Two points follow from this. The first is that experience may be taken up in reasoning, but that also it may not. Experience is a mode of learning that may go beyond what is already justified in reasoning – or in existing beliefs whether arising from reasoning or not – and independently ground a new belief. Something happens that incontrovertibly contradicts something previously held as justified. So, in this sense, experience can directly educate us. In more complex spheres of knowledge, beyond everyday practices, such experiences, though comprising knowledge, normally trigger further reasoning. For this, a new conjecture or projection is required whose validity may be tested; consistent with earlier terminology, a possibility is selected for examination. This selection is the process of *discovery*. Discovery rests upon the genetic significance of 'occult' qualities of mind resulting in the ability to see beyond anything that could logically be predicted on previous grounds. At the same time, discovery, beginning with and guided by abduction, entails the commencement of the further process of *logically* seeing beyond. Hence, inferential operations of logic fill in the initially vague 'discovery' and seek to ground it as justified belief, that is, knowledge. In this light, much work in critical theory only begins when discovery has already done its work or is assumed to have done its work. However, discovery is intrinsic to sociology, especially with its long-term and recently enhanced concern for the new (von Trotha, 2006). Discovery through abduction, building on the various steps of firstness, is also at the core of Peirce's theory of knowledge, providing ontological candidates – possibilities – for conversion by means of validated reasoning, ultimately inductively into applied knowledge, or actuals, of various kinds.

The second point arising is that reasoning may be defective, pathological, or at least challenged in a large variety of ways. Consider social objects such as the distribution of habitus relations in a social field. In the classical Peirce sense, signs mediate between such objects and interpretants. Confining attention to logical interpretants, that is, those used in reasoning, immediate, dynamic, and final, each of these interpretants makes sense of signs of objects – and hence of the objects themselves – by using the various kinds of inferences. Each of them is also set in relation to the others: the immediate interpretant to the dynamic interpretant in the context of the adjudicating final interpretant, and the dynamic to the immediate in the same context. The dynamic interpretant lives up to its name by having as many potential forms as possible interpretations. The final interpretant, as above, records the state of play of the relations between the dynamic interpretants with an impetus towards making abstract, that is, more general, sense, and ultimately fully justified validity. Habermas's account of yes/no validity claims can be partly set within Peirce's account of interpretants. The immediate interpretant of the speaker may be understood as a proposition raising a validity claim, that is, an abductive act. The interpreter may respond to this interpretant by agreeing

*Reasoning and Schemata in a Societal Frame* 171

with the responsive dynamic interpretant with this abduction, that is, accepting the validity claim of the immediate interpretant. Or the interpreter may disagree with the abductive claim of the speaker in the dynamic interpretant and develop in response a counter proposition, a new abduction. The interplay of these interpretants in reasoning potentially activates any component of Peirce's sign typology and sign relations; responsive interpretants thus can mobilize as interpretants signs other than logical interpretants, such as an index or an icon of some object. Such interpretants may serve as way stations for further reasoning activities of the recipient, but they also may not result in such activities due to reflexive and reasoning deficits on the part of the recipient in question. This way of thinking about 'interpretantation' is very important for critical thought. It suggests an asymmetrical power to produce certain kinds of interpretants. I will return to this theme later (Chapter 12) in discussing pathologies of reasoning.

Habermas's yes/no account of validity claims 'partly' mirrors Peirce's account of interpretants. Apart from the yes/no dimension, Habermas also emphasizes the moment of ideality associated with the unlimited communication community and the final interpretant. So, in this sense, Habermas's, like Peirce's, is a triadic conception, but it is not a completely convincing one. In the first instance, the articulation of the process of yes/no validity with that of shifting ideality – shifting because validity relations keep changing – is not well demonstrated, remaining something of a black box process. More seriously, the interpretant process in Peirce, unlike Habermas, is clearly and unambiguously both a medium and an outcome of reasoning. Crucially, it is a medium in the ever-present relational dynamic between possibility and actuality. It is an outcome in specifying those signs that variously settle validity claims, if they do indeed get settled, in the final interpretant and in the associated production of dicent symbols, also to be understood as various kinds of institutional rules. Due to this medium/outcome differentiation, there is permanent inter-operation between signs of possibility (and potentiality), necessity, and actuality. What Habermas has over Peirce is a clearer differentiation of the domains of validity, truth, rightness, and goodness. What is ultimately needed is a theory that emphasizes both and deals with the implications, something about which Habermas has recently made some suggestions that mark a start but are not by themselves sufficient (Habermas, 2019).

The various modes of inference that constitute the logic of relations are, as already suggested, all present in reasoning through logical interpretants. Provisionally bringing together the modes of inference with forms of the logical interpretant, abductive inference has an affinity with the immediate interpretant, inductive inference with the dynamic interpretant, and deductive inference with the final interpretant. Abduction adds a radical new premise and/or innovatively combines universes of discourse through identifying hitherto undeveloped inferential relations. Or induction also adds a hitherto unobserved premise or finds that the world is not consistent with the argumentation schema of abduction/deduction, possibility/necessity, as developed. Deductive conclusions can be changed on the basis of additional premises, and deduction across different universes of discourse is inherently challenging and constitutively unstable (Peczenik, 2008). The process

## 172  *Reasoning and Schemata in a Societal Frame*

of reasoning adds variation to inferential relations and results in shifts in interpretant relations, which, when extended over very large 'texts', ultimately involve a change in the order of discourse, including theories. Ampliative forms of reasoning, induction and abduction, through their respective world relations, are drivers of change, a change that deductive inference attempts to integrate through building and strengthening valid final interpretants.

Along with Habermas, modern normative philosophical approaches that have acquired traction within critical theory, such as Forst's account of justification and Honneth's account of recognition, can also be addressed within this Peirceian framework. If logical reasoning, on the one hand, is understood as using interpretants ('interpretantation') and the outcomes are 'chained' relations of interpretants in various schemas and models, then the justification paradigm emphasizes the reasoning process and the recognition paradigm its cultural ideal outcomes, which are also structuring inputs to further reasoning. The justification paradigm de-emphasizes the interpretant formation dimension and recognition theory correspondingly de-emphasizes the reasoning dimension. Nonetheless, both require, as does Habermas, that the focus be extended to include not only Peirce's predominant focus on truth but also that of Habermas on rightness and goodness. The essence of such a shift, anticipated by Peirce but not developed, is that the focus of the final interpretant, of transcendentally conditioned but immanent ideals, should also be addressed in relation to ideals of rightness and – in some respects – goodness. Habermas is right to think that the basic architecture of the theory can accommodate these discourses, at least those of truth and rightness, though the discourse of rightness does entail different considerations from that of truth that amount to a significant change (Habermas, 2019). The outcome of the theory in the second case requires normative intervention in the world and not only explanation of what is functionally operative in the world. For the discourse of rightness, reasoning has to do with the cognitive construction of what is right, as opposed to simply taking over normative ends from actual practices and using them as guides.

The latter also happens as the structural presupposition of both changed perception and reasoning, but the reasoning process, directed by the imagined possibilities that form before it properly starts, has consequences in bringing about legal, moral, and ethical potentials that in turn have direct implications for conduct. These implications must take account of the normative facticity of the world, but they are not bound by it. As Habermas mentions repeatedly in *Auch eine Geschichte*, innovation is brought about through learning processes (Habermas, 2019). Transposing this here, learning is a property of thirdness and is thus a manifestation of the power of reason.

Reasoning in the tradition of Peirce by no means operates within stable parameters. Van Eemereen, Grootendorst, and Grootendorst draw attention in their account of argumentation to the deeply recessed pragmatic premises that remain unexpressed, and for whose scholarly – or non-scholarly – identification deep exploration is required (van Eemeren et al., 2004). Even then, many could not be stated with complete certainty. For this, the construct of validity in formal logic is too strong. This is generally relevant to Peirce's semiotics, which offers an encompassing pragmatic frame that qualifies formal validity, more and more as his career went on, and applies to questions of both truth and rightness. Thus, normative learning processes depend on a vast range of conditions, such as instinct, guesswork, hope, chance, intelligence, nature, volition, and multiple other kinds of time-space contingencies. These conditions matter for normative learning and yet are very different from established models of law and democracy that privilege just procedures or constitutional texts. It is not that the above-listed conditions do not appear in formal arenas of rightness, but that they also and more fundamentally appear in non-formal, extra-institutional arenas. The hope of democracy has always been that collective intelligence can be sufficiently manifested so as to adjust to the ever-emerging new challenges and build or continue, in Peirce's term, states of 'concrete reasonableness' (Bidet et al., 2013). The challenge of the theory of society is to first adequately describe the state of the contemporary world, not just as it might seem to be but as it is becoming, and then to show how normatively it can evolve in a better way, keeping in mind that no description proceeds without some normative presuppositions. This does not mean that no normative progress has hitherto been made, nor does it deny the existence of good normative ideas that have not been adequately or at all realized. Yet, to develop an adequate description of society *in its becoming* is a prerequisite for bringing appropriate normative ideas to bear to determine a just becoming. Nonetheless, considered from the vantage point of critical theory, even to identify possible directions of becoming a just and good society inescapably entails normatively relevant activities of 'feeling' the pulse of just and good – or unjust – social change as a necessary prelude for the equally necessary activity of exploring and instituting them in knowledge formations.

**Interpretants, Schemata, and Social Theory**

The previous section began the task of addressing the relationship between the process of reasoning and the formation of interpretants. In this section, more is said about the nature of interpretants viewed from the vantage point of a general social theory. The idea lying behind the account is that, over time, interpretants can come to express regularity of meaning. This regularity of meaning is the product of justification (validation) processes that can be designated 'good' or 'bad' against a specified normative standard, whether the process of fixing valid interpretations is intellectual, popular, or both. Such normative standards are also interpretants. Interpretants are the product of signification in all its aspects, even if only in reasoning are they consciously considered as far as that proves possible at given times and places. Interpretants achieve stability through forming enduring signs of secondness. In line with the doubt/belief model of Peirce, they can become de-stabilized in episodes of doubting, where contradictory or different qualities of designated objects emerge compared to the existing interpretant forms and habits of action of secondness (Paolucci, 2021). Interpretants in this second sense, where there is recurrent channelling of signs and interpretants to generate regularity of outcome, are to be distinguished from the process of 'interpretantation' that occurs in reasoning.

174  *Reasoning and Schemata in a Societal Frame*

In this latter process, interpretants have a provisional status amidst the flux of argumentation. In interpretantation, some initially 'resonant' interpretants do not acquire regularity over time, whereas others do. The concept of interpretant is closely allied to that of habit – habits of action are concatenated interpretants that take on embodied form, individually and also culturally in the sense of the cultural embodiment of reason.

The concept of interpretant has great value for social theory, even if it is little used. In systems theory and Rosa's social theory, the concept of resonance is preferred, but interpretant has both much in common with it and is susceptible to high levels of analytic differentiation (Rosa, 2021). The location of societal, coordinating interpretants is the thirdness of secondness, the place of symbolic forms and associated habits of action. Interpretants that acquire symbolic stability mainly – become recurrent with small variations – are analogous to what is commonly called substantive dimensions of social theory, as distinct from those interpretants immediately associated with the *generative* activity of reasoning. The latter, by contrast with the substantive and recurrent, lies at the processual pole. Accordingly, innovative interpretants that emerge within processes of reasoning from conjectures striving to give coherence and legitimacy to the initial vagueness of an idea engage stable interpretants locked into stable, recurrent kinds, potentially changing them. The fact that stable interpretants, recurrent 'interpretant sets' such as ideals and norms, exist in relational forms that can become fluidized in reasoning and other cognitive processes does not mean they cannot impose regular effects at certain times and places. It is the combination of the two dimensions of interpretants, those that are bound up with reasoning and those that exert habitual force, that makes the concept so productive. This means that norms do not have to be identified as determining reasoning, nor can their social effectivity be denied by over-emphasizing interpretive fluidity. Peirce's model of signification, as outlined, renders both approaches reductive. The emphasis on regularized interpretants also reveals the nature of symbolic power, where it is precisely the regularized imposition of interpretants as belief commitments that enable various kinds of domination. Of course, merely pointing out that interpretants have power effects does not explain how they acquire those effects.

The generation of interpretants does not all happen through active reasoning in the sense that all could fully justify their beliefs, that is, habits of action, or that at least they could reconstruct the patterns of inference that led them to the belief. Instead, habits of action and dispositions to follow rules of certain kinds can be historically generated by long-distant reasoning – or other kinds of cognitive practice – and simply survive into the present in a way that nobody fully justifies, for example, certain signs of nations referring to a primordial past that never existed but which is nonetheless taken to have present implications (Hedetoft, 1995). There are also multiple kinds of pathological reasoning in which, variously, an agent or agents deceive themselves, some agents deceive others, or a range of agents disorient one another. More can be said on any of these complexes, which will be given further attention later. Paolucci also makes the acute point that Peirce's is less a theory of truth in reasoning than it is a theory of meaning linked to action (Paolucci, 2021). The implication is that, in many cases, agents cannot justify precisely why they act. They also act in ways that stand opposed to what they could justify in terms of truth, rightness, and goodness. This also shows the types of challenges that a sociological account of practical reason must face. It is not able to simply postulate moral obligations, being tasked also with addressing interfering conditions of many kinds that block moral or other kinds of appropriate action, while also facing the further challenge of specifying why it is appropriate, considering the multiple implications of practical reason in action.

From a social theoretical point of view, interpretants become concatenated into certain kinds of schemata or cultural models. The various kinds of cultural models that are pertinent to the normative coordination of society are introduced below. The three kinds of logical interpretants – immediate, dynamic, and final – have an affinity with the three kinds of inferences used in reasoning. This also allows the further identification of three kinds of compatible sources of schema-building given the intrinsic relationship between interpretant and schema, where schemata are themselves pathways that follow from previously validated interpretants over time, leading to the schematic pattern or structure.

Abductive inference, associated with the immediate interpretant, relies on a schema of feelings and abductive imagination. Later, I will distinguish this as a particular kind of 'quasi-schema', as it consists of the introduction of potentials into other schemas, where these potentials take the form of schematic variations. The play of innovation, selection, and stabilization involves the continuous interplay of feelings, reasons, and facts. The leading principle of abductive inference is the indefinite capacity to 'reason beyond' towards an ultimate validity that can never be attained but towards which knowledge may tend. It is associated with the immediate interpretant or validity claim. Deductive inference, associated with the final interpretant, draws from the transcendental cognitive schema of the cognitive order the claim to general cognitive validity of 'limit concepts'. The leading principle of deductive inference is accordingly those general principles on the basis of which reasoning proceeds. The validity of such reasoning, which can become effective in many different kinds of reasoning at many different levels, is not only formal but also allows situational elements to enter in as is also the case with Toulmin's warrants. These transcendental cognitive schemata become effective 'for us' as CCMs or immanent ideals Inductive inference, associated with the dynamic interpretant, is composed of the spectrum of interpretations of those cognitive ideals that become discursively manifest, ideals that as expressed in turn draw off the higher-level transcendent cognitive principles (validity concepts). The leading principle of inductive inference is accordingly approximation to an ideal towards which knowledge tends but which it never fully attains. The various schemata or cultural models associated with the above kinds of inferential processes act as a prelude to reasoning, on the one hand, localizing the relevance spectrum in various ways, and, on the other hand, guiding inductive reasoning and ultimately habits of action or norms that emerge from it.

In the original account of critical cognitive sociology by Strydom, and further elaborated on in my own work of 2013, the concept of cultural model or schema played an important role (O'Mahony, 2013, Strydom, 2011). Speaking to my own earlier work here, the idea of reasoning was partly, though far from fully, developed and related to that of the cultural model. Elsewhere, following D'Andrade, I 'distinguished' between cultural model and schema, with schema being understood as that used by a single actor, individual or collective, and models as the combination

## 176 *Reasoning and Schemata in a Societal Frame*

of such schemata (d'Andrade, 1995; O'Mahony, 2019). Strydom had originally taken over and developed Touraine's concept of cultural model with his idea of a societal stake contested over by two contending parties, for example, an older one of capital vs. labour and a newer one of technocracy vs. new social movements (Touraine, 1981; Strydom, 2000; Ballantyne, 2007).

This kind of critical cognitive sociology has emphasized two kinds of cultural models that would be comprehended as primarily inductive according to the distinctions offered just above: one more abstract and ideal, the cognitive cultural model (CCM), and another more substantive and concrete, the sociocultural model (SCM). I will go into the nature of these models in more detail shortly. At the most general level of coordinating the social world, these cultural models are not necessarily competing but frequently complementary, though operating at different levels. Through their respective forms, they structure the pragmatic orientation and semantic content of the social world. They are what is ordinarily understood to comprise the institutional features of culture, though they here play a distinctive semiotic function.

I am assuming that there are three such models, to which allusion has already been made above, comprising the CCMs and SCMs, and one other, the institutional model (IM). All these models are components of what Peirce understood in the 1903 triadic-triad account of signs as *the symbol*, the thirdness of secondness. The third model, the IM, is more specific to Peirce's understanding of the symbol. This model is close to action and contains beliefs that regularly result in actions of various kinds. In the account provided here, the additional models, the CCMs and SCMs, are introduced to fill the space, the actual, operational space, between formal thirdness, the signs that both build and interrogate schemata, and the teleological and normative levels of the socially operational schemata themselves.

The schemata, or cultural models, thus interpose in the space between indefiniteness and definitiveness. Definiteness is the characteristic of Peirce's *symbol*, taking the form of a validated set of non-contradictory factual relations, or relations at least assumed to be non-contradictory given the reasoning employed. The assumption of the non-contradictory becomes suspended in reasoning thirdness, and this suspension is captured through the form of the two additional models lying above the symbol just described: the more abstract CCM cultural models of teleological directedness following the ends of reasonableness and the more concrete SCM models that symbolically order various forms of coordination ranging from agreement to disputation, sometimes with provisional settlement between enduring 'fronts'. These two additional models, above the *symbol*, where the latter is here understood as the IM, the institutional model, thus give space for ends that are 'higher' than that of definite capacity for action represented in the validated beliefs contained in this IM. These cultural models, more indefinite than the IM but still normatively conditioned to some degree, specify relational templates for cognitive and symbolic practices, respectively, of ideal relevance and of the coordination of goals. The IM is a type of culminating model characterized by definite beliefs. Within this may be found a schema of action in which certain conditions will routinely trigger certain actions or reactions in agents. At this level, we reach 'down' to Bourdieu's idea of the habitus and the ingrained dispositions that decide types of action. Thus, there are four kinds of schema to be

*Reasoning and Schemata in a Societal Frame* 177

found in the general process of *actualization*, respectively guiding an ideal orientation, a goal orientation, a normative orientation, and an action orientation.[3] The next steps of the text will address three of these schemata in more detail, leaving out the last, the concrete context of action with the mobilization of habitual resources in pursuit of goals. The latter exclusion is simply a decision derived from available space, but it will enter the remaining text at many points.

## Coordinative Models and Schemata

The above three cultural models, along with the agent schema, are here described as 'output' schemata. They are outputs in the sense of rationalized outcomes of reasoning processes that progressively facilitate greater consistency of action, ranging from greater openness in CCMs to greater closure in institutional and actor models. In this respect, they are to be distinguished from 'input' schema formation, which I assume to accompany logical processes of abduction. Such input schemata will be addressed separately below in the concluding section.

The so-called output schemata at issue right now as various kinds of action-orienting and coordinating schemata have attracted the greater attention in the social sciences. Output schemata in these disciplines generally correlate with empirical-theoretical knowledge, though they are not merely constructs of the social sciences but are also actual cultural structures at work in society, including the various understandings of institutional orders. In one sense, the cultural models can be more than empirical-theoretical knowledge in that they operate beyond what is currently known through social scientific investigation. In another sense, empirical-theoretical knowledge can also reveal more than what is manifest to societal participants. This latter sense of offering more than what is apparent to participants provides the rationale for the intellectual reconstruction of cultural models, including the degree to which potential for normative innovation can be associated with them. Such innovation owes its directional thrust to the generative orientation provided by the input schemata of perception and abduction but must confront the path-embeddedness and power structures 'legitimated' in some way or other by the 'output' models and the institutional, including material, arrangements they have helped bring about and consolidate, which in turn consolidates them.

The account of these output models provided below will only touch on a fraction of what a full account of legal-political models of these kinds would consist of. It identifies the basic forms of these models rather than the shifting constellations associated with issues and, above the issues, the general normative culture that conditions them. Socially relevant output schemata, especially collective schemata like cultural models, are closely aligned to reasoning processes, together with other cognitive modalities such as developing conjectures, narrative revelation, and the unreasoned power of certain sentiments. Yet, as models with the relatively high patterns of endurance, they stabilize certain kinds of reasoning in the sense of socially aligning patterns of feeling, reasons, and facts that have a degree of consistency over time and space. From an inferential standpoint, output models are not to be understood only as templates that encode and organize 'data' about relevant worlds

## 178   *Reasoning and Schemata in a Societal Frame*

while themselves remaining relatively unchanging. They are instead dynamic relational fields of meaning that engage with possibilities, reasoning, and actuality.

They are output orders as action-orientating beliefs of various kinds that are embedded in relatively stable relational webs of objects and processes. As an output order, they ultimately conduce to habits of doing, anchored in common dispositions, reasons, and factual claims. Such a structure may be envisaged as composed on the societal level of models, for example, as generalized belief structures that take their form by virtue of existing in a common field with other opposing – or, at least, alternative – such structures. There is a vast multitude of such schemata/ models in operation in society. In relatively recent sociological literature, at least the space of such output models of this kind is present in Habermas, Touraine, and Bourdieu, though not explicitly. In *TCA*, both social systems and the symbolically structured lifeworld are reference points that correspond to the space of these cultural models.

The problem with Habermas's presentation of the lifeworld, viewed as a cultural model in the sense intended here, is that it lacks an intrinsic oppositional structure and thus tends towards overgeneralized idealization of background convictions without demonstrating their genesis and variation. Accordingly, though aligned with Habermas's emphasis on communicative reasoning, the concept of lifeworld does not convincingly demonstrate how the outcomes of such reasoning make their way into the three kinds of rationalized structures associated with that concept: those of culture, society, and personality. In other words, it does not show how reasoning leads to rationalization in these dimensions, or not. Somewhat differently, Touraine understands cultural models as conflictual and, at the highest level, part of the struggle of social movements to gain control over the direction of society. The conflictual structures he discerns within what are here called cultural models therefore exist at a very high level; for example, the opposition between two contending forces such as capital and labour over a societal stake leaves open the question of what is happening at lower levels (Touraine, 1981). Bourdieu's account of habitus and field does potentially extend to a wide range of social fields and offers both conflict- and power-based coordination models. The power/discourse nexus is nonetheless so strong that the different levels and kinds of discourse are diminished, leading to a failure to address reasoning with transformative normative goals.

Nonetheless, notwithstanding some of the limitations of these theories viewed in terms of an account of cultural dynamics and structures, they cumulatively take us a long way and point in the direction of a cognitively grounded theory of society. The above observations on the output side of schema theory in relation to a theory of reasoning can be turned around on the input side. Such is the case with Habermas's idea of the problematization of the lifeworld, more implicitly with Touraine's account of the battle for historicity, and in Bourdieu's account of the dispositional structures of 'habituses' set within contested fields. As Habermas recently observed, Peirce offers a model for the communicative integration of society, which, in his view, offers a basis for general normative integration beyond the mere assertion of plural perspectives (Habermas, 2019). The normative integration

*Reasoning and Schemata in a Societal Frame*  179

derives from the process of generating intersubjectively justified belief from reasonable doubt, doubt arising from the ground of existing beliefs, and not the radical doubt of modern scepticism with its assumption that nothing has gone before.

Extending this to the theory of schemata, both input (generative) and output (orienting) ones are apparent in Peirce's doubt/belief model and also in *Sundry Logical Conceptions* (Peirce, 1998 267–288). Addressing specifically the output models, their implications for reasoning can be stylized as either moderate or strong. If political models, say left/right for simplicity, are kept in mind, issues arise that trigger schematic responses on either side. In a moderate response, dispositions (reflecting settled feelings), reasons, and normative-factual orientations remain relatively aligned and can be adapted to deal with a contentious issue – for example, a new index of increasing poverty – while remaining within previously identifiable structuring parameters. In a strong response, of the kind that is perceptible in social arrangements for some time now, the existing schematic structure of left/right has come under tremendous pressure and its original relational formatting has begun to dissolve. This does not mean it has disappeared entirely, but it has become significantly recast. For example, a left-liberal model a half-century ago would scarcely have noticed let alone made central such considerations, now regarded as vital, as those of race, gender, and cosmopolitanism. These latter remarks are purely illustrative. A satisfactory account of political model change would have to go far beyond them. The implication for the relational structure of models is that, when confronted with strong perturbations that threaten their continuation, reasoning with wide societal resonance assumes a pivotal role. In the next section, I will outline the nature of these coordinative, output cultural models from the standpoint of a critical cognitive sociology. While these models are not described in their fullness, their architectonic significance for the advancement of a critical theory of society is demonstrated in their outline. These coordinative cultural models reflect the general thrust of the theorizing in the book. In a sense, they occupy the broad space of structure in sociology, even if this has been subject to considerable alteration. The direction of this change is to emphasize the interpretive uncertainty now assumed to characterize those structural forces that were once thought to be reliably causally determining. This applies to both general structural theory and institutional theory. The task of finding *some* order in the dynamic variation of social forces has replaced that of identifying *some* change within general order.

The approach taken here is certainly more grounded in the first of the above-mentioned tasks, but it does not neglect the older emphasis on the causal power of structures. The growth of interpretive openness is taken as a basic premise, but the relative closure of such openness in contexts of actions, decisions, and power imbalances cannot be ignored. Moreover, the underlying premise is that interpretive openness must be balanced with the cognitive and normative coordination of a common social life. At any level, such commonness requires capacity for generalization and endurance in social organization. The balancing of these tendencies is reflected in the cognitive sociological account of the basic coordinative models described below. This account of models is designed to be complementary to the general idea of bringing about a reasonable society.

180    *Reasoning and Schemata in a Societal Frame*

The coordination models described below range from abstractly general in the case of the CCM, through the coordinative modalities of the SCM, to concretely specific in the case of the IM. These models are meant to characterize the range of immanent normative ends that have made possible social coordination at various levels. They have an affinity with Kant's concept of the understanding, delineating the structure of knowledge in the movement from abstract to concrete, but they also with Peirce, and to some degree also Hegel, capture the reverse movement from concrete to abstract. They come after the input schematizing of abduction as well as providing cognitive foundations for all possible forms of knowing. In the next three steps of this chapter, I will outline these models in turn. Somewhat counter-intuitively, as it comes first in the sequence of generating meaning and validity, I will afterwards address abductive schematization in a further step. The rationale for following this order is to firstly follow what is most familiar in the general understanding of society, the output models, before then addressing its most implicitly operating and less clearly identified generative conditions of possibility in the input or process model.

### *Ideals as Cognitive Cultural Models*

The most abstract of the output models is the CCM, which has been associated with the ultimate logical interpretant in the Peirce architectonic of signification. This is the level of immanent cognitive generals, basic conceptual elements of thinking that derive from the transcending, evolutionarily established cognitive principles and that have been established as ideals to be striven for. They thus follow from initial processes of abductive/deductive schema formation that represent learning processes extended over time. The ultimate logical interpretant, as will be shown, captures the 'pragmatic' balance that stands between various argumentative positions. It represents the frame – or combination of frames – that makes the argument meaningful, for example, the frame of legitimacy on a political matter. It thus consists of outer boundaries of relevant statements, what is relevant to say within the semantic space of the ideal discourse. The argumentation positions are the spectrum of dynamic interpretants that take up the issue of legitimacy of a particular political act within the frame.

There is a further type of logical interpretant that lies beyond the ultimate interpretant in the above sense. It is the final logical interpretant. The final logical interpretant involves the limited concepts pertaining to transcendental ideas of reason, and it thus also pertains to the formation of abductive schemata in reasoning, whereas the ultimate logical interpretant pertains to schemata that participants can immanently recognize. Even if its horizons can never fully be reached, this is consistent with the inductive leading principle of approximation discussed earlier. It is the ultimate logical interpretant, the ideal interpretant, which is of immediate concern here, though they are at the end oriented by transcendentally anchored cognitive principles. The ideal of democracy, for example, involves selection from a variety of relevant, transcendental cognitive principles. Each of these cognitive principles 'codifies' distinctive reasoning capacities, for example, legitimacy, legality, solidarity, equality, freedom, and so on. This entails that agents both have an a priori sense of relevance and a capacity for logical argument for each of these

*Reasoning and Schemata in a Societal Frame* 181

principles and for using them in combination. These principles, and the capacities they represent, lie on the collective level in the sense that individuals are not born with them but acquire them as the evolving, collective, cultural a priori of the human form of life. They are thus culturally stored on the societal level not in individual minds. Ideals are a level down from such principles. They arise from the capacity to generate relevant possibilities and to logically select those that should be valid. Their form bears on the concrete social goals, yet as *anticipatory* forms, they exist before the goals. The activity of pursuing the goals over time results in shifts in the ideals consistent with the doubt-belief cycle. Such change can happen slowly, but at times, ongoing developments may be crystallized rapidly. Forst's account of the genesis and legitimacy of the ideal of general tolerance serves as a good example (Forst, 2013). Once formed, such an ideal can be opposed or denied, like any ideal, but it has nonetheless remained a normatively essential component of democracy, guiding practical discourse with its spectrum of opportunities and constraints.

Ideals should thus be distinguished from the transcendent cognitive principles that provide their conditions of possibility. In effect, immanent ideals take over the orientations provided by the cognitive principles, as stimulated by abductive conjectures, and then offer a 'teleology' of the cultural space regulating social life. In this process, it is the immanent ideals that change, not the overarching cognitive principles. The cognitive principles are evolutionarily stabilized and they change only very slowly. They are general and 'supermultitudinous' in the sense of being open to numberless interpretations. They are also acritical in sense of being involuntary, though they are also necessary. The ideals, by contrast, are critical in the sense of being contested attempts to occupy a determining cultural terrain, in other words, the attempt to specify the relevant cultural considerations that attend to human purposes. Yet, it is not only contestation, going against a contemporary tendency in certain social scientific and normative approaches. Contestation can also become resolved into consensus over certain interpretations of ideals. The consensus in question at the level of this model, the CCM, is not ultimate moral or functional consensus. It is 'only' the type of cognitive consensus that makes such further normative kinds of consensus possible, even if there is no ultimate and unchanging consensus, but only a consensus that can approach higher levels of agreement or 'finalization'.

Ideals are here understood as CCMs, and they are ultimately the expression of what has come to be deemed socially relevant. All types of societies have ideals of this kind. Only in democratic societies, following Habermas's extension of Peirce here, can these ideals, at least in principle, be established by means of an inclusive collective process. In fact, while all known democratic societies fall very far short of this standard, they remain capable of forming – but also regressing behind – a type of selective democratic model. Such a model involves a type of decision about a democratic space, a decision, or a series of rolling decisions, that is highly diffuse. The decision grants cognitive validity, that is, validity for legitimate pursuit, to a wide variety of ideals. The CCM in democratic societies, enjoying some measure of basic agreement, can be conceptualized as a vast loom of linked arguments, where

## 182 *Reasoning and Schemata in a Societal Frame*

each of the arguments is granted legitimacy *as an argument*. Together, they form a cultural model of what is validly *conceivable* within a democracy – the space of democratic reasons. These apply both to the deontic spaces of general rights and responsibilities as well as the specific, essential procedures of democracy itself.

CCMs of high generality, such as the democratic, implicate normative standards, in their selection, combination, and activation conditions. To speak of them being CCMs is therefore true, but nonetheless, they are also normatively restricted. Effectively, they have outer normative boundaries to their relevance. For example, few would assert that absolutely no consideration of equality should be considered in society. That such a view is practically unthinkable today prescribes the outer normative boundary of the ideal of equality. For the ideal of legitimacy, equally, few would assert that rulers should do absolutely what they want in democratic societies. Either of these extreme commitments would quickly undermine any semblance of democracy whatsoever, which has, of course, happened and could happen again. Ideals are thus cognitively open but normatively constrained in their operational sphere. The cognitive form, in addition to the normative constraint, canalizes reasoning into discourses that form the relevant horizons of democracies. The normative constraint is relatively 'light', not at this level specifying what concrete normative goal should be pursued but only what it is reasonable to raise. For example, the discourse of ecological responsibility has made its way into CCMs of democracy over the last half-century or so, and this implies that ecology, even ecological responsibility is legitimate to raise, though it may – and does – mean very different things, but also that there is no guarantee it has any significant effect on societal culture or policy output. The latter claim, the lack of effect, is not true of the example, but the degree of the effect remains open to further normative argumentation at 'lower', norm-building, and norm-setting levels on each of the respective lower models. Thus, ecological responsibility defines a cognitive space of ideal relevance that does not foreclose on how it may be normatively argued for or what institutional goals and cultural beliefs are justified. The normative levels, especially the SCM level, have their own autonomy. These levels exert normative constraint on the higher level of ideals, but this still leaves much space for further elaboration and innovation at this higher level. Nonetheless, the normative constraint can mean quite a lot; for example, in 'stronger' discourses like legal equality, the normative constraint is much tighter, even if much remains cognitively open in this instance too.

The democratic CCM, which is ever highly variable in actual democracies, is best understood as a *relational* cognitive model. To restate, it is a compendium of all positions that are generally accepted to be valid – in the light of general validity standards – within the space of an ideal (Forst, 2007). Such positions are those that all can accept as *validly asserted*. Validity asserted means that it is universally recognized that every such statement stands within the space of democratic culture is guided by democratically relevant immanent ideals of reason selected from overarching transcendent ideas of reason as the latter are activated in firstness before explicit formulation in abduction. Everything that can validly be asserted within a normatively circumscribed spectrum may be asserted. Such a spectrum presupposes agreement on what comprises a democratic

*Reasoning and Schemata in a Societal Frame* 183

normative culture, that is, agreement on certain orienting ideals, though there is almost invariably disagreement over the respective practical implications of all but the most basic. Even the general efficacy of the most basic constitutional and human rights and procedures can, at the margins of democracy, become threatened when democracy itself becomes threatened as a general cognitive-normative order.

The cognitive element is intrinsic to CCMs, since they are to be understood as cognitively open and only weakly normatively restricted, both in the sense of relevance criteria and of agreement to disagree. The 'agreement' in this sense has affinities with the idea of a basic structure of justification outlined by Rainer Forst (Forst, 2007). It operates as a weak normative force that allows multiple points of view to be legitimately expressed. New valid positions may always be added to the relational structure of the CCM or ideals may expand, for example, where equality reaches beyond distributive justice issues. Fundamentally, these ideals are cognitive in that they make possible a space of reasoning. The ideals are of the nature of 'why reasoning in the relevant dimension is required', 'what to reason about as characterized by the ideal' and 'how to reason' within a given discourse. To illustrate this further, take the example again of the ideal of equality within the conditions of democracy. Within the space of this ideal, a challenging experience first may involve the activation of pertinent feelings, for example, shock, anger, compassion, sympathy, and so on. These are immediate sensations, qualities of feelings that a situation brings to the fore, as in a perception of inequality. Impelled by feelings such as these, a conjecture is formed. In accordance with the doubt/belief model, the conjecture takes account of previous beliefs, attempting to move beyond them in some way. In this way, it is theory reconstructing since the pre-existing beliefs also rest on a theory of some kind.

The pre-existing theory, or range of possible theories that have effects on conduct, is what Peirce calls the 'fixing of belief' (Peirce, 1992). His account in this respect, though inspiring, is brief. For present purposes, all that needs to be said is that the theory is contained in the structuring of interpretants by means of existing output-side models. Specific theories also encounter other competing theories. It takes a very long time, cultural evolutionary time, to establish an ideal from such theoretical competition in its relation both to other ideals and the corresponding stabilization of action orientations. Thus, how the ideal of equality evolves with respect to the relevant environment of other ideals must be considered, together with its implications for schemata and models that are more 'concrete' than the CCM. Theory reconstruction occurs through a doubt-driven, critically elaborated, and challenging conjecture that potentially reorients reasoning processes. Conjectures and responses occur within the frame of an ideal and potentially change the guiding structure played by an ideal or set of ideals. The conjecture is the generative schema (the immediate interpretant), the ideal is the overarching cognitive schema (the ultimate interpretant, the CCM), and the action orientations comprise the substantive schema (dynamic interpretant, the SCM), advancing interpretations of the ideal. Ultimately, some results of this interplay lead to norm selection and thence habitual conduct, the IM.

## 184  *Reasoning and Schemata in a Societal Frame*

### *Structured Disputation: Substantive Cultural Models*

A second output schema is the substantive schema or substantive cultural model (SCM). As suggested above, this model is characterized by the play of dynamic interpretants. Such play occurs within the cognitive, coordinating space ideal order produced on the CCM level. So, for example, within a CCM of liberal democracy that enjoys the kind of minimal normative agreement advanced above, a corresponding SCM might comprise a political-cultural division such as the left/right split. This is purely an example, and such a 'neat' order should not be assumed as normal, at least not since the political de-alignment beginning in the 1980s. If there is no or very limited agreement on what should constitute a democratic CCM, or whether such a CCM is even desirable, then there cannot be a corresponding stable ordering of the SCM. The contemporary United States, characterized by constitutional disagreement – in the widest possible sense – provides a good example and serves perhaps as a harbinger of unruly times to come.

As with CCMs, SCMs are both reproduced and changed by forms of reasoning, where reasoning is given a wide reading to include pathological or unfair reasoning[4] and reasoning that has become reified over time. Typically, in the political realm, the variety of dynamic interpretants interpreting democratic ideals as a whole or an element within the democratic space of reasons, such as legitimacy or tolerance, can at certain times and places stand far apart or only be made 'closer' by suppression of dissenting opinion. Yet, at other times and places, consensus and rational dissensus over these ideals and their practical translation may be far-reaching. The CCM of democracy illustrates the power of political normative idealization to relatively bind itself off from the non-democratic context in which democracy must operate and thereby to create a specifically democratic 'normative force' in society. In previous work, I have sought to show how SCMs are organized through different coordinative modalities that make social and functional power central if by no means completely determining. The coordinative modalities that assume – and practically sustain – imbalances of power are compromise, hegemony, and zero sum polarization. Coordinating modalities that by contrast depend to a high degree on communicative power are those of consensus and rational dissensus (O'Mahony, 2013).

Frequently, SCMs reflect conditions in which the ultimate interpretant, the spectrum of relevant ideals in the CCM pertinent to a given discourse, may be interpreted in a variety of ways that cannot easily be reconciled. The cognitive relevance of ideals may be disputed in that there may be disagreement on what range of ideals apply and which should have priority. Anticipated in the idea of the CCM in the first place, normative differences over the interpretation of ideals, though not necessarily the ideals themselves, will often play an important role, in fact, such an important role that they tend to define the polarities of a political culture. The forms that these polarities take are expressed in the dominant modalities, whether, for example, they are at the agreement or conflict end of the spectrum, and the way opposing positions are aligned.

Commonly, the SCM follows the pattern of what political scientists describe as a cleavage structure, in other words, two dominant but opposed positions.

*Reasoning and Schemata in a Societal Frame*    185

Such opposing positions generate recurrent, opposing dynamic interpretants. Yet, this opposition frequently takes a relatively stable form rather than a chaotic one, though a stable form may be far from benign. Usually, this takes the form of a dominant tradition and a more or less influential opposing position, taking the form of binaries, such as, following Touraine's account of cultural models, capital/labour or technocrats/new social movements (Touraine, 1981). Stability within difference is also maintained in given epochs by the operation of certain agreed-upon or consensual modalities within the cultural model. So, a given left/right cultural model will be structured predominantly by the force of opposition, but, classically, it will also have in common the model of industrial society itself, the commitment to growth, the belief in strict scientific rationality, as well as accumulated legal norms and societal conventions, including constitutionally specified procedural norms built up over time. It may therefore be said that the SCM level, one of the two levels at which normative order is manifestly coordinated, is the space not just of organized disagreement but also partly of actual and potential agreement. By contrast, the weaker substantial and procedural normativity attached to the CCM level merely requires that certain cognitive-normative ideals be regarded as essential for the orientation both of material and procedural norms. There remains the issue of relations between the various ideals and what kinds of hierarchy can be established between them. This is where the type of reasoning that characterizes the SCM comes fully into play, as such decisions have historically been made in reasoning processes that stand at a distance from any universal justification, though the context of a democratic culture in the sense of the democratic CCM always makes its presence felt to some degree. Each contending position – again, for simplicity, left/right – within an SCM seeks to shape the institutional order – the body of rules backed by sanctions, material or cultural, or by incentives – to its own ends.

There is an 'internal' relationship between any achieved consensus within SCMs and the progression of a cognitive ideal in CCMs. The realization of a stronger consensual dimension indicates the gradual dissolution of dissenting opinion, never absolutely, but to all intents and purposes. In science, consensus on the law of gravity serves as example. The problem has been that examples such as this, correct on their own grounds, have abounded in those kinds of philosophy where the cognitive principle of truth has been elevated beyond all other principles. In traditional logic, this has helped suppress the discourse of rightness below that of truth, creating a distorted idea of cognition. In practical reason, certain rights before the law, for example, the right to a fair trial, serve as examples. There are multiple restrictions and variations on these rights across communication communities. Correspondingly, any degree of achieved universalization, such as legal freedom, tends to occur on the normative plane within concrete communication communities, though the relevant cognitive ideals stretch across them. At least this is the case until human rights are fully extended on the supra-national plane, because public spheres with adequate powers of discovery, justification, and application are normatively essential to reasonable ideal formation. In general, then, the fundamental distinction between CCMs and SCMs on the consensual dimension rests on the distinction between the argumentation-facilitating idealization pertaining to

# 186 *Reasoning and Schemata in a Societal Frame*

discourse as opposed to the normative fixity of agreement. The reference to normative fixity indicates that if there is consensus on the SCM level it could be 'pushed lower down' to the normative plane proper, where, as institutional rule systems, it becomes for a shorter or longer time embedded.

### *Institutional Models and Agents' Schemata*

Institutional cultural models comprise a third level of output schemata. Such an IM brings in a functional standard where consistent consequences derive from rules that are taken to be validated. They are taken to be validated in that it cannot be automatically supposed that they are normatively justifiable, even if they are de facto normatively justified. This is so in that social rule systems derive from the outcome of exchanges at the SCM level, where the various coordinative modalities determine different kinds of possible outcomes. The outcome, consistent with the modalities viewed at an inter-group societal level, can be one of sheer forced imposition of rules, of the mobilization of hegemonic power, of argued compromises, of rational disagreement, and of full agreement. Complex outcomes can also involve combinations of the above; for example, a consensual moral norm, such as the right to a fair trial, taking place in a wider context of injustice, say unfair treatment of the claims of asylum seekers, which occurs within a given raison d'état. The IM, whatever the modalities employed, depends on the production of rules with a high degree of unambiguous implications. Yet, these implications remain only as stable as the justification relations that underpin them. These justification relations are embedded in higher-level schemata and are outputs of reasoning processes in their fullness. The schemata in turn also canalizes, even in some cases absolutely exclude, the possibilities of reasoning. The pathways established in the output schemata constrain possible collective learning but still enable non-radical forms of such learning. For radical forms only emerge when the institutional relations built into the models are transformed by a process of radical, abductive schema formation, that is, radical abductive regressive or progressive learning identified against validity standards, a process that is happening to hitherto dominant models of liberal democracy at present from both 'left' and 'right' directions.

Functioning 'normally', IMs provide the descriptive, prescriptive, and evaluative rules that are specified in rule systems theory and that orient action (Burns and Dietz, 1992). These rules, in their different ways, take a yes/no form regarding what counts as valid. Modern developments in institutional theory make clear that such yes/no binaries are not absolute; in other words, rules are interpreted by those applying or subject to them. Such an understanding is greatly enhanced by the cognitive turn in institutional theory that precisely draws attention to the dependence of rules on cognitive frames and scripts. In the institutional field, this is generally only extended as 'high' as ideals in its equivalence to the framework outlined here. From the standpoint of critical theory, or any theory of radical collective learning, it must go yet higher to transcendentally enabled abductive schema formation if the innovating genesis of operating rule systems is to be fully understood, along with their distinctive patterning in various societies. A further important distinction is

*Reasoning and Schemata in a Societal Frame*   187

between intra-system justification in this multi-level sense and trans-systemic justification. For example, the latter distinction is important for understanding the wider context of the societalization of standards of legal justice compared to the routine operation of the legal system within established standards. Further, an assumption of theories of critique of any kind is that institutional norms may be contradictory, otherwise dysfunctional, and unjust, and, accordingly, identifying such problems becomes a basis for recourse to exposing critique. The implications of this remark are taken up in later chapters.

The fourth kind of output-side schema is the agent-level schema. I use the concept of schema rather than model here, as explained above, because it denotes not a complex relational structure as with the CCM or SCM but a minimally coherent kind of position that can be associated with a single, individual, or collective, agent. I will not expand here on the significant differences between one and the other, merely assuming that an agent's schema will result in a discernible degree of consistency of conduct, blending descriptive, prescriptive, and evaluative levels into a template for action. Agents' schemata are therefore composed of cognitive rule competences of various kinds that enable them to make sense of universes of discourse. The agent schema is not a derivative schema shaped by 'higher' ones; even where the higher schema is stable; the individual schema may still add internal variation to the worldview of the agent, as agents respond to experiences in their wider environments. Going the other way, in the construction phase of cultural models such as left/right on the SCM level, the agent level schemata have great impact, since it is partly out of the resolution of their differences that the SCM schema is constructed. Further, on the timing of schemata, the CCM schema comes first since its triggering premise is the translation of an evolutionary formed idea or ideas of reason that have consolidated on the transcendent plane into an immanent ideal that guides reasoning. Institutional and agents' schemata come second and become organized on the societal level when the various dynamic interpretants become aggregated into general positions. Finally, the SCM emerges as a consolidation of relational structures between dynamic interpretants over time, supplemented by the close relationship between the SCM and IMs that derive from it.

To restate the above, the various schemas/models are, in line with their role in inferential reasoning, types of medium. They interpose between immediate consciousness, understanding, and action. As media, they offer ways to stabilize inputs into reasoning and provide guidance as to how to reason and to act in specific universes. Read this way, they can be seen, in a classical Peirce sense, as interpretants; here they are interpreted as combinations of dynamic and final interpretants. As media, they also operate as modular inference sets that enable reasoning to proceed from a conjecture A to a meaning-distant final interpretant B to an inductively attained dynamic interpretant C without significant effort. The ability to proceed from A to B to C in this manner is indicative of a capacity for habitual interconnected inferential moves, which lies at the core of Peirce's account of reasoning. Extending this insight, schemata as completed sets of related inference chains organize diverse social fields, of which politics is just one. Further, taking over Peirce's insight in *The Fixation of Belief*, the different methods of fixing belief, in particular

## 188   *Reasoning and Schemata in a Societal Frame*

the last three, authority, a priori, and scientific, progressively involve a transition to democratic openness – where, admittedly, the explicit democratic emphasis derives more from discourse ethics than from Peirce (Peirce, 1992, 109–123). Hence, schemata are recurrent chains of interpretants that express the relational logic of fixing beliefs. In fact, the term 'fixing belief' could be extended to 'fixing' schemata. Schemata work with the logic of relatives in establishing relations between signs of objects that can endure over time, rather than, impossible from the standpoint of social coordination, be reinvented with each new act of reasoning. In this sense, schemata are intrinsic to the logic of relatives, being both generative on the input side and structuring on the output side.

### Abductive Schema Formation

In line with the triadic account of the derivation of schemata above, further kinds of schema must also be introduced. These additional schemata are the abductive schema and the transcendental schema. Both of these can be understood as fostering processes of schematization and schema-formation that are not understood in terms of the direct coordination of action as such, but of generating schematic innovation in such coordination; in other words, schema-transforming schematization. The abductive schema implicates two closely related kinds of schematization: the perceptual schema and the abductive schema proper. These are proto-schematic forms of generative schema formation that typically are shorter in duration than the 'output' schemas described above. They are also conjectural in form. In the first instance, the implications of what I perceive are not known, and my perception, or what I infer from it, may in fact turn out to be correct or incorrect upon further experience or reasoning. In the second, my conjecture, directed at a changed understanding of objects of any kind, is an exercise of the imagination whose truth only further reasoning can determine. In line with the doubt-belief model, abductive schema formation takes what is established in existing 'output' schemata and subjects it to transformation, ranging from almost imperceptibly modest to radical. This schematic conjecture on the input side is temporary, future-oriented, and conjectural.

The concept of schema goes back to Kant, where the transcendental moment was fundamental. It is recognized as one of the most difficult areas in Kant's philosophy. Apel argues that Peirce engaged in a detranscendentalization of Kant's categorial schema theory, though still operating within the framework of a modified transcendental philosophy (Apel, 1998). For Apel, Peirce supplements the subjective functions of intuition, understanding, and judgement with dynamic, semiotic relations. The emphasis on relations attests to an open-ended interpretive process of adding interpretants to continuing processes of signification, where such interpretants are not simply pre-decided by the history of that discourse but also dependent on the constitution of the object and the context of interpretation. A transcendent element remains in Peirce in the assumption of evolutionary formed capacity to build logical relations within universes of discourse. What today is called extended mind was already in play with Peirce, for the building of logical

*Reasoning and Schemata in a Societal Frame* 189

relations arises from the capability to reason in common using collective habits of thought. These collective habits of thinking are predicated upon the logical capacity to establish valid relations within the logical space of transcendentally anchored validity concepts.

Peirce's account of sign-based inference renders the concept of schema more fluid. With the addition of his pioneering account of abduction as part of the semiotic transformation of logic, there are now three kinds of inferential operations involved in building knowledge: abductive, deductive, and inductive. Meaning is accordingly dynamically shifted through successive semiotic movements, potentially enriching cognitive relations to objects in the world, and hence both comprehension and action in relation to those objects. In the cognitive revolution in the second half of the 20th century, still going on, where Peirce is becoming a growing influence, the schema emerged as a pivotal concept. Schemata were extended into social domains to try to teach computational systems how to interact with humans in human-like situations, such as ordering a meal in a restaurant. An entire vocabulary of concepts such as frames, scripts, rules, roles, and events emerged. Within the human and social sciences, the constructivist turn took such ideas and linked them to the idealist tradition where, in the extreme version, the schema that agents have of the world was the reality of the world, or, in the more moderate one, world descriptions were enriched by understanding the mediating power of schemata.

Perception and abduction succeed one another in cognition – though it does not follow that an imaginative abductive schema always emerges from a perceptual one. For this to happen, certain propitious conditions have first to be present. For example, agents can *feel* injustice but not be able to turn it into a rational conjecture as to why this injustice has occurred and/or how it could be ameliorated or removed. The critical difference is that perception as the culmination of firstness has a mostly acritical quality, whereas abduction manifests itself in a different kind of explicit rational projection. Taking this on further, acritical, or non-conscious, elements are prominent with the crystallization of perception, the selective concatenation of myriad feelings into an idea that can be grasped in abduction. Nesher describes this kind of reasoning as acritical, and Pietarinen within the frame of logica utens describes it as neither good nor bad (Nesher, 2002; Pietarinen, 2005).

To speak of acritical schematization does not mean that its reconstructed quasi-intentions cannot be criticized, simply that its performance is beyond conscious control, though indirectly influenced by already explicated cultural beliefs and by mediating cognitive principles. This entails a kind of rationalization of firstness by acritical *inference*, the habitual cognitive penetration, the attempted bringing of order, to firstness, an order that nonetheless it regularly escapes. Perceptual schematization is iconic in form, resting on associated images that are loosely inferentially related. It is not entirely iconic in that it remains perception of an external world, and therefore indexical elements enter in together with volition towards this world. Further still, general elements that give form to particulars are also present. Its possibility is far from only that carried by a single agent. It also has a collective expression that could take the form of a generally held perception that opens the way to a transformation of knowledge, such as Barrington Moore's perception of

## 190    Reasoning and Schemata in a Societal Frame

injustice and multiple other kinds of collective sentiment (Moore Jr, 2015 (1978)). To become fully socially effective, such sentiment must acquire traction on beliefs, and hence must draw off forms of reasoning that have been completed, either resorting to 'conservative' belief or opening towards possible transformative belief projection.

This last remark above leads into the second kind of input schematization, abductive schematization, which, building on the perceptive schema, implies conscious control of a reasoning process. Peirce's architecture in this instance, and in the previous case of perceptual schematization, is different from that of Kant. In his later work stemming from the logic of relations, he breaks away from the paradigm of judgement towards the idea of a reflective building of relations upon relations. The latter can be understood as schematization that projects *possible* semantic relations into a future in which they may be confirmed. Whether they will or will not be depends on the type of possibility in question, the nature and quality of reasoning, and the factual situation as it stands now or might be in the future. Thus, judgement is deferred and only finally takes form at the end of inductive reasoning in the formation of beliefs. Reasoning thirdness in this account therefore remains a mediated and open process of possible learning throughout. Abductive schematization does not depend on definite judgements but on possible relations that may conduce to the truth – or the right, or the good. In this respect, abductive schematization depends on critical engagement; it is not that something can simply be asserted to be true on appearance, as in empiricism, but it requires a process of valid reasoning to demonstrate it is so. It depends on an imaginative projection of something that could be into the future without yet being able to comprehensively demonstrate that, under given conditions, it would be, that is, not before demonstrating it through reasoning, especially inductive reasoning, even in circumstances where the proponent is convinced of its necessity. By contrast, it is possible to routinely observe in political discourse judgements made at this level that could not possibly be justified, or at least they are made without any such demonstration. Accordingly, such premature judgements are not judgements at all, merely sentiments, and exhibit a pathological form in the claim to be judgements rather than what they are, untested conjectures or even dogmatic assertions.

Alternately, abductive schematization can open the possibility of building radically new knowledge. Peirce, following Kant, emphasizes its aesthetic form, mediating between acritical and critical, and guided by the summum bonum, the ultimately right ideal, which can never be fully realized but towards which thought must tend or risk becoming anomic, insincere, or false. The imagination allows the modal projection of something that *could be* turned into something that *would be* given certain conditions, in other words, a movement from the indefinite to the definite. Such a schematizing impulse has become central to modern social theory, for example, the idea of a social imaginary in the tradition emanating from Castoriadis (Castoriadis, 1998). The persistence of orienting feelings resulting from perception, continuing through abduction, and remaining ever present in reasoning is intrinsic to Peirce. The way we feel objects and states of affairs conditions the way we think about them. Such figurations are powerfully present

*Reasoning and Schemata in a Societal Frame*   191

in abduction. They are permanently present even where the feelings change under the light of critique. All that happens is that other feelings replace them, ones better suited to building desired or needed sets of world-oriented understandings and interventions. Notwithstanding its dependence on orientation by feelings, abductive schematization is at the very heart of rational autonomy, at least when guided by the scientific mode of fixing beliefs that Peirce believed was coming to dominance. The infinitude of possibilities requires a rational conjecture to be formed for which autonomy is an essential condition, bearing in mind that such autonomy may not be institutionally enabled but is in fact forged against prevailing institutional conditions.

Perceptual and abductive schematization are generative in nature. In both Peirce's and Kant's reflective judgement, they are at the same time conjectural and yet engage ultimate horizons of possible knowledge, in other words, transcendental ideas of reason. The universalism is a cognitive and not a normative universalism at this stage. In the end, since knowledge rests on the quality of this generative schematizatioin, normative universalism in turn rests on its cognitive condensation of rational possibilities. Some of these possibilities are utilized, some remain potentials that could be instituted, and some remain diffuse feelings that are unable to rationally present themselves at a given time. It is at this point that what Kant calls transcendental schematism, and here the cognitive order, is engaged. The power of the aesthetic in Kant's reflective judgement and in Peirce's idea of aesthetics as the first of the normative sciences serves a similar purpose. It involves the capacity to think beyond all levels of the existent, including the other output schemata, by engaging transcendent schemata in the form of: What do I or we want to achieve that is not currently in existence but could be brought into being if I or we make these interventions? Mostly, engaging the transcendental schema leads to only infinitesimal changes as existing schemata and the corresponding ordering of knowledge are not fundamentally changed, even if something always minutely changes. However, sometimes, radical innovation does take place. In this case, those transcendental schemata that act as presuppositions or anticipations of human purposes are *fundamentally* engaged. They are of evolutionary standing as cognitive universals and change only over very long time-scales – achieving a type of secular transcendence. Nonetheless, radical reflection mediated through them can bring about transformative socio-historical change in certain conditions, which those social scientists and historians concerned with long-term social change have extensively studied. The challenge, though, beyond this work is to examine the dynamics of these generative processes. If Bourdieu is followed, socially formed dispositions underpin and are thus more fundamental than norms. Yet, these dispositions are also pluralistic, reflective of the worlds in which they are embedded and the range of possibilities that allow its further construction. If we follow Peirce beyond Bourdieu into the reasoning process, they may not stay pluralistic, or even antagonistic, but become reconciled according to various possible outcomes of such reasoning. Only at this latter point are fully fledged *normative* universals achievable. Even without the full completion of normative universals, even if certain ones are indispensable and all must be present in some meaningful way,

## 192 *Reasoning and Schemata in a Societal Frame*

it remains possible to have a reasonable society. However, it is an open question for all societies, and today more and more insistently for world society, as to how far they have gone along that path.

### Notes

1 Garfinkel is an obvious exception.
2 Proposals along these lines are advanced in Chapter 12 in the account of reasoning pathologies, building on the path-breaking work of Max Miller on communication pathologies (Miller, 2002).
3 It would take too long to do this here, but, along with the general theoretical approach documented here, developments over the last few decades in the sociological theory of institutions, in addition to revisiting the Parsonian model following Munch and others, would allow a more gradated account of institutionalisation spanning all the models to be advanced.
4 Pathological reasoning will be addressed in Chapter 12. The emphasis on reasoning both includes a wide reading of reasoning and, implied, the assumption of a wide range of other genres, such as narratives and iconic schemes, that animate and guide such reasoning.

### References

Apel, K–O (1998) *Towards a Transformation of Philosophy*. Milwaukee: Marquette University Press.

Ballantyne G (2007) *Creativity and Critique: Subjectivity and Agency in Touraine and Ricoeur*. Leiden: Brill.

Belvedere C (2023) *Collective Consciousness and the Phenomenology of Émile Durkheim*. New York, NY: Springer.

Bidet A, Boutet M, and Chave F (2013) Au-Delà de L'intelligibilité Mutuelle: L'activité Collective Comme Transaction. Un Apport Du Pragmatisme Illustré Par Trois Cas. *Activités* 10(1): 1–46.

Brandom R (2000) *Articulating Reasons: An Introduction to Inferentialism*. Cambridge, MA: Harvard University Press.

Burns TR and Dietz T (1992) Institutionelle Dynamik: Ein Evolutionärer Ansatz. *Journal für Sozialforschung* 32(3/4): 283–306.

Castoriadis C (1998) *The Imaginary Institution of Society*. Cambridge, MA: MIT Press.

Chevalier J-M (2016) Forms of Reasoning as Conditions of Possibility: Peirce's Transcendental Inquiry Concerning Inductive Knowledge. In: Gava G and Stern R (eds) *Pragmatism, Kant, and Transcendental Philosophy*. Abington, PA: Routledge, pp. 114–132.

d'Andrade RG (1995) *The Development of Cognitive Anthropology*. Cambridge: Cambridge University Press.

Forst R (2007) *The Right to Justification: Elements of a Constructivist Theory of Justice*. New York, NY: Columbia University Press.

Forst R (2013) *Toleration in Conflict: Past and Present*. Cambridge: Cambridge University Press.

Forster P (2011) *Peirce and the Threat of Nominalism*. Cambridge: Cambridge University Press.

Foucault M (1972) *The Archaeology of Knowledge*. New York, NY: Pantheorn.

Habermas J (2019) *Auch Eine Geschichte der Philosophie*. Frankfurt: Suhrkamp.

Hedetoft U (1995) *Signs of Nations: Studies in the Political Semiotics of Self and Other in Contemporary European Nationalism*. Dartmouth: University of Michigan Press.

Lane R (2007) Peirce's Modal Shift: From Set Theory to Pragmaticism. *Journal of the History of Philosophy* 45(4): 551–576.

Miller, M (2002) Some Theoretical Aspects of Systemic Learning. *Sozialer Sinn.* 3(3): 379–422.

Moore Jr B (2015 (1978)) *Injustice: The Social Bases of Obedience and Revolt.* New York, NY: Routledge.

Münch R (2010) *Theory of Action (Routledge Revivals): Towards a New Synthesis Going Beyond Parsons.* London: Routledge.

Nesher D (2002) Peirce's Essential Discovery: "Our Senses as Reasoning Machines" Can Quasi-Prove Our Perceptual Judgments. *Transactions of the Charles S. Peirce Society* 38(1/2): 175–206.

Nööth W (2011) From Representation to Thirdness and Representamen to Medium: Evolution of Peircean Key Terms and Topics. *Transactions of the Charles S. Peirce Society: A Quarterly Journal in American Philosophy* 47(4): 445–481.

O'Mahony P (2013) *The Contemporary Theory of the Public Sphere.* Oxford: Peter Lang.

O'Mahony P (2019) The Theory of Symbolic Universes and Cognitive Sociology. In: Salvatore S, Viviana F, Mannarini T, et al. (eds) *Symbolic Universes in Time of (Post) Crisis.* Switzerland: Springer, pp. 317–331.

Paolucci C (2021) *Cognitive Semiotics.* New York, NY: Springer.

Peczenik A (2008) *On Law and Reason.* New York, NY: Springer Science & Business Media.

Peirce CS (1903) *A Syllabus of Certain Topics of Logic.* Boston, IL: Mudge.

Peirce CS (1992) *The Essential Peirce: Selected Philosophical Writings. (Vol. 1) (1867–1893).* Bloomington, IN: Indiana University Press.

Peirce CS (1998) *The Essential Peirce: Selected Philosophical Writings (Vol. 2), (1893–1913).* Bloomington, IN: Indiana University Press.

Peirce, C (1998) Sundry Logical Conceptions. In: The Essential Peirce: Selected Philosophical Writings (Vol 2), (1893-1913). Bloomington, IN: Indiana University Press, 267–288.

Pietarinen A-V (2005) Cultivating Habits of Reason: Peirce and the Logica Utens Versus Logica Docens Distinction. *History of Philosophy Quarterly* 22(4): 357–372.

Rosa H (2021) *Resonance: A Sociology of Our Relationship to the World.* Cambridge: Polity.

Rose G (1981) *Hegel Contra Sociology.* London: Verso.

Shalin DN (1990) The Impact of Transcendental Idealism on Early German and American Sociology. *Current Perspectives in Social Theory* 10(1): 1–29.

Strydom P (2000) *Discourse and Knowledge: The Making of Enlightenment Sociology.* Liverpool: Liverpool University Press.

Strydom, P (2011) *Critical Theory and Methodology.* London: Routledge.

Touraine A (1981) *The Voice and the Eye: An Analysis of Social Movements.* Cambridge: Cambridge University Press.

van Eemeren FH, Grootendorst R, and Grootendorst R (2004) *A Systematic Theory of Argumentation: The Pragma-Dialectical Approach.* Cambridge: Cambridge University Press.

von Trotha T (2006) Perspektiven Der Politischen Soziologie. *Soziologie* 35(3): 283–302.

Zalamea, F (2001) *Peirce's Continuum: A Logical and Mathematical Approach.* University of Bagota.

# 7 Towards a Sign-Mediated Societal Ontology

In the last 60 years or so, under multiple internal and external disciplinary pressures, sociology has begun to reorient itself away from structural analysis of social causes to move lower down the ontological landscape, emphasizing individual and inter-individual interpretive processes. In so doing, it frequently understood itself to be moving from static, teleological, evolutionary, structural, and causal modes of theorizing to more processual, open-ended, historical, agential, and circular ones. This has facilitated a re-figuration of the theoretical and methodological landscape to emphasize dynamics, processes, micro power, and indeed a range of acutely relevant phenomena of the kind that cannot easily be generalized. With it came a renewed nominalism emphasizing the power of the particular over the general. What was most under assault was a macro-sociology that emphasized the compatible formation of cultural and social structures in various combinations. These structures had been assumed to have routinizing effects on social action. For a half-century or so, presumptions about their explanatory power have been weakened, and in some cases, they have been simply abandoned entirely. There has also been a cognate intellectual tendency, combining critiques of figures, such as Kant, Parsons, Rawls, and Habermas, to oppose the very idea of reason as a repository of an alleged neutral authority. In the hands of the powerful, reason is taken to operate as a hegemonic force that excludes through the device of apparently including.

While many of the implications of the changed mode of theorizing should be defended in general, both the rather arbitrary use of structural claims in micro-sociological accounts – for example, to explain uneven power distributions – and the assault on the very idea of reason are not convincing. With the lack of attention to reason comes the inescapable limitation of the applicability of the social sciences to democratic argumentation. It is not that the new theoretical ventures cannot be made relevant to this overarching question. It is rather that, ironically, other than as a point of critique of anti-democratic tendencies, democracy is not much considered at all, not even in political sociology that might be considered its home domain. The micro-sociological tendency to oppose structural explanation, even what it might conceivably propose based on its own methodological stance, has led to distance from such generalizing ideas as social integration, social order, or anything that could open insight into normatively justifiable macro-social

DOI: 10.4324/9780429060571-8

*Towards a Sign-Mediated Societal Ontology* 195

arrangements in much critical thought and practically any kind of macro-social relations in much interpretive thinking. Hence, for example, the relationship of democracy to social integration, however, conceived, does not appear high on the current theoretical or research agenda, yet it subsists in some form as a vital issue for society.

Critical theory cannot readily settle for such a situation. Macro-sociological evaluation of the state of society was intrinsic to its modus operandi from the very beginning. Much later, in the influential, contemporary writing of Honneth, for example, significant attention is given to a neo-Parsonian account of appropriate and inappropriate societal conditions for achieving solidarity through reciprocal role coordination (Honneth, 2011). Yet, viewed from an 'internal' sociological perspective, characterized by its distinctive phenomenological and linguistic turns, many attempts at macro-micro integration appear unconvincing. *TCA* addressed a new foundation for understanding social integration with its emphasis on communication, an integration that would be built from the compatible integration of macro and micro levels within the shift inaugurated by the linguistic turn. This quest for integration on new foundations was shortly afterwards extended by Habermas to embrace the question of democracy, a move away from reliance on negative critique towards the 'affirmative', institutionally specific introduction of law and democracy as intrinsic modes of procedural integration. Though, as argued here, this project was a considerable success in its conception, few would argue that it does not remain incomplete. Nonetheless, it did centrally pose the post-Peirce frame of the way linguistically operating cultural capacities acquire orienting power within a sociocultural lifeworld. The lifeworld is an implicit, background cultural resource reproduced and changed through communicative action. Habermas deeply enriched the grounding resources of critical theory, and potentially a critical sociology, by showing how functional and phenomenological currents could interact within an overall linguistic paradigm.

The important point to take from these initial remarks is that critical theory cannot abandon its concern for the macro-social, or merely turn it affirmative as in procedural theories of law and democracy. Honneth is quite right on this point (Honneth, 2014). Neither can it ignore the wide implications of recognizing the significance of linguistic nor, more widely, sign-mediated transactions in coordinating social life. This general communicative turn has major implications for the conception of the macro-level and of micro- and macro-integration. Both the perceived range of human cultural forms has been extended, and the relationship between macro- and micro-levels has become re-conceptualized within this cultural-communicative frame. Giddens sums up a relevant current in social theory that bears on this when he speaks of social structures being enabling and not just constraining (Giddens, 1984). From another theoretical perspective, critical realism, Archer, as outlined in Chapter 3, is indicative in differentiating but also rendering compatible what she describes, respectively, as cultural and social structures. These changes lead to a greater elaboration of cultural structure and, at the same time, its dialectical interplay with dynamic sense-making practices of all kinds. The implication is that the generalizing quality of social structures was historically set too cognitively

# 196  *Towards a Sign-Mediated Societal Ontology*

low down in the mechanical conception of social laws, whereas something akin to it can be retained if any such laws are shown to substantially depend on cultural arrangements higher up. From the vantage point of a critical theory concerned with deepening democracy, much more extended consideration of cultural levels and cognitive praxis would also reflexively open a theoretical-methodological space for addressing the self-constituting normative power of society by means of its public.

The approach crucially involves reconstructing the idea of the general, for which now, on the immanent plane, ideal generals would have pride of place. Such ideal generals, consistent with the CCMs of the last chapter, are mediating and evolving cognitive generals in the sense of a teleology that cannot be denied since it can be made demonstrable. This may seem overly strong. It involves two claims. The first is that basic ideal concepts, or concatenations of concepts that characterize an ideal such as democracy, cannot be dismissed without impossible to recover normative loss, whether for the intellectual logic of inquiry or society as a whole. The second is that while they can be multiply interpreted there remains a moral core that imposes 'limits' on conceptions of rightness, on what is truly general is the concept of justice, or, for that matter, that of truth, legitimacy, legality, publicity, and so on. These are normatively applicable and intellectually general concepts. The general, at this level, entails that concepts specify core elements of all possible objects to which they may refer, though these core elements allow for many possible and potentially competing accounts of the appropriate implications. The social facts, including normative facts such as value patterns that were previously assumed to comprise the general, are only general to a lesser degree than conventionally supposed, and their efficacy depends on variability higher up. This higher-up variability has at its core the mediating generality of evolving ideals that have both a structuring force and responsiveness to dynamic restructuring in learning processes.

And more fundamental still than these cognitive generals that structure human thought and action lie another set of cognitive universals on the transcendent level. Following Kant's distinction, these are unconditioned, as opposed to conditioned, generals, indicating their status as that without which human forms of life could not exist, for without them present and possible human purposes could not be generated. These transcendently located generals, the cognitive capacities and principles of the cognitive order, enable 'thinking beyond' when they are triggered in episodes of abduction. The generality subsists in the capacity to think beyond anything that exists, to be able to add something fundamentally new, something not previously thought about in the same way, something not culturally present before brought into being. An interesting example at present is the concept of cosmopolitanism. As an ideal on the immanent, convergent level of the CCM, cosmopolitanism has a growing structuring impact on human goals. Yet, when symbolically packaged at the SCM level, its power becomes revealed as less than other competing concepts such as national sovereignty or a civilizational worldview, for example, 'the west'. However, the ideal of cosmopolitanism is evolving, its potential lies beyond its existing ideal, yet it is coming into being ever more powerfully on the margins. It is rarely spoken about directly in relation to the current multi-stranded ecological crisis, yet any solution to that crisis requires its widespread recognition. This level of cognitive 'generalization' thus involves a type of emergent abductive schema formation, a process of innovation that exceeds the current structure of ideals. This kind of schema formation, as outlined in the previous chapter, emphasizes the generative process of schematization.[1]

Apel's idea of co-responsibility, taking up the concept of collective responsibility for the unforeseeable consequences of modern civilization first developed by Jonas, but reaching beyond that to an innovative, democratic concept of co-responsibility, illustrates how the cognitive order engages with such ideal formation processes. It is thus necessary to be aware of emergent potential, realize the role of the abductively mobilized cognitive order in conceptualizing it, and be willing to probe what may initially be the margins, but perhaps the significant margins, of ideas and contexts of reception in milieus. The range of concepts and processes already outlined in the last chapter, viz., transcendentally anchored cognitive universals, the innovative quality of abductive schematization, ideal formation and transformation, and the various lower level output schemata, indicate the needed scope of theorization. It also begins to show how intrinsic reason and the reasonable must be to human forms of life, for without appropriate democratic validity standards and processes, modern forms of life will become increasingly unjust, unecological, and generally dangerous.

Modern social ontologies are far from the older ontological model of representing the reality of an external world assumed to be beyond direct human control yet fateful for human action. In the social sciences, these social ontologies do not deny the significance of epistemic processes in their relational and processual claims (Renault, 2016). In these accounts, the power of mind, including extended mind, is recognized but seldom explicated. A social ontology of a reasonable society must recognize this power of mind and identify its primary expression as extended rather than individual mind. In modern scholarship, this does not represent an unusual emphasis, and Habermas has laid important foundations for a theory of communicative reasoning that would carry intersubjective processes. Nonetheless, the Habermas synthesis, while a vital lodestar, is not fully adequate in a few important dimensions, including the tendency to rely on the individualist and situation-specific tendencies of speech act theory rather than inferential relations, tendencies that are in variance with the general thrust of Habermas's theory. It also includes other nominalist residues, as, for example, in the corresponding individually centred learning theory employed or his later explicitly nominalist account of the external world (Habermas, 2003). Furthermore, the systems theoretical perspective is granted excessive autonomy from normative orders, albeit qualified in writing after *TCA*. The lifeworld acquires a rather static quality, with the way it emerges from communicative action not adequately demonstrated. The brilliant account of rationalization is highly suggestive, but the gap between communicative reasoning and such rationalization is too wide for a convincing generative account. Finally, there is insufficient attention to the nature and consequences of unjust and pathological reasoning and to related forms of critique.

What is here proposed is instead a more emphatic realist logic following the post-Kantian linguistic or, with Peirce, sign-mediated, radicalization of ontology. Peirce views the core of logic as consisting of inferentially structured arguments.

## 198 *Towards a Sign-Mediated Societal Ontology*

Communicative reasoning within a communication community is both autonomous and general. The priority and autonomy of the general organizes particulars, not the other way round. Sociologically translated, this means that the social-inferential form of argumentation is decisive for the generation of knowledge (Apel, 1995). What is knowable must be generated and justified according to this *social* understanding of logic to become known. However, the sociality of logic does not stand on its own. It is bounded, on the one hand, by the embodied quality of feelings that are variously naturally grounded, socially conditioned, and epistemically orienting. On the other hand, it is bounded by its applicability to the actual situation of the world, which can be either consonance with existing facts or carry normatively distilled potentiality to go beyond them in multiple registers. What emerges nonetheless is the sense of a world that is comprehensively permeated by the social logic of reasoning, always bearing in mind that reasoning in some of its forms can be unjust and pathological. Yet, the cognitive form and normative implications of reasoning have been consistently diminished, even ignored, by sociology with implications for the kind of systematic social theorizing required for any new flourishing of the theory of a reasonable society.

In certain key respects, the outline societal ontology proposed below stands outside the mainstream of social theory in dimensions such as the immanent-transcendent architecture, the modal quality, the respect for experience and immanent cognizability without jettisoning the a priori, the emphasis on validity, and the semiotic inferential realism as opposed to nominalism. In other respects, though in altered form because of the differences just emphasized, it moves in broadly similar directions: the relational emphasis, the constructivist or generative quality and the concern for the dispositional, the emphasis on process over substance, and the doubt-belief model that is implicit in the social sciences. The ontology that emerges based on these themes provides a preliminary skeletal model of the theory of society, a theory of society meant to be applied in normatively guided critical diagnosis and prognosis.

The exposition of the social ontology is guided by Figure 7.1, *Sign-mediated Societal Ontology*. In the next section, I will describe the main dimensions of the figure. In the subsequent section, I will describe the individual signs. In the concluding section, I will emphasize the main implications for a sociology of reason.

**The Societal Ontological Framework**

The task of outlining a communicative social ontology must strike a balance between description of, on the one hand, the sign-mediated communicative process and, on the other hand, the general social theoreticaly depicted context from which such an ontology might emerge. Here, the outline first moves relatively quickly to technical description of the sign-mediated process to clarify the very idea itself. Preliminary work has been done in the outline and application of the cognitive theoretical framework in Chapters 2 and 4, and what follows below was also anticipated in the

Towards a Sign-Mediated Societal Ontology 199

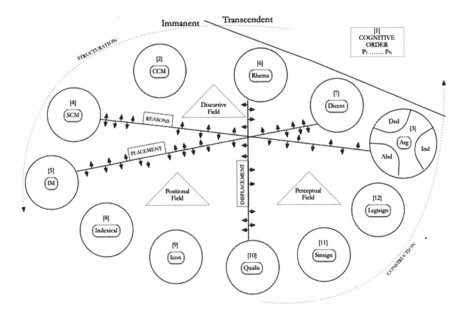

*Figure 7.1* Sign-mediated Societal Ontology

chapter on Peirce, Chapter 5, and on reasoning and schemata in Chapter 6. These background contexts will re-emerge in the later development of the ontology as a *critical theoretical societal ontology*, with the account of sign-mediation offering a crucial bridge. At the outer limit of ambition, lies the goal of showing how the normative order of society – and its component spheres – might be adjudged reasonable or unreasonable, a goal that could not be reached without such a sign-mediated ontology.

I will thus proceed to describe the dimensions of Figure 7.1. The most basic dimension is the distinction/relation between transcendence and immanence within the general critical theoretical frame of immanent transcendence. This is indicated by the slanted line that separates the transcendental, T, from the immanent, I, in the figure. This key concept has already been discussed on several occasions, including in this chapter with the distinction between the types of cognitive generals, so I will not address it directly here, though it remains essential to that which is represented. In extreme simplicity, what is designated above the line as the *cognitive order* formally separates transcendence from all the rest, which is immanent.

As well as this basic immanent/transcendent distinction, several structuring features of the figure may be noted. It is based on Peirce's sign topology of 1903 (Peirce, 1998; Short, 2007). Accordingly, there are the signs of thirdness, [3], [6], and [7], the signs of secondness (from Peirce), [5], [8], and [9], and the signs of firstness, [10], [11], and [12]. In line with the description of cultural models in the

## 200 *Towards a Sign-Mediated Societal Ontology*

last paragraph, the sign typology has been extended. The cognitive cultural model (the CCM of the last chapter), sign [2], and the sociocultural model, sign [4], lie between thirdness and secondness as intermediate signs that are consistent with the form of interpretants, the ultimate logical interpretant in the case of the CCM and dynamic interpretants in the case of the SCM.

The immediate interpretant, which is the direct and possibly also intended interpretant of the sign, emerges from the process of abductive schema formation described in the last chapter and is associated with perceptual and logical (abductive) innovation. Such an interpretant – of a previous sign – can either be transformed quickly in the cognitive process or endure as a type of accumulated emergent proto-schema, such as a sense of injustice or dysfunction leading to an explanatory conjecture or modal projection, for example, the early stages of the limits to growth movement in the environmental field or the rise of perceptions of various kinds of inequality from the 1950s onwards through the prism of social movements. The signs of secondness are the schematic – or rationalized – signs in Peirce. In the figure, through the addition of signs [2] and [4], two additional such signs are added that lie beyond the symbol, the thirdness of secondness in Peirce. Such signs draw both on the implications of the theory of interpretants as developed in the later Peirce – outlined in the Peirce chapter and below – and on frame theory in the social sciences. In the language of frame theory, these additional schematic signs are, in the case of the CCM, *frames*, and in the case of the SCM, *frame positions*, most simply articulated as the positions various agents hold within the frame (Skillington, 1997; Wood et al., 2018). Ultimately, these signs remain in the space of the secondness of thirdness, the space of the symbol, but they are progressively nearer to thirdness proper – going from the SCM to the CCM. The penetration of active thirdness into these schematic signs indicates that they are open to logical innovation through reasoning guided by abductive schematization.

The signs of thirdness are *formal* signs signs that mediate between the other sign categories, the signs of firstness and of secondness, to connect these other categories of signs in various possible ways. The forms of mediation involve the mediation of firstness, the generation of feelings, through the rhema [6], the mediation of secondness, the articulation of propositions, through the dicent [7], or the mediation of thirdness, the assertion of the rational, through the argument [3]. The signs of firstness are generative signs, signs that originate possible perspectives and begin to shape them into recognizable forms. The processes are very complex because feelings continue into thirdness, where their formal possibility is present in the rhema, which in turn draws off the substantive content of signs of secondness. The signs of secondness are schematic signs that purport to represent factual states of affairs. What Peirce calls the symbol is here called the institutional model, sign [5], and represents the social rule systems, descriptive, prescriptive, and evaluative, at which society has 'arrived'. The institutional models are therefore signs that grant validity to various kinds of conduct that are in conformity with the selected rules, or, in other words, the disposition and expectation to follow certain kinds of rules. These signs of conduct represent the 'what' of social coordination, whereas indexical signs, [8], represent the 'that' of the 'what', that is, particular instances of the 'what'. Iconic signs represent those images and metaphors that make the 'that' conceivable. The 'what', for example, is the concept of an empire and what knowing this concept means for conduct. The 'that' is an instance of an empire, 'that empire'. The image of the 'that' is the sensuous construct of an empire in many ways, such as images of slaves in chains or colonial big houses, or even images of benign domination, a delusion that is all too common in former colonizing countries.

The figure further has three lines, respectively indicating spaces of displacement, placement, and reasons. The positioning of these lines is inevitably inexact, given the difficulty of demarcating such spaces in contexts of fluid interaction. They each emanate from one of the signs of thirdness, displacement from the rhema [6] (signs of feeling), placement from the dicent [7] (signs of facts), and reasons from the argument [3] (signs of thought). Displacement, as firstness, comes first in the interpretive sequences – It can also be conceptualized as coming first in evolutionary time – initally as singular instances of phenomena without apparent connecting order that potentially become increasingly culturally structured. The space of placement, as secondness, comes second to that which is encountered when a feeling complex meets a reality beyond its own singular property or ensemble of singular properties. Reasons come third as the basis of explication and mediation of this encounter. Less technically, the space of displacement assumes the mostly unconscious activity of perceiving the world from the ultimate standpoint of acting in it in some way, including thought action. The space of placement specifies the relational placement of every possible object of common understanding. The space of reasons explicates not the 'what' and the 'that' but the 'why' and 'how' of possible actions at any conceivable scale. The space of displacement generates feeling states, for example, a diffuse perception of injustice. The space of placement is the 'what' and 'that' of unjust experiences that can be referenced. The space of reasons offers a reasoned interpretation, or even a possible explanation, for the fact of injustice. Modally speaking, the space of reasons is also characterized by the power of negative suggestion, the assertion of something that could or should be that builds on the coalescence of initially diffuse feelings brought into relation by an effort of mind and then explicated.

In the figure, there are also three kinds of fields, here represented as triangles, that broadly correspond to the above three vectors. These are the *Discursive Field*, the *Positional Field*, and the *Perceptual Field*, each designated by a triangle. The concept of field has become widely used in the contemporary social sciences to indicate a space of relations between those entities that could be said to exist in the same action-reaction space. The *Positional Field* is the one most utilized in sociology; for example, Bourdieu's concept of social field. Actors, endowed with various material and symbolic resources, contend in such fields, which are unified by certain stakes or forms of social capital. Positional fields are also structured by characteristic kinds of arenas or contexts of action, such as markets, bureaucratic processes, associations, and modes of interaction. The institutional cultural model represents the general culture of the field, those rules guiding various distinctions, for example, efficiency or its opposite, good or bad, fair or unfair, that characterize it. A comprehensive account of the cultural and organizational dimensions of fields,

## 202 *Towards a Sign-Mediated Societal Ontology*

the possible positioning strategies of the actors, and the range of possible media that structure interaction within them would indeed be a long one (Bourdieu, 1987; Dezalay, 1990; Emirbayer, 1997; Patterson, 2014). Even though it was already modified in Bourdieu and many others in the second half of the 20th century reaching up to the present, the space of placement was for a long time at the very core of sociology. Prior to various cultural and agential turns, it largely operated without an emphatic relational and dynamic form. Yet, the positional field, or positional fields, drawing from the space of placement, remains pivotal both to sociology and critical theory. The space of placement specifies the object worlds that sociology observes, and fields are assumed to coordinate them and imbue them with regularity. Critical theory has always relied on sociology, along with other social sciences, to provide the means to account for what it understands as the general 'existent object' of society (Adorno, 2019 (1964)). For critical theory, this existent object is assumed to be currently substantially characterized by deep injustice, contradiction, and pathology. Admittedly, with the development of both society and the social sciences, the identification of existent objects in their relational fields has become progressively more difficult. Yet it remains essential to the sociological enterprise.

The second field complex is the *Perceptual Field.* The significance of this field has grown progressively in the human and social sciences with the now widespread phenomenological turn. Here, the perceptual is understood as a mode and perspective of experiencing social life. The components of this field and the relations between these components are much more diffuse than the positional field. Here we have to do with entities mostly operating below the level of direct awareness. Frequently, their form is so diffuse and rapidly evolving that it is difficult to get close to the basic feelings deployed. The most basic kinds of social interactions between, say, two persons will involve a vast range of feelings about, for example, the dignity of the other, the nature of the object, the positions to be ascribed to other actors, previously known sensitivities, and so on. In something as complex as a perception of injustice, it ranges far wider and brings in the generalized other – an institutional schema – as well as the self and concrete other and a vast range of other considerations. The sense of the importance of such perceptual fields has grown dramatically in recent decades. In critical theory and other disciplines, the ground was already well-trodden with the reception of psychotherapy as early as the 20th century. It was carried powerfully forward by the embracing social phenomenological movement in sociology emerging from the 1960s that was inspired by developments much earlier in the century. It is also advanced with the sociology of embodiment as a mode of being that is separate from the explicit dictates of the mind, operating either as a repressive or emancipating force 'behind' the mind in elementary social forms that are beyond conscious control. As understood here, the perceptual field involves the immersion of subjects into contexts they do not consciously control but nonetheless have powers of determination over how they will consciously think. Of great interest, beyond the individual subject, is how groups subconsciously, or, at least, only partly consciously, emotionally respond to situations based on what they collectively 'feel'. This capacity for common feeling suggests that unconscious inference is at work leading to the emergence of common perception across groups or sub-groups at certain times and places, even though in early stages this is not consciously elaborated. This also suggests that the inferential mechanisms that allow for 'free' suggestion and those that 'inhibit' it involve much more than control over explicit symbols but extend to control over consciousness itself. As a field, perception has a real and observable status, using phenomenological, hermeneutical, psychological, and linguistic methodologies to assess, variously, its source as impending episodes of creativity, epistemic challenge, moral consciousness, and pathology. Such methodologies involve the 'objectualization' of the field of subjectivity with a view to revealing emerging and potentially transformative sensibilities.

The third field complex is that of the *Discursive Field*. This field is primarily associated with the signs of thirdness, especially those of *argument* or *reasoning* and with the CCM. This field, when understood as being in the space of reasons, is concerned with the advancement of normative ends. In the Kantian tradition, such normative ends have the form of an irrevocable commitment to normative goods beyond inclination or interest. Both inclination and interest can inform us about possible normative ends, and influence their form, but they cannot stand above the freedom to commit to other-advancing or society-advancing standards of reasonableness standing above interests and inclinations. To speak of a field of reasons thus involves understanding those multiple fora of discursive exchange that foster the possibility of such reasonableness. In other words, those fora should support the full realization of the signs of reason, especially the triad represented by the cognitive order, the CCM, and *argument*. However, the field should also be regarded as comprising not just such institution-bound fora as law and formal democracy but also, above all, the public sphere of the public of publics in its widest sense. Peirce's signs of thirdness, complemented by the additional schematic signs outlined above, the CCM and SCM, capture the relatively stable cultural foundations of this field. However, the distinctive characteristic of this field is its overarching power to form socio-mental relations that both 'capture' worlds taken as objective – natural and relatively stable social worlds – or that, more fundamentally, still have the conceptual power to imagine new worlds that potentially regulate interpersonal relations in myriad ways.

## Component Signs of the Societal Ontology

Figure 7.1 is ultimately centred on the possibilities and modalities for the realization of reason, thus on signs [1], the *Cognitive Order* [2], the CCM, and [3], *The sign of argument*, but also on signs [6], *Rhema*, and [7], *Dicent*. In this respect, it is differentiated from the two dominant traditions in advancing a theory of society, functionalism and Marxism. These latter theories tend to be mainly associated with quite different variations on operations [4], the SCM *or symbolic struggles and coordination modes*, and [5], the *institutional model* or *normative order*. Yet, the operations [4] and [5] are here, by contrast, not the centre of gravity of the theory and, by implication, the social order, but are instead regarded as conditioned by the overall sign-mediated logic of reasoning. As explained, operations [4] and [5] are

## 204    *Towards a Sign-Mediated Societal Ontology*

both expressions of what Peirce understood as the symbol. The symbol, located in secondness, was a temporally, but also temporarily, stable outcome of operations of thirdness of all kinds, but especially outcomes of reasoning. While the sign of reasoning has the greatest interest for a critical theory of societal reasonableness, the Rhematic and Dicentic signs are also essential. As specified in Chapter 5 on Peirce, his account of logic did not follow the nominalist direction from terms to propositions, to arguments, but operated the other way round. Thus, argument weakly determines dicents (dyadic propositional forms) and rhemas (monadic qualitative forms). This is key to understanding his emphasis on general principles, taken to be real in themselves, as the most fundamental building block of knowledge. It is also key to understanding his immanent-transcendent architecture since form ultimately derives from the infinite, transcendent, *general* continuum of meaning possibilities that enable the equality-infinite process of building epistemic relations on the immanent plane. The Dicent sign, [7], the secondness of thirdness as per the account of Chapter 5 and Peirce's 1903 model, is a formal sign with the capacity to build dyadic propositional relations. In such relations, the law of non-contradiction and of excluded middle applies. It converts outcomes of reasoning taking place within the sign of *argument* [3] into propositional forms that result in symbolization (Institutional Models]. The *Rhema*, [6], the firstness of thirdness, entails the formal capacity to utilize 'singular' feelings as, for example, the verbal constructs 'loves' or 'hates', elementary primitives that can exist abstractly as a possibility, including possibilities that exist but are not yet known, prior to any application. Both Dicents and Rhemas derive their positional meaning from within relations of general thirdness, which can be understood as an infinitely expanding relational cultural structure that organizes argumentation through concepts, propositions, and terms. The whole must be grasped before the parts, the general before the particular and singular.

Both secondness, the realm of the *institutional model* (instituted habits/beliefs) [5], the *index* (referential relations to objects in the external world), [8], and the *icon* (images of such objects), [9], and thirdness, comprising the *argumentative* capacity to generate coherent cultural order, the *dicentic* capacity to form propositions, and the *rhematic* capacity to feel are understood as relational forms. Operations [4] and [5] therefore represent relational secondness, that is, symbolic structures that both shape reasoning – of all kinds, good and bad – on the input side and are altered by it on the output side. This kind of relational secondness involves a 'fixing', a relational stabilization of the logical operations of thirdness in all its facets. Once rationalized in secondness, relations take on the form of relations between particulars that are crystallized in the relational forms of [4] and [5]. Ontologically, in terms of the interests of social theory, such particulars, the vast range of what Peirce calls habits of action and volition, thus include specific norms, values, attitudes, moral and ethical commitments, and entitlements. What these orders of belief have in common is that, as particulars, they have a definite force. They are relationally structured dyadic forms whose action/reaction set is habitual in the sense of habits of conduct. Such forms are particulars that have congealed in the social world, or at least are assumed to have done so. They are relationally generated, are internally relational forms, and enter relations with other forms, but they nonetheless have a distinctive force recurrent over time. Anything that manifests or impels habits of volition-driven action over time has such force. A particular norm, a value, a personality type, an individual or collective identity, a substantive moral commitment, and a political ideology may thus be identified. To use the terms forces understood in this way is not therefore incompatible with a relational approach, as Emirbayer and Mische claim, illustrating a type of general presumption of relational approaches (Emirbayer and Mische, 1998). It instead retains the substantive or concrete dimension, indispensable to agency and vital for critical thinking, but shorn of the encompassing essentialism often attributed to it.

These forces enter into the relational operations [4] and [5] to form practical relations between humans and objects, between objects and objects, and within institutionalized human-human relations. The intrinsic difference between thirdness and secondness is that the 'mental' relations of thirdness, especially those of reasoning, entail a reflexive 'take' on what secondness assumes to exist, a take that can either reproductively utilize or change the world-understanding built into the relational and rule order of secondness. The inferential relations of reasoning that constitute logical thirdness therefore potentially render fluid the relatively stable positional relations of secondness, encompassing the distinction between the *Discursive* and *Positional Fields* described in the last section. Both in the reflective possibilities of everyday life and of the social sciences, theories constituted in thirdness mediate the institutionalized relations and forces of secondness. Thirdness is therefore what enables the regularities and transformations of secondness to be theoretically grasped. The corresponding distinction between imaginatively guided reflection and institution is vital in building a theory of society, an approach similar to that of Castoriadis (Castoriadis, 1998; Arnason, 2023). That is not all; the operations of firstness also come into the picture, as will be explored.

Modern phenomenological and hermeneutically inspired sociology has been in the main indifferent or even antipathetic to a normative theory concerned with the general conditions for the realization of a reasonable society. Yet, these approaches generate indispensable orientations and forms of knowledge for an appropriate understanding of what one might consist of. In the figure, operation [8], taking pivotal works as illustrations, corresponds to Garfinkel's ethnomethodological concentration on indexicals and operation [9] to Lakoff and Johnson on metaphors (Lakoff and Johnson, 2003 (1980); Garfinkel et al., 2015). The *index* refers to the worlds of existence as they are thought to be in themselves. It refers to everything that can be thought of as actual, that is, has been the case, is the case, or will predictably be the case. It can encompass such varied existents as the British Empire, the me, the door that resists opening, and the real movement of the economy. Metaphors and narratives, both immensely influential in social thought today, involve an iconization of indexicals within a timeline (Ehrat, 2005). They serve as background images that provide individual or group orientation. What are the images that come to mind when the contemporary discourse of refugees is raised? It could be of wretchedly suffering people trying to gain some foothold in the world or as 'invaders' or 'hordes' in the lexicon of the radical right. Icons prefigure reasoning on the

## 206 *Towards a Sign-Mediated Societal Ontology*

input side and represent its outcomes on the output side. Narratives 'legitimate' a particular conception of the reference of indexicals, such as the emotional resonance of an event with an audience of some kind. When taken together, the signs [1], [2], [4], [5], [8], and [9] delineate the space of the lifeworld in Habermas, combining the space of reasons with the space of placement. The operations of signification within these signs, though subject to change, nonetheless become fixed through habits – individual and collective – of feeling [12], thought [2], and action [5] within the respective integrated communal contexts, or lifeworlds, of feeling, thought, and action.

The cognitive operations of firstness, [10], [11], and [12] are intrinsic to the constructivist moment in the figure. Constructivism has become influential in social theory since the loosening of the dominant science paradigm after the Second World War. It has taken many forms, all influenced by phenomenology, from various kinds of subject-centred constructivism to systems constructivism in Luhmann, to Bourdieu's structural constructivism. By now, it has a long and complex history. In the figure, though generally mindful of its complex history, a particular kind of reading of constructivism is presented in the tradition of Peirce. Relatively late in his career, further developing his scholastic realist philosophy, Peirce underwent a modal turn (Lane, 2007). This led him to assert both the reality of 'vagues' or possibility, not just the reality of (general) necessities. In operation [10] in the figure, this is characterized as pure possibility. Possibilities are general because they are not individuals but singulars, elementary qualities that could inhere in an object. However, even where they do not currently exist, that is, where they are not embodied in objects, they remain real, that is, possibilities. They are the other side of the reality of necessary generals in reasoning, that which pushes such generals towards the attribution of new meaning or, over time, leads to the formation of additional, necessary generals. Operation [10] is termed *Quality* by Peirce to signify the qualitative possibilities that are ascribed to objects. Qualities are feelings bearing on the possible cognitive construction of objects, such as the sense that the action of another requires responsive ethical, legal, or moral cognition, and in which direction to look. Such qualitative feeling, consisting of idea potentiality, is at the very base of cognition and applies whether the cognition is relatively routine or innovative in some way.

In operation [11], the above immediate feeling of a possible quality encounters the existing world, a world that is viewed now from the implication of the emerging feeling. In [11], feeling encounters the world, grasped through indexical signs, and that interaction shapes what to address in the world in the gathering cognitive process. Proto-suppositions about the nature of reality contained in feelings crash upon the reactive force of the actual world encountered, inducing perceptual orientation. Many qualities of feeling and many perceptual orientations are possible, and for any kind of effective cognition to transpire, they must be organized in the 'synthesis of the manifold' generated by the 'lawlike' nature of habits of feelings and associated perceptual judgements. Habits of feeling [12], akin to Bourdieu's habitus, are those orientations that result from previous interactions with the social and natural world, the distillate of experience, but also the capacity to feel beyond the existing limits of experience by engaging a priori categories and semiotically organized continua represented in the quasi-transcendental *cognitive principles* or meta-cognitive frames [1], P1....Pn.

Perceptual judgement represents the beginning of conscious thought. The habits of feeling that underpin it allow condensation of perception. These habits are the residue of much trial and error, not just arising from individual experience but also drawing off group experience and socialization patterns and embedded in supra-individual social and natural evolution. Following Nesher, inference is already at work in the process of firstness that leads to perceptual judgements, which emerge from the confrontation of the senses with external reality within the frame of habits of feeling. Hence, Peirce concludes that the distinction between, to use the title of Nesher's article in turn taken from Peirce, the 'senses as reasoning machines' and conscious logical reasoning is only relative (Nesher, 2002). Habits of feeling organize perceptual judgements that, in the initial logical process of abduction, cumulate into abductive – or generative – schema formation. This is where, viewed in a Peircean light, Bourdieu's theory of the habitus should be further developed as a basic component of a theory of society. It is the most developed account of this space in sociology, though it lacks the inferential dimensions of conscious reasoning and unconscious quasi-reasoning. Nonetheless, it forms a foundation for considering how the perceptual process of firstness leading up to abduction, a selected way of relating to the world, is embedded in quasi-determinate relations of secondness that condition it. Such relations of secondness seek to grasp the 'object world' which is organized into three kinds of fields: perceptual, positional, and discursive, as discussed above.

The challenge for a theory of society that incorporates the combined unconscious and conscious perceptual processes that lead up to abduction is that it is difficult to access. It remains below the level of conscious thought until a perceptual judgement is formed that brings in a dimension of 'law' – the generality of thirdness – and hence opens the way to possible explication. Here, interdisciplinary cooperation with, among others, aesthetics, phenomenology, and various kinds of psychology is called for, as well as examining the dispositions that must be assumed to exist given actions of all kinds and their consequences. Such work characterizes much ongoing activity in the cultural and social sciences. These investigations are also necessary to shed light on those unconscious codes that, in structuralist and neo-structuralist theories, are assumed to be lodged in the symbolic order, operation [5] in the figure, habitually guiding volition and action (Foucault, 1972; Frank, 1989).

Constructivism, associated with the generative process outlined earlier, viewed from the Peirce approach, does not remain confined to the operations of firstness but continues into reasoning. The fact that in Peirce, the activity of cognition moves from the subjective context of firstness into the – for him – through and through social property of reasoning is of the first importance. The subjective moment of rationalized feeling continues into and throughout the social moment of logical, intersubjective reasoning. Thirdness, the space of reasoning, is a space of social construction that does not depend on a nominalist interpretation of an

## 208 *Towards a Sign-Mediated Societal Ontology*

assumed determining psychological foundation. Yet, there is a *psychic* moment, the moment of feeling in perception and beyond perception in reasoning, but this psychic moment does not *justify* the validity of logical claims. Such claims can only be justified by *public* validity standards in communication communities. The bridge between the proto constructivism of firstness and the social constructivism of logical thirdness lies in the first abductive logical step. This abductive move, conjectures or modal projections about *possible* realities, tallies with the modern sociological emphasis on reflexivity and, at the same time, recapitulates and goes beyond the Kantian critical moment in establishing a plausible critical *sense* beyond the formal possibility of critique. It is deficient in the historically dominant theories of society. In functionalism, it is at most weakly present in Parsons's voluntarism, and in Marxism, it is also weakly present in the account of praxis, even if more could have been taken from Marx in this regard. It is present in Castoriadis. It is also present in critical realism, but with too great emphasis on a backward-looking idea of 'retroduction' rather than a more emphatically future-oriented practice of abduction (Bertilsson, 2009). The Kantian constructivist moment is retained in the necessity of *social* justification, whose transcendent influence is here not understood as the transcendental subject, but as the collective evolutionary inheritance of reasoning capacities and associated, orienting cognitive principles [1].

In social theoretical terms, and here consideration of reasoning [3] is fully enjoined, abduction involves the crystallization of new ideas. In some form or other, such a crystallization involves contesting existing orders of knowledge, represented by operations [2], [4], and [5]. Abduction is closely associated with the 'cognitive praxis' of social movements of various kinds (Eyerman and Jamison, 1991). This does not mean only the progressive movements emphasized critical thought; there were also conservative and reactionary movements. At the most radical level, though, emphasized by critical theory and other critical movements, it encompasses the cognitive challenge that emanates from movements seeking fundamental social change, a challenge that must also be normatively justified. More generally, abduction involves the ongoing construction of the social world based on dispositional schematization, schematization that minutely or significantly changes existing cultural models within the willed construction of orders of 'mental' relations in thirdness. Constructing such relations entails the presence of freedom, even manipulatively or regressively oriented use of freedom. It then becomes a normative task of critical theory to identify and justify what it deems to be normatively *progressive* relational possibilities arising from abduction and emergent abductive schema formation. Following Apel's account of Peirce, conjectures or hypotheses associated with abduction have an experience-transcending quality, the capacity to generate new conjectures or modal projections that go beyond existing knowledge and which give rise to validity claims that must be inductively evaluated to assess their actual or possible traction in the world (Apel, 1995). This experience-transcending quality is associated in the figure with recourse to the transcendently anchored cognitive principles of the cognitive order [1]. Such principles are the outcome of evolutionary sociocultural learning processes. They underpin, within the assumed immanent-transcendent form of knowledge, the continuum of possible learning.

With the constructivist moment of abduction at its core, thirdness comprises the essence of social theorization. Specifically, regarding the theory of society, third-ness integrates the various moments of theory-building: the determinative moment of 'what is' of secondness, the perspectival moment of what 'could be' of first-ness, and the generalizing moment of what 'would be' of logical thirdness. This entails a seminal change in the theory of society away from its traditional concentration on the first determinative moment to also incorporate the other moments, the modal-phenomenological moment of firstness and the generalizing logical and normative moment of thirdness. The distinction between thirdness and secondness in Peirce also marks a distinction between theorization, belonging to thirdness, and knowledge, embodied in secondness. Therefore, the theory of society should be understood as a theorization of the process of constructing society, intellectually and practically, that is *partly* conditioned by existing knowledge but, as a construction, always exceeds it.[2] This remark encapsulates the cognitive-processual emphasis above. The form of theorization entails reflection on the relations identifiable through the signs of secondness, for example, production or consumption relations, or, generally, any trends of objects that are or predictably will be the case. In addition to reflection on these relations of secondness, theorization involves the construction of further cognitive relations 'beyond' them. It represents a 'critical interpretation' by a communal mind of existing relations of secondness in the form of relations of thirdness. As reasoning, thirdness potentially further entails the building of critical relational forms that bring about cognitive and then social change by transforming what counts as legitimate knowledge. For this, Wright-Mill's discussion of master symbols of legitimation in *The Sociological Imagination* is instructive (Mills, 2000; Bagnoli, 2016).

The references to critical in the last sentences above do not per se denote a critical approach in the normally understood sense of critical thinking today. Rather, in the Kantian sense of critical, the operations of thirdness animated by any of an infinite range of possible conjectures can animate critical reflection. Putting it simply, it is as likely to emanate from 'conservative' positions as from 'radical' ones, as thirdness is shaped by a variable quality of mind operating within interpretive communities. Nor can the 'right' kind of critique be identified strictly according to the logical soundness of arguments, for arguments that have regressive conclusions can also be logically sound. By contrast, the critical forms of critical theory depend on the conditions of argumentation, their cognitive forms and contents, and the normative validity standards that are deployed within them. Normative validity standards do not simply exist 'out there' ready to be deployed. They must be cognitively generated and applied over time in collective learning processes, for which cognitive praxis is of the essence.

For all this, normative validity standards that are transparent and inclusive play a special role in critical theory. The above-referenced cognitive learning processes that accompany their gestation and ongoing application stand on an interesting fault line between constructivism and the other major axis in the figure, that of

## 210 *Towards a Sign-Mediated Societal Ontology*

structuration, which at its poles can be either rational or irrational. Such structuration is intrinsic to any treatment of normative validity. The account of constructivism so far offered here has considered the construction of possibilities in situations. Beyond this, yet not inconsistent with it, another kind of constructivism, Kantian constructivism, should be regarded as intrinsic to the normative stance of critical theory (Bagnoli, 2016). Peirce was in the Kantian tradition in emphasizing the necessity of an objective ethics of reasoning, that is, an ethics whose standards and objects would come from reasoning itself and could impose obligations of certain kinds of rational conduct.[3] If this position is accepted in second-generation critical theory, radically foreshortening what should be a long exposition here, then the next consideration bears on what is necessarily implied in realizing it. In turning to this issue, I will sidestep but indirectly incorporate the relatively well-trodden question of the conditions of communication in the public sphere at the core of critical theory (O'Mahony, 2013, 2021).

### Pivotal Vectors: Constructivism and Rational Structuration

The figure entails two main vectors, lines of force, that are designed to both represent essential dimensions of theoretical cognition and practical realization. These, *constructivism* and *structuration*, have already been addressed just above, but here they will be taken up more systematically. Drawing on the vectors here is intended to show how the emphasis on generalizable outcomes of the older sociology with its concern for the normatively rational grounds of action – affirmatively in Parsons, critically in Marx – must find alignment with the constructivist impulse of the new sociology. The bridge between them must be understood through the mediating power of a justifiable use of reason, always mindful, as will be shown below, of the power of unjustifiable reason or the attempt to bypass reason.

Regarding the two vectors, one, *structuration* runs along the left-hand side of the figure, as observed above, while the other *construction* runs along the right-hand side. 'Downstream' symbolic versions of such structuration have always been used in explanatory sociological accounts of social arrangements, where the supra-individual structures, cultural or material, are assumed to cause patterns of action. Such accounts have tended to understand structural presuppositions of different kinds as historically established conditions that organize ongoing social activities from 'behind' or 'before'. It is the congealing of structures that determines the possibilities of action. The task of the observing social scientists is to use a scientific approach to identify those major social trends that have such structural force. It is certainly a concomitant of the constructivist revolution in contemporary social thought that the cogency of such assumptions has been substantially eroded, even if they continue in an auxiliary role, for example, in the way the concept of capitalism is frequently employed in micro-level studies. The cultural structuralist intellectual transformation in the mid-20th century progressively opened the way to increasing emphasis on cognition-guiding structures rather than determinative social structures. In the critical theoretical tradition, such cognition-guiding structures are considered, at least potentially, to occur in line with the directing will of human agents. In this

*Towards a Sign-Mediated Societal Ontology* 211

tradition, while the account remains underdeveloped, such cognitive structures, both of evolutionary origin and historically shaped, are deployed and modified in human praxis. Their modification emanates from normative learning processes with short-, medium-, and long-term effects. Such normative learning processes occur through the interplay of unconscious feeling and conscious reasoning in the wider context of social and natural forces. This interplay is guided by habits of feeling and of thought, though the recurrence of such habits may be punctuated by learning about and hence revision of the habits. The theory of a reasonable society is therefore based on identifying and normatively advocating those mutually intertwined dispositional qualities and modes of reasoning that make the most appropriate use, within society's organizational principles, of the evolutionary-formed capacities and historical potentials of the human cognitive endowment.

In the figure, the constructivist moment, whose vector runs along the right-hand side, is understood as the creative and dynamic product of human activity. Kantian constructivism, taken further in Peirce, Apel, and Habermas, draws attention to the evolutionary establishment of modes of reasoning and justification that are necessary for achieving normative reasonableness. This type of constructivism combines with rational structuration in the operations of the transcendently anchored cognitive order. The cognitive order, those evolutionary established principles that emerge from the temporally extended rationalization of human reasoning processes in multiple dimensions, is the essence of reason, [1] in the figure. It involves the selection of those cognitive principles that are essential to the common life of humans. It is important to note that they are cognitive principles that serve as structural conditions for feeling, thinking, and communicating, and not normative prescriptions. They give indispensable cognitive orientation for the formation of norms even if they cannot decide what they should be, for such deciding comes about immanently and normatively. Speaking of the combination of construction and structuration in the cognitive order means that the cognitive order principles give form to the potentially fully inclusive reasoning, the Kantian constructivism moment, but also represent, as structuration, a quasi-transcendental a priori that imposes orienting limits on the infinitude of possible societally relevant feeling and thinking. While on the one side, the principles represent *limits* to possible meaning, on the other side, their very limits are presuppositions of the creative mental powers that humans possess, in line with the kinds of structure/practice formulations to be variously found in Chomsky and Piaget. The theory of a reasonable society must therefore ask: What are these limits that serve as enabling conditions for generating knowledge in the actual and potential forms of collectively organized sociation?

To speak of limits as enabling conditions may seem paradoxical. Limits in this sense are to be understood as sense-making structures that orient possible meaning from the random infinity of possibility. Thus, to speak of a cognitive principle such as that of legitimacy entails understanding how such a principle can be logically employed within systems of meaning and to what it refers in the world. Transcendent limits of this kind that implicitly operate both as presuppositions and anticipations in cognitive practices are mirrored on the immanent plane by another kind of limit concept that is susceptible to conscious inferential explication.

## 212    *Towards a Sign-Mediated Societal Ontology*

These immanent limit concepts, [2], are, as explored, ideals that guide thought, communication, and action. These ideals, unlike transcendent cognitive principles, are directly graspable and enter societal application, including disputation. In the figure, they are represented by operation [2] and, as idealized validity standards, deductively enter reasoning. These ideals are the general 'purposes' of society. They form variable patterns with differing relative power across societies. Following the theme of structuration, they make possible two kinds of orientation. The first is the a priori orientation that emanates from settled consensus on beliefs, moral and functional, and the second is their role as cognitive orientations that define the space of argumentation – the frames – for the interpretation and application of the ideals. In the first instance, examples are 'all swans are white' or 'all should be equal before the law' and, in the second, an example is moral disputation over the level of material equality that should be brought about through policies and other actions. Ideals are not necessarily democratically 'positive'. A negative or regressive ideal is that of the moral necessity of social hierarchy, a viewpoint that is growing in potency once again at present in some quarters, as from others it becomes ever more resolutely opposed.

The selection of appropriate ideals underpins society-wide normative standards since ideals translate the validity of concepts instantiated in cognitive principles into valid achievement standards (Strydom, 2019). In line with the above, the continua of meaning supply conceptual orientations and the selection of ideals are convergent limits within such standards that specify what should be striven for immanently. Equality is a universal validity concept, whereas specific dimensions and degrees of equality are general immanent validity goals. The dimensions and degrees of ideals in the plural go to form *idealized* cognitive cultural models, [2] in the figure. Such models provide general immanent orientation and are continuously further elaborated in societal argumentation and practices. This further elaboration leads to the formation of nearer-to-action social cultural models, SCMs [4] in the figure, which consist of modalities of coordinating different validity preferences arising from the higher level of ideals, [2], with a simple example being the historical left/right split in normative culture. Once elaborated and selected in the relational fields of these 'lower' kinds of cultural models, the outcome leads downwards to institutional norm formation and to those concrete beliefs that underpin habits of action in institutional models, [9]. At least for the actors who have such habits, these manifest 'achieved validity' a power of action has been acquired, that is, eked out of the social-relational process. Such achieved validity though, contrary to Parsons and the functionalist tradition, should not be assumed to be either consensual or functionally necessary, as extensively, though far from entirely, it is shaped by asymmetrical power relations of many possible kinds. These last remarks also bear on 'materialist functionalism' within Marxism and various other traditions. The semiotic realism of the theory proposed here encompasses the permanent independence of natural objects and the acquired independence of social objects, so far as the latter have either unintended consequences or consequences intentionally visited by some agents on others through disparities of power. The production of consequences is nonetheless bound up with human purposes and

*Towards a Sign-Mediated Societal Ontology* 213

learning processes, though in conditions of social and natural constraint, including egregious asymmetries in access to resources. Contrary to strong materialist theories of Marxism, this is consistent with Marx's account of capitalism, variously as ideology, unintended consequences of the practices of capitalists, and the power of the willed purpose of transformative socialist praxis.

The reference to ideology immediately above echoes earlier references to regressive processes and outcomes. To attach centrality to reasoning does not entail that reasoning can always be assumed to act as a normative corrective to injustice, alienation, and dysfunction. Pathological or unjust reasoning, reflecting the state of the public sphere and societal conditions generally, pervades societal discourse (see Chapter 12). Within the general framework of a reasonable society, such reasoning entails constructing 'bad' inferential relations of various possible kinds. To speak of 'bad' in such a context does not automatically entail unsound, for, to take an example, reasoning that asserts the virtues of extreme hierarchy can claim soundness on its own terms, following its particular ends. To find such reasoning pathological or unjust still requires demonstrating its implications for the relevant situation (as revealed by secondness) and appropriate critical sentiments (as emerging from firstness). Such sentiments can be the outcome of prior experience or emerge from fundamental critical learning that reaches beyond it, and recasting it in a new way in line with Peirce's doubt-belief model (Peirce, 1992, 109–123).

From a critical-empirical standpoint, the analysis of pathological and unjust reasoning is paradoxically essential to theorizing a reasonable society. Such analysis can reveal the kinds of bad organization of society that follow from asymmetrical discursive power. The various critical standards of critical theory, reification, alienation, dysfunction, non-inclusion, and so on, can be expressed as inferential relations that generate and sustain societal pathologies, injustices, and contradictions. This will be taken up further in Chapter 12. In the tradition of Kantian constructivism, modified through Peirce for the import of conditions and feelings, reasoning can embark on reconstructive self-critique. Reason is to be equated with the quasi-transcendent implications of the evolutionary-formed cognitive principles that underpin human sociation, to whose immanent translation into democratic ideals modernity gave impetus, even if ambivalently, as the existence of contradictory ideals and bad reason attest. I cannot follow here all the implications of this expansion of the normative foundations of reason, for indeed, that would be a very long undertaking. To illustrate, it can readily be asserted, notwithstanding background beliefs in hierarchy, that it is not easy for anyone to publicly assert in democratic contexts that some citizens should be regarded as less worthy of equal treatment before the law. This illustration, to which many more could be added, suggests a democratic 'hardening' over time of certain commitments, an ongoing process with losses as well as gains and many enduring blind spots. Some ideals harden to the point of universal necessity and achieve the status of functional or moral a priori commitments, while others simply open cognitive spaces of contention with open and variable outcomes within certain limits.

The vector of structuration generally provides insight into the relationship between freedom and constraint. Reversing the upper numbers of the component

## 214  *Towards a Sign-Mediated Societal Ontology*

signs, that is, going from [5] back to [1] involves gains in freedom and rational capacity for action in multiple dimensions. Viewed this way, it is apparent how empirical-analytical sociology started too low in its concentration on combinations of norms, values, and rules, which were perceived as necessary, constraining standards for social organization. Modern forms of sociology, in seeking to escape this, took an antagonistic attitude to such assumptions of 'rational constraint', emphasized their embedding in power constellations, and sought to pursue freedom, mostly without calling it that, by emphasizing the active individual or collective subject (Rose, 2006). What is required is an elaboration of cultural structure that encompasses the possible kinds and levels of human social purposes and shows on the constructivist side how freedom and action are not alien to higher levels of structuration but, in the right circumstances, can be made possible by it. This critical theme, and its implications for validity, will be taken up in the next few chapters.

### Notes

1  This is just an illustration. All such 'strong' abductive schemata will be opposed by counter-schemata. The contemporary world now experiences elaborated counter-ecological schemata. One of the principal critical tasks of critical theory is to make sense of these debates within a developed normative perspective.
2  To exceed it is not necessarily to better it. Bad abduction, to be encountered later (Chapter 12), leads to reasoning pathologies.
3  As will be explored in subsequent chapters, the issue of validity within the frame of critical theory requires extensive exploration.

### References

Adorno TW 2019 (1964) *Philosophical Elements of a Theory of Society*. Cambridge: Polity.
Apel K-O (1995) *Charles Peirce: From Pragmatism to Pragmaticism*. New York, NY: Prometheus.
Arnason JP (2023) Lessons from Castoriadis: Downsizing Critical Theory and Defusing the Concept of Society. *European Journal of Social Theory* 26(2): 180–200.
Bagnoli C (2016) Kantian Constructivism and the Moral Problem. *Philosophia* 44(4): 1229–1246.
Bertilsson TM (2009) *Peirce's Theory of Inquiry and Beyond*. Frankfurt: Peter Lang.
Bourdieu P (1987) Towards a Sociology of the Legal Field. *Hastings Law Journal* 38: 814–853.
Castoriadis C (1998) *The Imaginary Institution of Society*. Cambridge, MA: MIT Press.
Dezalay Y (1990) The Big Bang and the Law: The Internationalization and Restructuration of the Legal Field. *Theory, Culture & Society* 7(2–3): 279–293.
Ehrat J (2005) *Cinema and Semiotic: Peirce and Film Aesthetics, Narration, and Representation*. Toronto: University of Toronto Press.
Emirbayer M (1997) Manifesto for a Relational Sociology. *American Journal of Sociology* 103(2): 281–317.
Emirbayer, M and Mische, A (1998) What is Agency. *American Journal of Sociology*. 103(4): 962–1023.
Eyerman R and Jamison A (1991) *Social Movements: A Cognitive Approach*. University Park, PA: Penn State Press.
Foucault M (1972) *The Archaeology of Knowledge*. New York, NY: Pantheon.

Frank M (1989) *What Is Neostructuralism?* Minneapolis, MN: University of Minnesota Press.

Garfinkel H, Rawls A, and Lemert CC (2015) *Seeing Sociologically: The Routine Grounds of Social Action*. London: Routledge.

Giddens A (1984) *The Constitution of Society*. Cambridge: Polity.

Habermas J (2003) *Truth and Justification*. Cambridge, MA: MIT Press.

Honneth A (2011) Verwilderungen des Sozialen Konflikts: Anerkennungskämpfe zu Beginn des 21. Jahrhunderts. Report: MPIfG working paper. Max Planck Institute for the Study of Societies. Cologne.

Honneth A (2014) *Freedom's Right: The Social Foundations of Democratic Life*. New York, NY: Columbia University Press.

Lakoff G and Johnson M (2003 (1980)) *Metaphors We Live By*. Chicago, IL: University of Chicago Press.

Lane R (2007) Peirce's Modal Shift: From Set Theory to Pragmaticism. *Journal of the History of Philosophy* 45(4): 551–576.

Mills CW (2000) *The Sociological Imagination*. Oxford: Oxford University Press.

Nesher D (2002) Peirce's Essential Discovery: "Our Senses as Reasoning Machines" Can Quasi-Prove our Perceptual Judgments. *Transactions of the Charles S. Peirce Society* 38(1/2): 175–206.

O'Mahony P (2013) *The Contemporary Theory of the Public Sphere*. Oxford: Peter Lang.

O'Mahony P (2021) Habermas and the Public Sphere: Rethinking a Key Theoretical Concept. *European Journal of Social Theory* 24(4): 485–506.

Patterson O (2014) Making Sense of Culture. *Annual Review of Sociology* 40(1): 1–30.

Peirce CS (1992) *The Essential Peirce: Selected Philosophical Writings. Vol. 1 (1867–1893)*. Bloomington, IN: Indiana University Press.

Peirce CS (1998) *The Essential Peirce: Selected Philosophical Writings. Vol. 2 (1893–1913)*. Bloomington, IN: Indiana University Press.

Renault E (2016) Critical Theory and Processual Social Ontology. *Journal of Social Ontology* 2(1): 17–32.

Rose N (2006) *Power of Freedom: Reframing Political Thought*. Cambridge: Cambridge University Press.

Short TL (2007) *Peirce's Theory of Signs*. Cambridge: Cambridge University Press.

Skillington T (1997) Politics and the Struggle to Define: A Discourse Analysis of the Framing Strategies of Competing Actors in a 'New' Participatory Forum. *British Journal of Sociology* 48(3): 493–513.

Strydom P (2019) On Habermas's Differentiation of Rightness from Truth: Can an Achievement Concept Do without a Validity Concept? *Philosophy and Social Criticism* 45(5): 555–574.

Wood ML, Stoltz DS, Van Ness J, et al. (2018) Schemas and Frames. *Sociological Theory* 36(3): 244–261.

# 8 Reason, Communication, and Validity

## Introduction

This chapter, the first of several on the theme, explores the critical concept of validity in terms of the overall goal of the book, an inferential semiotic representation of the normative implications of a cognitively grounded communicative reason. It explores how a reasonable society can be envisaged on this theoretical foundation and, within it, how critique fits with validity, given that their relative disjunction is, to some degree, at least a source of theoretical disablement in contemporary critical theory. The theoretical account begins with a focus on validity over the next three chapters, building on a previous book (O'Mahony, 2013). A comprehensive turn to emphasizing communicatively constructed validity was put in place in Habermas's *TCA*, and, as explored, important arguments were there advanced. However, this approach only took the critical task so far. It came before Habermas's normative philosophical turn, and he appeared to leave the project undeveloped. Though the account of communicative action was indeed innovative and intricate, it lacked the focus on inferential processes of schematization that could throw a generative light, in the sense of how they come to be and what brings about their change, on the pivotal concepts, respectively, normative and non-normative, of lifeworld and system. Further, later in *BFN* and beyond, when Habermas moves in a normative-democratic direction, the divide between a procedural normative philosophy and the social scientific logic of inquiry grew relatively wider, even if in his case far less wide than most moral and political philosophy, critical theoretical or otherwise.

One casualty of this, vital for critical theory, is that the link between validity and critique was not fully explicated, nor has it been adequately since. This has much to do with the particular way in which validity was developed in *TCA* as a theory of validity claims within speech act theory. This account was accentuated by the encompassing tendency in critical theory not to systematically address the relationship between validity and critique, a relation at the heart of any account of critical reason. This is not to say that there has been no development in this space, but that it is relatively insufficient with respect to both dimensions, separately and in their interpenetration.

This theme has already been enjoined in previous chapters, but it is more systematically addressed in the current one. Regarding the approach to validity here,

DOI: 10.4324/9780429060571-9

a few key points arising from preceding chapters may be of value. Habermas has identified validity claims associated with the truth, rightness, and sincerity of propositions. Propositions raise yes/no validity claims with respect to each or all of the validity conditions, all in the case of full-blown communicative action, and each in the case of various kinds of possible actions: teleological, normative, and expressive. The approach here, taken from Peirce, while far from separating fully from this framework, substantially substitutes an inferential approach based on the logic of argument. Arguments are integrated chains of inferentially established meaning regulated by orienting concepts that bind propositions and terms together. Accordingly, the general, inferentially structured schemata arising from and implicated in reasoning take logical precedence over individual propositions and singular terms. This is by no means a recipe for methodological holism, since changes in individual terms and propositions – altered consciousness, new empirical circumstances – modify the implication of general concepts. However, they can only do this where there is established general meaning, regulated by validity conferring general concepts. It is on the basis of this general meaning, constitutive in the case of divergent cognitive principles and regulative in the case of regulative ideals, that their individual meaningful form has been established. Where a proposition has valid meaning, therefore, it is already part of a general conceptually organized schema, but its meaning may change in the light of new information that brings into question its precise place within the schema. This will lead to changes in the schema as well, and, in cases of radical learning, changes in its form. This is as characteristic of the 'lower' cognitive levels as of the convergent cognitive cultural model (CCM).

Individual propositions thus gain their validity from their positioning within general schemata that circumscribe their possible relevance to the external world. Cognition is thus not fully comprehensible as only the yes/no testing of the validity of individual propositions serving as an inductive basis for establishing generality. Rather, the general itself is cognitively active and real. Generals have their own distinctive cognitive operations that sapient actors must be able to master in common. It must be clear, for example, what a relevant general context is, especially when that context is rapidly evolving under the pressure – for political issues – of public discourse. Formats for coordinating collective learning in the light of such extended and evolving discourse must also be generally shared, for example, coresponsible insight into a public issue such as climate change. Accordingly, general concepts and the immanent schemata on which they rely (the CCM) have their own cognitive status and operations that can be assessed as rational, just, or otherwise. Downstream, the outcomes of these operations, the cultural forms of a society, a normative order, a political party, and a social movement can be shown to *potentially* achieve some degree of reasonableness judged by some defensible standards. They can also be shown to have failed to achieve any defensible degree of reasonableness.

To conceive of generals as real is essential for viewing argumentation as the integral foundation of propositions and terms rather than the other way round. Individuals (in the logical sense) acquire validity in view of their relation to generals. This shift in focus requires a different way of thinking about validity and about the

218  *Reason, Communication, and Validity*

cultural forms that carry it. The semiotic logic in Peirce and the role within it of innerworldly cognitive processes and their outcomes both characterizes thought in the world and also the special kind of thinking that is reasoning that enables transformative reflection. The outline of fields, spaces, schemata/models, and vectors in the last few chapters also shows that logical discourse (logos) does not subsist on its own. It is conditioned by self-consciousness (including group consciousness) and existent – material and socially materialized – forces. In this chapter, the differentiation and potential integration of forms of reason – subjective, intersubjective, and objective – can also be brought into the picture and matter for further treatment.

The relevant comparison between this approach and that of Habermas then, in substantial part, falls on perceived limitations in his account of reasoning – communicative action – specifically, the failure to extend consideration of yes/ no validity claims to the 'triadic' elaboration of steps of reasoning. The speech act theoretical framework, even when quasi-transcendentally extended, results in isolation from both self- and trans-consciousness, respectively, represented in the process of abductive schema formation and of mediating and organizing cultural models. Extending the framework in the Peirceian direction accordingly allows these dimensions to be included and, within them, two divided moments of sociology, structural-explanatory and phenomenological-hermeneutic, to be better integrated within a more developed, and essential, third dimension, that of concern for the reasonable by means of valid reasoning in accord with appropriate validity standards. This third dimension was present in classical sociology, the meta-conceptual standards of justice and solidarity in Marx, solidarity in Durkheim, and the charisma of reason in Weber. This kind of sociology of reason is practically everywhere misrecognized and diminished within the abiding assumption of a discipline-defining struggle between the 'rationality' of empirical-analytical approaches and the 'hermeneutics' of interpretive sociology. It is further diminished by the tendency within critical sociology to gravitate towards negative critique without any clear attempt to specify corresponding validity standards.

These problems were not satisfactorily overcome by the relationship, traced by Habermas, between communicative action and, respectively, lifeworld and system complexes in *TCA*, even if it was creatively elaborated. The problems that lay unresolved were to clarify how system and lifeworld were constituted in relation to reason or unreason, and also how either concept could be empirically employed within the theory of society. The respective formulae of 'problematization of the lifeworld' and 'societal rationalization' were prominent and have served as important lodestars of a critical theory of society ever since, but were not integrated adequately into the role reason played in the integration and transformation of society. Hence, validity was principally placed on the transcendent, conceptual level, and immanent ideals and goals that could capture both stable *and* dynamic features of social reproduction and change remained underdeveloped.

The core of the cognitive thrust of this book is not to be confused with the standard assumption about the 'cognitive'. Mostly, the cognitive in this latter sense is opposed to the normative or the aesthetic given the premise that it pertains only to

*Reason, Communication, and Validity*   219

alethic rationality. By contrast, cognitive forms are here understood as evolutionary-formed real transcendentals – for example, ideas of truth, dignity, efficiency, control, critique, and legitimacy that have a presupposing and idealizing force. These real transcendentals offer conceptual foundations for validity. They present infinite possibilities of logically distinctive interpretation within a specific continuum of meaning. Their evolutionarily formed role is to make possible immanent discourses of certain kinds and thus to constitute multiple orders of knowing. Metacognitive concepts of legitimacy, privacy, and publicity, for example, accordingly have a general transcendent form that has been crystallized over human evolutionary time.

Strydom, as already outlined, has made an important contribution to extending the theory of validity by distinguishing between validity as a concept and validity as a goal (Strydom, 2019b). Validity concepts exist in this cognitive approach condition but do not determine validity goals. In a Kantian sense, the concepts offer conditions of possibility for the goals. This means that validity goals, which are present at different cultural levels of societal coordination, are immanent specifications of the overarching validity concepts, with many variations at different times and places. Validity as a concept thus pertains to the activation of cognitive principles of the widest generality. Such principles are products of cultural evolution and have a presupposing or idealizing quality in delimiting possible human purposes. In Peirce's terms, they condition the spectrum of qualitative perceptions right at the beginning of cognitive episodes, the qualitative possibilities of the previous chapter. Humans perceive the things they do – I am thinking here of social objects – because they are certain kinds of beings whose socialization makes certain qualities of these things relevant to their practices. Validity as a concept is first immanently experienced as qualitative feelings that become more general as perception proceeds before finally transposing into reasoning and its world application. Hence, validity as a concept pertains to the sense of relevance of a presupposing quasi-transcendental cognitive principle to a social situation. Validity at this level is a quasi-transcendental concept with a bivalent quality that specifies its designation value, its sphere of validity, and a negation value, the sphere in which it is not valid. Putting it more simply, each cognitive principle specifies a validity concept for certain cognitive operations. At the most basic level, this means the competence to distinguish between what makes sense and what is non-sense in a particular conceptual register, for example, political legitimacy or legality.

In complex discourses, like the discourse of democracy, different validity concepts move in and out of focus as the discourse progresses. The validity concepts are discrete, like the codes of DNA, but together, when spread across a complex discourse, they form a dense interpenetrating web. Their discrete quality is owed to their status as the cognitive principles. As such, they are the most abstract of generals, that which is absolutely foundational to the capacity for thinking in indispensable ways, its condition of possibility. These conceptual capacities ultimately become immanently manifested in argumentation schemas, but they have an underlying transcendental logic. The actual principles are shared world-related 'mental' constructs that have grown up in the course of evolution from protracted

## 220 *Reason, Communication, and Validity*

immersion in worlds of all kinds. As foundational, here following Peirce's three categories, the transcendentally located validity concepts have, firstly, inductive world-relevant properties; secondly, they offer a criteriology of perceptual relevance; and, thirdly, they are underpinned by acritical deductive capacities for diagrammatic integration of premises into conclusions. In their relatively structured and unvarying properties, they are similar to the Kantian transcendental noumenal schemata, elaborated further by Hans Lenk (Lenk, 2003). In essence, then, validity concepts prescribe a spectrum of bivalently valid cognitive principles that are perception-guiding, reason-orienting, and world-relevant. They are at the very core of what may be designated as the capacity for reason as opposed to reasoning, yet they historically emerged from immanent processes of signification, including reasoning, and their reception changes with ongoing signification.

Turning to validity as an achievement- or goal-concept involves a move to the immanent plane, but an immanent plane conditioned by these validity concepts in a manner similar to the DNA metaphor. Validity concepts get 'moved about' according to the societal construction and implications of immanent cultural orders. Though they delimit common cognitive capacities, they are open to a wide range of interpretations, in principle, an infinite range. This quasi-transcendental realm of validity concepts is contrasted to the immanent level of validity goals, in which the varied interpretations and ultimately normative fixing of the concepts take place, so far as that can be achieved. I use the term 'quasi' to distinguish between metaphysical rationalist supra-mundane conceptions of transcendence from those that emerge within intra-mundane evolutionary time. Along with the validity concepts, there are also capacities of mind, both the minds of individual persons and interlocking capacities of extended mind. Such interlocking mental capacities are transcendental products of evolution. Peirce's account of the intrinsic categories, firstness, secondness, and thirdness, is intended to capture the process whereby symbol-using creatures construct meaning conditioned by the world beyond the mind and by their own natural and cultural evolution. Both the concepts and capacities are a priori. Being evolutionary, they are subject to change, but this change is slow, relatively faster for the concepts than the capacities, but still slow.

The above-sketched distinctions do not sit well with the dominant architectonic of the social sciences. Any a priori transcendent element in social theorizing is routinely dismissed. The corresponding immanent emphasis on the potential rationality involved in *constructing* the future, arising in some critical theory approaches, is deemed to deviate from the reigning concern for the relentless critique of an overbearing reason. This orientation has been examined in earlier chapters. The challenge before critical theory is to contribute to creating a just world, and, as Apel has emphasized, today the question of planetary responsibility, among all the other reasons, compels attention to the general normative order. To grasp this order requires attention to generals, both those that have an evolutionary cognitive quality and those historically constructed and granted the status of extended validity, the CCMs of the previous chapter. In the very long run, both are the product of inferential operations of reasoning, congealing respectively in cognitive structures that enable knowing and in their product, knowledge, where the latter is understood

*Reason, Communication, and Validity*  221

as temporarily 'settled' normative orders of all kinds, communities of volition and action that establish ongoing, settled practices.

The above distinction between 'live' reasoning processes and instituted orders of knowledge allows a shorthand distinction to be made between the two *validation* processes and *validated* practices. As explored earlier, neither validation nor validated presuppose consensual agreement, though that is also possible and, to some degree at least, even indispensable to any prospect of a just society. These two concepts, validation and validated, together go all the way from the initial vagueness involved in the process of contesting pre-existing instituted validity at the phenomenal level, to addressing validity claims in reasoning processes, to institutionally concretizing newly validated normative orders. The realization of valid orders, in other words, the power to shape order, can be achieved as much, in contemporary conditions perhaps more, through pathological and unjust validation processes as through any kind of defensible concrete reasonableness consistent with the validity standards of critical theory. The entire process of settling validity, viewed through the framework of the previous chapter, which distinguished between perceptual, discursive, and positional fields, is complex. It is also reciprocal in the sense that what is validated may become unstable, for example, through societal crisis leading to altered or transformed perception and potentially from there into ongoing contested learning processes over what should be institutionally validated.

In the following parts of this chapter, and in the chapters to follow, the overall frame of discourse ethics guides the approach. In a modified form, the discourse ethical approach has the form of a defensible normative democratic theory that can be transposed into a logic of inquiry. The specification of validity standards, the normative dimension, that could guide such a logic of inquiry is outlined in the next chapter. In this chapter, first of all, some basics pertaining to the discourse ethical account of validity are outlined in the next section. This introduction of the normative standpoint of discourse ethics moves the account of validity from documenting outcomes to assessing how validity standards can be brought to bear within a communicative, inferential logic. The thesis asserts that the relationship between reasoning and validity is at the core of second-generation critical theory, and that it is essential, if the potential of that second generation is to be fully realized, to the future of critical theory as both a democratic and, at the same time, a social theory. The core is not complete by just emphasizing validity standards. It also requires a concern for specifying those dimensions of critique by virtue of which existing validity standards can be deployed or altered over time. Validity and critique are inextricably intertwined. The dimensions of critique are thus considered along with those of validity, but their fuller development awaits subsequent chapters.

**Discourse Ethics and Validity Standards**

Discourse ethics[1] is a philosophy advancing a distinctive normative account of the democratic organization of society. As such, it postulates a desired relationship between democracy and other social spheres. A just society can be brought about through building universal reflexive capacity into political

## 222 *Reason, Communication, and Validity*

institutions that are broadly understood to include the public sphere. In a radical Kantian line, it is concerned with rightness as the self-legislation of citizens, advancing a normative thesis as to how inclusive, deliberative democratization can bring about the just organization of society. Its challenge is to show how deliberative democratic designs, in the widest understanding of deliberation, could transpose into a just society in conditions of complexity and pluralism? This is a notably cross-disciplinary challenge, for it raises the question beyond the immediate remit of normative theories of how can the path to application of a universally agreed norm be elucidated by means of the objectivating filter of the social sciences? This interdisciplinary challenge is also a rationality challenge; how can the claims of different kinds of rationality be reconciled? Even more fundamentally, it asks how can the ideal of a reasonable society be anticipated against the ever-present danger of regression to non-rational, or only selectively rational, value preferences and normative orders?

Two broad options for deciding the place of discourse ethics within these characteristic challenges emerge. The first is a strong democratic theory that is firmly located in rightness over against, though not entirely disregarding, the functional and the good. The second is a type of 'weaker' democratic theory, in part dependent upon social processes, shaped by the functional and good as well as the moral-legal. Such social processes cannot be fully regulated in advance, and in the light of their dynamics, democratic society must constantly adjust its forms, if not its basic precepts. Even Habermas, whose contribution to the social sciences and to these very questions has been extensive and path-breaking, may be variably positioned between these two poles of a strong and weaker democratic theory. In his attempts to reconcile them, the deontological normative claims of the first tend to override dynamic societal processes. Yet, such processes both have emergent normative implications and also condition how norms are practically utilized. In spite of many attempts at reconciling the deontological and the processual from *TCA* onwards, he has never fully succeeded to the detriment of social theoretical application. Such a reconciliation is essential as discourse ethics is at base a strongly participatory democratic theory, even if this participatory quality in practice appears less than commensurate to its abstracted inclusion principles, as illustrated by the deliberative turn that brought it closer to institutional liberal theories and away from institutional designs based on radically extended participation, towards institutionalized political-legal deliberation and away from public deliberation.

This core question of discourse ethics thus extends to the issue of whether the democratic forms present in society are adequate or whether, quite differently, more participatory forms are required? In my view, the second choice is the more promising, though it should be guided by a stronger participatory democratic theory. In turn, such a participatory theory should build on rather than attempt to disregard existing institutional forms of democracy. The requirements for integrating participatory innovation within liberal institutions were explored in depth in my *Contemporary Theory of the Public Sphere* from both a normative theoretical and social theoretical vantage point (O'Mahony, 2013). The existing democratic centre of gravity cannot hold, because the highly indirect, representative institutions

Reason, Communication, and Validity 223

of liberal democracy as they stand do not foster popular self-legislation. Without more advanced capacity for self-legislation on different societal levels, below, at, and above the nation-state, the institutional elements of democracy become more and more a veneer that does not penetrate into multiple social spheres, especially those high-consequence spheres such as security, economy, and information that globalized first, and generally show accelerated development. Yet, emerging in the broader democratic space are the deliberative and participatory germs of an altered democratic form. This view requires rethinking the relationship between discourse ethics, or Habermas's later deliberative theory, and social processes generally. It proposes that discourse ethics be pushed in a more radical participatory direction, impelled by the depth of contemporary problems. In important respects, this lies in line with Apel's more teleological approach to the relationship between democracy and societal challenges, for example, the challenge of co-responsibility in the face of planetary destruction (Apel, 2001).

The focus of discourse ethics lies on two kinds of interrelated 'principles', namely, unconditioned cognitive order principles, lying on the transcendent plane, and immanent, conditioned cognitive-normative ideals lying on the immanent plane. The differentiation and integration of these have already been addressed at a general level. For present purposes, the transcendent plane specifies those evolutionary-formed competences that provide necessary orientation for a good common life and, when translated into the architecture of appropriate general ideals on the immanent plane, provide a foundation for democracy. Both the transcendent and immanent components of the theory turn on communicative reasoning, the first providing the basic communicative orientations (the communicative validity concepts) and the second the specific singular and interpenetrating ideals that underpin an appropriate kind of democracy. Together, these form three essential levels of theorizing, the unconditioned, transcendent, level, the conditioned immanent level, and the reproductive and transformative power of reasoning.

It is intrinsic to the original intentions of the theory that its core ideals can only be realized by means of a participatory transformation of democracy. The rationale for such a participatory transformation is already implied in the basic inclusive norm-setting ideals that would be manifest in a certain kind of universalistic reasoning. This is not easy to accomplish, as the recent history of the participatory theory of democracy illustrates. Any progress in the narrow political arena would mean little if function systems, everyday life, and civil society were not to be themselves compatibly minimally democratized in a participatory direction. The increased level of difficulty in moving towards such a level of democratization has much to do with the institutional success of radical liberalization as privatization advanced by the new right over the last half-century. Yet, such liberalization offered today represents only one direction forward. Another is the democratization of national and macro-regional welfare states, accompanied by a different kind of solidaristic globalization, which has been left relatively unconsidered. Indeed, the advent of liberalization was a historical 'choice', as another such choice involving the deepening of the welfare state and a different form of globalization was actively possible at the same time. There is no doubt that neoliberalism won

224 *Reason, Communication, and Validity*

the ideological battle and, also, was easier to realize by providing monetary and status incentives to important demographics, along with the new acceptability of marginalization and relative pauperization of others. Of course, the radical liberalization wave has now gone on, particularly influencing allocative institutions and great swathes of culture, and it has made further democratization appear very difficult, especially when globalization and the letting loose of a wave of democracy-sceptical neoconservativism are taken into account. At the same time, society is polarized, and the effects of the counterculture of the sixties, as elaborated in subsequent decades, are also pervasive, though not as institutionally powerful. These remarks suggest that discourse ethics cannot simply understand itself as a normative position advocating the progressive finalization of certain ideals, but it also has to engage substantively with those societal tendencies that could advance or inhibit its normative project.

In this respect, in his late work, Apel proposed a double emphasis on discourse ethics, both deontological in the sense of the specification of those democratic principles that are 'uncircumventable' and teleological in the sense of a transformation of both democratic institutions and social spheres beyond them (Apel, 2001). The teleological dimension advances the necessity of actualizing the basic moral principles of discourse ethics in societal arrangements, with most decisively comprehensive democratic participation as a moral imperative. Once again, in the basic Kantian sense, what is at issue is the universalization of moral principles, while allowing for alternative societal mechanisms and general complexity. Habermas's solution in *TCA*, relatively long ago now, was to concede the autonomy of social systems built around the media of power and money. This led him into a contradiction taking the form of how systems, thus autonomous, could be normatively regulated. The solution that followed was to advance the idea of a stronger institutional democratic presence between system and lifeworld, chiefly through deliberative theory. It was further supplemented within critical theory by Klaus Günther's distinction and reconciliation between justification and application discourses that Habermas also took over ((Günther, 1993; Habermas, 1996).

These efforts, though important steps away from the de-contextualizing tendency of normative philosophies, suffer from a few shortcomings. The first is that the agency of situated actors in the here and now is positioned too remotely from the democratic core, as Habermas has specified it. What appears instead are 'counterfactual persons' who can be hypothetically invested with the necessary dispositions and competences. It is a variation on Rawls's veil of ignorance, and it suffers from a similar limitation of such counterfactual persons being taken to leave their concrete experiences on the outside of hypothetical procedures. It is highly limiting, even if it is more 'realistic' than the participatory claims of discourse ethics, that is, more realistic in conformity with existing institutional orders. Such an approach advances the claim that deliberation is already strong within such existing institutional orders and that the corresponding task is to advance it still further. However, this kind of institutional deliberation, while in some cases extremely important, is nonetheless not the dominant way in which democracy conducts itself

*Reason, Communication, and Validity*   225

as a practice, and it tends to neglect the wider kind of public deliberation emphasized by Bohman, partly as a critique of Habermas (Bohman, 2000). It thus serves as an important stepping stone, but not at all in conformity with the original ideals of discourse ethics. On this narrow deliberative, already institutionalized, basis, it has proven extremely difficult to actualize basic principles of discourse ethics. In fact, under the assault of the new right, some aspects of their force have been weakened, for example, universalistic solidarity and legitimacy. It leaves a democratic vicious circle, in that the institutional legal-political forms cannot sufficiently shape the societal conditions, and the worsening societal conditions, or their perceived worsening, undermine the existing forms.

The second is that generally defensible, readily identifiable, moral principles – Rawls's difference principle, neo-Marxist anti-exploitation, the inalienable dignity of discriminated groups – have at most an indirect presence. These and other absences ensure the purity of the principle, and in this respect, they are illustratively defensible on the highest level but immediately reveal a situationally indifferent account with the change in perspective from the pure procedure to its application context. This is exemplified in Habermas's shift in focus from 'the ideal speech situation' to deliberative democracy. Present basic liberal democratic institutions, or only modest deliberative modifications of them, do not vindicate the inclusive participatory norm of discourse ethics. This could only be achieved, so far as it can really be, if these institutions were to be substantially altered in a participatory direction. Internally, Apel has proposed a distinction between the pure reason of discourse ethics, part A and impure application in part B, but this distinction and part B itself are generally underdeveloped (Apel, 2001). For this, social scientific theories of a kind compatible with discourse ethics would be intrinsic, but by and large, they have not yet been developed. This is not just a pressing problem but also an opportunity if it could be grasped.

The third is that law, even if critical, cannot be seen as a *sufficient* solution to the double problem of the ideal mediation and concrete application of moral principles. Social forces emanate elsewhere that substantially condition law, and law cannot be considered as superordinate to these conditioning forces in all cases, since just as often its operations are either subordinate to them or unaware of wider, emerging moral ideas in society generally. Of course, this does not deny the possibility that law encapsulates and institutionalizes collective learning taking place elsewhere, as is manifest in the new environmental legal activism (McMurry, 2023). Nor does it deny that innovative currents in law, academic and practical, may actually mean that law might be the arena in which fundamental collective learning takes place. A great deal depends on what is considered to be the medium of law and its demarcation from wider public discourse. It is contended here that this demarcation leans too much towards the formal context of law itself after Habermas's democratic turn.[2]

And, finally, since discourse ethics, formed in the tradition of Peirce, assumes the power of future-oriented reasoning, it cannot do this without a sophisticated theory of collective learning. A normative science such as discourse ethics must fully incorporate the diagnostic and prognostic power of the social sciences

## 226  *Reason, Communication, and Validity*

by demonstrating how normative principles are or can be embedded in collective learning processes and downstream institutionalization. In this way, the emergence of history-related capacities for normatively directed social change can become manifest as potentials with prospects of realization, or, alternatively, can be blocked (Eder, 1985).

To elaborate on the core principles of discourse ethics, universality and inclusion in norm-determining discourse, in such a way as to do justice to the above implied need for reorientation is a challenging task. Such reorientation must address both the innovation and application problems of the theory. The innovation problem has to do with the fact that the context in which validity claims are being raised is constantly evolving, hence requiring a quality of conjecture that is adequately world-defining or appropriately world-creating. The application problem relates to the world understandings that must be adequately anticipated in the combined normative and empirical-theoretical projections of the theory. Innovation arises with abduction, where the validity standard, as explored further in the next chapter, is in the form of a conjectural claim to validity. The corresponding type of critique, emphasized by both Kant and Peirce, is aesthetic critique, the crystallization of what is possible as a conjecture that either criticizes an existing state of affairs, or knowledge of such a state of affairs, and discloses the possibility of a new one. In the logic of inquiry, deduction explicates the implications of an abductively revealed conjecture. The corresponding type of critique is ideal critique, in the light of the implications of the abductive conjecture for the normative quality of one or more ideals. It is also the locus of the idea of reconstruction in critical theory, where reconstruction is applied to the configuration of ideals that could, would, or should be brought to bear on the actual world. Application – or actualization – has to do with induction, where the validity standard is actual validity and the type of critique is applied normative (actual) critique. This kind of critique addresses the facticity and potential transformability of the social world, deriving from the reconstructive ideal critical process.

Since Peirce's logical theory, as Habermas also outlines it in his 2019 book, was ultimately concerned with questions of establishing what is true in the external world, his account of deduction correspondingly focussed on truth as an ideal validity standard (Habermas, 2019). The key to integrating formal pragmatics into Peirce's logical theory is to expand the deductive level to include the other validity standards as well. In other words, the ideal standards of rightness and ethical appropriateness must also be accommodated. Habermas has pioneered an approach in which rightness claims should be given the same importance as truth claims. His formal pragmatic validity claims of truthfulness or authenticity, truth, and rightness are idealizations that provide validity standards for reasoning. At the deductive level of ideal concepts, they point to different intrinsic groups of Strydom's account of cognitive principles, with truth being associated with principles bearing on the objective world such as control or efficiency, truthfulness with principles bearing on the subjective world such as authenticity or dignity, and rightness with principles bearing on the social-normative world such as

*Reason, Communication, and Validity* 227

legitimacy, solidarity, or legality (Strydom, 2019a). A further point to emphasize is that these distinctive sets of principles are often not clearly separated in contexts of application, a variation of the problem of interpenetration addressed in Chapter 3, following Munch.

Ideal validity standards are, first of all, cognitive validity standards. Such ideals cognitively orient but do not determine normative conclusions. They nonetheless have a minimum normative force that recognizes what has either become a moral or legal 'grounding' consensus. Such a consensus, operating in a given space and time, orients further discourse, that is, constrains it while also opening further possibilities within the range of its constraint – its limit concept. Also, on the ideal plane, a point emphatically introduced by Max Miller, one must also allow for what he describes as 'rational dissensus', that is, where respect is accorded to different accounts of specific principles, for example, legitimacy, or combinations of such principles, for example, democracy (Miller, 1992). Beyond this, there are commonly different normative interpretations of the various ideal standards, where these differences are 'settled' at the next level down, the sociocultural model, according to the various coordination modalities described in the last chapter. This level throws up alternative possibilities *in actu* for either an agreed or coercively attained conclusion. Such conclusions, instanced in radically different cases of a generally agreed constitutional norm or a successful ideological promulgation of a factually false norm, mean that ideals can become norms. In other words, the cognitive space of an ideal can become shrunken to only one interpretation, which is manifested at the level of the institutional model (IM). In general, regarding validity claims, the abductive-deductive moment of conjectural thematization is a moment of cognitive opening, and the deductive-inductive moment is a moment of normative closing, though final closure is not attainable in many cases. The latter moment of closing involves the process, intrinsic to discourse ethics as a theory but little demonstrated in practice, of forming an appropriate norm from a general, and in this sense unspecific, cognitive-normative ideal.

To summarize the development of the chapter thus far, firstly, there has been some general indication of the account of validity as developed in the book in the first section above. In this current section, such an account has been elaborated in relation to the normative programme of discourse ethics, specifically with a view to re-examining Habermas's account of validity as ultimately dependent on communicative reasoning. Some further remarks were also offered on the discourse ethics approach as a whole, indicating the need for its further development. Further, in this emerging account, validity was embedded, as of now merely suggestively, in Peirce's three categories of inferential reasoning within an accompanying logic of inquiry. This captures the double aim of advancing an account that would be theoretically-empirically fruitful as well as normatively appropriate. In the next section, which is a type of orienting reflection that both points back to what has been done as well as forward to subsequent chapters, a further development of the semiotic figure introduced in the last chapter (Figure 7.1) is presented. A variation on this figure, Figure 8.1, *Validity and Societal Ontology*, this time will be specified for the issue of validity.

228  *Reason, Communication, and Validity*

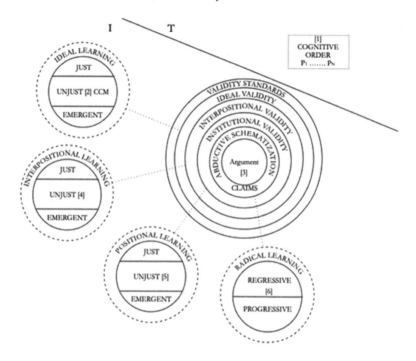

*Figure 8.1* Validity and Societal Ontology

**Validity and the Reasonable**

Figure 8.1 is a variation on Figure 7.1, this time specialised for the issue of validity. All the basic features and dynamics that were described in Figure 7.1 are also taken to apply to Figure 8.1. and they will not be specifically outlined here except where essential. Furthermore, the figure will at this point be specified only in minimal, architectural outline, as the dimensions bearing on validity arising from it, and represented on it, will be given extensive attention over the next two chapters.

The validity-specific innovations bear in particular on a number of components of the figure. This applies, firstly, to the three cultural models, the cogntiive cultural model, the CCM, the sociocultural model, the SCM, and the institutional model, the IM. It applies, secondly, to the component of reasoning or logic proper. Of course, emphasizing how validity operates for each of these components also has implications for all the other components. Nonetheless, the critical theoretical understanding of validity has basic affinities with these particular components.

Though the CCM bears on 'the reasonable' as a general cognitive horizon that comes before any specific acts of reasoning, giving them form and direction as discourse ordering ideals, I will, first of all, concentrate here on reasoning understood as the distinctive *process form* of discourse ethics and of critical theory more generally, and where the complementary term of justification is often used.[3] Figure 8.1 distinguishes within *Reasoning (3)*, assumed to take place in the discursive field, between three modes of validation: conjectural, ideal, and actual. These modes of validation, the subject matter of the next chapter, are not simply associated with the validity standards of discourse ethics but also serve as general modes of reasoning even where the concerns of discourse ethics are entirely sidelined. The focus on what follows allows for the assumption that some kind of reasoning has 'gone on' before any specific intervention of the normative standards of discourse ethics, and it must be assumed that it has not gone on entirely well and often very badly. So, the validity standards also harbour within them distinctive moments of critique, aesthetic, ideal, and actual. The further outline of the dimensions of critique will be the subject matter of later chapters and will build on the completed analysis of validity.

The assumed improvement on Habermas is that this specification of validity standards extends the lens beyond the 'mere' raising of such claims in a transcendental validity frame. Nonetheless, such a frame is vitally important, as it is the means to consider what general principles pertain to the raising of a validity claim and that activate evolutionarily endowed reasoning competence. Given that this is the basic starting point of any societal reasoning whatsoever, it is noteworthy that the contemporary social sciences to a very great extent, indeed almost universally, ignore or diminish it. Within critical theory, and moral and political philosophy more generally, it is often dismissed as supra-contextual and thus inapplicable. This is clearly not a position held in the current book. However, it is also the case that it is not sufficient on its own. The crucial 'hinge' insight is that whereas Habermas utilizes this quasi-transcendent, supra-contextual move as the foundation of validity, and then considers rationalization from this standpoint, there are other moves, also entailed within reasoning, that he does not equivalently consider. The first such move is to explicate the precise immanent validity standards of discourse ethics, contained in its interpretation of the democratic CCM. It may be said this is implicitly done, but it does not issue in systematically addressing how validity analysis should be pursued that would properly combine immanent and transcendent within the conditions of actual or foreseeable societal arrangements. The later analysis of detranscendentalization, in reality immanent transcendence, does point in this direction but is more of a call to arms than a systematic account (Habermas, 1992). Difficulties also arise when analysing either validity in conflictual situations or the validity of instituted norms. The reasoning process that corresponds to this is 'actualization', the consideration of the implication of modal normative projections in societal contexts. The typical response of discourse ethics is that these are 'material' norms best left to participants themselves to decide once the framework conditions are themselves decided, but this strategy runs the acute risk of de-historicization and loss of clarity of objects of critique – unjust, reify alienating, exploiting, etc. – arising in the positional field. It thus deviates from the long-running left-Hegelian critique of deontological formalism from the standpoint of both objects of critique in the positional field and responsive possibilities arising in the perceptual field. This has, in turn, given rise to a new debate within critical theory on these matters, especially taking the form of ideal versus non-ideal theory, a debate that still lacks some clarity. In my view, both ideal and non-ideal theory assumptions are requisite. The normative core of critical theory must balance ideal and non-ideal considerations, as Thomas McCarthy already emphasized some time ago (McCarthy, 1993; 2009).

230　*Reason, Communication, and Validity*

This means that the question of actual validity, and the potentials present in existing social forms, must become intrinsic to the reasoning process and, by extension, the logic of inquiry of critical theory. The three kinds of validity associated with the different kinds of reasoning – abductive (conjectural), deductive (ideal), and inductive (actual) – will be explored in Chapter 10. While for analytic purposes they will be examined individually as well as interdependently, the latter is pivotal to understanding the role of the various kinds of inference in reasoning.

Reverting to Figure 8.1, I want to draw attention now to four concentric broken lines that surround the sign of *Argument*. These lines capture the particular architecture of discourse ethics. Each of the spaces within the lines relates to a dimension of schematization, what I have been calling, on the one hand, abductive schema formation in the very inside space operating on the generative or constructivist plane and cultural models occupying the further three spaces on the plane of structuration. The lines are specifically placed around the sign of argument to indicate a distinction between the general societal form of the various schemata, how they appear as signs in themselves, as opposed to the way they are being 'localized' in an episode of thematization, of cognitively processing a theme. Thus, what the device of the concentric broken lines indicates is the thematic selection of what is being made relevant in discourse. It advances the doubt-belief model towards a cognitive process model. That which is contained in these lines is an episode of thematization, approximating to what is sometimes called an issue culture in the literature on media communication and social movements. It involves particular selections from the universe of actuality and from the infinite vastness of the universe of possibility. This combined effect is to create a space of temporary schematization within the space of displacement and bringing it to bear on the discursive field. It offers direction to the abductive logical processes that open up the space of reasons.

The space within the inner line is therefore, as earlier described, that of abductive schematization. This is the most creative of schema-forming processes, condensing the thematization process within the discursive space of potentiality that, through logical means, will over time, short or long, be further explicated and tested. The second space out, addressing the issue of – in some way, validated – normative validity, corresponds to the *institutional model*; the third space corresponds to the differentiated validity standards present in society, and correlates with both the cognitive cultural and sociocultural models. Finally, the space within the outer line is taken to signify the various validity standards of discourse ethics, to be specified in the next chapter.[4] This last space is meta-normative in the sense of normative proposals that stand beyond current cultural orders and institutional arrangements. All of these spaces in which validity of one kind or other is arrayed are ultimately conditioned by the cultural evolutionary principles located on the transcendent plane, without which they would not be immanently recognizable.

These four 'spaces', in the wider frame of their transcendent conditioning, are intended to capture the particular normative architecture of discourse ethics. It involves both identifying the validity of the societal standards that are obtained and that are, so far as they are just, a product of historical democratic learning processes.

*Reason, Communication, and Validity* 231

These standards, the matter of the third space out, are themselves subject to critical reconstruction according to the procedural standards of discourse ethics, the outer space. The second space, that of normative validity, will evince more or less reasonableness in relation to the variously present – even if not fully implemented – validity standards held in society, but, according to the normative standard, could only reach something approximating full reasonableness if the procedural validity standards of discourse ethics were comprehensively put in place within a reasonable societal environment.

I remain in broad agreement with important elements of this normative architecture. However, as I hope to gradually bring out in later chapters, I do not consider it adequate on its own. Chapter 6 already identified some limitations of discourse ethics, further developed in the last section. One essential requisite is the need to address the nature of societal learning of the requisite kinds within the theory. To achieve this, a socially theoretically relevant kind of attention to the logical process is needed. It must address the implications for such learning of societal actuality as well as normative projections explicated in reconstruction-oriented reasoning for a potentially different future. The further implication is that a comprehensive normative theory, fully attentive to the possibilities of the theory of society, must advance an encompassing framework that does not neglect those conditions of life that either do or could enable or block democratic procedural innovation. Formal-procedural democratic innovation, for all its importance, cannot be the only normative goal. For society more generally, it is pervaded by a democratic culture, even though it is also structured by non-democratic or democracy-indifferent cultures. Thus, the conditions of democracy in these spheres, the popular capacity to intersubjectively imagine, reason, and act in a democratic way, must also be addressed.

A limitation in the discourse ethics approach made manifest in the different structure of validity proposed there, lies in accounting for the actuality of social arrangements of all kinds, that from which normative theory starts and in relation to which it ultimately must conclude. Such a normative theory must make full use of variegated capacities for reasoning in multiple social contexts and their complex implications. Validity must therefore be considered, not just in terms of quasi-transcendentally justified procedural normativity on the interactionist plane, but also in terms of the ever-evolving cultural foundations of such normative validity through the permanent reconceptualization of concepts. These concepts do not stand by themselves. They must be discerned in actually operating 'empirical' conditions of validity that may or may not contain elements of reasonableness. For this further consideration, all the identified cultural models must be intellectually engaged, and, beyond this, so also must the wider assemblage of signs outlined in the last chapter.

**Collective Learning and Validity**

Looking more systematically at the relationship between collective learning and validity as it appears in Figure 8.1 the various types of collective learning are outlined around each of the three cultural models, and, additionally, around abductive

## 232 *Reason, Communication, and Validity*

schema formation. Before specifically addressing these various kinds of collective learning and their import for validation processes and validated outcomes, the three kinds of models and the one kind of schema formation can, in a preliminary step, be related to the spaces and fields discussed in Figure 7.1. Thus, the CCM stands in the space of reasons and in the discursive field and the IM stands in the space of placement and the positional field. The sociocultural model can be understood as occurring in both these spaces and fields, characterized as it is by a discursive quality, though it is a discursive quality that becomes inter-positionally stabilized, or, at least, relatively stabilized. To that extent, it incorporates structuring fixed commitments that have historically been concretized. They are the background structuring contexts that animate interventions in discourse. They tend to become generalized over time, so that at the macro-political level there is a consistent tendency for only a few powerful ones to structure the field, for example, formerly the left-right split and currently techno-conservatism versus radical pluralism.[5]

Proceeding upwards from the IM, these respective models can be thought of as the normative, relational placement of entities in the IM, the normative relational positioning of these entitles in the light of structures of contestation in the SCM, and the cognitive conditions of possibility of this argumentation in the CCM. Finally, abductive schema formation, viewed collectively, is a more transient kind of collective operation that belongs in the space of displacement and in the perceptual field. Viewing all of these in terms of Peirce's three categories, the three models are respectively supportive of thirdness proper in the case of the CCM, the thirdness of secondness or the symbolic in the case of the IM, and intermediate between these two, partaking of both, in the case of the SCM. Abductive schema formation belongs jointly to the thirdness of firstness, habits of feeling, and perceptual judgements and, more intricately to grasp, is also bound up with the beginning of logical operations, the immediate mediation of what is possible, and hence the beginning of conscious logical discourse involving a reconceptualization of the object. In Peirce, this involves the onset of abduction, conjecture formation, and transcendental engagement with possibilities.

The four components, viz., the three kinds of models and the abductive schemata, are, from a normative standpoint, characterized in Figure 8.1 as either just or unjust. This is an extreme simplification of what would have to be an intricate set of distinctions and conclusions in a given empirical instance. In other words, the distinction between just and unjust is extremely complicated to justify, as legal discourse makes abundantly clear. For any given issue, there is a wide spectrum of dimensions. These include dimensions of principles and ideals, legality, legitimacy, solidarity, equality, dignity, and so on (the space of reasons), dimensions of inter-positional coordination (the space of reasons and of placement), dimensions of norms and beliefs (the space of placement and of subjectivation), and abductive schematization including perceptual judgements (the space of displacement). There are also multiple reflexive levels that accompany the task of normative theorizing from within the participant's perspective of discourse ethics. These include, in no particular order, giving due autonomy to various participatory standpoints; judging the implications over space and time of various standpoints or, for that matter, the absence of standpoints in an inchoate debate; considering the accounts given by other theorists; assessing the overall situations in their theoretical-empirical fullness; and, finally, coming to a normative viewpoint of what is reasonable and unreasonable consistent with its validity standards. In the self-understanding of discourse ethics, or what discourse ethics has inspired, speaking very broadly here from Apel, through Habermas, to Forst, among others, this is mostly a procedural perspective of various kinds. As explained, this cannot serve on its own to make sufficiently telling arguments for non-procedural change, or indeed for those non-procedural changes where shifts in worldviews on various matters may induce procedural change. Regarding the latter, a procedural theory does have much to say. However, it is not sufficient on its own to address the implications of issues such as climate change, decolonization, the dangers of nuclear war, identity struggles, and global inequality, beyond its procedural focus.

It is for reasons such as the above that I single out the importance of collective learning as a relatively underdeveloped concept of discourse ethics, though not of critical theory, sociological critical theory almost exclusively in this regard (Eder, 1985; Miller, 1986, 2002; Strydom, 1987; Forchtner et al., 2020). Collective learning refers to the formation and utilization of those societally essential collective feelings, conceptualizations, and actions, together with associated habits, that underpin coordinated forms of life. Right away, it must be said, collective learning does not automatically equate with a 'progressive' shift in capacities, for regressive and authoritarian learning is also possible. Normative standards have to be justified to in turn justify what is considered appropriate collective learning, such as would open the path to a more reasonable society. Nor does collective learning mean that inevitably, the learning will be fully implemented. There are many instances of partial societal learning, as is the case today in the environmental field. Learning in this instance is both partial and highly confined, and evinces the ever-likely gap between understanding and practice that prevents the learning being realized. It is almost trivial to suggest that in this case the kind of eco-systemic collective learning that characterizes the growing scientific consensus in the field can be opposed by other forms of operational collective learning, such as the continuing seductive power of functional technical innovation and its ideologies. Collective learning can also be blocked, and this is quite apparent in the environmental case in a myriad of ways that perhaps do not need explication here.

Conceptually, *learning* is a process form, a modus operandi, to be distinguished from what is learned and already embedded in practice, opus operatum. Collective learning as process can either be regressive or progressive. As used in conformity with the validity standards of discourse ethics, especially as revised in this text,[6] the intention is to identify learning that points in a normatively progressive direction, where 'progressive' is defined by the validity standards of the theory and includes its methodological demonstration. The validity standards also entail critical identification of those that block their progressive realization in the form of critical standards. Collective learning processes refer to what takes place in certain fields and spaces, most essentially the discursive field and the space of reasons, though also in the perceptual field and space of displacement. The interplay of

## 234   *Reason, Communication, and Validity*

progressive and regressive within the theory does, in a way somewhat contrary to Bourdieu's, emphasize such learning as at least a partly conscious activity. However, it is far from entirely a conscious activity, since it is characterized not just by a rationally controlled procedure of knowing but also by an unconscious – or partly unconscious – phenomenal searching for appropriate meaning. To speak of learning in this way involves a type of emergence, respectively the interplay of knowledge, confidence in the directions in which knowledge may be found, and indefiniteness, uncertainty, and vagueness. As collective learning, it is also differentiated, where some parts of it are collectively shared but other parts are fragmented across social space.

Collective learning is bound up with various kinds of emergence, as indicated in Figure 8.1. More precisely, emergence must be understood as 'possible emergence', as possibilities that *might* eventuate into various kinds of cultural structures and models. Such learning is typically general societal learning before it enters into learning associated with democratic procedures. General societal learning is assumed to take place in civil society itself, including the mass and differentiated public spheres. Such an idea opposes an overly proceduralist reading of normative innovation that characterizes much contemporary political philosophy. This philosophy characteristically misses the cultural emergence of progressive and regressive movements with their innovative schemata congealing in diffuse societal or sub-societal learning processes. Might it be claimed that fully realized participatory democratic procedures could be the site of such learning?

A first response would be to accept that the thrust of critical proceduralist theorizing requires the participatory extension of democratic forms. Nonetheless, there are two counterarguments to the idea of relying on counterfactual procedural innovation alone to underpin its validity standards. The first counterargument is that fully realized participatory, procedural innovation, or even substantially realized such innovation, is far distant and it is unclear as to how it would work, even if continued experimentation in this direction remains essential. Such experimentation, though, must emerge from a general society-spanning critique of the *general* conditions of possibility of a reasonable society, including the obstacles to such a society. The second counterargument is that it is practically inconceivable that collective learning would be confined in any possible future to democratic procedural contexts. These would then have to encompass all important societal norm-setting and norm-monitoring exercises, and beyond these, the vast apparatus of operations of non-conscious feeling and conscious reasoning characteristic of societal arrangements. In fact, the original proponents of discourse ethics, Apel and Habermas, both found various ways to detach themselves from such an extreme position, Apel in his distinction between part A and part B of discourse ethics, and Habermas, even more radically, by emphasizing the significance of democratic counterfactuals for existing liberal democratic institutions, institutions that in his view harboured the potential to become more deliberative and hence participatory up to certain limits. From *TCA* onwards, it was also clear that the recourse to systems theory meant the abandonment of the ideal of full participatory democratization at every level. Yet, the vast amphitheatre of discourse that is society in all its myriad forms and the embedding of this discourse in the 'material' order formed by interlocking practices escape the active lens of the theory, while paradoxically at the same time is regarded as lying at its core. To the contrary, the idea of civil society itself as a differentiated but interlocking complex of collective learning processes must be made visible, accompanied by the historically informed recognition that ultimately nothing endures in democratic societies beyond the contexts of such learning, whether historical or contemporary, enabling change or reifying order.

At multiple points in his voluminous works, Peirce refers to the quality of thirdness as being composed of such activities as growth, evolution, memory, and learning. Thirdness is a dynamic or processual activity characterized neither by isolated feeling whose import is not known (firstness), nor by action/reaction relations characterized by a causally detectable lawfulness (secondness), but rather by intended, or at least – for humans – conscious, reflection. Thirdness is a relation-forming and hence also relation-changing power of mind. Though individual humans can occupy thirdness, and utilize its power, indeed they must do as that is intrinsic to the kinds of beings they are, as a vast network of semiotic relations, thirdness extends far beyond any individual mind for its radical relation-forming capacity is constructed over time and by means of inferential sign system. The cogitations of individual minds resonate on this vast, ever-expanding network, absorbing available parts of it and actively changing it according to the infinite range of possibilities thrown up in firstness. Yet, thirdness needs consistent collective orientation, and for this Peirce developed the concept of habit in the threefold form of habits of feeling, habits of thought, and habits of volition and action. These habits may be particular to individuals, but this is not their most important locus. This lies in the collective, social spectrum, hence collective learning. These shared habits, whether generalized individual habits or actual habits of collectives, representing capacities to feel, to think, and to do. Habits can of course be changed, and indeed are regularly changed over shorter or longer time periods.

To speak of *progressive* collective learning, then, in line with the validity standards of a democratic theory, involves the formation of habits of the above kinds, respectively of possibility, thought, or action, that conduce to general societal reasonableness. The ultimate locus of learning lies in the dynamic relation-forming power of thirdness. Thirdness is therefore a kind of processual cognitive capacity that can conceptually mediate between feelings and action consequences. In the next chapter, I will attempt to show how validity of various kinds of bad or good rationalization can be understood in the light of cultural models and their possible change. Such change is initially activated through firstness, congealing in the kind of abductive schematization that relates perceptual judgements to logical conjecture. In the subsequent chapter, I will have more to say about thirdness and, by association, learning through considering the various components of reasoning in the light of those normative validity standards guiding semiotic relation-forming activity. For these reasons, the exploration of Figure 8.1 will continue through these subsequent chapters. Specifically, there too, in partial culmination of a train of exposition, the advantages of considering learning as co-original with democratic procedural innovation will

236  *Reason, Communication, and Validity*

take clearer shape. In the following set of chapters, on critique in the light of validity standards, the learning accomplishments that define societalization will be made fully apparent.

## Notes

1  Discourse ethics is chosen as a general frame here for second-generation critical theory, notwithstanding the somewhat different paths adopted by Apel and Habermas from the 1980s onwards. It is not intended to suppress these differences by using the common term, which retains generalizing value, to describe what both authors share. Where different viewpoints emerge, these are specifically addressed.
2  This is a point also stressed by Honneth, indeed emerging as a distinction for him between a wider social philosophy and a narrower, proceduralized moral and political philosophy (Honneth, 2014).
3  While I will not hold to strong distinctions between reasoning and justification as cognitive process modes, I will generally emphasize the former. This is for two reasons. Firstly, reasoning, as abductive reasoning, is more easily tied to the generative level, with the emphasis on how potentially transformative idea potentialities enter the logical process. And, secondly, reasoning may be directly associated with the idea of reason itself.
4  Discourse ethics is the projective validity standard preferred here. In principle, and in fact, there are others with different projective standards. Of course, in a wider discussion, the derivation of discourse ethics out of the spectrum of normative pathways has to be defended against these others. My *Contemporary Theory of the Public Sphere* addresses this task within a sociological frame, but far beyond this attempt it remains a matter that is ongoing in the interaction of these normative theories (O'Mahony, 2013).
5  See O'Mahony for a detailed account of these two political 'cleavages' (O'Mahony, 2014). These structuring forces must be understood as, in part, products of particular electoral systems as well as relatively long-established social structures. A quite different structure of forces could well emerge with greater societal differentiation and different, more participatory, democratic forms.
6  See, in particular, Chapter 10.

## References

Apel K-O (2001) *The Response of Discourse Ethics*. Leuven: Peeters.
Bohman J (2000) *Public Deliberation: Pluralism, Complexity, and Democracy*. Cambridge, MA: MIT Press.
Eder K (1985) *Geschichte als Lernprozeß? Zur Pathogenese Politischer Modernität in Deutschland*. Frankfurt: Suhrkamp.
Forchtner B, Jorge ME, and Eder K (2020) Towards a Revised Theory of Collective Learning Processes: Argumentation, Narrative and the Making of the Social Bond. *European Journal of Social Theory* 23(2): 200–218.
Günther K (1993) *The Sense of Appropriateness: Application Discourses in Morality and Law*. New York, NY: SUNY Press.
Habermas J (1992) *Post-Metaphysical Thinking: Philosophical Essays* Cambridge: Polity.
Habermas J (1996) *Between Facts and Norms: Contributions to a Discourse Theory of Law and Democracy*. Cambridge, MA: MIT Press.
Habermas J (2019) *Auch Eine Geschichte Der Philosophie*. Frankfurt: Suhrkamp.
Honneth A (2014) *Freedom's Right: The Social Foundations of Democratic Life*. New York, NY: Columbia University Press.
Lenk H (2003) *Grasping Reality: An Interpretation-Realistic Epistemology*. New Jersey, NJ: World Scientific.

McCarthy T (1993) *Ideals and Illusions: On Reconstruction and Deconstruction in Contemporary Critical Theory*. Cambridge, MA: MIT Press.

McCarthy T (2009) *Race, Empire, and the Idea of Human Development*. Cambridge: Cambridge University Press.

McMurry N (2023) *Participation and Democratic Innovation under International Human Rights Law*. London: Routledge

Miller M (1986) *Kollektive Lernprozesse: Studien zur Grundlegung einer Soziologischen Lerntheorie*. Frankfurt: Suhrkamp.

Miller M (1992) Rationaler Dissens. Zur Gesellschaftlichen Funktion Sozialer Konflikte. In: Giegel HJ (ed) *Rationaler Dissens. zur Gesellschaftlichen Funktion Sozialer Konflikte*. Frankfurt: Suhrkamp.

Miller M (2002) Some Theoretical Aspects of Systemic Learning. *Sozialersinn* 3: 379–421.

O'Mahony P (2013) *The Contemporary Theory of the Public Sphere*. Oxford: Peter Lang.

O'Mahony P (2014) Europe, Crisis, and Critique: Social Theory and Transnational Society. *European Journal of Social Theory* 17(3): 291–304.

Strydom P (1987) Collective Learning: Habermas's Concessions and Their Theoretical Implications. *Philosophy and Social Criticism* 13(3): 265–281.

Strydom P (2019a) Critical Theory and Cognitive Sociology. In: Brekhus WH and Ignatow G (eds) *The Oxford Handbook of Cognitive Sociology*. Oxford: Oxford University Press.

Strydom P (2019b) On Habermas's Differentiation of Rightness from Truth: Can an Achievement Concept Do without a Validity Concept? *Philosophy and Social Criticism* 45(5): 555–574.

# 9   Validity, Schemata, and Reasoning on Moral-Political Issues

The previous chapter concluded by drawing attention to the learning processes arising within thirdness, notably the logical process of reasoning, the schemata and models that serve as its immanent context, as well as the transcendental capacities that serve as its conditions of possibility. Further, it has been stressed through the text that logical thirdness has a generative function, recontextualizing and potentially transforming received understandings through its various possible communicative genres. In the next chapter, I will turn to outlining revised kinds of validity standards directly associated with reasoning and close to those of discourse ethics, especially regarding its procedural democratic aims. In the current chapter, I will complete the account of the role of cultural models and abductive schema formation in validity-forming processes in the light of various forms of collective learning. Here, the schemata are laid out before the cognitive processes, especially reasoning, though it might be argued that historically, if reasoning is indeed generative of far-reaching societal rationalization it should come analytically first. It probably matters little in the grand scheme of things, and, in any case, it illustrates very well how reasoning, or any cognitive activity, is embedded, on the one hand, within transcendentally anchored cultural-evolutionary forms extended in time, forged in the past but enabling a future through their constant extension, and, on the other hand, within immanent ideals that have mediating teleological import.

Essential therefore to grasping moral-political validity is the relationship between the cognitive capacity to reason, thirdness, and the various kinds of schemata and cultural models that stand as initiating, mediating, coordinating, and instituting conditions of such reasoning. The three cultural models are assumed to occupy the sub-category of the thirdness of secondness in Peirce's three-triad system, as described in Chapter 5. Classically, in Peirce's account, this sub-category was understood to be the repository of provisionally settled beliefs or habits of action. Here, this element is expanded to cover not just habits of conduct in the sense of institutions carrying specific action-directing norms of various kinds, the institutional model, but also the two other specified relational cultural models, the cognitive cultural (CCM) and substantive (SCM). As outlined earlier, the first, the CCM, is more general and necessary and is composed of ideals within the space of reasons. The second, the SCM, substantive and interactional-perspectival,

DOI: 10.4324/9780429060571-10

*Validity, Schemata, and Reasoning on Moral-Political Issues* 239

corresponds to what Touraine describes as the social stake in the legal-political order, for example, technocrats versus new social movements or capital versus labour (Touraine, 1981; Ballantyne, 2007). Touraine introduced this second kind of cultural model – not his words – as an expression of the need to move sociological, and specifically institutional, theory away from the consensual normative assumptions of Parsons.

From the standpoint of validity, these relational cultural models, the institutional, sociocultural, and cognitive cultural models, range downwards from greater uncertainty to greater certainty regarding the context of action. In the case of the cultural model of ideals, the cognitive cultural model, the CCM, ideals are not understood as higher-order values but as general, minimal cognitive orientations to possible normative goals that allow for interpretation and conflict. Ideals have the minimal but vital role of specifying valid modes of consideration of issues. Ideals are thus not only shared themes in public discourse but shared themes imbued with a *minimum* agreed normative orientation. They are both constraining and enabling. General societal ideals normally entail a complex architecture as in, to take a straightforward example, responsible ecological democracy. This general ideal is composed of three ideal elements – responsible, ecological, and democratic – that are combined into a single ideal. The uncertainty lies in that the ideal is general and as general subject to different interpretations. The validity of ideals hence rests on the public acceptability of the ideal as something for which to strive, but the mere acceptability of the ideal does not imply agreement on how it should be interpreted. In the above, for example, the ideal of democracy, resting on a large variety of subsidiary ideals, can be specified in many ways. Accordingly, ideals are not univocal. In fact, their societal purpose would become inoperable if this were the case. There may be, for example, completely different accounts by different agents of each of the elements of the triad: responsible, ecological, and democratic. Some may even prefer a different ideal, such as responsible ecological hierarchy. Ideals are thus subject to contestation, but the most important aspect of their validity *as ideals* is where they are generally considered *cognitively* legitimate as discourse frames within the space of reasons.

The validity of the second cultural model, the *substantive cultural model* (SCM), is characterized by structural alignment of agreements and differences. The reference to structure refers to the structure of positions within both the positional and discursive fields. The SCM is thus the locus of the operations of the public sphere in the widest sense. Those particular alignments where some kind of at least minimal agreement is possible as opposed to confrontation, domination, and violence open up potentials for establishing general validity.[1] A significant, explicit sense of the moral, ethical, functional, and legal stakes, including their interpenetration, is manifest, though that does not deny that there are latent, implicit forces also heavily involved in positional structures, notably concentrated in adherents to positions (followers) as distinct from exponents of positions (actors). The degree of explicit sense possible in this cultural model, though limited, is much more difficult to achieve at the 'higher' levels of ideals (CCMs). The binding quality of ideals mostly operates implicitly in the space of reasons, but at crucial junctures, the force

240 *Validity, Schemata, and Reasoning on Moral-Political Issues*

of ideals comes explicitly into focus; for example, democracy itself, ecological responsibility, freedom, justice, and so on become explicitly thematized.

The potential for some degree of reasoned validity at the SCM level does not suppose that there is 'positional enlightenment' everywhere and that all that is at stake is explicitly understood in conditions of relatively fair contestation. This is a type of pluralist myth insofar as it claims to be general. Nonetheless, contestation in conditions of relative fairness is indeed partly the case, and to be understood as occurring within a range of generally justifiable ideals. These are not the only kinds of ideals. There are also negative or problematic ideals, such as belief in intrinsic hierarchy, that arise from bad societal conditions exacerbated by bad reasoning. In this case, validity may lose its connection with justice and result in a de facto structure of unjustifiable domination-based validity.

At the SCM level, there are differing degrees of freedom and domination across different societies and across different issues within a society. Each of the positions within an SCM, such as left/right to take a simple example, claims that their position should enjoy overall validity. In actual contexts where some approximation to legitimate pluralism is present, actors know that their claimed validity must be understood relationally in the light of the power of other actors, including publics, to block it or force its adaptation. The reconciliation of validity claims is, however, not necessarily the realization of a normative standard. When speaking of validity in the context of the model of ideals above in the cognitive cultural model, or the model of worldviews here at the level of the SCM, what is *manifestly* at issue is the self-ascribed claims to validity and the relational positioning that leads to various kinds of outcomes. Beyond this, and at all levels of cultural models, another kind of validity must also be countenanced. This is whether such validity claims can meet wider normative standards of the kind erected by various normative theories? This type of 'external' assessment of validity claims raises the further issue as to whether these wider assessments are constrained by context or they have a wider supra-contextual reach?

The approach advanced here contends that similarities and differences between contextual and supra-contextual validity standards can be reconciled, not permanently held apart. A comprehensive logic of inquiry of the kind proposed seeks to demonstrate exactly how these serve as compatible operations. In much of critical theory, and in most sociology, there is a distinct animus against the idea of supra-contextual sources of cognitive operations. By contrast here, the very ideas of immanent transcendence and the associated distinction between validity concept and validity goal clearly attest to commitment to a supra-contextual level. However, any such supra-contextual level must be shown to be immanently operative, and that is the hard but completely necessary part requiring demonstration.

The third cultural model, the *Institutional Cultural Model*, is closer to the original meaning of Peirce's symbol than the other two, the SCM and the CCM. It seeks to be definite, though, as suggested, ever only provisionally, whereas the other two have pronounced elements of indefiniteness that make them more open-ended cognitive operations. The institutional model is generated from that which is validated in the validation processes of the 'higher' cultural models, but it still retains

*Validity, Schemata, and Reasoning on Moral-Political Issues* 241

its own capacity for change in its response to indexical variation, which indicates what is or predictably will be the case, and iconic variation, the mental imagery that ground what is the case. Notwithstanding this context of self-transformation, the institutional model is, at its core, the action-guiding outcome of societal-political signification in the discursive field applied to the positional field. It is constituted by what can be described, following Burns and Dietz, as social rule systems (Burns and Dietz, 1992). The three kinds of rule systems identified in this tradition are descriptive rules for classifying objects of any kind, prescriptive rules as normative rules that should be followed in morals, laws, and conduct generally, and evaluative rules for conceptions of the good. A significant part of the story of critical social thought over the last century emphasizes the impossibility of limiting these rules to one or two, say descriptive and prescriptive rules, where all three are required to capture social processes of institution. Nonetheless, prescriptive rules have a particular salience for a normative science such as critical theory, as well as other social philosophies that seek to prescribe better forms of social organization. Generations of scholarship have shown that such rules, even where they have sanctionable force as in legal rules, continue to be interpreted and to elicit highly variable levels of compliance. Thus, merely specifying prescriptive rules is not necessarily sufficient for them to be consistently applied. Nonetheless, following or not following various rules does have consequences. Correspondingly, rules give rise to a hierarchy of beliefs, where hierarchy in this instance means 'higher' validity. That the validity is higher, however, does not necessarily mean more just, since rules can be formed from the higher cultural models in unjust or pathological ways that serve domination.

Closely associated with this *Institutional Cultural Model* is also to be found the subject, individual or collective. At this level, we find those habits of action that make themselves consistently felt in interactions with self and others. It is the consolidated idea of the 'me' arising first with Peirce but made famous by Mead. Thus, the subject at this level is objectified, whether by the self or by others. To speak of 'objectified' in this context involves the presumption of certain consistent competences and associated habits that conduce to regularized patterns of conduct. The micro-sociological revolution, emphasizing the processual freedom of agency, has made so much ground in sociology that one is immediately obliged to say that while there may be high levels of variation in patterns of action by subjects, there are also very powerful forces of cohesion and regularity. Bourdieu's habitus theory, or anything like it, would make no sense at all without such an assumption, secured for Bourdieu by the recursive operations of social fields in which actors are embedded, creating an interaction space both of conformity and possible non-conformity. It must also be borne in mind that patterns of non-conformity, for example, the tendency of youths of certain backgrounds at certain times and places to *regularly* deviate from the views of figures of authority, may also have, if not a conformist, at least a habitual character once the specific genre has become socially manifest.

The above-sketched cultural models construct validity in a variety of different ways. Within them, among many others, can be found at one extreme the most abstracted ideals of a civilization, at another level, the type of general moral-legal

## 242 *Validity, Schemata, and Reasoning on Moral-Political Issues*

precepts to be found in constitutions, and, at the other extreme, rules imposed through monopoly of power. The models are operations of the most general level of public association in Dewey's sense (Dewey, 1927). Validity claims can also be raised by groups that, at the outset, seek to transform any settled societal validity present in the models, and therefore more or less consciously stand outside them. This is the realm of transcendental engagement through the abductive building of radical schemata.

The crucial distinguishing hallmark of these latter radical schemata is that they are not institutionally implicated – or at least not strongly – in the here and now of established societal validity. There are a wide variety of such forms, ranging from group political claims that have for long been excluded from rec-ognition and have little real prospect of gaining it to those of groups of all kinds that have an emergent status. That such groups have such an emergent status does not guarantee that they will succeed in changing cultural models and insti-tutional norms, but it means that they can mount societally resonant arguments that might in time have this effect. The contemporary operating ideals and insti-tutional rules in many parts of the world and in many different spheres are quite different from those of even 40 years ago. This change was powerfully driven by originally abductive schemata of different and opposing kinds, such as neo-Hayekan 'social' theory, by the environmental movement responding to climate change risk, and by movements of feminism and decolonization, to name only a few. These abductive schemata generate new kinds of modal imaginaries and conjectures that are consistent with the logic of abduction outlined at length in earlier chapters. In certain cases, the abductive process gains cultural and insti-tutional traction and begins to shift what counts as valid within cultural models at different levels.

These abductively arising 'validity claims' have something in common with Habermas's account of validity in *TCA*. They bear on communicative reasoning; they have a conjectural, intersubjective quality; they operate through proposition-ally raised illocutionary claims; they proceed from a collective, though differ-entiated, background context; and they have an immanent-transcendent quality. However, the account of validity proposed here is to be distinguished from that of Habermas by addressing not just propositions understood in the sense of proposi-tional speech acts but inferentially linked arguments at all levels from abductive modal projections onwards. The account of the background context, attempting to advance Habermas's account of the lifeworld, is also regarded as generatively intertwined with the reasoning process. Reasoning is thus circularly related to these contexts, not just on the input but also on the output side, leading to more dynamic possibilities in the analysis of validity. The quasi-transcendent validity concepts are also more extended than Habermas's three formal world concepts, embracing the multiple transcendent validity concepts of the cognitive order, which come to a long list but to which additional concepts can always be added. Also different, and significant from the point of view of critical *analysis*, is the specification here of the relational *cognitive* models that serve as constructions of objects and of rela-tions between objects. Such objects are also themselves understood as conditioned

*Validity, Schemata, and Reasoning on Moral-Political Issues* 243

by their own objectual properties. These changes are designed to make the account of validity more amenable to societal application.

To speak of levels of validity does not mean that distinct cognitive operations taking up different validity claims separately and exclusively happen on each of these levels. It is rather a matter of the operations – incorporating interactions – being determined by and determining in turn multiple levels, as, for example, a cognitive ideal being further developed in the midst of an issue culture that manifestly, if misleadingly, appears to be happening entirely on the substantive level. Each level is developmentally shaped by higher levels, reaching down from cognitive order principles. To speak of developmental in this sense is to suggest, in a manner with affinities to Piaget, that higher-level structures or models 'call forth' developmental tendencies at lower levels. While this tendency in socialization, whether ontogenetic or collectively developmental, is an important force, it should also be kept in mind that societies regularly deviate from existing developmental structures. Issues accumulating 'lower down', such as contradictions and dysfunctions within institutional orders, input into perceptual and reflective processes, and they potentially result in the reorientation of the validity relations in the various models. One implication of emphasizing fluidity up and down levels, and for that matter across different cultural spheres, is that, from a democratic theoretical perspective, the true role of the ideal general public can become manifest. This perspective is designed to overcome a certain partial quality to some modern accounts, for example, over-strong assumptions about the integrative power of law or the 'negative' autonomy of the capitalist economy. Such accounts, valuable in their own right, can nonetheless serve as an imagination-restricting impediment to the further theorization of the public sphere and to proposals for more radical democratic experiments that might follow such theorization. More generally, it is still too restricted a base for understanding the power of public reasoning, for good or bad, in a democratic order. The mediating function of cultural models is designed to unify different discourses in another way, as cross-discursive sets of provisionally validated meaning interfaced with 'live' actions of validity innovation, contestation, and potentially settlement, where the latter follow the format of coordinative modalities that are next to be discussed.

**Validity, Coordinative Modalities, and Collective Learning**

Forming and utilizing validity standards of all kinds, from initial claims to general ideals, interactional perspectives, or institutional norms, are integrally related to the idea of what is called here modalities of coordination. In the classic literature on discourse ethics, consensual normative coordination, establishing the one right norm, was emphasized. This has been routinely criticized, often on the mistaken grounds that it depended on a type of de facto consensus, whereas it was in reality put forth as an ultimate standard, a final interpretant in Peirce's term, operating through the counterfactual force of recognizing the necessity of the right argument towards which agreement should tend. In *BFN*, Habermas expands on that model with his *Process Model of Political Will Formation* (Habermas, 1996, 162–168).

## 244  *Validity, Schemata, and Reasoning on Moral-Political Issues*

Other levels of political discourse within the model were outlined, ranging from the presumed pragmatic origin of an issue to its expansion through ethical political discourse and/or through political bargaining leading to morally guided reflection within the system of rights before finally taking the form of coherent legislative expression. This is a deliberately idealized model. In it is to be found an account of a number of modalities of coordinating normative agreement, viz., pragmatic, ethical-political, compromise, moral, and legal. There is an idealizing assumption that these coordinative modalities both rest on agreed-upon – or at least acceptable – processes and procedures, as well as existing substantive commitments, and that they conduce to a justified outcome. While an idealized model, one that here takes on a distinctive formulation, it is one that is also widely shared in liberal – in the widest sense – conceptions of the political process.

While recognizing the status and value of Habermas's account, there is still a need to add further dimensions. In the first place, certain assumptions in his model rest on a prior moral-political formation of the right kinds of agreed-upon, orienting norms. It is not a criticism of the model as such in its idealizing quality to assert that such agreed-upon norms, substantive, procedural, and processual, are far from always in place. To demonstrate this in depth is perhaps not necessary, as it is only too apparent from enduring ethical and moral conflict lines, factual disagreements, divergences on the actualization of existing or possible rights, and incoherent legal formulations that break down in application and/or simply ignore the various steps in the will formation model. To list these qualities does not mean that the idealizing model is wrong on its own terms. It is a validity standard, and, as such, given the nature of the legal-political situation, it meets a recalcitrant reality. This reality can be understood as, in part, a pathological one that is parasitic on the model, but also in part points to a lack of completion of the model. It follows that there are two reasons to go further. The first is the theoretical-empirical requirement to add more downside assumptions to the model, for example, pathologies and injustices at every level, while the second is that the model as it stands remains far from complete even as an ideal. In the latter respect, it needs to be shown above all how what comes before and after reasoning, respectively perception and actualization, shaping it on the input and output sides, where the output side also forms a context for the beginning of the next cycle of potential knowing on the input side.

What has been addressed in the last number of chapters already incorporates important dimensions of a process model of rational political will formation, though one that has not been directly shown to apply to the political process. I will not be explicitly outlining such a process model in this text. Instead, it is intended to offer essential considerations for actually doing it, taking account of the existence of pathology and injustice, and also through extending the understanding of reasoning to address the role of its relevant perceptual and positional fields and associated spaces of placement and displacement. The dimensions so far outlined in the text already involve a significant expansion of what Habermas emphasizes in his process model. The first dimension of such an expansion is to incorporate more clearly the domain of firstness and its implications for conscious coordination. Here, what might be called the 'vaguely conceptual' as opposed to the non-conceptual is to be

*Validity, Schemata, and Reasoning on Moral-Political Issues* 245

understood as making its way from an unconscious inference to a conscious one, moving from diffuse and ineffable feeling to explication by means of logical conjectures and modal projections. The second is to emphasize the potential *generative* power of transformative ideas as they make their way from unconscious qualitative feeling, to reality confrontation, to perception, then through the various phases of reasoning, and potentially, if the collective learning achieved is taken on board, into institutional orders. The third is to recognize that the institutional order thus generated in its multiple instantiations from organizational to personality structures and much else is part of a circuit of 'effectivity', shaped by the generative process that comes before it, though once formed it is consequential for action in its own right, and received as secondness, actual relations to the objectual figurations into the new belief/doubt process beginning again in firstness. If this circuit is expanded onto the societal plane, the best-case scenario of a collective competence for rational will formation is seen to be bounded by pre-rational sensibilities, on the input side, and by institutionally embedded belief systems and habits on the output side.

What has been referred to as coordinative modalities have an intrinsic relationship to validity. They are consensus, rational dissensus, convention, compromise, hegemony, and, at the limit, undisguised, enforced domination. In shorthand, *consensual* validity refers to ideal of reaching universal or near universal agreement regarding various descriptive, evaluative, and prescriptive rules. Another kind of consensual validity arises from *conventional* validity regarding matters that are taken for granted, taking the form of everyday conventions, say greeting conventions, generally in line with some features of Habermas's account of the background context of the lifeworld or certain kinds of hermeneutics. The ideal of *dissensual* validity refers to situations where there is acceptance of both the relevantly operating ideal or ideals and of the legitimacy of other positions, that is, their right to be asserted, but no final agreement on rules; rather, instead, there is agreement to disagree. The ideal of validity through compromise involves strategic bargaining over preferred norms of many possible kinds between self-interested parties, though that self-interest is constrained by moral, ethical, and functional norms. The ideal of *hegemonic* validity involves the presence of ideologically developed, or at least naturalized, assumptions of the dominance of some positions over others. This is not the naked imposition of force, but the articulation of what Bourdieu calls symbolic power. *Enforced* validity involves the naked use of force over others without any meaningful kind of justification. It is therefore to be differentiated from Weber's idea of the legitimate monopoly of violence, which rather belongs under hegemonic validity or could be regarded as a mixed-mode format, part hegemonic, part enforced. Consensual and rational dissensual validity have the highest justification requirements, and enforced validity has the lowest, little, or none, depending on circumstances.

These various kinds of coordinative modalities involve transactions between agents in contexts of systems, structures, and institutions. They serve as immanent validity goals for coordinating social action. In the coordination process, spanning the three core cultural models, cognitive, substantive, and institutional, all manifest positions on all possible issues are present, while also latent, dissident positions

## 246  *Validity, Schemata, and Reasoning on Moral-Political Issues*

may be repressed but still weakly present as potentials. Thus, cultural models are not simply the expression of what has been made manifest but of other positions and insights that are either vaguely formulated or repressed. These various kinds of positions are present either as autonomously articulated and interpreted through the modalities of consensus, rational dissensus, and certain kinds of compromise, or as repressed, either manifest or latent to various degrees, through the modalities of hegemony and conflict/domination. To speak of existing positions means positions that have existing social force and are institutionally present in social arrangements. As above, these may be either manifest or latent. The latent/manifest distinction is not absolute. Historically, many forms of idea-potentiality may in the end flourish despite their initial vagueness. They represent precisely the kinds of possibilities that could mature into true societal significance under the right conditions. Such societal significance needs the presence of a 'social movement', one grounded in characteristic collective habits of feeling, to develop in this way. Such a social movement, which has overlaps with the general understanding of social movements in the social sciences and elsewhere, is instantiated in a collective learning process and moves between these gradually crystallizing habits of feeling and the characteristic habits of thought of thirdness, gaining in insistency to the extent that the movement is accompanied by wider collective learning. As movements grow stronger, they begin to develop and, if successful, to societally institute schemata at the level of the various output cultural models. They are accordingly triggered by habits of feeling and abductive schema formation and mature in reasoning processes before being potentially instituted in the structure of cultural models and patterns of volition and action affecting society generally. The presumption here is that social movements are much more than the kind of coordinated agency that commonly appears in the literature. In addition to manifest forms of agency, they also draw off, mobilize, and even create an alternative structure of feelings, reasons, and facts. In this respect, 'social' movements can exist broadly in the realm of ideas, even where they lack an easily defined collective agent to carry them. Indeed, it may be noted in passing that the insufficient attention to cultural mediation in the various ways in which coordinated social movements are addressed throws light on why there are such problems in explaining their societal resonance through learning processes, and hence their true influence over time, even in conditions of demobilization of the manifest carrying form of a movement.[2]

In Figure 8.1, *Validity and Societal Ontology*, presented in Chapter 8, the coordinative modalities appear in each of the cultural models. Before I delve into their respective roles at these levels, I first must offer some general remarks on the representation of the models in the figure. Consistent with previous remarks on reasoning, the cultural models are respectively divided into a part emphasizing intellectually derived normative standards of societal reasonableness and the normative validity standards of society itself. The latter is divided, via a simplified binary criterion, into just and unjust validity standards.[3] Of course, to some degree, the selection of what counts as just or unjust derives from preferred theoretical validity standards of the first kind, that is, those that emanate from the normative sciences of which critical theory is the exemplar here. Notwithstanding, interpretations of the validity of normative standards, those that are present in actual societal arrangements, can be independent and relatively objective. That which is deemed to be reasonable is then taken to be already partly manifest in society – or not – and prescriptions offered on the part of normative theories as to what should replace or emend such manifest standards. From the vantage point of any normative theory, but especially critical theory, it cannot be supposed that the way in which democracy has 'gone on' is entirely without merit or entirely without its own endogenous learning capacity through its publics that cannot be supplied from the outside. This is what is 'manifest' in the justice component of cultural models and it provides a realist filter to normative prescriptions. What could be deemed to be just has emerged to some degree in a multitude of social spheres, some of which are only indirectly democratic, for example, the family, as explored by Honneth in *Freedom's Right* (Honneth, 2014). These are therefore endogenous areas of learning whose particular make-up regarding the degree of manifest justice and the avoidance of pathology indicates the autonomy of social spheres, a lesson from both the polycentric societal conception of Luhmann and the later Habermas. Standards of reasonableness must therefore take at least some account of what is possible in the light of what has proved feasible, crucially when it cannot be reasonably shown that a total transformation of existing culture and institutional collective learning is foreseeable. This by no means excludes the normative projection of potential alternative arrangements, the very essence of critical theory, and, to some degree, general to normative philosophies of most kinds. In the critical theory lineage, this is at the heart of what first Peirce, then Dewey, and finally Honneth understand as experimentation, more explicitly democratic experimentation in the latter two cases (Honneth, 2016). It is precisely to normatively allow for such projection and to empirically allow for cultural orders of society that make it possible, that various 'schematic areas' have been outlined in Figure 8.1, Chapter 8, viz., a transcendent space of reason, a space of immanent democratically relevant ideals (the CCM), a space of democratic reasoning and conflict in the discursive and positional fields, an institutional model that regulates the space of placement, and abductive schema formation that opens up collective learning within the space of displacement.

Following these last remarks, it may be noted that in each of the three cultural models as represented in the figure there is a category marked 'emergence'. The concept of emergence, important both in critical realism and systems theory, often refers to collectively operating causal capacities that lie beyond or behind what is empirically manifest. As deployed in both systems theory and critical realism, albeit in very different ways, it signifies the capacity of supra-individual systems or structures to determine the forms taken by practices and experiences. In these formulations, it attempts to break with the classical methodological holist type position towards a mediated type position, the structure/action paradigm as taken up in critical realism, and the system constructivism of systems theory. Both positions on emergence have affinities with Peirce, in the critical realist case directly and in systems theory indirectly.[4] They respectively advance the case for generals that come before worldly appearances of phenomena, even individual human beings as phenomena. The type of emergence that comes with critical theory in the line

248    *Validity, Schemata, and Reasoning on Moral-Political Issues*

from Peirce, or, in the first generation, from Hegel and Marx, asserts that while the human subject is certainly conditioned by social forces that tend to reach beyond individual or even group control it can also collectively respond to those forces. Most fundamental for this is the evolutionary transcendent form of the capacities of common humanity to strive for a just collective life lodged in its powers of reason, capacities that are nonetheless regularly blocked in social practices. Emergence in Figure 8.1, Chapter 8, thus refers to the interchange of relations between those cultural templates that 'happen beyond' democratic control and those normative capacities to potentially respond and justly order them and also to pre-empt bad outcomes. In this way, the kind of emergence assumed here is connected to capacities for innovatively reordering relations of democratic reason.

The nature of collective learning, viewed in the above light, lies, firstly, in capacities for learning within specific social spheres that regularly go beyond the epistemic and volitive capacities of democratic orders to regulate or otherwise control them. Secondly, as normative collective learning, it must democratically find a way to respond to the kind of non- or anti-democratic learning that frequently runs ahead, for example, the contemporary problem of globally regulating social media. What is critical is that democratic collective learning 'reasonably' prevails and penetrates into 'extra-democratic' social orders, increasing their level of justice. In later critical theory, there tends to be less and less said about this latter dimension, though how to begin to think in this manner is precisely the legacy of Marx and of first-generation critical theory. No doubt a major reason for this is that societal complexity is growing as the different media of money, power, opinion, and trust, to name only a few, work through social spheres, endlessly differentiating and reintegrating them. This calls forth the need for an emancipatory theory of equivalent complexity, not the abandonment of the enterprise altogether. At the general level of cultural form at issue here, collective learning may be specified for each of the models. The key to this is to understand collective learning as tied to the coordinative modalities. In order to come to this, something more needs to be said of the modalities themselves in relation to each of the models.

Each of the models is assumed, as in Figure 8.1, Chapter 8, to contain all the various modalities, but with different implications in each case. For each model, beneficent use of the modalities is associated with consensus and rational dissensus, while maleficent use is associated with hegemony and unproductive conflict. At the CCM level, using the language of frames here to clarify, it is a question of those cognitive frames that should or should not coordinate democratic discourse. At the SCM level, with its inverse normative-cognitive ordering, it is a question of argumentation between normative frame positions. At the level of the symbolic in the Institutional Model, it is a question of those normative frames that are taken to have – or actually have through power arrangements – direct reference to the state of external worlds or acting in them in any one of a multitude of ways.

The 'lower' models, the substantive and the institutional, 'absorb' the cognitive orientations deriving from the ideal model and add to them the classical sociologically identified cultural properties, viz., values, interests, beliefs, habits (of action), and norms.[5] They do so in highly variable ways across discourses and

*Validity, Schemata, and Reasoning on Moral-Political Issues*   249

societies. These models also add strategic, other-oriented discourse to the puta-tively free and autonomous discourse level of ideals. Even where the ideals are opposing, they each stand on their own ground. There is the potential of commu-nicatively forging common ideal spaces out of differences through the modalities of consensus and rational dissensus. Understanding ideals in this way helps to clarify the goals of discourse ethics without necessarily always extending analysis in search of 'agreement on the one right norm'. A more attainable standard for general agreement is the appropriate space of reasons of democratic discourse, including positions within that discourse that are granted to be legitimate artic-ulations of preferences. These preferences, if they are to serve as the basis of reasonable argumentation, do not presuppose full agreement on moral matters, but they can stand within moral boundaries. In other words, different preferences within these boundaries are accorded reciprocal respect (Forst, 2013). Such ideal boundaries are constantly evolving in response to cultural construction and social change. Thus, in the Kantian lineage of discourse ethics, morality ultimately rests on the collective capacity to bring about reasoned agreement and not on the gen-eral norms that are obtained at given times and places. Nonetheless, established and generally accepted moral commitments in the form of institutionalized norms at the symbolic levels, including also here the legal enactment of moral rules, also feature at the ideal level as cognitive presuppositions. As already normatively instituted, they serve as the solid ground underpinning ideals to which new po-tentialities are constantly being added. These serve as consensual presuppositions that are supplemented also at this level by rational dissensual presuppositions. The latter do not assume agreement, merely respect for the positions of others with which there is disagreement.

Differentiating the operation of coordinative modalities between the CCM and SCM levels in the light of the above indicates first of all a distinction to be drawn between the cognitive and the normative. The cognitive, located on the ideal level, answers to those orientations that remain open, that have their raison d'être in bringing about norms and other symbolic standards but whose function is not to maintain the standards themselves. This ideal level is the level of cognizing rela-tions of reason, related to but still distinct from the activity of specifying right relations. For example, to take two largely opposing ideals, those of hierarchy and equality, the ideal level concerns the ultimate justification of equality. It is com-mensurate with Kant's concept of the understanding, that which is universal or common to a phenomenon. Thus, it supposes that those who hold hierarchy as an ideal can also understand the nature of equality as an ideal, though their interpreta-tion of equality may be minimal. The space of ideals is here analytically separated from the comprehensive cognitive *and* symbolic operations of the SCM. In the latter, the normative spectrum of goal-oriented argument is in play. It is entangled in complex relations with the ideal level. The ideal level strives towards cognitive clarification, but such clarification does not mean foreclosing on the settling of normative commitments that emerge in the light of the ideal. How to normatively validate the ideal remains an open question when posed from the vantage point of the ideal level itself. It is a process that requires forms of reasoning that are guided

## 250   *Validity, Schemata, and Reasoning on Moral-Political Issues*

by the forms of the 'lower' cultural models, by the interactional and pluralist form of the SCM, and by the implications of norm-setting and validated action of the IM.

Common, general ideals are constructed from idea potentialities and abductive schemata, while the task of normatively structuring argumentation on the ideals involves the normative fixing of distinctive interpretations of the ideals. Thus, ideals have autonomy at the level of creation, including creative configurations of existing ideals, but their social implications are more directly specified by the manner in which the modalities of coordination work on the normative, SCM level, and, lower down still, on the institutional level. The implications of these modalities at the various model levels are by no means confined to those of consensus and rational dissensus. They can also extend to compromise, hegemony, and conflict/domination. At present, for example, the ideal democratic space, as it previously existed in contemporary societies, has lost traction, and ideals have become starkly opposing. In these circumstances, ideals are emerging that exclude the operation of previous democratic ideals. For example, equality before the law is now contested in authoritarian regimes in many parts of the world. Repairing this fragmented order is difficult and involves learning from conflict so as to rebuild ideal configurations, which involves moving them towards consensus and rational dissensus.

These modes of fixing validity are of a cognitive nature. As such, they are modes of thinking and arguing rather than normative modes of directly guiding action. As cognitive, they are idealizing forms, but when socially employed, they produce normative outcomes. In all cases, even the consensual case, they assume ongoing transactions between agents. At the SCM level, the coordinative modalities operate within forms of 'schematic contestation'. Such schematic contestation, using the language of validity claims, could be said to be among agents' schemata replete with validity claims. On all sides, these are presumed by the advocates to be valid, but these advocates also know that they routinely are not so regarded by others, and must take account of this. The coordinative modalities are means of fixing validity, where the fixing accordingly utilizes a wide range of modes from consensus to violence or the threat of it. Discourse ethics places its emphasis on the consensual mode as an ideal democratic standard that depends on the capacity to find moral agreement. Others sympathetic to this tradition have additionally emphasized rational dissensus as also depending on moral agreement but with greater emphasis on contextual differences (Miller, 1992). A sociological approach, fortified by realist assumptions, must place these modalities, granted the highest normative status, into the wider context of the other modalities, variously understood as regressive, authoritarian, pathological, or unjust. From the perspective of analysis, understanding just arguments as in contention with unjust ones adds a necessary dimension of normative realism, and it reduces the dangers of hidden, that is, not justified, teleological normative standards being projected.

The coordinative modalities can be integrated with Peirce's concept of interpretant. In his essay on the fixation of belief, Peirce put the scientific method at the pinnacle of the ways of fixing belief (Peirce, 1992, 109–123). This method would assume a comprehensive reasoning process in which immediate interpretants responding to signs would be subject to a range of dynamic interpretants,

*Validity, Schemata, and Reasoning on Moral-Political Issues* 251

all regulated by the mediating final interpretant. In the scientific method, made into an explicit democratic approach in a line from Mead and Dewey to Apel and Habermas, all possible interpretations would finally lead to a resolution, the realization of fully tested knowledge and associated conduct. Knowledge of this kind would rest on 'finalization', a stable, if always provisional, state of integrating all known conjectures, modal projections, and consequences. This would also reflect the role of the normative sciences, aesthetics, ethics, and logic. With finalization on a given issue, the aesthetic exploration of ideals would no longer be disruptive, the various normative ends, ethical, functional, and moral, would be respectively incorporated depending on the issue, and the ultimate interpretant would be provisionally concluded. I am assuming that Peirce's concept of logical truth could be extended across the classical normative domains of the functional, the moral, and the ethical. Finalization, nonetheless, is always fallibilistic. Even belief in the non-disputability of certain fundamental human rights is not always given and is subject to change. What finalization means in this sense is the Peirce idea that in the interplay of discourse and experience within the cultural structure of coming to know and coming to agree certain 'truths' become established, and these truths reach the threshold of enduring agreement. Such agreement is not permanent, for it remains subject to potential contestation, and, as Foucault has shown, such contestation may result in epistemic discontinuity when viewed over the 'longue durée' (Foucault, 1972). However, over historical time so long that it gains cultural evolutionary significance, it does mean that ideas such as, for example, reflexive freedom and equal dignity of persons become incorporated into cultural evolutionary cognitive principles. As immanently operating but transcendentally grounded cognitive principles, such a second nature exerts a directive force on humans' affairs, even if, as experience abundantly shows, these principles do not have permanent traction on societal norms across space and time. What they do is to provide orientations and 'expectation expectations' over historical epochs of human forms of life. Modernity is one of those forms of life for all its ambivalences and tragic consequences, and the one in which immanent ideals forged from this second nature have the most explicit prominence.

To speak of societal coordination by validity claims, as Habermas does, is analogous to speaking of coordination by 'mature' or stable interpretants, that is, interpretants that group together and aggregate other interpretants. Such aggregating and orienting interpretants are schemata. Such schemata range from the strong cognitivism of the transcendental cognitive principles to the strong normativism of institutional models, the latter including habits of conduct. CCMs and SCMs occupy intermediate positions. Validity claims, first explicitly articulated in abduction, advance a possible new line of validation. Such 'new lines' can endure for a time in the form of emergent abductive schemata engaging with the transcendental schemata of cognitive principles. In this sense, the interplay between habits of feeling that drive abduction and the transcendental cognitive principles opens up a space of habits of habit change (West and Anderson, 2016), which I interpret as transformative, transcendentally constituted engagements that spring from

## 252  *Validity, Schemata, and Reasoning on Moral-Political Issues*

abduction and, where persistent, take the form of abductive schema formation that criticizes existing habits of thought and action, separately or jointly.

The net implication of this double differentiation of the concept of validity into validity concept and achievement concept and into different levels and modes improves its utility for societal analysis. This is further improved by placing it in the sequential context of argumentation by means of inferential chains rather than in individual binary yes/no propositions. No longer does validity need to be only regarded as being about universals that would be the outcome of sufficiently long and fairly organized argumentation; it can also be about what is claimed to be valid but is clearly not universal. As an achievement concept, validity can therefore be claimed in the name of the nation, the class, the gender, the family, and innumerable others. It could be argued that this was always implicit in Habermas's account, provided that validity claims arising in societally dispersed locations should still be capable of being universally justified. This is a normatively reasonable position, but it has not translated into associated studies that show how different claims to validity in different social spheres could be so justified. However, the problem is even deeper. In complex societies, what should count as valid is not always apparent; important validity claims can be bundled into discourses that do not advertise their universality. Moreover, we also need to know, beyond universality, how claims to validity are actually made socially manifest, and especially how to address non-moral claims to validity, such as ethical claims or asserted functional imperatives of various kinds. Fundamentally, for a critical theory, we need to know when validity is inadmissibly, unjustly, or pathologically claimed. Without a comprehensive theory of validity that allows for such critique of validity claims, not just at the level of the individual proposition, as is at least formally catered for in Habermas, but at the level of the argument or schema as a whole, critical theory cannot properly fulfil its mission. Extended critique of certain claims to validity, which would amount to a critique of certain kinds of reasoning, has not been developed in any sustained way within recent critical theory.

Finally, the issue of collective learning can be related to the various models and to abductive schema formation. I will begin with the latter, for here is the locus of all and every kind of, in the widest sense, epistemic innovation. Collective learning here involves building conjectural schemata or modal projections that are both normative and explanatory. For example, a group might ask why they are poor and accept it as their fate for a long time before eventually developing a concept of exploitation that they then come to regard as explaining their condition, thus putting it in a wider frame. This may be a new idea at the time and place, or an idea already with normative traction but not hitherto applied to this group. It is normative in its implications and contains also an explanatory conjecture that extends to the social order, to other agents, to public discourse, and so on. Its mere assertion is nonetheless far from its institutional realization, but it is an illustration of schematic learning. Such a development can frequently lead to antithetical schematic learning arising from different, emerging social positions, creating a set of emerging positions within the discursive field. Normative and explanatory positions seek to support one another, frequently by what Forst describes as justification narratives (Forst, 2017). Eder also draws

*Validity, Schemata, and Reasoning on Moral-Political Issues* 253

attention to the transformative power of narratives to stimulate reasoning, arriving potentially at achieved learning as learning on which action can follow, so some part of the learning dimension is narrative learning that is anchored in collective life experiences (Eder, 2023). Not just narratives but multiple other genres contribute to stimulating the imagination to project beyond what is 'known' to exist, therefore bringing modal considerations into collective learning, what could or may be (Strydom, 2023). For this, the essential element is the engagement of the transcendentally anchored cognitive principles that epistemically structure possible knowing. In Kantian language, this is the constitutive cycle of learning. These embrace, in a manner that has already been outlined, firstly, collective learning as the production and application of general ideals, as in the case of *ideal learning* in the CCM. As learning contexts, such ideals can be potentially reasonable, actually reasonable, actually unreasonable, and emerging. Secondly, they embrace *inter-positional learning* arising from the structuring of public culture into positional fields structured by meso-level cultural models, the SCM. Thirdly, they embrace *positional learning* in the IM, bearing on what beliefs action should follow in the light of external conditions, which often prove recalcitrant and tilt the orbital path of collective learning in a new direction. Each of these is represented in the broken circular lines surrounding the cultural models in Figure 8.1. Underlying all of the above-sketched loci of collective learning, lies the core element of triadic learning arising in cognitive-normative reasoning processes. Such learning is cognitive by virtue of a form that is open to the reconstruction of knowledge as much as its confirmation, and it is normative by virtue of the ends that guide it.

In Figure 8.1, accordingly, the icons of the cultural models surround the icon of the sign of argument. This sign is the locus of reasoning, and reasoning is inextricably intertwined with schematization process and schematic outcomes. Schemata are the scaffolding from which reasoning, the use of the logical categories, builds. In second-generation critical theory, Peirce's account of the doubt-belief model is engaged. The outcome, linked here to the role of the identified schemata, is represented in concentric circles around the sign of argument, where the various validity dimensions associated with them are represented. There are three fundamental divisions in these concentric lines. The first is the existing structure of actuality, both in its lifeworld and system dimensions, which is represented by the circles of ideal, inter-positional, and institutional validity. The second is the validity claims associated with abduction, the inner circle. The third is the overall validity standards associated with critical theory, but it could equally be any other normative philosophy. This is the outer circle. For the first and second divisions, each of the concentric lines is associated with each of the schemata, the abductive schema and the models. The third division, the subject matter of the next chapter, represents those validity standards that should rightly be obtained at the levels of models and schemata. To say they should rightly obtain is to identify the preferred process and outcome standards that a normative philosophy emphasizes. In the doubt-belief sequences, the existent order is represented by the cultural models, the potentially changed order by the abductive schema, and the regulative instance of the validity standards supplies the 'leading principles' that thread the relevant discourses

## 254   *Validity, Schemata, and Reasoning on Moral-Political Issues*

together, various feelings, facts, and reasons, ultimately guided by the discourse of reason, good or bad.

## Notes

1 The issue of alignment is elaborated in terms of modalities of agreement and difference in the next chapter. This applies not just to the SCM but also to the other cultural models.
2 O'Mahony and Delanty provide an account of this dimension of movements illustrated by the Irish national movement, which, characteristic of social movements generally, was not merely one unified force but broken into various 'wings', some of whom became dominant and repressed the other wings once the initial goal, in this case Irish independence, had been reached (O'Mahony and Delanty, 1998). See also Rainer Forst for a quite different, but still complementary account of an intellectual idea, that of tolerance (Forst, 2013).
3 A fuller account of the meta-theoretical foundations of standards of justice and injustice in the context of critical theorizing will follow in the next chapter.
4 Regarding critical realism and its relationship to Peirce, see the remarks on Margaret Archer in Chapter 3.
5 Mostly, the preceding dimensions are referenced further as norms, simply as a shorthand.

## References

Ballantyne G (2007) *Creativity and Critique: Subjectivity and Agency in Touraine and Ricoeur*. Leiden: Brill.
Burns TR and Dietz T (1992) Institutionelle Dynamik: Ein Evolutionärer Ansatz. *Journal für Sozialforschung* 32(3/4): 283–306.
Dewey, J (1927) *The Public and its Problems*. Pennsylvania: Penn State Press.
Eder K (2023) Pandora's Box: The Two Sides of the Public Sphere. *European Journal of Social Theory* 26(2): 136–152.
Forst R (2013) *Toleration in Conflict: Past and Present*. Cambridge: Cambridge University Press.
Forst R (2017) *Normativity and Power: Analyzing Social Orders of Justification*. Oxford: Oxford University Press.
Foucault M (1972) *The Archaeology of Knowledge*. New York, NY: Pantheorn.
Habermas J (1996) *Between Facts and Norms: Contributions to a Discourse Theory of Law and Democracy*. Cambridge, MA: MIT Press.
Honneth A (2014) *Freedom's Right: The Social Foundations of Democratic Life*. New York, NY: Columbia University Press.
Honneth A (2016) *The Idea of Socialism: Towards a Renewal*. Cambridge: Polity.
Miller M (1992) Rationaler Dissens. Zur Gesellschaftlichen Funktion Sozialer Konflikte. In: Giegel HJ (ed) *Kommunkation und Konsens in modernen Gesellschaften*. Frankfurt: Suhrkamp.
O'Mahony P and Delanty G (1998) *Rethinking Irish History: Nationalism, Identity, and Ideology*. New York, NY: St. Martin's Press.
Peirce CS (1992) *The Essential Peirce: Selected Philosophical Writings. Vol. 1 (1867–1893)*. Bloomington, IN: Indiana University Press.
Strydom P (2023) The Critical Theory of Society: From Its Young-Hegelian Core to Its Key Concept of Possibility. *European Journal of Social Theory* 26(2): 153–179.
Touraine A (1981) *The Voice and the Eye: An Analysis of Social Movements*. Cambridge: Cambridge University Press.
West DE and Anderson M (2016) *Consensus on Peirce's Concept of Habit: Before and Beyond Consciousness*. New York, NY: Springer.

# 10 Reasoning and Validity Standards

The task taken up in this chapter is to elaborate on each of the three dimensions of validity associated with reasoning and to begin the task of addressing the associated dimensions of critique. This entails further taking up the theme of reasoning processes, which are also potential learning processes as they seek embodiment in cultural models. In this sense, learning processes, especially at the societal level as societal learning processes, are expressions of a struggle to comprehend and disseminate preferred validity standards. Earlier, I outlined the intertwined relationship between Peirce's three logical categories: conjecture (abduction), ideal formation (deduction), and actualization (induction). Each of these categories will be associated with a validity standard or set of standards bearing on reasoning. This assumes that, from one vantage point, reasoning can be isolated into three distinctive moments, abductive conjecture (modal projection), explication, and actualization, each with its own set of validity standards. Even if the moments can be separated out for validity analysis, they make no sense on their own, either logically or in terms of the wider implications of reasoning. The divided moments must come together in reasoning as a general, interrelated process. At the same time, the individual moments highlight critical processual validity standards amidst the wider general reasoning process.

The approach seeks to embed formal pragmatics in a more defined logical frame. This has the advantage of relating the normative emphasis of discourse ethics, present in its conception of validity, to the three basic ontological elements of feelings, reasons, and facts that respectively condition the logical moments of abduction, deduction, and induction. These three moments constantly interweave, and as they do, they may produce reasoned validity, always taking account of the possibility that reasoned validity may, in given circumstances, actually prove unreasonable depending on the form of cognitive ideals (the CCM) and actual societal conditions. To adjudge what is reasonable or unreasonable, hence criticizable or not, requires the availability of validity standards of democratic reasoning that claim to lead to general reasonableness in society. Such standards must also have traction in the many worlds, possible or actual, to which they could be applied. They must have appropriate normative potentiality but also feasibility in the light of actual or emerging societal conditions. For both tasks, they need to draw upon the specialized theories

DOI: 10.4324/9780429060571-11

## 256   *Reasoning and Validity Standards*

of the social as well as normative sciences. At the same time, they must intrinsically allow for reflexivity, a reflexivity that spans from the perspective of the investigator to the critical self-understanding of members of society generally.

In what follows, standards of normative reasonableness that arise from modal normative projection – what may, could, or should be – are placed in the context of existing normative standards of society, both those that specifically offer validity standards for reasonable social arrangements and those that stand as social facts. In the case of the latter, there is a high likelihood, a presumption indeed of critical theory, that what operates as social facts can be unjust and pathological. So, the task that follows is to show how this comes to be and to propose normatively directed social change. The emphasis on the relationship between validity and *social* change is because the kinds of democratic change emphasized by much contemporary critical theory would be blind if it did not take sufficiently into account the wider development of society. While a relatively sociologically distanced, normative-democratic approach characterizes much of critical theory today, its historical legacy leads to a troubled conscience in this respect. It is 'irritated' by the insufficient clarity on the societal implications of its normative claims, though often convinced of the necessity of its deliberative democratic claims. What follows, then, is a version of the modal normative projection of critical theory taking the form of sign-mediated, reflective reasoning, yet reasoning that must also have implications for societal reproduction and change. It is inspired by discourse ethics, interpreted 'generously' across the careers of both Apel and Habermas, but it presents itself as a discourse ethics newly conceived to deal with earlier identified concerns on the generative – creative, abductive – and applied levels.

The chapter accordingly advances three kinds of validity standards, conjectural, ideal, and actual, that stand somewhere between, on the one hand, substantive conjectures or modal projections (in abductive schema formation), ideals in the cognitive cultural model (CCM), and, respectively, discourse structures and action-ready beliefs in the sociocultural (SCM) and institutional (IM) models. On the other hand, it explores their communicative fluidization in reasoning processes. This has clear analogies with Habermas's distinction between communicative action and the lifeworld in *TCA*, but, as explained earlier, it also has several differences, including, above all, the desire to demonstrate the generative powers of reasoning for societal coordination and to better integrate feelings and facts with reasons with all their wide theoretical implications. The focus on reasoning is intended to bring out its significance set within the two other contexts, those of consciousness (feelings) and actuality (facts, including the facticity of the normative). Reasoning, as emphasized throughout the book, has a distinctive power of its own as argumentation, thus as a process of raising, examining, and settling validity. While such a process of potential and actual validation stands forth as a social achievement, it is, at least in the encompassing sense developed here, little present in the contemporary social sciences, and above all, not in the form of validity conceived of in an inter- and transsubjective manner. The most striking reason for this state of affairs, touched on at many points in the text above, is the inattention to multi-level cognitive structures and the corresponding non-recognition of epistemic processes in

*Reasoning and Validity Standards* 257

utilizing and transforming these collective cognitive structures, ranging from the collective transcendent to the infra-individual. In the social sciences, this dimension is either vaguely presented or, mostly, ignored by the form of a dominating ontology of either the object or subject or both. To the contrary, both Apel and Habermas are right to emphasize it as a vital power of human agents to be able to transform the sociocultural world and its relation to the natural world, with recognition of necessary limits to the employment of such powers of transformation in many cases.

In its unfolding steps, the chapter will work its way through the three categories of Peirce's account of reasoning, using validity standards for each that emerge from a modified account of discourse ethics. It will, in a final step, attempt to show at least the bare outlines of a transversal standard and associated processes that would build from the three analytically isolated standards.

## Conjectural Validity

Text Box 10.1 addresses the abductively formed conjectural validity standard. Overall, what is contained in the text box conforms to what has already been addressed in this and previous chapters. The emphasis is on 'positive' normative

---

**Text Box 10.1:   Conjectural validity**

- Rationalized habits of feeling (appropriate level of self- and hetero-criticism); relational structure of conjectures – adequacy (truth, rightness, and sincerity) of perceptual judgements that underlie them.
- Veracity of implicated percepts (indexes).
- Modal (epistemic and normative) quality of possibilities and real vagues.
- Relational structure of conjecture – judgement-like inference in relation to appropriate ideals (established or possible).
- Comprehensibility (hazarding by 'the mind' conducive to intelligible order) of transition from habits of feeling to habits of thought.
- Empirical-theoretical adequacy of critical societal imagination.
- Presence of conditions of comprehensive reflexive freedom and associated innovation capacity.
- Openness to intersubjective testing and fair inclusion.
- Appropriate volition (including negation).
- Avoidance of bad or inadequate habits of feeling (alienated, regressive, ad hominem, discriminatory, etc.); 'civilizing' of limiting or destructive elementary social forms, for example, rivalry, competition, violence, discrimination, etc.
- Critique: habits of feeling and conjectures can take regressive, ad hominem, reifying, alienated, dysfunctional, and dominating forms, which may block or inhibit the disclosure of meaning.

## 258    *Reasoning and Validity Standards*

orientations essential for a critical theoretical approach. Validity standards respond to the general direction of its critical intentions. Of the various possible dimensions of critique, abduction at its core is concerned with the aesthetic dimension, in important respects consistent with Kant's idea of reflective as opposed to determinant judgement. Though abduction draws on feelings that reach beyond existing societal validity, once in conformity with appropriate validity standards, it need not in itself be unreasonable. Of course, it often is unreasonable when pathologically or unjustly intended. To put it differently, a validity standard for abduction depends on establishing a standard of reasonableness for it, a standard that sets processual parameters for reflection but does not attempt to absolutely constrain it. This observation is broadly consistent with the 'procedural' emphasis of discourse ethics. Such a standard must take account of the inferential chaining process that abduction initiates or varies. Conjecture is therefore not merely a chance effect of qualities of mind but contains within it what had hitherto lain beyond rational demonstration but which was nonetheless diffusely and inchoately experienced. Such experience, though, is not beyond *possible* rational apprehension, as the conjecture attests, and *could*, in the right conditions for society-wide reasoning, prove itself, and then, if justified as a conjectural validity claim, become accepted as a reasonable societal innovation. A reasonable innovation would be obtained at some possible level of the output cultural models, initially normally at the ideal level (the CCM), where it is first postulated as a potential. Mostly at this level, only perturbations to existing ideals occur, but in the case of fundamental learning, it goes much further than this, and altogether new ideals may emerge, such as, in relatively recent history, feminism or ecological responsibility. This happens in the case of radical learning, going 'beyond' what already exists by engaging cognitive principles and literally transcending the previous state of understanding resulting from the prior operations of the cultural models.

The rationality of abduction is derived from a specific type of normative validity standard that, like Kant, is of an aesthetic kind. For Peirce, aesthetics is the first of the normative sciences, where it represents the capacity for reflective judgements that bring particulars into line with concepts. The law-like quality of habits of feeling, enabling the bringing together of multiple sensations into coherent perception, animates the abductive quality of mind. These habits are on the feeling side of abduction, so to speak, while the explicit quality of what is conjectured lies on the logical side. Abduction, as the vehicle of the conjectural validity standard, is the locus of reflexive freedom in projecting candidate ideas for possible rationalization, a process that itself builds on the even more basic reflexive working through of feelings. As conjectural, in other words, to do with new knowledge, it is intrinsically bound up with the integrating standard of deduction, pushing forward on a continuum of knowing ultimately structured by cognitive principles or ideas of reason, to generate a new ideal or, more commonly, a new interpretation of an ideal. Hence, conjecture is, as previously, also essential for the 'opening up' cognitive operations that engage with the principles that populate the transcendent cognitive order, pushing in the direction of one or more continua of meaning, for example, legitimacy, dignity, or equality. This allows the modal imagination to come into play, which is vital in both

Kant and Peirce. This cognitive, modal imagination reveals the capacity from a position within the world to reach beyond it. Here, the cognitive order principles provide continua for imaginative thinking, operating as collectively shared capacities for cognitive operations. For Peirce, such productive imagination leads to provisional judgements. Judgement therefore operates together with the imagination and is not separate from it, as in one ending and the other beginning. The logical operation of abduction involves the transition from habits of feeling to habits of thought. However, even 'good' abduction may not be proven true or right. Its success in a relevant sense of the word depends on the remainder of the logical process. Such success depends on whether the altered ideal can indeed 'bear' the reconstructive import and, perhaps more fundamentally still, to what extent the inductively located play of 'dynamic interpretants', emanating inside the mind or from external sources, will *productively* relate to the 'immediate interpretant' that is what is contained in the conjecture.

The response of the dynamic interpretant comes after the conjecture, which is mostly not simply baldly stated but built into its own inferential logic, whether explicated or implied. In other words, the conjecture is embedded in both an ideal and a preferred normative interpretation of that ideal. The response, assuming it accepts the broad space of the selected ideal, can either accept, reject, or modify the conjecture. Frequently, the new interpretation of the ideal is not accepted; for example, the rejection of a cosmopolitan ideal in preference for a nationalist, sovereign one. Such a promulgation and acceptance/rejection of a conjecture/ideal homology can be explicated through the relationship between the relational structures proposed by the conjecture in the light of the 'relations of relations' or meta-relations constituted by the ideal. The conjecture thus resonates with the ideal. Ideals acquire the refractive power of integrating relations over time. For example, imagine again taking the 'nation-state' as an 'ideal' form of self-government that has been built up through a myriad of historic or ongoing conjectures, related ideals, competing interpretations, and normative selections over time. A conjecture, assuming for simplicity that it is confined to the space of one ideal, postulates a set of inferential relations that should be obtained in relation to the ideal. For example, it may postulate that a national ethical community should break any transnational interdependencies in operation to make its own laws. In so doing, the vast body of ideals and norms that pertain to transnational law-making legitimacy, and all that goes with it, is brought into question. The relations built into this conjecture are vast, and the space of ideals and norms, in operation or possible within existing arrangements, may be even vaster and, correspondingly, have attached to them normative powers. This scale entailed in this example gives a sense of the significance of inferential relations over the paradigm of individual judgements, whether of Kant or of Rawls's reflective equilibrium. With the logic of relations, the implications of relations must be made publicly manifest, not reduced to the deliberate judgement of a single individual within their own sense of harmony. Yet, judgement does also enter intrinsically into conjecture when conjecture is understood as the aesthetically guided condensation of those possible relations of reason that *could pertain* to an object. Only the completion of the full process of reasoning, though, can

260    *Reasoning and Validity Standards*

confirm whether this relational judgement has logical validity. It cannot be settled inside the mind. It is rather a collective process of justification, a justification that, in inductive reasoning, will be tested against facts of relevant external worlds as represented in indexical and iconic signs.

A certain type of critique specifically attends to the conjectural validity standard. It has some associations with Habermas's formal pragmatic validity claim of truthfulness or sincerity. A first consideration, therefore, is whether the conjecture, understood more generally as the intention of the speaker, is sincere. If the speaker – more broadly to be understood as the subject position that may amalgamate the perspectives of many like-minded agents – is perceived to be insincere, it opens a vista of interrogation of their statements. However, how can the speaker's lack of sincerity be demonstrated? This leads back to the kinds of reasoning pathologies listed in the text box and to be outlined in Chapter 12. It invokes those that have an important abductive moment, such as understanding alienation as a deficit of reflexive perspective taking, including lack of perspective on the self. Conjecture, as here understood, using Weber's metaphor, lies on the switching tracks of culture, in the tendency to move reasoning in a new direction as part of the knowledge construction process. The various kinds of reasoning pathology arise when the achieved switch, by accident or design, ignores certain important aspects of the validity standard, such as comprehensibility through lack of intelligibility and transparency, freedom by false or disorienting suggestion, lack of attention to hetero-criticism, lack of capacity for self-criticism, incapacity for necessary negation, inability to develop real vagues, and so on. These syndromes issue in combined habits of feeling and conjectures that are unjust, distorting, or pathological in any of the various ways outlined. The significance of this validity standard for the general purpose of reflection that may become critical lies in its pivotal status for cultural reorientation; it is the entryway to the initiation of relational chains of reasoning that may in time – short or long – lead to new knowledge. It may also lead to not just new knowledge about society but also new states of society itself if the anticipated capacity for action is realized.

Sociologically, this conjectural moment is like what Wright-Mills described as the sociological imagination, that quality of mind that could forge connections between distant conditions and proximate experience (Mills, 2000). It is also what, following Castoriadis, has become known as the social imaginary (Castoriadis, 1998). Beyond this immediate intellectual context, this state of mind also extends to the 'lay' capacity to obscure such connections, deliberately or otherwise. Further, there is that limited capacity that merely gets to the point of sentiment, settles habits of feelings, and is unable to move from there to engage in any true process of reasoning. The sway of sentiment over reasoning may serve perfectly reasonable functions, those that are practically indubitable and do not require further thought, but it can also sustain an oppressive lack of awareness that negatively affects oneself and others. Following Wright Mills's thoroughly pragmatist understanding, the proper exercise of the sociological imagination entails bringing forth good conjecture, that is, not just the conjectural capacity to 'suddenly' see

*Reasoning and Validity Standards* 261

relations of knowing differently through a new insight, but also the capacity to articulate that insight coherently within the concepts of a scientific mode of knowledge. Conjecture must therefore be articulated in a way that bears relation to a conceptually organized mode of knowledge that it seeks to influence in some way. This conjectural inference arises from the distillation of unconscious inferential processes, animated by a sense of the need to go beyond what is conceptually understood. It therefore does not simply succumb to concepts in the process of ideal explication, but it coexists with them until there is satisfaction that the impetus to change has in some way been met, or, alternatively, that its need has not been demonstrated. This continuation of a feeling that cannot be fully explicated is what Peirce understood by the continuation of feelings – or vagues – throughout the process of forming generals, losing intensity as the explication process progresses. It does not mean that conjecture is wholly unconscious, but that some part of it remains so while the ultimate validity status of the conjecture remains incomplete.

Conjecture and reflexivity are intrinsically related. Reflexivity is to be understood in a double sense: as the reflexivity of intellectuals establishing an orientation towards an object of research and as an assessment of the reflexive capacity of other agents in situations under analysis. The latter kind of reflexivity is influenced by whether the thrust of the interpretation of agents by the researcher is critical or affirmative. Critical theory is particularly engaged with reflexivity because of its basic premise of the capacity of agents to intersubjectively agree on norms in the right deliberative and general conditions. Hence, intellectual reflexivity is at least partly constrained by the priority accorded to the reflexive capacity of actors. In my view, already articulated above, the strong assumption of discourse ethics regarding the high capacity of actors, while at the limit correct and normatively justifiable, comes at the cost of its capacity for its exposing critique of the mechanisms of non-ideal domination. The discourse ethics approach tends to limit critical capacity by virtue of its normatively formed 'epistemological optimism' and, consequently, ontological operations on the input and output sides of reasoning receive insufficient attention. Ontological constructions are thus prominent in the conjectural input moment of intellectual critique and condition the epistemic operations of reasoning. If this is put with the above remarks on the persistence of feelings within these epistemic operations, the modern disjunction between epistemology and ontology becomes allayed, a disjunction that persists also between Kantian approaches in critical theory and modern sociology. The latter arises notwithstanding how important neo-Kantianism has been in the history of sociology, from Durkheim through Weber to Parsons.

I have drawn attention to the role of conjecture in critical theory to illustrate dimensions of normative and social theorizing that are often addressed only implicitly and in a very restricted fashion. This is even where they are at all addressed. Drawing attention to conjecture as a validity standard is first of all meant to address a distinctive kind of critique at the very origins of critical reflexivity in general. It involves the attempt to identify and normatively adjudicate, on the one side, the motivations that apparently animate newly formulated validity claims and, on

## 262 *Reasoning and Validity Standards*

the other side, to consider their likely societal import. This directs attention to the very wellsprings of social change, the postulation of new ideas to be judged as defensible or indefensible. Critical theory has an array of distinctions, historically especially concentrated on the indefensible side, such as reification and alienation, but Apel and Habermas have added more clearly outlined defensible ones to them, for example, in Habermas's case, sincerity and appropriateness. The conjectural validity standard can therefore be used to direct a wide range of critical prognoses. If this is the intra-theoretical function, analogous to Mills's sociological imagination, then the societal function is to critically assess abduction at work in society and its effects. This is where the dimension of aesthetic revelation comes to the fore, as a means of apprehending highly embedded and intricately connected permutations of emergent feelings, reasons, and facts. In recent decades in the social sciences, building on a resonant earlier history, this aesthetic dimension has been given greater prominence with the rise of various kinds of social phenomenology. While this is generally a progressive development in itself, few are the cases in which this has been coupled with an analysis of reasoning, an analysis that remains the key to the societal diffusion of innovative ideas. It is also where the concern with consciousness of embodied experiences, which both attach to bodies from outside and are generated by sensibility from within, dialectically encounters logical operations. Critically, it is also the locus classicus of the generation of negative ideologies, the application of distorting habits of feelings – and their further extension – in formulating distorted consciousness. Finally, conjectural validity involves the assertion of critical validity claims involving new standards or the innovative application of existing standards. Such standards, both in the moments of constitution by engaging the transcendent and in the moment of regulation by societally applying it in further logical operations and in action, are pivotal to critical theory and the reasonableness of society alike.

### Actual Validity

Text Box 10.2 summarizes the important elements of ideal validity. Though ideals have normative import, they are, in the first instance, cognitive. The building of norms ultimately depends on the prior establishing of an ideal, which first of all defines a space – a space of reasons – in which norms can emerge. Ideals are akin to 'ultimate interpretants' that allow many interpretations arising from different normative tendencies. These interpretations actualize the potentials contained in ideals. Yet, possible interpretations of the ideals always remain greater than actual ones, following the inductive leading principle of approximation towards the completion of an ideal that can never be finally attained. Viewing the cognitive dimension of ideals as 'above' norms places methodological emphasis on viewing social objects as in states of becoming rather than concretely actualized. In capturing states of becoming, ideals encapsulate normative *potentials.* What if *this* interpretation of the ideal beyond any other were to be implemented? Or what imaginable norm would be a satisfactory interpretation of *these* multiple ideals?

**Text Box 10.2:   Ideal Validity**

- Identification of ideals as encompassing discrete and hybrid relational continua (superordinate intellectual concepts with implication of appropriate general behaviour, necessarily or modally) within a learning community.
- Generalized (inclusive, reciprocal, reflexively, and thematically adequate) reasoning processes carry explicit (or implicit that could be made explicit) learning processes, reasoning through principles, and associated habits across key domains (aesthetic, normative, and functional).
- Appropriate ideal-forming capacity is required on consensual and rational-dissensual planes (requisite habits of thought or capacity for corrective reasoning); appropriate ideals taken sufficiently far become universalist and of evolutionary significance.
- Such ideal-forming capacity as orientations to truth, rightness, and goodness should be appropriately grounded in the normative sciences and empirical-theoretically guided analysis; from evolutionary formed transcendent presuppositions and formal properties to historically orienting ideals and then to inclusively grounded norms; in this progression, ideals balance deontology and teleology.
- Adequacy of inferential relations ranging between vagueness (potential implicit sense) and generality (explicated, abstracted ideals); appropriate general ideals stand as ultimate interpretants of inferentially culminating sense-making processes; they thus claim historical validity as validity standards set appropriately within transcendent validity concepts (final interpretants).
- Democratic ideals on convergent plane with capacity to explicate appropriate conjectures and thus to guide the formation of needed democratic innovations; appropriate ideals of rightness at core of just societal validity standards, where such ideals should fully embrace evolutionary formed, transcendently located cognitive universals to serve democratic participation.
- Critique: bad habits of reasoning, pathological learning (reasoning pathologies).
- Qualification: ideal-formation only partly corresponds to the above even in good cases; ideals also formed in context of power, inequality and domination, imperfect knowledge, bad motives, etc.; ideals applicable only mediately through taking account of the effect on others of co-responsible norm-formation (intersubjective and collective proviso).

## 264  *Reasoning and Validity Standards*

As already stressed, despite the generally positive connotations of the word, ideals are not of necessity normatively positive. In fact, depending on the normative vantage point, ideals can be regressive as well as progressive. Thus, a normative theory like discourse ethics must identify which ideals are progressive and under what conditions they arise. It also must find a means of identifying and criticizing problematic ideals and downstream norm selections arising from them. The efficacy of ideals is very hard to properly establish. Peirce identified ultimate interpretants, which in this reading are ideals, with habits of thought. Agreed upon or generalized habits of thought produce rules, but ideal rules are in the first instance cognitive rules, as with the procedural rules of discourse ethics. Such procedural rules, which are ways of fixing ideals, are also ways of fixing norms based on ideals. Discourse ethics emphasizes consensual norm fixing conditioned by the exhaustiveness of the procedure. Even within the broadly understood discourse ethical tradition, others, also including this text, additionally stress normative rules that depend on disagreement or rational dissensus. Beyond that, there are other modalities of fixing norms that could be deemed progressive and yet cannot be established in either of the above ways, such as norms that depend for final decision on the voting hegemony of a majority who reason justly. Beyond these kinds of progressive ideals that critical theory finds reasonable, there are also those that it finds unreasonable. Thus, the incorporation of ideals into reasoning as media of deduction can be either reasonable or unreasonable.

The general precepts of a modified discourse ethics are specified in Text Box 10.2. The modifications to the theory underpinning the text box relate partly to the greater emphasis on contingency in ideal formation. It also assumes a necessary transsubjective dimension arising from the cognitive nature of ideals rather than the classical discourse ethical emphasis on norms intersubjectively formed through exhaustive procedures. These remarks bear on the observations about law in the last chapter, where the cultural effects of the medium of law were taken to be much wider than legal procedures can ever fully reflect. As a result, the public sphere concept, which has moved about considerably in Habermas's treatment over time, gains greater centrality (O'Mahony, 2021). The deontological sense of norm-forming forums that appear to hover above society is diminished with the greater centrality of ideals as part of an open-ended logical 'interpretantation' process. The temporal underpinning of ideal formation becomes extended due to a more realistic account of how various institutional modalities of exploring agreement and disagreement are embedded in collective learning processes that extend over time. With this emphasis, the teleological task comes to the fore of generating the kinds of ideals that are adapted to multiple moving parts of society as they evolve in time and the associated reasoning and learning processes. Out of this multiplicity and pluralism, the ideal limit of normatively comprehensive communication can be held fast, without its over-strong deontological manifestation in the classical theory limiting the cognitive-semiotically oriented social scientific exploration of its full, historical context.

The original vision of discourse ethics entailed radical democratic participation. Yet, this vision was more an implication of the theory than an explicated commitment. The vision could only be realized if there was a thoroughgoing participatory democratization of society in all its aspects, yet only tentatively could any indications of such a transformation be drawn from the movement of history. Habermas's theory can be read to a degree as a gradual distancing from that vision, with the renunciation of the idea of complete democratization at every level in the period around *TCA* and the advancement of a deliberative model more associated with liberal democratic legal and political institutions in *BFN*. Notwithstanding, his distinctive procedural theory taken forward from the discourse ethics period remained different from the Rawlsian social liberal account, compatible as it and some other liberal accounts were in some ways. The enduring difference was the degree of emphasis on the intersubjective epistemic and participatory implications of the linguistic turn in Habermas, even where the participatory standard has been significantly weakened over time.

Nevertheless, because the sociological translation of discourse ethics was never extended beyond the original work of the founders, there remains an empirical-theoretical gap that also has normative implications. This gap could be filled in if the transcendental foundations of discourse ethics, the basic presuppositions of speech and action, were to be regarded as cognitive rather than, in the first instance, normative. There is a human social obligation to make sense, but such sense-making is compatible with many different normative outcomes when the full panoply of human purposes is considered. This amounts to proposing that the core of discourse ethics should no longer be regarded as normatively transcendental in a direct sense. Thus, instead, the 'first' normative space of discourse ethics entails the use of evolutionary-formed, transcendent, cognitive presuppositions and principles that bear on *normative culture* rather than norms per se. Such cognitive principles give orientation but leave final outcomes open to multi-level discursive settlement with different coordinative modalities. This implies that the level of democratization compatible with such a normative culture must be seen as *evolving* in society and accordingly to be studied on those terms, not already there, nearly there, or even readily specifiable. This would also be compatible with using this account of ideals as the base of a reconstructive democratic theory since its flexible design would confer advantages in this respect.

Ideal validity standards present in the text box are, following from the above, embedded in an emergent process. References to ideal formation and collective learning processes reveal the extent to which understanding emergent process depends on social scientific elaboration. Existing ideals are constantly reassessed, intentionally negated or elaborated, and re-instituted. For this process, the opening-up abductive-deductive cycle involves conjecture, and generative schematization is intrinsic.

Reflexive 'surplus' is derived from the transcendent cognitive principles, for example, something not thought before about ecological responsibility is now made salient. This is manifest, to take one example, in the relatively recent foregrounding of ecological responsibility emanating from figures such as Apel and Lenk (Apel, 1987; Lenk, 2007). This also goes on beyond the intellectual realm to the vast thought experiment that is society. The building of a convergent, immanent ideal of ecological responsibility from a cognitive principle, or a suite of

## 266 *Reasoning and Validity Standards*

such relevant principles, is therefore a result of extended argumentation over time. Following this example further, for Apel, the survival of the species depends on arriving at an adequate recognition of the ideal. It requires a certain kind of evolutionarily significant, temporally extended stabilization of the ideal (Apel, 1975). Sociologically, since the knowledge generated in the academic context is only part of the knowledge needed to construct the ideal, the entire societal construction process must be explored. In this process, what must be reconstructed is a version of the ideal of responsibility that is adequately infused with other necessary ideals. Apel, for example, distinguished his ideal from that of Jonas's principle of responsibility due to its democratic emphasis on co-responsibility. It might also be ventured at this point that the way the concept of sustainability has been advanced in the last 30 years has distracted from an appropriate realization of the ideal of responsibility. It has advanced the idea of responsibility as not essentially requiring profound democratic change to enable the requisite collective learning. This could be summed up by saying that the ideal of sustainability, if not entirely, substantially provides an inadequate validity goal for the validity concept of ecological responsibility. It does this because sustainability substantially draws off a different kind of abductive conjecture: that the goal of ecological responsibility can be attained without substantially changing economic and political arrangements. Indeed, the idea became widespread that market actors' self-regulation and state de-regulation were together sufficient to reach ecological goals. The reason why sustainability, more especially its original formulation as sustainable development, operates with a different conjecture is that it has assumptions about what can and must be done that significantly deviate from Apel's account of co-responsibility in discourse ethics. The ideals of sustainable development and ecological co-responsibility have a type of in-between status; they might be called, in this regard, conjectural proto-ideals that are both reciprocally competitive and yet also partly complementary.

Taking the case of co-responsibility as an example and putting it in the context of the internal structure of cultural models in the previous chapter, it entails both a claim to an ideal of reasonableness and also to various elements of actuality. The former, the 'co' part of co-responsibility, is a call for participatory democratization that is a minimum condition for addressing the ecological crisis. The issue of actuality goes three ways: that of real ecological progress through agreed upon – in the end – steps; that of ongoing or new practices based on ideals deemed legitimate that actually make matters worse; and that of emergent challenges to the ecological status quo from groups on the ideal periphery whose voice has become ever more insistent. However, the growth in insistence of the voice does not translate into institutional influence, partly because this emergent ideal is not remotely as strong as opposing industrial and technocratic ideals – to express them in a very limited way. Further, spanning Apel and Touraine, different ideas of the subject – writ large – are brought into play in the sustainability and co-responsibility ideals. In this respect, sustainability by and large carries on the western tradition of emphasizing clever beings, whereas discourse ethics emphasizes sincere beings, one of the basic formal pragmatic validity standards (Cortina, 1990). Of course, as the sustainability ideal becomes expanded with the crisis-driven transformation of ecological discourse, what is today understood as sustainability takes on part of the co-responsibility ideal, but a lot of time has passed, and ecological problems have intensified.

It is already implied in the above that ideal validity cannot be separated from conjectural validity and the kinds of theoretical assumptions subjects associate with the latter. I will return to this while addressing its actual validity in the next section. For now, one point must be emphasized. Following Peirce's model of real rather than radical Cartesian (sceptical) doubt, knowledge already pre-exists cognitive endeavours. This knowledge is associated with what I have called the 'closing down' phase, a phase ultimately characterized by the inculcation of institutionally organized habits of volition and action. These latter habits are the product of previous cognitive operations that have resulted in the discursive selection of ideals. However, 'worlds of objects' change in unexpected ways, and the habits no longer work and become normatively questioned. Contradictions appear, either manifesting as direct crises, such as climate change or poverty, or more diffuse dissatisfaction with the 'spiritual situation of the age'. Thus, feelings of dissatisfaction or crisis emerge towards what has served as a previously acceptable standard of actual validity. It is the crystallization of these feelings in explicated logical argument that then commences the opening-up abductive phase, with ineluctable consequences for the action-orienting structure of ideals and the relevant standard of ideal validity.

Second-generation critical theory in its early stages – let us say to in or about the 1980s – above all else is a theory of democratic idealization, specifically a theory of participatory idealization, as is revealed in Text Box 10.2, Ideal Validity. Habermas certainly began to lean away from these participatory aspects from *TCA* onwards, but they remained – sometimes awkwardly – present in the idealizations of his later theory. It is certainly true that full participatory democratization could not be enacted right away in contemporary societies. Still, participatory democratization must remain at the core of the theory, even as a graduated intercept strategy. Even the fullest version of the ideal of deliberation must contain, in the situation of the world today, much stronger participatory elements. For all the problems with participatory experimentation – time commitments, realism, and representativity –, the contemporary situation of highly indirect, globally hollowed-out, and communicatively deficient democratic forms simply cannot cope, and certainly offers no utopian horizons. Honneth, following Dewey, makes an interesting suggestion in his book on socialism, a suggestion that ultimately goes all the way back to Peirce's experimental philosophy (Honneth, 2016). This is to conduct a range of experiments that would explore the participatory quality of democracy in the context of other social spheres, for example, those represented in Figure 7.1, Chapter 7, *Sign-Mediated Societal Ontology*, as discursive, positional, and displacement fields. This suggestion is broadly consistent with that which is explored here, an approach that would open the social sciences to what Touraine calls sociological 'interventionism' (Touraine, 1981). The implication for ideals of the reasonable in critical theory, continuing with the example of ecological co-responsibility, would be the place

## 268   *Reasoning and Validity Standards*

the idealized standard in the broader sign system outlined in Chapter 8 and in the account of validity emerging in the last few chapters. The outcome would be directed towards, using the words of Rawls, progress towards realistic utopias, but, unlike Rawls, envisioning utopias with strong democratic participatory qualities (Rawls, 1999). The line of work pioneered by Tom Burns in this regard holds out some promise, but critical theory, as the most insistently democratic theory present in the social sciences, must develop its own blueprint and associated studies and actions (Burns, 1999).

### Actual Validity

The last two sections of this chapter have addressed conjectural and ideal validity standards. Conjectural validity standards seek to normatively order the relations of reason that take explicit form in abductive inferential processes. Validity at this first level has both autonomous grounding as a specific kind of inference carrying new idea potentiality. It is also oriented to the reconstruction of general ideal relations, relations that organize relations. Though Peirce's logic of inquiry can be represented as a movement from conjecture to ideal, to fact, this is not entirely adequate. The dynamic interpretant – rather simplified in standard examples in the Peirce literature such as that of 'ground arms' where it is reduced to an inevitable, in the circumstances, response – is in fact for any complex issue more likely to be a field of interpretants that carry opposed or at least varying interpretations of the conjecture-ideal relation. This idea of a field of contestation of dynamic interpretants that have ongoing implications for conjecture-ideal relations opens the possibility of charting a more dynamic relationship between the logic of ideals and the logic of application, where the latter is the focus of actual validity.

Actuality is the manifest sphere of the social where 'interactants' of all kinds encounter one another with – by then – pre-formed belief systems and commitments. In this latter sense, it is social institution, the outcome of 'old' reasoning that pre-exists 'new' reflexive reasoning. Actuality can be grasped as existing societal rationalization. Institutional norms, belief systems, habits, and dispositions are products of rationalization and structure ongoing interaction to generate recurrent and predictable results. There is no impassable wall separating actuality from perceptual innovation (firstness) or from reasoning (thirdness). Actuality generates the conditions in which reasonable doubt arises, leading to the 'agitation' of sensibility, perception, and reasoning to generate new knowledge. In the realm of human knowledge communities, the crucial distinction regarding such new knowledge lies between the reproduction of orders of knowledge with incremental variation, or their critically induced transformation. In the first, sensibility and reasoning are necessarily employed, but within established cultural – both normative and cognitive – boundaries. In the second, sensibility and reasoning generate collective learning that, in certain instances, leads to radical social change. I enter the caveat, as always, that viewed from the normative perspective of discourse ethics, the kind of learning and rationalization that ensues may not represent progress.

*Reasoning and Validity Standards* 269

From the standpoint of discourse ethics, there is no doubt that concrete interaction will deviate from its ideal horizons. Yet it is critical to know, on the one hand, how and to what extent ideals it regards as reasonable ideals have become socially embedded, as opposed to other ideals that are not consistent with its validity standards. To acquire knowledge in both dimensions is essential. It is also essential that such knowledge be brought together in assessing the normative state of society so as to break the rival tendencies towards normative horizons without content or negative critique of content without reconstructive specification, either of ideals or procedures for realising them. This integrated double focus defines what it is to specify actual validity.

Klaus Günther proposes that, beyond justification, an additional consideration arises at the level of application, here called actuality, that is, of the coherence of already justified norms with one another (Günther, 1993). Such coherence is necessary for democratically grounded, 'equilbrated' normative rule systems. However, can individual norms be justified independent of such striving for coherence in the first place? In some cases, they can be. Fundamental human rights, for example, should not depend on whether other less important norm complexes impinge on them in application. While this applies most obviously to such fundamental norms, even there, the question of how they should be applied is often far from easy to establish. Gunther's important insight must be taken further. In the light of the above and generally, discourse ethics, while emphasizing universal participatory *communication*, nonetheless relies on *judgements* and decisions on rules deemed justified. Judgements within ongoing ideal contexts rely on the ever-expanding chain of arguments that compose them and connect them to other relational chains. So, we need to know how judgements, such as constitutional principles, relationally operate, even of what they relationally consist of, not just in legal contexts of argumentations but also in actual social spheres. Judgements, in this sense, are just one dimension of relations of reason, those that have become actual. Discourse ethics makes provision for such wide relational fields by virtue of its emphasis on exhaustive argumentation procedures. However, there is a difference between the positing of the possibility of such relations and the theoretical-methodological demonstration of their reality. It is the *generative* foundation of rationalization – the logical-projective account of future relations – that follows from Peirce's logic of reasoning that opens the way to the necessary sociological and social semiotic intervention. Discourse ethics does not exclude this possibility, but it does not show how it can be done either. This matters for an account of validity; otherwise, the entirety of validity appears to only consist of the transcendental relation to validity concepts. These validity concepts must be set in their relation to validity goals; otherwise, the validity concepts will remain problematically indeterminate with no demonstrable teleological moment.

Text Box 10.3, *Actual Validity*, following the specified standards should involve the translation into responsible conduct of that which is ideally possible. Modes of conduct therefore involve taking responsibility for actions that can claim to be right, true, or good. Responsibility is confronted most acutely at the point of action, whether the action is to act physically or communicatively or to decide on a norm.

270 *Reasoning and Validity Standards*

---

**Text Box 10.3:   Actual Validity**

- Justifiable outcomes of idealization (interpretant stabilization) manifested in coherent rule systems and habits of action (e.g., ethical, aesthetic, legal, moral, functional, and various combinations).
- Institution of responsible modes of conduct – is true, is right, and is good – that can offer reasonable self-justification (responsible individual or co-responsible collective/group justification) within the ideal standard.
- Adequacy of realization of theme and actor inclusive public sphere that enables 'progressive' collective learning.
- Adequacy of realization of ideal of participatory democratization, action coordinating power (immanent limit), essential for justified, knowledge-able actions in contexts of modalities of agreement.
- Inter-positionally justified models of reasonableness and rationality guiding selection from ideals in dimensions of functional, ethical, moral, and combined (e.g., reciprocal and general in moral matters).
- Appropriate equilibration of ideals and facts; inter-positional fixation of key beliefs in context of ideals that shape them.
- Adequate integration of rules of conduct and motives (responsible individual or group) in context of common world and inter-positional relations.
- Avoidance of genealogical proviso (ideals subverted or one-sided in practice, for example, Honneth's social pathology of law).
- Non-contradictory relationship of indexes (objectual relational variation) to habits of volition and action.
- Non-contradictory and semantically adequate relationship between indexes and icons (predicates) (e.g., real facts of empire vs. imperial nostalgia).
- Critique of unjustifiable actuality, that is, contradictions/injustices between social relations and materialized forces; for example, domination (including racism, sexism, exploitation, and others), contradiction, dysfunctional organization, hermeneutic and testimonial injustice, reification, alienation, mis-development, and pathology.

---

In the logic of Peirce, it is through induction that the consequence of acting is truly confronted and responsibility, or with Apel co-responsibility, asserted or ignored. For reasons that Günther has generally highlighted, the need to take multiple possible consequences into account along with the need to preserve the moral content of important ideals, induction is a very exacting kind of reasoning. Accordingly, the application problem is far from being 'mere' application of norms already set in some higher-level process. Rather, in application, whether in setting norms or learning from their implications, very complex problems arise. Norms bearing on climate change, for example, carbon taxes, require, inter alia, political legitimacy

*Reasoning and Validity Standards* 271

from those already relatively poor, who stand to lose more, implementation capacity, responsiveness to targets for reducing $CO_2$, dealing with pressure from affected industries and from environmental movements, conformity with existing and emergent ideals, and much else.

In dealing with issues characterized by this kind of complexity, inductive reasoning must take account of existing factual states of all kinds, cultural, technical, natural, and various hybrids, and also any consequences of actions that would affect the future. The future orientation is the real one in that the past has already happened and states of affairs deriving from it already exist, whereas the future is open to volition and action. In this inductive moment, the true difference between Peirce and discourse ethics, on the one side, and the predominant temporal strategy in sociology become apparent. Whether in empirical-analytical sociology, where the future appears to follow from the past, or in phenomenological sociology, where the future appears as a type of intense present, no engaged sense of reasoning about the past from the vantage point of the future is properly addressed. It is intrinsic to discourse ethics, bringing forth the emphasis on future-oriented co-responsibility that Apel pioneered.

This text proposes several changes of emphasis on discourse ethics arising from the above distinction between opening up and closing down phases of reasoning, respectively associated with the abductive-deductive and deductive-inductive cycles. Regarding the first cycle, the focus shifts to a more emphatic cognitive emphasis, as outlined, both applying to transcendent principles and to immanent ideals as the cognitive foundation of normative culture. In the closing down cycle, empirical-theoretical considerations need to be fully incorporated to help shape complex normative judgements. If semiotics is truly to realize its potential as a meta-paradigm, emphasizing reasoning mediated through signs as an evolutionary universal that is generative of social forms, then it must find a way to incorporate the empirical-theoretical logics of the natural, social, and normative sciences. This challenge becomes pointed on an issue such as climate change, where, for example, the complex natural and social causality whose understanding should orient the human response is extremely hard to decipher. Taking some profit here from considerations outlined in Text Box 10.3, indices must become aligned; for example, indices on carbon emissions must go down, but these indices can be in tension with resultant indices pointing to potentially increased welfare loss of the poorest. The price mechanism may not work for a variety of reasons. Taking another category from the previous chapter, *iconic* images of the challenge of climate change vary widely; for some, they are utterly secondary to the seduction exerted by high-consumption lifestyles; for others, they carry the grim foreboding of vanishing biodiversity and natural and bodily vulnerability (Skillington, 2023). It matters greatly whether the institutional modality thought to deliver emissions reduction is predominantly through the financial and market systems or through regulations and laws of states and other political bodies. This also suggests that with inductive reasoning, knowledge must be generated about relevant, interpenetrating natural and social laws, that is, recurrent forces in the

## 272  *Reasoning and Validity Standards*

light of a dynamic, changing world forever generating new indexical and iconic symptoms. Depending on the level of political polarization, the same indices will be interpreted differently by different political and social groups. This leads to difficulty in seeking stable, agreed upon outcomes except through mechanisms of domination, despite an escalation in reasoning.

Contradictions and other problems in inductive diagnosis, whether done by an individual researcher or through collective democratic mechanisms, are listed in Text Box 10.3. On many political matters, the circumstances in which inductive reasoning occurs allow only defeasible general rules to be established. Such rules could change if the inductive premises were interpreted differently. Thus, the relationship between inductive premises and deductive rule formation is made technically impossible, at least with a strong concept of deduction as the invariant application of rules in like circumstances. Therefore, only some ideals, chiefly moral and functional, reach the threshold of consistent deducibility. Such ideals tend to be those stressed by discourse ethics in the normative sphere.

In the normative political world, fundamental moral rules that would ensure universality have the greatest priority. They are ascribed deontological status; that is, they are regarded as being of the kind that is permanently valid irrespective of circumstances. It is also supposed that such moral rules, principally those of communicative universality but also other rules that make such universality possible, are at the core of societal coordination. What the inductive dimension shows is just how hard it is to demonstrate how the relationship between moral and other rules can be achieved, even when supplemented by law and democratic coordination. Discourse ethics, and critical theory more generally, have explored many pathways to reconcile the relationship between morality and other rule systems. Yet none has been fully sociologically convincing. By the latter, I do not mean by the existing standards of sociology, but by the standards of the sociological innovation that critical theory requires. That is a sociology that allows for emancipatory possibilities that are not yet actualized, for extended reasoning, and for establishing democratic validity standards that, in some cases, are not just projective but actual in their implications. In this sense, the elusive and much-contested goal of a normative sociology remains essential. Such a normative sociology cannot just entail the demonstration of normative potentials given the 'right' normative preferences but also the demonstration of how the selected normative complex *could operate* in concrete cases. The idea of operation here is understood both diagnostically in relation to actual conditions, including latent social potentials, and prognostically in relation to the implications of appropriate normative interventions.

The inductive moment of reasoning is an integral part of general reasoning. In such general episodes of reasoning, which, in complex political or social issues, carry the same content into a range of different arenas, all the moments of reasoning are successively engaged. Though the inferential moments of reasoning cannot be easily separated, the inductive moment has a distinct affinity with actual procedures of settling a norm in the light of ideals, on one side, and facts on the other side. Therefore, induction can be institutionally conceived in relation to both cultural models and transactional fields outlined first in Chapter 7. These fields range

*Reasoning and Validity Standards* 273

in dynamic capacity from settled relational fields in which strongly patterning institutional rules apply (the institutional cultural model) to more loosely organized, yet still institutionally patterned, political and legal fields in which agents operate from relatively stable argumentation positions (the substantive cultural model). Located in contested fields, the inductive moment cannot be seen as only the consideration of a single actor or group on what to say and do. Inductive reasoning in political contexts involves the interaction of multiple actors with various levels of power. Whether individual or multiple, actors always draw off the stock of settled inferences, or, at least, *their* stock of settled inferences that must ineluctably include some part of a common stock. In inductive reasoning, these background contexts, which also include the results of the opening-up phase of reasoning, are brought together in contestation or in concert. The relation to the world beyond, set in this transactional setting, is structured by the operation of the coordinative modalities, viz., agreement, rational disagreement, compromise, domination, and permanent conflict spread across the cultural models as described in the last chapter. Yet, it must also depend on fresh judgements about the external situation supplied by various indices and icons as signs of actual states of affairs that enter reasoning via abduction.

The inductive moment of reasoning, thus described, challenges the normative philosophical tendency to separate deontological procedural norms from material norms. If the complementary teleological moment is to be fully included, it should also address the relationship between procedural and material norms. The inductive moment brings constantly shifting magnitudes of forces and interpretations of forces into play, set within empirically operating ideals. A social theory of important societal processes still requires intrinsic and sustained attention to material norms in all their facets for issues such as those Apel considers the most pressing: ecological capacity for self-destruction through nuclear annihilation, global poverty, and ultimately the kind of procedural co-responsibility he advocates. It is also unclear what kinds of procedures are needed and how they would balance the myriad existing commitments and roles of present procedures. Such present procedures have evolved in relation to existing issues and their institutional structuration; future procedures will have to evolve in relation to the pressing issues confronting humanity and their normative and factual structuring. It is, of course, the case that in democratic theory, and specifically in the area of deliberative democracy, such work is ongoing. Nonetheless, within it, a recurrent tendency is the absence of a general theory of society that would correspond to its intellectual premises. Such a theory is ultimately needed for questions such as: what is deliberative democracy *for*, what problems could it solve, and how could such potential solutions be institutionalized?

Little has been said here about the actual relations of reasoning or discourses that could contribute to addressing the challenge. In the tradition of Foucault, albeit differently, what is needed is a sustained analysis of existing such relations, their historical genesis, and their cultural-institutional implications. What would inevitably emerge is that ideals, positional commitments, and norms of many kinds are at work in the world. Moreover, new kinds of positional commitments are struggling

## 274 *Reasoning and Validity Standards*

to be born. The reasoning spans legal, natural scientific, social scientific, cultural scientific, political, and a multitude of other kinds. Each of these kinds of reasoning must be described according to a common format. Of course, the different kinds of reasoning will not be identical, but their distinctive operative conditions should broadly conform, if the overall hypothesis is correct, to the general format of reasoning proposed here. Each will involve conjectural, idealization, and actualization processes, albeit of different kinds, functional, nature-related, moral, legal, and aesthetic, among others. In any such undertaking, two kinds of short-circuiting are to be avoided. It should avoid the sociological short-circuiting that simply starts with an inventory of forces that are mainly downstream consequences of the reasoning processes in all their forms, just as well as unjust, true as well as false, and so on. It should also avoid the normative philosophical, along with cognate disciplines, short-circuiting that confines itself to the level of ideals, understood strictly normatively and including procedural ideals, with insufficient consideration given to consequences in the positional field. Actual validity thus should be seen to emerge from the reasoning process so far as it concerns the human capacity to act in social and natural environments, but also to be circumscribed in its possibility by the real constraints present in these environments, as they are naturally or as they have humanly evolved.

### Reasoning and Integrated Validity Standards

In this chapter, in the context of the previous two chapters, validity standards for democratic reasoning have been outlined that follow the inferential forms of reasoning in general. This has sought to place the issue of validity beyond the relatively narrow and individual-centred context of speech act theory and into the inferential logic of collective argumentation. Viewed from the latter standpoint, reasoning becomes a generative process carried on by collectivities within multiple contexts and associated capacities, viz., evolutionary, qualitatively felt, logically constituted, explicated, evaluated, and socially stored and applied. Theoretical-methodologically grasped, validity may be thought of as occurring within a vast complex of relations, both intellectually forged discursive relations and material objectual relations. The latter derives from the direct experience both of outer nature and of states of inner nature hardened into quasi-natural, rationalized forms. Behind both of these lies a vast complex of world-constituting and world-disclosing feeling relations where meaning itself is being generated and relevance established, a sensorium of all that is possible, with some of it moving in the direction of idea-potentiality by acquiring traction in cultural models sufficient to directly influence practice.

It is perhaps not too difficult to discern in the immediate above the influence of the three Peirce categories, firstness, secondness, and thirdness, that recent chapters have sought to apply, both socially theoretically in an expository sense and normatively in terms of validity standards. From this standpoint, validity derives from an integrated complex of dynamic processes within constituting and regulating forms, individual consciousness, collective consciousness, transcendent cognitive principles, logical states of reasoning, and various immanent cultural models leading

*Reasoning and Validity Standards* 275

down to capacities for action. Put more schematically, relations of validity start out with an initially ineffable sense of disturbance, and they progress through reasoning as reconsideration of what was previously accepted as given, a progression that could result in potentials for normative change. Validity thus traverses through the extended range of ends of human forms of life, from the evolutionary established potentiality of reason itself right down to rigid habits of belief. It also reaches beyond these ends and the cognitive structures that sustain them towards its own critique, where, starting from what is prescribed as valid, new considerations begin to be interposed in episodes of sensibility and perception, which are often extended episodes. All of these steps in part point towards an idealized picture of the role of validity as ultimately about producing rational, that is, valid, knowledge as a guide to reasonable action. Validity may also, in part, be conferred on actions that, by some validity standard, may be deemed unreasonable or irrational. If critical theory has often operated with a strong normative dichotomy between just and unjust, valid and invalid, there are also those states of validity where it is very difficult to discern what is valid and invalid from the standpoint of justified reasonableness, as, for example, the relative claims of ethical and moral standards in bounded communities. Accordingly, the consideration of validity brings in its train a vast range of considerations that point not only to clearly distinguishable yes/no distinctions on validity claims raised intersubjectively but also to intricate, extended, and indefinite consideration of validity in situations where clarity, in the words of Yeats, comes dropping slow. In these contexts, intersubjective, co-present communication constitutes only some of the relevant operations and even then utilizes only a relatively small part of the general context that reaches far beyond them.

Habermas's formal pragmatic understanding of validity nonetheless contains an important insight. Validity is guided by supra-contextual orientations to distinctive kinds of principles, in this case, truth, truthfulness, and rightness. Strydom's account of a wider variety of cognitive principles supplements this. These principles nonetheless go beyond the narrow sense of only three basic validity claims set within the three formal pragmatic principles to represent a potentially infinite set of validity concepts, what might be understood as presuppositional and directive orientations for their immanent utilization. Further, by following the distinction, he makes between transcendentally anchored validity concepts and immanent validity goals, and by adding to it the consideration of non- or partly conscious perception of validity, the field of validity opens up (Strydom, 2019). The way in which this 'opening up' has been considered above further allows the distinction to be made between validity in the service of the reasonable and the unreasonable. Hence, to distinguish reasonable from unreasonable, the additional idea of what constitutes validity standards that conduce to ideal reasonableness must be brought into play. This idea of the reasonable is set within the cycle of continuously moving from validation to validated and back again, where every iteration of the cycle infinitesimally shifts the ideal relations, whether located within one validity concept, for example, solidarity, or many, for example, democracy. Overarching this cycle, validity is the translation of validity concepts into immanent kinds of validity that can variously be understood as goals, ends, ideals, or motives. To make the claim to be

## 276 *Reasoning and Validity Standards*

reasonable, the pattern of their justification must be demonstrated, not just in the context of other scholarship but in the more important context of societal learning processes and their outcomes.

In all of this, validity retains an intrinsic relation to reasoning. However, it is no longer only, as, in subjective reason, the means to arrive at preset ends; subject to its consideration must also be the very reasonableness of the ends themselves. This consideration opens up a whole new vista of validity in reasoning, where such reasoning validity must be positioned in its generative aspect, its ideal aspect, and its applied aspect. All these condition the role of validity in reasoning. By understanding validity in reasoning in these three ways, not only can Horkheimer's call for the mediation of subjective and objective reason be addressed, but through Peirce and Habermas, the intersubjective dimension of reasoning comes into play (Horkheimer, 1974 (1947)). Then, objective reason in the post-Enlightenment context no longer need be dismissed on the grounds of being an unjustified metaphysical construct but retained in its context as something that must be true of worlds of experience if they are to be able to responsibly continue. In this sense, objective reason has never really departed the social sciences, however much they have sought to accommodate one or another kind of subjective reason, whether in the means-end schema of positivism or the attribution of phenomenal freedom to the subject. It is only with the addition of intersubjective reason, what Peirce calls 'dialecticism', that the mediation between objective and subjective reason that Horkheimer advocates becomes possible (Peirce, 1998, 59). Intersubjective reason emphasizes the dimension of coming to agreement, ultimately settling the outcomes of validation processes characterizes by differences of both subjective and objective kinds. Thus, intersubjectivity must be addressed within the context of the other moments of reason. It is guided by these other moments but ultimately retains an autonomous capacity.

Within this architectonic of the various moments of reasoning, validity becomes radically extended beyond its formal role in truth-setting, which is far too limited, as positivism and its ultimate rejection abundantly demonstrated. It now becomes the means of not just evaluating but, through valid inferences, *building* schemata and models that ultimately have normative implications for regulating possible forms of action and interaction. These schemata can be determined as reasonable if they pass 'tests' of validity, the appropriate use of basic validity concepts within their immanent cognitive and symbolic instantiation. Any such judgement of appropriateness must allow for the fact that validity, as here described for the normative social world, has been fluidized. That is to say, it has been freed from formal meta-standards of reasoning that could confer objective validity on accounts of world relations. Rather, validity standards must be reflexively worked up spanning the three moments of reason, subjective, objective, and intersubjective, in this case, semiotically elaborated through Peirce. As with judgement in Kant's Third Critique, validity rests on the conjectural relevance of its initial projections (Ferrara, 2008). It also depends on the capacity to formulate ideals and on how these ideals can be applied to coordinating the social world. If the concept of reason is brought in at this point, it becomes not a question of just any validity at all, but validity according to standards that encapsulate the necessary reasonableness to survive all possible challenges arising from relevant immanent deployment of validity concepts. At least, such standards should not be formulated that are known to evidently fail such challenges.

The validity concepts, once evolutionarily stabilized, continue to provide orientations over time. As evolutionary, the basic form of these validity concepts does not significantly change for long historical periods. What does change is how the concepts are discursively constructed, placed, and displaced in the immanent world. Such processes generate a vast web of possible, necessary, and actual relations over time. The schematic outcome of such processes in the form of cultural models, the merest outline of which only has been provided, involves a multiplicity of actors operating in extended historical time, penetrating all areas of societal coordination, and being sustained and changed by experience-driven reflection. Thus, to take any concept from the cognitive order, say solidarity or legitimacy, to describe its immanent validity deployment requires a long exercise of inquiry. In reality, the methodological process could not be only description that would simply go on forever; it would be description guided by normative standards operating as ideal limits. In this sense, description has its determinate place, for it alone allows a credible account of what has been, is, or might be the forms of that deployment. As a learning process that must be apprehended and perhaps also, depending on its outcomes, respected, understanding such deployment must educate intellectual attempts at clarification and normative redirection. Yet, this is also the foundation on which reconstruction must commence, intended as the reconstruction of ideals to add to their reasoned validity or reasonableness. Critical intellectual reflection must guide the process of such reconstruction, informed by existing outcomes of collective learning processes with the intention of setting other learning processes in motion that are projected as better. Such learning processes depend on validity-guided reasoning that can comprehensively show the grounds of reason on which it variously rests, knowing that ultimately, as reasoning, it is appealing to potential future states of affairs. What has been attempted over the last few chapters is merely to clarify some basic meta-theoretical preliminaries. It calls forth the need for methodological innovation of a kind that follows from these insights.

### References

Apel K-O (1975) *Diskurs Und Verantwortung: Das Problem des Übergangs zur Postkonventionellen Moral.* Frankfurt: Suhrkamp.

Apel K-O (1987) The Problem of a Macroethic of Responsibility to the Future in the Crisis of Technological Civilization: An Attempt to Come to Terms with Hans Jonas's "Principle of Responsibility". *Man and World* 20(1): 3–40.

Burns TR (1999) The Evolution of Parliaments and Societies in Europe. *European Journal of Social Theory* 2(2): 167–194.

Castoriadis C (1998) *The Imaginary Institution of Society.* Cambridge, MA: MIT Press.

Cortina A (1990) Diskursethik und Menchenrechte. *Archiv fur Rechts- und Sozialphilosophie* 76: 37–49.

Ferrara A (2008) *The Force of the Example: Explorations in the Paradigm of Judgment.* New York, NY: Columbia University Press.

278 *Reasoning and Validity Standards*

Günther K (1993) *The Sense of Appropriateness: Application Discourses in Morality and Law*. New York, NY: SUNY Press.

Honneth A (2016) *The Idea of Socialism: Towards a Renewal*. Cambridge: Polity..

Horkheimer M (1974 (1947)) *Eclipse of Reason*. London: Bloomsbury.

Lenk H (2007) *Global Technoscience and Responsibility: Schemes Applied to Human Values, Technology, Creativity and Globalisation*. Münster: LIT Verlag

Mills CW (2000) *The Sociological Imagination*. Oxford: Oxford University Press.

O'Mahony P (2021) Habermas and the Public Sphere: Rethinking a Key Theoretical Concept. *European Journal of Social Theory* 24(4): 485–506.

Peirce CS (1998) *The Essential Peirce: Selected Philosophical Writings (Vol. 2): 1893–1913*. Bloomington, IN: Indiana University Press.

Rawls J (1999) *The Law of Peoples*. Cambridge, MA: Harvard University Press.

Skillington T (2023) Thinking Beyond the Ecological Present: Critical Theory on the Self-Problematization of Society and Its Transformation. *European Journal of Social Theory* 26(2): 236–257.

Strydom P (2019) On Habermas's Differentiation of Rightness from Truth: Can an Achievement Concept Do without a Validity Concept? *Philosophy and Social Criticism* 45(5): 555–574.

Touraine A (1981) *The Voice and the Eye: An Analysis of Social Movements*. Cambridge: Cambridge University Press.

# 11 Reason and Critique

## Critique and General Reasonableness

Critique has always been a contested term in philosophy and the social sciences, and never more so than at present. Some assert from the respective vantage points of empirical-analytical and interpretive social science that critique is not needed, and when it arises, it is distorting and leads to opposite outcomes from the intentions of the critique. Even the last point may be deemed too charitable by the critics of critique in that it is also supposed that those engaged in critique ignore either necessary institutional rules or the duty of charity towards their interlocutors. The genealogical critique applied to liberalism is generalized to critique as a distinctive philosophy of social science; its claims to validity in fact turn into their opposite, a type of authoritarian judgement. The claim to autonomy as a validity standard within critique is regarded as merely a claim on behalf of privileged elites, who do not adequately reflect on their privilege. Autonomy in fact becomes subverted and is assumed to be associated with a kind of permanent arrogance on behalf of those who 'know best', Another variation of the critique of critique, with Luhmann, is that it fails because it can only ever be one more perspective where none can be endowed with normative privilege. Overarching normative standards have no place in an assumed to be emerging functionally differentiated global society organized by the logic of systems against the disappearing authority of state-organized societies built upon the outmoded law-politics couplet. If critique tries to assert itself in these conditions, it denies the kind of epistemic pluralism that must characterize modern society and will do so increasingly as contradictions mount. Luhmann, along with many others, also extends the line of critique that is crystallized in Marx – though understood and applied very differently in Marx –, the critique of the imposition of normative standards that seek to hide their arbitrariness by claiming epistemic objectivity. Luhmann's view is ultimately directed at the ethical objectivity that has historically been the self-understood function of the enlightenment version of reason to uphold.

From the vantage point argued here and critical theory generally, critique is justified, even and perhaps especially, radical critique. This means not that all and every kind or act of critique is justified; simply, critique is inextricably bound up with learning and validity. Validity is fundamental to the functioning of society,

DOI: 10.4324/9780429060571-12

280 *Reason and Critique*

which cannot stay in a state of permanent antagonism. If a society, including and especially global society, is to be called reasonable, such an assignation must depend on general acceptance that it is reasonable, not just fleetingly but over extended time. For it to be so, a just normative order must accordingly be consistent with such extended time a normative order that can be recognized as one thing and not another thing. In other words, a normative order – an institutional cultural model – would be recognized over time as being just by all affected parties. Or, if not fully just, then containing some greater or lesser measure of justice as well as domination. Both justice as norm and domination are outcomes. They are symbolic forms that find resonance in social objects such as the elements of society and the iconic schemata that allow them to become effective as action. As the outcome of other, more dynamic, cognitively structured processes, they are actualized particulars. There are many such particulars, institutionalized symbolic forms with material socially coordinating, consequences. So, society cannot be understood as the repository of unlimited pluralism or unlimited individualization, but as an ensemble of social relations that must exhibit some kind of directionality, a social logic, *in the end.* Such directionally is what Adorno calls the 'existent object', which is the object both of critique and potential reconstruction according to the import of validity standards (Adorno, 2019 (1964)).

But the object of critique is not itself critique, for critique involves a distinctive stance on the status of the object from a wide range of possible vantage points. Objects of critique of all kinds potentially call forth a wide range of critical objections. This is an everyday social fact that is scarcely to be denied. It indicates that the cognitive apparatus for offering critique is not just an unwarranted preserve of some ordinary actors and some intellectual actors, but a general capacity and widely distributed set of competences. It is only if we take the functionalist route of assuming laws that utterly constrain society, however much it tries to wriggle free, or the interpretive route of positing situations that contain all in themselves, that critique can even appear optional. The view that critique always and everywhere is either an illusion or a dangerous conceit can only belong to those who oppose critique, either in the name of a liberalism that demands adaptation to quasi-natural social forms or a 'conservatism' that stays resolutely rooted in the local and the ineffable.

More interesting is the question of which kinds of critique are justified and which are not? And together with this is the question of whether critique has any potency, though it may continue to happen, and how any such potency can be realized as reasonable social change? What is at issue here regarding the first question is the legitimacy of the characteristic type of critique of critical theory of the unreasonable forms of society as an 'existent object'. For various reasons, this object, or set of objects, has become more distant and harder to specify. The Marxist focus on critique of capitalism has shrunk to merely one kind of critique, albeit still of great importance, in the light of the plurality of identified objects of injustice amid societal complexity (Honneth, 2016; Delanty and Harris, 2022). The relative intellectual decline of the theory of society, especially Marxist but also functional, including the sweeping judgements of modernity of those, like Weber, who did not offer a theory of society per se, has played a part (O'Mahony, 2023a; 2023b).

In this situation, much of critical theory, animated in some part by the new kind of political philosophy inspired by John Rawls, has turned instead to focusing on democracy as the key, above all, with a strong emphasis on normative conceptions of justice (Renault, 2020). In this, the set of dependent objects that constitute the 'base' of society is more distant, and getting democratic procedure abstractly right mostly takes precedence. Observing long-term social change, it is true that democracy indeed holds the key to the critical theoretical idea of a reasonable society. Marx's focus on association already points in that direction. As with the general argument of this book, democracy cannot just be regarded as a procedure to be idealized, but as itself a complex object, a regularized process form, within society more generally understood, including those societal spheres that have presently only an indirect relationship to democracy, or indeed an indifferent, even hostile, one. In this light, any justifiable version of democratic reasonableness is far from the democracy that currently exists, and there is no shortcut to its possible realization by simply insisting on the right normative conception. To show that what might be reasonable cannot remain within the intellectual confines of theories of law and democracy as currently developed, even with deliberative modifications. The challenge is far greater than that and pertains to the imaginary construction of a democratic future *society*.

The dilemma of critical theory may be summed up in relation to the object of its critique as either that the original object identified with a class-organized societal base has become too heterogenous, complex, and diffuse, as well as plainly insufficient, or that the new kind of object ignores the base of society as any kind of general sociological object and moves upstream to normative conceptions of democracy. The problem is intellectually cognate with the history of political sociology going forward from the 1950s that in the neo-Marxist-influenced phase turned to the left/right account of the social base to explain the social-political rather than settle for an intra-political conception such as the previously dominant pluralism. With the evident decline in confidence about the existence of a class-defined social base from the late 1970s onwards, political sociology was forced to think again and turned increasingly to a mix of phenomenological, deconstructionist, and rational choice theories. The idea of a vertically structured social base in society has lost much credibility, yet there is little doubt that societies across the globe show evidence of increased domination. The idea that this simply takes on a new class-based general structure is not credible either.

Following the vantage point offered here, the set of objects that constitute society is composed of states of feelings, states of beliefs, and states of reasons in complex relational configurations. These configurations are constantly changing, but still, at given times and places, allow sufficient regularity to be identified as one thing – one relational configuration, including its institutional conditions of existence – and not another. Moreover, such configurations also include states of nature as well as human technical organization. They are frequently diffuse objects, hard to specify, but nonetheless capable of being specified as constellations of force, regularities with predictable effects though within assumed rapid social change. The crucial question for critical theory arising from these objects – for

## 282 *Reason and Critique*

example, states of democracy, states of economic organization, states of subjectivity, and states of nature – is whether they can be said to evince reasonableness in the light of reasonable ideals, where the ideals are bound up with the understanding of the objects and also with more general validity standards, possibilities, or could be's, that potentially point beyond existing forms of reasonableness. Where they do not achieve sufficient reasonableness, including where they are in their repressive forms the very antithesis of any reasonableness whatsoever, they are opened to the kind of reconstructive critique that characterizes critical theory.

Viewed in terms of the above remarks, the fault line that currently runs through critical theory, not to mention the wider divide between political philosophy and sociology, is that between the preference to concentrate on the right kinds of ideals that would bring about, at least in tendency, a reasonable society, or to concentrate instead on the unreasonable state of society as a corrective to the hegemony of ideals. The path chosen here has been to accept that the formation of ideals (cognitive cultural models) is fundamental both to critical theory and society, and further that it proceeds from general evolutionary formed, mediately operating, universally available cognitive principles. It is also to track the relationship between the selection of ideals and societal outcomes viewed from the standard of reasonable states of affairs, where reasonable means generally just. This is not to accept that a given society as it exists, in the sense of a set of regularized objects, defining predictable action-reaction sequences, contains all that is necessary for its own transformation. Any such transformation depends on the capacity for radical collective learning beyond what exists as factually identifiable objects, and the epistemo-methodological challenge that understanding such learning poses for normative social theorizing. It is precisely this that characterizes critique as immanent transcendent and thus reconstructive in that light. Yet, the path of potential reconstruction must be shown through the analysis of both existing and possible states of society. For this, a new kind of theory of society is needed that can deal with contemporary societal complexity from a normative standpoint. One must stand humble before such a task. All that has been done, can be done, is to here point towards its need. Its delineation, even partial, illustrative, delineation, must wait for another day.[1]

The term unreasonable rather than the more common, unjust, has been used in the remarks above. This is the case for two reasons. The first is that the reasonable extends beyond what is just in the strict sense, though justice is often critical to the reasonable. The reasonable also extends to what societies, groups, or individuals get wrong, not in this instance because they intend to perpetrate injustice, even if unjust consequences flow from their actions. Such an extension of the reasonable covers the space of social pathology in the Hegel-derived idea that bad consequences might arise not from a will to dominate but from unintended consequences of action, in whole or in part, or from a specific inability, of the kind Honneth explains in-depth, to 'make sense' of historical circumstances to attain an ideal (Honneth, 2014). In other words, the sensorium for the reasonable extends more widely than that for justice. Frequently, the two overlap, as in incapacities that arise from injustice coexisting with available other capacities that cannot be utilized because they are in some way 'internally' blocked or inhibited. If societal objects are

*Reason and Critique* 283

thought about with the suggested complexity, there are many imaginable instances when unplanned contingencies with the potential to generate unreasonable outcomes on the widest scale that cannot be adequately anticipated or even foreseen. However, they can be identified as unreasonable, in potential tendency or fact, from a situation-transcending vantage point.

The second justification for the use of the term reasonable is that it leads back to communicative reason itself. This is why I do not follow Honneth and others to the standard of recognition, though I do not at all deny its value for characterizing ideals. It is rather that recognition as an already operating societal ideal, or set of ideals, is downstream from the constitutive activity of forming such ideals in the first place. We need to know how ideals that deserve recognition come to be as a response to the unreasonable, and for that, the transcendent core of reason must be engaged. In other works, we must engage with recognition standards as fallible learning processes that are open to the future and not only to the historically established, partly suppressed standards of modern forms of life. It is not just a question of how ideals come to be. A further question is also raised about the implications of these ideals for unreasonable downstream social objects. Thus, to speak of the reasonable attests to the 'epistemic dependency' of normative standards, whose origin and mutation depend on collective learning, which in turn draws from those transcendent, cognitive validity principles that underly human capacities and purposes of all kinds. What emerges as reasonable ideals ultimately depends on what is established by reasoning in the light of such principles. This applies both to the long process of interaction and refinement of the core human and democratic ideals over time and to the ongoing process of their further specification in encountering the world. The cognitive ideal only creates a circumscribed interaction space for interpretations of the ideal, while these further specifications constantly redefine what it means in practice. The ideal is applied and reconstructed in ongoing communicative processes, part radical and transformative and part constrained by existing norms and associated validity standards.

As outlined at length in Strydom (Strydom, 2011; Chapter 7), there are a range of types of critique: reconstructive (immanent-transcendent), immanent, explanatory, and transcendent. Whereas strictly transcendent critique, for which he gives Rawls as an example, is not core to critical theory, the Kantian tradition has had a profound influence, and with it comes a tendency to postulate necessary moral laws for a reasonable society, as in Forst's right and duty to justify (Forst, 2011). Immanent transcendence has already been stressed as core to critical theory, uniting its various generations, and with it comes an emphasis on reconstructive critique that combines a transcendent dimension in the tradition of Kant with critique of the existing state of society. Also prominent in critical theory is a type of immanent critique that either eschews the transcendent moment or, at least in practice, de-emphasizes it (Jaeggi, 2018; Arato and Cohen, 2021). The type of immanent critique developed in critical theory follows from the Hegelian assumption of the potential of existing social arrangements to transform themselves towards the reasonable. There is also an explanatory critique, stemming from Marx, that emphasizes the inhibiting and oppressing power of identified causal structures and offers explanatory

## 284  *Reason and Critique*

conjectures, socialism pre-eminently, that would guide their transformation. Finally, there is a disclosing critique guided by a hermeneutics of being that seeks to identify intrinsic and essential but, in part, unrealized human potentialities.

Debates on the nature of its critical preferences, among the above and in relation to other non-critical theoretical uses of critique, tend to be relatively scarce in critical theory. There are, nonetheless, apparent paradigmatic differences. A prominent one is the fault line between an 'ideal theory' that examines the critical potential of conceptions of justice and a deontological focus on inclusive communication, 'non-ideal theory' that understands itself as starting from both the facts, mostly repressive, power-saturated facts, and the potentials of extant historical forms of life. This is a manifestation of a long-running debate in critical theory and beyond, arising from interpretations of the Kant-Hegel relation, including the liberal and communitarian debate and the democratic-theoretical versus emancipatory struggle debate. This division sometimes overlaps the differences between mainly normative disciplinary orientations such as political philosophy, political theory, legal theory, and disciplines and orientations more manifestly starting from the objects of critique embedded in historical states of the world. In a rather general way, it can be said that an elaborated form of immanent transcendent critique is used in what is deemed ideal theory, whereas immanent critique is offered on the other side, and in the contemporary variation different from its progenitor, Adorno, confining itself to strictly immanent standards. A further delineation can be made between an emphasis on disclosing as opposed to negative critique. Disclosing critique focusing on the transformative power of the imagination in the light of human potential contrasts with a negative critique identifying repressive mechanisms so that negative syndromes associated with them can be appropriately identified and in some way also transformed. The distinction tends to work itself out as the difference between those who emphasize imaginative powers to transcend present cultural constraints and those who focus on exposing repressive social mechanisms.

What is also relatively clear is that critical theory is today more diffuse in the sense of absorbing influences from a wider range of disciplines, whose varying epistemological practices and normative commitments often create reciprocal disorientation. Such disorientation at its root lies in differing opinions on the idea of modernity itself. The issue of the status of modernity in critical theory was re-initiated by Habermas from the *TCA* period onwards in his identification of a progressive import with further emancipatory potentials, opposing the more negative judgements of the first generation. Much of the discussion and application of critical standards in critical theory today breaks down into different opinions on the normative import of modernity. Disciplines, or disciplinary traditions, such as critical structural sociology, critical phenomenological studies of various kinds, decolonial theories, and critical political economy tend to be sceptical of attributing modernity general progressive import, while disciplinary traditions such as political philosophy, the Honneth strand of social philosophy, and legal theory grant it an emancipatory potential, in spite of various regressive historical trends, that is assumed to be partly realized. As is already apparent from these comments, the terrain is more fissured than any short summary can address. Moreover, it is not the case that views on modernity correlate neatly with views on, say, the ideal/non-ideal theory division. The focus on modernity raises the question of whether, however conceived, critical theory should become some form of revolutionary project, or whether the gradual, 'evolutionary' transformation of existing institutional arrangements, both legal-political and others, should be the ultimate end. There seems little doubt that critical theory is not clear about its ultimate end, and perhaps it is best formulated in terms of the depth of transformation required. Clarity is urgently required as the world grapples with issues such as the essential requirements of democratization in a planetary civilization, including the rapid destruction of its biosphere, massive levels of violence at all levels, and the growth of irrationalism. These issues seem rather clearly to point towards the need for radical transformation that neither a focus on the older existent object of critical theory, capitalist social relations, nor on small-scale, indicative procedural innovations of deliberative democracy can alone address, even if they will play their part. The companion of deliberative democratic theorizing within critical theory should be at least as much the theoretically-methodologically revealed cultural-political state of society, as it is the 'base' offered by existing legal and democratic institutions.

To pose a rather naive question, in what way could sociology, understood along the lines pursued here, help? Already, I have outlined the social ontological frame of a communicative, critical theoretical sociology and documented its significant departure from major traditions in that discipline, though I am still building from them. Within that project lies a cognitive and socio-epistemic core. The essential focus is to show how this core is indispensable to identifying both reasonable and unreasonable forms of life. I have taken this through the basic architectonic (Chapters 5–7), and its concern for validity (Chapters 8–10). The task for the remainder of this chapter is to consider how critique can be addressed on this basis.

### Critique as Epistemo-Methodological Activity

Critical reflexivity abductively presents itself in the form of a revealing insight that, in some cases, may lead to a process of transformation. Frequently, though, critical insight does not open up the possibility of transformation, either internally due to incomplete learning processes or due to external impediments. The first is often stressed by Honneth, though he does not use the concept of collective learning, while the second is stressed by critical sociologists like Bourdieu and by many other intellectual figures and traditions more pessimistic than Honneth about the achievements, or even the ideals, of modernity. Following the Peircean frame of social theorizing outlined here, reflexivity begins well before critical awareness. It begins in the unconscious depths of first consciousness and involves infinitesimal but cumulatively significant reorientation regarding the object forms of existence. When it turns out to have substance in the light of the actual situation, the first reflexive moment, a different way of feeling towards an object, leads to a perceptual judgement and begins the journey into critique proper as a conscious negation, at least conjecturally, of what previously stood as knowledge. In its infinitesimally evolving path, it is a mode of disclosing in the light of ultimate potentials – ideas of reason – an alternative within being, a different way of being. Conscious negation

## 286 *Reason and Critique*

marks a shift from a recessed process of disclosure to direct critique, thus from disclosing to exposing (or negative) critique, that is, critique of an identified existing object and potentially offering proposals for reconstructing it. And 'reaching beyond' the 'merely' critical, realizing idea potentiality in cognition, involves collective learning processes that have general societal implications. If Peirce's doubt-belief model in his famous essay *The Fixing of Belief* is used as an exemplar, then all critique involves both critique of existing knowledge of an object (negation) and an attempt to project 'corrective' normative potentials that lie behind it (Peirce, 1992, 109–123). Both steps require disclosure in the sense of opening up evolutionary formed and transcendentally anchored cognitive capacities.

According to the approach presented here, the steps of critique follow the logical steps for validity previously outlined, that is, conjectural, ideal, and actual. All critique begins abductively and leads to the building of a theory, that is, precisely, a *critical* theory directed at unreasonable states of existence according to some explicit standard and accompanied by a sense of the imperative to get beyond or transcend it not just in thought but in fact. Such theories correspond to abductive schematization with the power of potentiality. Abduction opens up the space of critique, a critique that can be more or less radically judged by its implications for ideal and actual – or normative – orders, once again following the scheme as previously outlined for validity and extending it to cultural models. The ideal moment of critique is a distinct step yet closely integrated with the abductive departure. Both ideal and actual critiques are necessarily already present in abduction, but they are initially only diffusely present. As expressed, critique departs negatively in some respect from actuality, ensuring there is already an actual moment in abduction. That is its backwards chaining moment; its forward chaining is inextricably bound up with its relation to ideals mediated through ideas of reason. It is through this step that generality, anticipated in the first operations of abduction, begins to become a concrete generality. Once it has been first formulated as diffuse critique, it must begin the path towards explicated ideal theorization. Abductively, in its first manifestation, critique can present itself as having normative implications in some way, but, ideally, it must then justify this way, that is, it must justify what universe of discourse it will follow in its critique. Further still, it must project forward to the actuality of existing norms, offer an interpretation of this universe, and, yet further still, specify normative consequences that follow from the critical-reconstructive theorization.

Thus, in a potentially long series of iterations, critique recurrently moves from a critical conjecture to criticizing the present operations of ideal universes of discourse and onto specifying normative consequences. In these iterations, which will be repeated and thus elaborated many times, a theory is gradually built. At the same time, critique must reflexively justify itself regarding its various moments in line with the previous account of validity. Such justification must address not only the worthiness of the critique but also the worthiness of the intention behind the critique, that is, what should follow from the critique in terms of change. It is for these reasons that validity is so tightly bound up with critique. When they are decoupled, critique becomes aimless and potentially dangerous, for some kind of

*Reason and Critique*   287

claim to validity is intrinsic to any and every critique, but these can dramatically vary. Critique is therefore fundamentally *both* a question of the quality of the validity standard as well as the quality of the critique advanced on its basis. Of course, reflexive critique, as the exercise of self-critical reason, can also bring into question and change its own validity standards.

Critique intends to open epistemic uncertainty so that a critical theory can be fully developed and that the critique can gain empirical traction. As understood in the Peirce sense, this is the space of logical reasoning. More precisely, critique must first emerge as a critical conjecture that *might* be justified, and hence must merely postulate a claim to validity. The multiple iterations of this conjecture that follow, which can be of long or short duration, determine whether this validity claim is justified at all and, if it is, how and to what extent. In addition, and fundamentally for critical theory along with some other democratic theories, critique must allow for both contestation and associated revision. This implicates both the critique offered internally within the frame of the theory, the critique offered by other theories, and the critique of others in society. As these processes play out and a critical conjecture accordingly evolves, it moves towards maturity as a critical theory. The references to uncertainty implicate a triadic, dialectical, and democratic account that stands opposed to the binary forms of many contemporary critical theories. The threefold logical form of both Peirce and discourse ethics is designed to incorporate dialectics of societal participation. It is not just an issue of what is deemed problematic in society, and in need of criticism on behalf of its members, but also of the criticisms of these members themselves. A logic of critical inquiry that assumes a space of uncertainty and collective learning replaces the certainties of subject-object approaches. Critique is accordingly intrinsically bound up with collective societal learning processes.

These last remarks also bring into play the nature of intellectual critique. In many cases, intellectual critique is harnessed to an attempted objective specification of states of affairs that become the direct object of critique. This type of external, objective critique can bypass the exploration of doubt and the implications of societal preferences in problematic ways. It is bound up with approaches, such as those of Bourdieu and critical realism, that do not specifically articulate its normative preferences, at most only doing so negatively in terms of what it criticizes. An ontological emphasis, together with a narrowed epistemology confined to the justification of the theory itself and its methodological implications, preclude such articulation. Much of the hitherto existing authority of critical sociological theorizing rests on this kind of objective claim to truth. A consequence is that this kind of sociology, relying on identifying causal forces beyond agents' knowledge, operates relatively speaking 'lower down' the epistemic chain to structuring forces that allow only strategies and implicit practices by agents. All that exists higher up, the constitutive, regulative, learning, and reasoning processes stressed in this text, is not directly theorized. Intellectual critique of this kind then has a narrow epistemic focus on criticizing other theories and states of the object world. Even with this limitation, theories of this kind provide important insights because the object world has been substantially constituted beyond the will of dependent agents in the first

## 288    *Reason and Critique*

place, resulting in a second nature at least partly consistent with those structuring forces that dominate them.

This kind of intellectual critique is not sufficient for critical theory. It is not that critical theory is always able to directly include the perspectives of its addressees, but that it depends on a theoretical-methodological architectonic that makes space for a plurality of perspectives. This combining of concern for plurality with critique has grown in importance in critical theory over time. In one sense, it was always there in the first-generation emphasis on the threatened autonomy of subjects, including their self-consciousness. In the second generation, deeply influenced by pragmatism, it became an imperative with its various intersubjective, communicative, and democratic themes. It did not merely rest on the plurality of perspectives, a common emphasis in modern liberal political philosophy, but also in figures such as James Tully, in neo-Wittgensteinian language game theory, and in sociologists such as Boltantki, who directly set out to oppose Bourdieu in this regard. None of these has the theoretical comprehensiveness of neo-Peircean critical theory, as developed by Apel, stressing all the factors: evolution, immanent transcendence, idealization, abductively guided, intersubjective reasoning, disputation, and symbolization. This version of critical theory inevitably arrives at a different account of intellectual critique to either externalist versions discussed in the last paragraph or 'merely' pluralist ones referenced in this. Intellectual critique, which in any version seeks to penetrate that which remains hidden or repressed, in the critical theoretical account seeks to uncover the suppressed potential of subjects acting together with will and consciousness. It is thus, pre-eminently, the barriers to this kind of solidaristic, communicative relations that should be exposed. This is far from only a normative precept of social or political philosophy, but an entire methodological programme. Intellectual critique thus confronts a world that has gone on, substantially in the wrong way, to disable these common powers of subjects and with it the evolutionary-endowed capacity for reason. It also supposes that, beyond but also respectful of pluralist difference, a fully reasonable *common life* can, in principle, be restored. Thus, intellectually, the theory must both identify the distorting mechanisms that have blocked and continue to block appropriate validity standards and postulate normative arrangements sufficient for the emergence of reasonable collective rule systems.

Justifying intellectual critique in the above sense requires steering a path between negative, explanatory critique and a hermeneutically grounded pluralism that, as the wider debate vividly shows, are often assumed to pull in opposite directions (Apel, 1984). It requires retaining a critical impulse that does not dissolve itself by merely handing over evaluative authority to existing publics that are currently far from ideal, general publics in Dewey's sense. For critical theory, this has proven an uneasy space to occupy, concerned as it is, on the one side, with epistemic authoritarianism (Cooke, 2006) and, on the other side, with dissolving its own critical purpose. The space of intellectual critique for such a theory thus must involve abductive and projective schema formation addressed at distorting mechanisms that preclude its validity goals. These can be considered quite widely to include forces such as colonialism, patriarchy, racism, and capitalism in their many independent and interacting facets. Its emphasis on common deliberation must be extended well beyond the liberal democratic frame in a participatory direction, a participatory direction that has only existed historically in relatively weak forms. Accordingly, the revealing of distorting mechanisms already embedded in forms of life involves negative intellectual critique, and reaching beyond it in the direction of radical participation involves an experimental form of disclosing intellectual critique in the revealing of realizable potentials.

The complex of exposing/disclosing critique set within the normative ends of critical theory ultimately requires the immanent-transcendent reconstructive critique that is core to it. If the above-outlined modified validity standards of a communicative critical theory are to be met, this will, first, require abductive leaps, the projected transposition of diffuse conjectural 'hopes' for greater enlightenment into the guiding cognitive structures and institutional arrangements of societies. Given its tentative nature, such a projection cannot be understood as grounded on firm normative standards that point clearly to what should be done. It requires instead the spatially and temporally extended and empirically sensitive tasks of reconstructing the conditions for the exercise of communicative competence and showing how such competence should manifest itself in multiple spheres of life. Such reconstructive critique must start with existing conditions that, in various ways, continue to cause human suffering, even if in modern societies there is manifest evidence too of reasonable outcomes of collective learning. It also must show how those outcomes have been generated within a power-saturated relational complex. It thus needs a sufficiently sophisticated architectonic to capture the historical generation of such outcomes, for which, in another way, Foucault has already laid a trail. Then, beyond this, it must suggest an intervention into this complex that promises to address such suffering by means of epistemic and democratic enlightenment.

If the above suggests a blending of ontological and epistemological tasks, it also implies methodological recourse to an appropriate logic of inquiry. The abductive moment of critique brings to bear epistemically relevant feelings that emerge from the immense sensorium lodged in the collective unconscious and initial perception. This sensorium is the product of an experience that has already been influenced by sign-mediation but, at the same time, is not exhausted by what has historically existed, whether rationally willed or contingently formed. The intellectual critic takes account of these developments and seeks to grant them argumentative cogency. Thus, the moment of abductive critique carried out in such intellectual criticism is lodged in a corresponding schematization and involves a sense both of repression and potentiality that must be further developed. Development embraces both the social scientific identification of the problematic mechanism – for example, over-extension of the market mechanism – and suggestions for its normative transformation.[2]

Modifying a little the threefold lifeworld spheres lodged in Habermas and others, problematic mechanisms could lie in subjective dispositions, in institutional norms, in ideas, or in various combinations of these. Each of them individually, and the possible combinations, entail limitless possible relations. Abductively, the specification of the problematic mechanism and the further elaboration of how it might be addressed have to be, respectively, constructed and reconstructed through the prism of

290 *Reason and Critique*

the general architectonic. The construction process involves identifying, through the theory, how pathologies and injustices are embedded in the problematic mechanism. Similarly, the reconstructive moment, through the theory involves a modal specification of alternative potentials that specifies both actual existing and potential new relations. Both the phases of construction and reconstruction should be shown to respond to the validity standards previously specified. Both stand interdependently as conjectures that belong to the unfolding logic of inquiry, but once elaborated constructively and reconstructively through the structure of cognitive principles, cultural models, fields, and actions, they become, or seek to become, mature conjectures with potential explanatory force. In the logic of inquiry of Peirce, loosely taken over by critical theory, it is not enough simply to suppose the truth of explanatory conjecture; it must be tested before both the community of scientists and the general public. Thus, great attention must be given to both.[3] What is distinctive about the critical theory approach is that construction and reconstruction must take account of the generative process at work in society and view that as fluid and dynamic. It can nonetheless neither settle for only understanding society as fluid and dynamic (the interpretive mistake) nor only as institutionally sedimented (the scientistic mistake). It is also tasked with advancing the standard of a reasonable society, knowing that must consist both of coordinative regularities as well as capacities for critical transformation towards reasonableness. If the latter cannot be any more recognized, nor achieved even if recognized, then critical theory loses its rationale and is fated to wither away. Those like Luhmann would say we are already beyond that point; the point of the theory is to demonstrate we are not.

In summary, the position advocated here, first, attempts to bridge ideal and non-ideal theory. Negative critique, whose modern roots lie in Hegel's idea of negativity, carries within it the critique of social relations in general. It also carries in this process, though mostly not properly acknowledged, the desire to bring about a different *possible* world, a world that, not yet formed, can only be imagined as an ideal or set of complementary ideals. It is not properly recognized because, in line with Apel's idea of avoiding performative contradiction, negative critique contains an unacknowledged potential *reconstruction* of the problem situation to be able to make the critical argument in the first place. This dimension of reconstruction is often left unexplored. In any case, what is advocated in non-ideal critique in its assumptions of injustice or disagreement, opposing what are assumed to be pre-existing models of justice, is the potential that reaches beyond what exists. However, it can at least be imagined, perhaps even conditionally projected. Therefore, the validity standards of ideal theory and the negative critique of non-ideal *potentially* stand towards one another in a reciprocally replenishing relationship. The deep roots of symbolically shaped consciousness confronted with an unjust or pathological world may result in negativity that takes its first explicit form in perceptual judgements before becoming explicit as conjectures about injustice. In this way, negativity enters logic through abduction, though it pre-exists in consciousness, and within the conjectural validity standard that seeks to reorientate the logical and institutional order. This negativity, following the analysis, an analysis also aligned with Adorno's ideas of thinking in contradiction and the non-identical, then explicitly meets the standards of the ideal, which, like all validity standards, is not intrinsically 'progressive' but requires further argumentation before reaching the threshold of justified normative claims (Adorno, 2004). It is this and all that follows from it that qualifies the claims of especially non-critical ideal theories, for example, Parsons in sociology and, in some respects a cousin, Rawls in political philosophy. These theories lack a sufficient genetic dimension embedded in the contingency and creativity of social innovation and social change. The key to the productive combination of ideal and negative critique therefore lies in regarding this conjectural moment as intrinsic. It is where the negating and the potential meet and confront together the existing structure of ideals in the cognitive cultural model and field of reasons. The projection extends from there to the other models within the field of positions. In this process, the existing negative implications diagnosed by the critique and the potentially positive implications if the critique were socially 'successful' are alike assessed.

In all of this, the conjectural moment is the abductive moment, the ideal moment is deductive or conceptually generalizing, and the applied or positioning moment is inductive. Given this logic, which is mostly implicitly understood and applied, no form of critical theory can properly be understood as an ideal theory. Ideals are only one moment, the *cognitive* coordinating moment, of validity, and they are subject to the discursive logic and associated collective learning processes that decide their form and relative importance. In this sense, there is a very big difference between Habermas and a liberal political theory such as that of Rawls, whose constructivism is of a largely non-dynamic kind, a difference that in the frame of social theory also distinguishes Habermas from Parsons. Nevertheless, because of Habermas's incorporation of systems theory and later of a proceduralized democratic theory into a central role, even if in certain respects these moves are defensible as theoretical departures, uneasiness persists that unreasonable objects of critique drop from consideration. The relative loss of the unreasonable object leads to the lifeworld being idealized, on the one side, and, on the other side, the sensorium for revealing the unreasonable, the operation of feelings, and the emergence of critical abductive schematization being correspondingly sidelined. It also has the further effect of diminishing the role of generalizing, generative cognition, whether guided by reasonable or unreasonable validity standards. The net outcome is a degree of unresponsiveness to, variously, the object of critique, the form of the contemporary subject, regressive cognitive operations, and the role of conflict.

## Notes

1   A general overview of the field of critical theory of society is the focus of a special issue of the European Journal of Social Theory (O'Mahony, 2023b).
2   See Strydom for an account of the status of problematic mechanisms within the logic of inquiry (Strydom, 2011, Chapter 7).
3   In my own *Contemporary Theory of the Public Sphere* (O'Mahony, 2013), for example, seeking to identify the significance of public deliberation to legal-political normative orders, I also examined a range of rival theories and sought to build in insights arising from these theories.

292   *Reason and Critique*

## References

Adorno TW (2004) *Negative Dialectics*. London: Routledge.

Adorno TW (2019 (1964)) *Philosophical Elements of a Theory of Society*. Cambridge: Polity.

Apel K-O (1984) *Understanding and Explanation: A Transcendental-Pragmatic Perspective*. Cambridge, MA: MIT Press.

Arato A and Cohen JL (2021) *Populism and Civil Society: The Challenge to Constitutional Democracy*. Oxford: Oxford University Press.

Cooke M (2006) *Represesenting the Good Society*. Cambridge, MA: MIT Press.

Delanty G and Harris N (2022) *Capitalism and Its Critics: Capitalism in Social and Political Theory*. London: Routledge

Forst R (2011) *The Right to Justification: Elements of a Constructivist Theory of Justice*. New York, NY: Columbia University Press.

Honneth, A (2014) *Freedom's right: The social foundations of democratic life*. New York, NY: Columbia University Press.

Honneth A (2016) *The Idea of Socialism: Towards a Renewal*. Cambridge: Polity.

Jaeggi R (2018) *Critique of Forms of Life*. Cambridge, MA: Belknap Press.

O'Mahony, P (2013) *The Contemporary Theory of the Public Sphere*. Oxford: Peter Lang.

O'Mahony P (2023a) Critical Theory, Peirce and the Theory of Society. *European Journal of Social Theory* 26(2): 258–281.

O'Mahony P (2023b) Introduction to Special Issue: The Critical Theory of Society. *European Journal of Social Theory* 26(2): 121–135.

Peirce CS (1992) *The Essential Peirce: Selected Philosophical Writings. Vol. 1 (1867–1893)*. Bloomington, IN: Indiana University Press.

Renault E (2020) Critical Theory, Social Critique and Knowledge. *Critical Horizons* 21(3): 189–204.

Strydom P (2011) *Contemporary Critical Theory and Methodology*. London: Routledge.

# 12 Critique and Reasoning Pathologies

The analysis of reasoning pathologies plays an important role in any account of the potential realization of reason or, alternatively, the realization of unreason. This can be done in a highly general way through the analysis of general pathologies of interaction that have psychopathological consequences (Watzlawick et al., 2011). It can also be done through the analysis of pathologies that arise from the non-application of validity standards deemed essential, as with the validity standards for discourse ethics outlined in Chapter 10. In the latter sense, the focus here is a double obligation to address both, on the one hand, the reflexive justifiability of any critique built on the basis of validity standards and, on the other hand, the actual critique of specific kinds of societal reasoning pathologies and their implications. Thus, the perspective of the critique must not be neglected in justifying the critical analysis of pathologies. Nonetheless, it is the latter, the kinds of possible critique of reasoning pathologies, that is specifically at issue here, though the former, the reflexive justification of the critical stance, must inevitably be kept in sight of and must accompany any such exploration of critical possibilities. Further, as explored in the last chapter, the exposure of reasoning pathologies in the light of the validity standards must therefore also serve for establishing non-pathological potentials, that is to say, reasonable reasoning.

How does such a critique of reasoning pathologies bear on unjust or unreasonable societal arrangements? Identifying reasoning pathologies, on the one hand, exposes the failure to realize existing societal standards of reasonableness consistent with widely accepted validity standards. An example here, at least for some countries, is the relatively wide contemporary feeling of the unacceptability of diminishing workers' rights, accompanied by the attempt to expose – as pathologies – arguments that advocate such diminution. A reasoning pathology could therefore serve the will to inflict injustice by those interested in maintaining or expanding it, even though those interests might be quite indirect and diffuse. A different example is when existing reasoning is deemed to be pathologically reproducing an unjust and/or dysfunctional rationality. An example here is the kind of environmental reasoning that challenges the subjective, instrumental, and strategic rationality that dominates contemporary resource utilization. A diagnostic frame for identifying such deficient rationality, which is pathological in the light of the extreme urgency

DOI: 10.4324/9780429060571-13

294 *Critique and Reasoning Pathologies*

of planetary needs, is that of Apel's concept of co-responsibility towards nature (Apel, 1987). Co-responsibility seeks to reconfigure and fundamentally change existing forms of rationality, where rationality, first established through various stages of reasoning and practical experimentation over time, has become lodged in institutional models. In this case, what was once collectively learned has now to be collectively unlearned. Such a pathology diagnosis, based on an immanent-transcendent prognosis of likely consequences, ineluctably leads to critique of cultural models and their associated discursive and positional fields.

Conceptualized in these ways, and especially the latter way, reasoning pathologies are either already deeply embedded in institutional arrangements and social systems by virtue of the – bad – rationality they support and that in turn underpins them – the outmoded assumptions of industrial society –, or, in the form in which they emerge, they potentially carry negative implications, such as the kinds of preliminary discursive legwork that seeks to legitimate recent political authoritarianism. The whole effort of this book is to open a path towards understanding how reasoning is at the centre of society, and, accordingly, also at the centre of critical theory. Its explication is not confined to legal-political institutions, even 'supplemented' by the public sphere as widely supposed, but suffuses every dimension of social being. It does not necessarily only suffuse it in a reasonable way. It also does so in unreasonable ways. Reasoning pathologies are thus to be understood as using ideas of reason (validity concepts) ultimately to deny their potential progressive normative import. Such denial arises from selective or manipulative reasoning, whether its consequences are properly grasped or not. The idea of being 'properly grasped' is a relative one, for even strategically elaborated intentions can fail because of unexpected patterns of resonance and reaction. At least in those cases it can be said to be intended in some defined way. Pathologies of reasoning may also arise, neither due to the inability to attain available rationality standards nor due to manipulative intention, but because of reasoning incompetence. These individual or group specific reasoning deficiencies lead to a characteristic type of disorientation for which the way out is often dangerous simplification. It is not easy to disentangle incapacity for appropriate reasoning in public spheres from mere detachment from relevant contexts of reasoning. While the latter is different, it is also a type of reasoning pathology, such as civic privatism, that impedes the will to reason, a type of structural reflexivity deficit associated with alienation.

Generally, the approach taken here has not been directly concerned with formal logical analysis. Its concern has been to examine how validity is actually logically claimed in cognitive processes that are set within socially extended inference chains, or schemata. Validity used in this non-formal, or partly formal, way is consistent with general practical political discourse and, beyond that, everyday discourse of most kinds. A simple example may help clarify this. Black people in the United States have claimed, reasonably in the light of the evidence, that to be seen wearing a mask in a retail setting in the context of COVID-19, especially black males, would open them to the risk of being shot by security personnel assuming they were going to commit a robbery. Looking at this from the vantage point of the so-disposed security personnel, as concerned black people do, these personnel draw a perceptual judgement leading to the abductive conjecture that a black male wearing a mask poses a threat. The abductive conjecture in the Peirce cycle of inferential reasoning then translates into a deductive 'would-be', showing under what conditions the presumed risk would hold good. If the would-be for the relevant, assumed white, security person in question was 'deductively' that undoubtedly or highly probably a black male wearing a mask in a retail environment posed a threat, that person might conclude that there was sufficient cause to act – completely unreasonably and illegally, it goes without saying. Actual action of a violent kind might be supported or inhibited by a type of inductive reasoning in which various actual cases flashed before the mind of the security person, video news footage or movies seen, patterns of accumulated experience interpreted in a racist manner, training advice, likely consequences, and so on. So, it can be seen from this short example that deeply flawed and dangerous inferences may amount to a kind of reasoning that is taken to justify certain actions.

From the vantage point of a constrained formal logic, for example, based on the ineluctable necessity of deductive conclusions, this example might seem to lie beyond the bounds of logic altogether. However, logical theory in application increasingly makes allowance for arguments that are not deductively secure but defeasible (Pollock, 1987; Peczenik, 2008). Two strategies seem possible: either to claim that defeasible arguments are not deductive, claiming that they use abductive or inductive reasoning only, or to modify the understanding of deduction so as to regard it as a possible *progression* towards greater and, in the end, *potentially* complete validity in the right – socio-epistemic – conditions. It is in the second broader sense of extending the reach of deduction that is taken up here, already delineated previously through the differentiation of the ultimate (really applying) and final (infinite potentiality) interpretants. This changes the nature of deduction, at least for many 'impure' cases, away from necessary truths that must be followed because they are true in all circumstances to viewing deduction as a type of reasoning that does not only include those conditionals that would inevitably prove to be valid but also those conditionals that may or could prove to be valid but are notwithstandingly taken as valid. This in turn changes the form of reasoning in those latter cases from reasoning with certainty to defeasible reasoning, that is to say, elaborating possible deductive rules that might possibly serve as a conclusion of inference. It could be argued that hypothetical reasoning in Peirce's account is already addressed in the logical form of abduction and is therefore redundant for deduction. Including this 'weaker' form of 'open' deduction acknowledges that a form of generalization of the argument has been applied, a form that is not certain, at least not now, but is strong enough to explicate certain testable conjectures. In fact, this train of thought reveals that deductive certainty – underpinning the a priori – is itself a set of rules that must be built up over time, not presumed (Calcaterra, 2011). In this sense, potentiality is a form of deduction in process. For ethical-political questions in particular, where there is frequently ongoing contention over normative concepts, some are 'more prevalent' at a given time and accordingly take on quasi-deductive status. Thinking in this way goes beyond the Humean fact-value distinction and opposes the idea of logical certainty, opening instead to community-determined normative ends that condition logical operations (Toulmin, 2009). There is no overarching criterion of rightness that can be deployed to ascertain indubitable truths, an insight consistent with Peirce's hierarchy of the normative sciences, where logic comes after aesthetics and ethics (Liszka, 2021). Nonetheless, in a pragmatist vein, already explored in depth, there remain both evolutionary capacities to deploy potentially valid arguments and immanent capacities to come to agreement. Thus, uncertainty does not necessarily lead to a permanent vacillating pluralism, which is so often taken as a corollary of the turn to a fully relativist logic.

Thinking along this path opens the way to understanding deduction as a process of reasoning that could be logically sound but nonetheless pathological. It would be logically sound in the 'language game' or 'universe of discourse' in which it was employed, but the wider normative implications could be argued to be pathological, as, for example, arguments for the necessity of extreme hierarchy. Such arguments could find favour with some, yet still be opposed by most by contradicting other norms that emphatically speak against it: rights to freedom, solidarity, equality, publicity, dignity, and practically every basic modern norm. This general presumption about sound but pathological reasoning entails a type of deductive pluralism, a pluralism that could be resolved into consensus over time, but with this outcome far from certain. Peczenik's analysis shows how the deductive rule that justifies a conclusion can vary across individual judges in legal contexts (Peczenik, 2008). In other words, the conclusion does not automatically follow from the premises. It would take further collective learning, a learning that might never happen, before such different judgements would be reconciled into an invariably agreed judgement. In the meantime, or in many cases more or less forever, differently conceived and applied deductive rules would show variance deriving from the nature of aesthetically formed modal projections together with the prescriptive normative ends that initially enter the logical process from the outside.

The above remarks open the way to consider pathological reasoning, where the pathology lies not in the use of the formal rules of reasoning but in the overall conditioning import of certain normative ends. It is also true that the normative ends are in turn conditioned by the reasoning process, forming an unending reflexive chain of justification. Earlier chapters laid out the fields of signification – discursive, positional, and displacement – that bear on reasoning, extending to the analysis of validity types and then to conditions and forms of critique. New episodes of signification-carrying learning processes can change the form of these fields. The fields accordingly exhibit both stability and instability, since periods of relative stability may be followed by periods of learning-driven critique resulting in instability. Reasoning can therefore be constrained in various ways for long periods owing to assumptions about validity contained within cultural models. Change in these cultural models results from sustained critique made possible by innovative abductive schematization animated by critique of various kinds. Critique takes the initial form of changed perception that then becomes logically elaborated, first of all through the abductive process of asserting possible innovative relations of validity and later through altering the form of cultural models. Such changed relations interrupt the validity of existing patterns of interpretation (interpretant chains) that are tied into hitherto institutionally stable cultural models. These existing interpretants, previously held to have general validity, canalized the signification process into settled interpretations that allow for recurrent coordinated actions. At periods of rupture, the interpretation process becomes destabilized, and with it, so do cultural models, as their instituted relations of validity come under pressure. In other words, critical signification can negate existing validity relations, and by correspondingly changing the nature of characteristic interpretants, it can ultimately change cultural and institutional models and habits of action. There is nothing in this process that in any way guarantees reasonable outcomes. This depends on the validity standards being deployed through critique and reconstruction. Bad, or one-sided, validity standards will produce unreasonable outcomes, as illustrated, for example, in Horkheimer's critique of the hegemony of subjective reason (Horkheimer, 1974 (1947)).

Discourse ethics certainly operates within this tradition of Peirce-inspired thinking, that is when validity standards understood in the context of 'logical socialism' are used in the critique of pathology (Wartenberg, 1971). However, it attaches such normative force to the long-run end of those validation processes that conform to its validity standards that everything that could be critically analyzed is made to seem merely intermediate on the path towards the final outcome of such standards. The final outcome therefore appears above the process. The consequence has been that 'deviating' pathological utilization of reasoning is insufficiently elaborated compared to the standard of the 'forceless force of the better argument'. This last observation does not mean there is not something important, even essential, in the idea of the force of the better argument. Habermas, for example, interpreted Peirce correctly in supposing that he sets the universality of the search for truth through reasoning against the merely self-interested use of reason (Habermas, 2019). An analogous figure of thought already appeared in *TCA* in the distinction between communicative and strategic action and the corresponding emphasis on mutual understanding as the telos of communicative action. The corollary is that strategic action, a legitimate kind of reason in itself, can become pathological if inappropriately pressing on the space of communicative action. Reasoning associated with strategic action is only one kind of reasoning, one whose excessive or inappropriate use can be pathological. There are other kinds of reasoning that are intrinsically pathological, and these are not equivalently elaborated within the theory; for example, ideological, regressive, or alienated reasoning. I will address these kinds of reasoning in more detail later in the chapter.

Consideration of the distinction between communicative reasoning, justifiable or pathological, or some combination, ineluctably raises the question of the relationship between theoretical and practical reason. Their ideal forms can be distinguished as practices of reasoning bearing on questions of truth and rightness. Judgement of where one ends and the other begins is extremely complex in practice. The logic of interpenetration, raised above in Chapters 3 and 4 arising from Munch, raises further questions about when different, potentially opposing, ideal forms arise at the same time. Peirce's account of the relationship between theoretical and

## 298 *Critique and Reasoning Pathologies*

practical reason and between theory and practice is notably complex, perhaps even ambivalent and contradictory. Stepping away from this debate, it is perhaps reasonable to claim that Peirce's distinction between theoretical and practical reason was different from Habermas's Neo-Kantian one. Peirce did not distinguish between theoretical reasoning as operating from a detached observational perspective with practical reason arising from the self-understanding of participants in their practices. The practice of theoretical reason requires participation, and practical reasoners require theories. In Peirce, both of them commence with a type of 'faith', a type of conjecture that has not yet been fully explicated that something could be true, good, or right. Even with the assumption of a common methodology of theoretical and practical reason, there remains a potential gap between reasoning and action. This gap cannot be closed by either a type of existential 'decisionism' or by moral postulates, even procedural ones. It can only be closed, ever more and more, by turning conjectural moral engagement into justified moral conduct within a logic of inquiry. This, whether carried out in a laboratory, a social science institute, or everyday life, is a process of inclusive, democratic inquiry and appropriate collective learning.

Discourse ethics can indeed be read as a set of normative prescriptions for good, that is, inclusive and responsible democratic reasoning, but with the intention that the normative prescriptions can also be used to identify bad reasoning. The most important distinction that discourse ethics draws in this regard is that good reasoning is better adapted to the second nature of human beings and must come to the fore in the long run if society is not to degenerate, even to disappear. While all of this is entirely consistent with that which is advanced here, it is also true that discourse ethics concentrates on the conditions for realizing good reasoning and has not adequately developed its account of reasoning pathologies, a lacuna partly remedied by the well-known work of Honneth on social pathologies and by the undeservedly less well-known work of Miller on communication pathologies and collective learning (Miller, 2002; Honneth, 2004; Zurn, 2011). It is also manifested in Habermas's 'outcome' pathologies in *TCA*, loss of meaning, anomie, and psychopathology. As outcome pathologies, these are not generative reasoning pathologies as developed here. Nor are those of Honneth. Nonetheless, the existence of instituted pathologies of these kinds consistently generates pathogenesis in reasoning, so these conceptual registers and domains are closely related. Instituted social pathologies are located in the space of placement within the positional field, and reasoning pathologies are process forms that are located in the space of reasons and the discursive field, as outlined earlier. The path between them is of the first social scientific importance.

In the last chapter, the validity standards of discourse ethics were outlined within the frame of Peirce's three-level account of reasoning: abductive (conjectural validity standards), deductive (ideal validity standards), and inductive (actual validity standards). Such an approach combines what is possible and what is actual, that is, what is possible but foreseeably 'actualizable' and with an emphasis on what is deemed, by the standards of the theory, normatively progressive. The selection of progressive validity standards does not imply that reasoning is only guided by such standards. It can be applied to them only because of a prior selection of normative goals that itself is the result of previous reasoning, where potentials are formulated over a long evolutionary and relatively long historical time before being crystallized in the specifically selected here-and-now validity standards. The focus on reasoning does not only apply to validity standards deemed progressive. Reasoning can also be guided by validity standards deemed regressive, where a fundamental task of the critical analyst is to specify the existence and implications of such regressive standards. Thus, the frame of reasoning can be used for either purpose, and with it, the teleological implications of *claims* to reason are significantly weakened. There is no security that what is operative in the world as a claim to reason is in fact reasonable. There is no way out such as the Kantian idea of a transcendental ground of reason that can be counterpointed to the misleading effects of our inclinations. There are no transcendent moral norms beyond our human powers that make their presence felt and from which deviation can straightforwardly be regarded as immoral. Rather, we are burdened with the task of constructing relevant distinctions that support such moral norms, whose principles must be publicly and not privately justified. Admittedly, what we construct is guided by a structure of cognitive orientations, but these orientations do not themselves specify what are appropriate moral norms, the prerogative assumed by the older metaphysics, only what diversified capacities for feelings, facts, and arguments can be used to develop them. Of course, the very existence of transcendental properties that could produce moral laws is a moral orientation that is taken to be at the heart of a species-embedded second nature distilled over evolutionary time for what Rainer Forst calls 'justificatory beings' or, with Apel or Peirce perhaps, we could say for argument-oriented beings (Benhabib et al., 2015).

## Reasoning Pathologies in Intellectual Context

At the beginning of Thomas McCarthy's *Ideals and Illusions*, he shows how Kant's idea of the deceiving power of inclination, on one side, and, on the other side, the rational power of thought still resonates (McCarthy, 1993). This is so even if the conception of reason at issue is considerably changed from Kant's in a variable, embodied, collective, and culturally embedded direction. McCarthy identifies a deconstructionist strand among those who hold that ideas of reason lead to permanent illusions and those who hold that they can be rationally reconstructed to provide guidance for reasonable conduct and a reasonable society. In one sense, Kant had it right in assuming that inclination can pervert ideas of reason, a view that can be socially scientifically elucidated through Durkheim's concept of elementary social forms, for example, the implications of those in a negative register such as conflict, competition, and narrow self-interest. Of course, the deconstructionist critique, beyond inclination in this sense, further extends to the very idea of reason itself, which is assumed to have no independent existence that can assure anything, and that postulating such a possibility is a smokescreen for unreasonable claims to the authority of 'reason'. It can be easily admitted that reason – frequently understood as limited kinds of rationality – has indeed historically often worked up in that way, and accordingly the deconstructionist position has societal value in exposing manifest pathologies of reason. Something akin to this critique of reason was present in Adorno and Horkheimer, even if it remained a project internal to reason. Without a

## 300 *Critique and Reasoning Pathologies*

concept of reasonable reason, we are left without any validity standards that could set things right, eventually lost in a confusing world either of unending domination or undecidable pluralism, in which nonetheless forms of unjustified rationality may hold sway. Neither is a good formula, however partly true they may be, for the task of advocating a better possible world that cannot simply be relegated to consisting of another point of view or another strategy of domination. Yet, from the alternative standpoint of rescuing a reasonable idea of reason, in another sense, the dynamic, that is, historical and evolutionary, secular, and inter-subjectivist caste of the post-Kantian conception of reason from left-Hegelianism to critical theory, also calls for a radical change in intellectual architectonic. If an overarching concept of reason may still be defended, such a concept must be displaced from individual mind to that of extended social mind, of which individual reasoning is only one part. Moreover, Kant's own distinction between pure and impure ethics (Horn, 2014), viewed in this broader context, emphasizes the intertwining and reconciliation of the generation of new knowledge with forms of deontological commitment, reducing the divide between theoretical and practical reason. An intersubjective logic of inquiry thus underpins the possibility of normative innovation, where the validity of norms remains conjectural and contested until sufficiently justified in *world-embedded* reasoning processes.

Such a conception of normativity is de-transcendentalized. In discourse-ethical terms, de-transcendentalization, as expressed, means that the norm itself is not transcendental. Rather, what is transcendental are those capacities and orientations that go to make the norm possible, the basic frame of reason itself. The norm is established through an intra-mundane logic of inquiry. Those norms that are counted as deontological commitments must now be shown to originate and be consolidated within a fallible reasoning process that can always be revised. Some dimensions of such commitments may endure over an extended time, for example, fundamental human rights, but are still woven into discursive processes embracing other norms in ever-changing situations. The characteristic of norms that could count as functionally or morally beyond doubt in the here and now is that they can be *explicitly* justified, that is, fully comprehended in their moral force within intra-mundane contexts.

The above remarks can be set within the context of later disagreements between the original proponents of discourse ethics, Apel and Habermas. Apel articulates this disagreement as opposition between his own continuing transcendental pragmatics and Habermas's strategy of the detranscendentalization of practical reason (Apel, 2007, 50). Transcendental pragmatics insists on the transcendental but not metaphysical foundations of certain fundamental norms or argumentation, that we are all partners of an unlimited communication community, having equal rights and equal co-responsibility. For Apel, these norms follow the necessary shift from the solipsistic 'I think' of Kant and Descartes to Peirce's 'I argue' within an unlimited communication community (Apel, 2007). In this different setting of the 'fact of reason', reason remains non-empirical and thus transcendental, in this sense consistent with Kant. It therefore operates as an 'a priori' that does not depend on contingent empirical contexts. This is a complicated and underappreciated debate whose intricacies need not be fully followed for immediate present purposes.

*Critique and Reasoning Pathologies* 301

What I do wish to highlight is Apel's contention that Habermas moves the issue of the validity of practical reason away from the transcendental normative argumentation commitments of discourse ethics, as above, towards the application context of a morality that can only be immanently redeemed through the responsibility ethic of law. Habermas can thus also assert the separation of theoretical reason – operating still with the transcendental principle following truth – and practical reason operating without it (Habermas, 2003; Apel, 2007; Strydom, 2019). Apel's position, in line with Peirce, is that theoretical and practical reasons emerge from the same procedure, and that ultimately, theoretical reason must just as much be subject to intersubjective validation as practical reason. By extension, the a priori commitments of practical reason only make possible a set of moral commitments to the procedure of argument that must be met, just as with theoretical reason. Kant's non-empirical 'fact of reason' can be retained, but only to the extent that it guides certain fundamental moral conditions of democratic argumentation, not that it pre-decides outcomes, including moral outcomes. Even if a Kantian riposte could be that it is ultimately a procedural moral theory, it still leaves open the issue of how it becomes societally effective, both procedurally and substantively.

In the light of the interest of this chapter, the question arises as to how exactly a theory built on orienting validity standards can accommodate an account of unjust and pathological reasoning? Axel Honneth, whose critical social philosophy extensively incorporates social theory, opens a path. For him, the failure to realize a possible rational societal universal must be explained by those social pathological obstacles that prevent it from forming (Honneth, 2004). Honneth here distinguishes between social injustice, which arises in the context of the denial of existing recognition standards, and social pathologies, which call for an ontological critique of over-institutionalization. Social pathologies arise as reflexive incapacities to grasp what could and should be grasped. That such grasping is possible represents the horizons of validity and critique, without which the identification of a pathology would not be possible.

Reasoning itself is a social process where the social form is intrinsic to the generation of valid knowledge. However, sociality arises in another sense too. The deliberate misuse of reason by some individuals or groups can be designed to lead to the creation or maintenance of reasoning pathologies by others. Capacities for needed reflexivity can be deliberately prevented from forming, or existing capacities can be disabled. This can happen, for example, in conditions of ethnic tension where capacities for tolerance are deliberately subverted. In such cases, there is an internal relation between pathological and unjust reasoning. Marx's analysis of capitalism can also be read in this light. The reasoning of capitalists makes possible exploitation even if their manifest understanding of the crisis-prone, cyclical economic process is itself flawed. More interesting in this connection, though, is that the capitalist ideology of fair appropriation of labour, a product of ideology in Marx's view, is also the source of misrecognition among workers so far as they willingly accept the terms of their own exploitation. Such misrecognition is a more or less deliberately inculcated social pathology. In Honneth's account, they show a lack of ability due to social causes to adequately practice the normative grammar

302 *Critique and Reasoning Pathologies*

of a form of life that should be available to them. Without this normative grammar, they are unable to engage in a struggle for recognition. This group pathology, which could lead workers to accept the unjust status quo as just, unravelled progressively in the second half of the 19th century and onwards as they acquired the necessary reflexive capacities in changing conditions to work on the kind of encompassing domination that hitherto enfettered them.

The kind of pathology, simply illustrated above, can be described as a particular relational group pathology. It consists of the inability of a particular group to avail itself of the necessary reflexive capacities to identify and act on injustice that they experience. It is relational in that both injustice and pathology serve the interests of other groups. In general, the idea of a social pathology takes the social distribution of reflexive capacities to depend on structural conditions. In Honneth's formulation, for example, the ideals that underpin the social spheres of market, law, and state are not pathological per se. They are taken to be imbued with rationality derived from their modern form. Instead, what occurs are pathological deviations from the ideals of such social spheres manifested as a failure to realize them in practice. The pathology is more general and encompassing of a social sphere as a whole than characteristic of particular groups within it. While Honneth's account of social pathology is remarkable in its quality and depth, its emphasis on the fact that pathologies emerge from already-constituted social spheres with established principles is constraining. Quite apart from the optimistic insight that the rationality of the social spheres has already been appropriately constituted and stands potentially available, it diminishes insight into collective learning processes, above all those aimed at reconstructing the rationality of social spheres themselves, that emerge from inter-group dynamics (Freyenhagen, 2015). Being open to such learning processes opens the way towards viewing reasoning as continuously occupied with reconstituting, transforming, or replacing the potentiality of social spheres. Modernity is thus regarded as not constituted once but many times over and recurrently. Less is assumed to be carried through instituted cultural and social structures, as with Honneth, and more through reflexive cognitive operations guided by generative and coordinative schematization. It is this that makes future-oriented collective learning, that is, radical potentiality, possible. Of course, in keeping with the generally expressed view here, collective learning is not only 'progressive' in line with the validity standards proposed earlier; it can just as easily be regressive.

Ricouer's account of freedom also offers interesting possibilities for further clarifying the idea of pathology. For him, the possibility of freedom arises in the human capacity to transcend a particular situation and state of knowledge and to incorporate the reason potential of the infinite into finite practices. Yet, the gap between the infinite and the finite also reveals the fallibility of human cognition. Freedom can accordingly be misused in the quest for possessions, power, and prestige (Ricouer, 1965). The misuse of freedom thus has transcendental conditions of possibility that evince the same structural form as any other utilization of the power of freedom. The cognitive principles, which are the a priori of reasonable reasoning must also be capable of serving as the a priori of unreasonable reasoning. Hence, to speak of an a priori principle of legitimacy, efficiency, control, equality, and

*Critique and Reasoning Pathologies* 303

freedom must allow for their 'dialectical inverse' to be countenanced. Knowing how to make claims to legitimacy means also knowing how to subvert claims to legitimacy. The misuse of freedom in Ricouer can thus be extended to the misuse of reason in general. Social pathologies are thus not only a question of deviations from existing societal rationalities; also to be considered are pathological incapacities to learn or pathological capacities to regressively learn. Both are upstream of institutional rationalities in Honneth's sense and have generative consequences for the formation, transformation, and change of those rationalities. Grasping reasoning pathologies in their fullness therefore requires understanding the blocking of collective learning potentials as well as the inability to reflexively grasp established institutional rationalities. The first calls for a different kind of task to the second, the modal task of charting rational potentialities out of possibilities. For the goals of critical theory, it is the more fundamental task, even if it cannot be executed without adequate attention to the second task, that of addressing existing rationalities, including the unreasonableness that they spawn.

**Reasoning Pathologies in Practice: First Outline**

Turning then on the above foundations to the task of specifying reasoning pathologies and also of showing the implications of such pathologies for sustaining problematic or disabling structures, I propose the following – provisional – list. The first four pathologies outlined below are taken over from Max Miller's account of communication pathologies, which I also built upon in an earlier publication (Miller, 2002; O'Mahony, 2013). The remainder are characteristic foci of critical theory that are here addressed as reasoning pathologies. The first two pathologies below are described by Miller as consensus pathologies, and the latter two as dissensus pathologies. They emerge from his research programme exploring the role of collective learning within the structures of coordinated dissent, in part an attempt to modify the degree to which discourse ethics operates as a theory of 'consensus'. The manner in which they are described here is, first of all, to offer a rough outline that is broadly consistent with Miller's approach to the four pathologies, though placing them in a logical frame consistent with the current approach. The same rough outline is provided for the remaining three, which are classically associated with critical theory: reification, alienation, and dysfunction/material crisis. Following these broad introductory remarks, the pathologies are then elaborated upon in line with the general features of the approach.

The first two pathologies, respectively, authoritarian and defensive, are described by Miller as 'consensus pathologies', either involving a type of authoritarian fiat, elitist-individualist or institutional, or, alternately, a type of incorporation that is widely manifest in conservative populism. The consensus is such that, in the first case, it cannot be disagreed with for fear of sanctions, or it should not be disagreed with because it has already included possible objections seamlessly. In the latter case, it should be supposed, as is often the case, that consensus is asserted so strongly, backed by either emotional or material sanctions, that any lurking dissent often remains unexpressed. In the first, authoritarian, case, collective learning

## 304 *Critique and Reasoning Pathologies*

is assumed to be deductively complete, that is, that deduction has already absorbed possible discord arising from abductive or inductive inferences. In the defensive case, there is nominal openness but effective closure with a similar structure of inferences. In this latter case, though, there is some scope for escaping the symbolic entrapment. A further basic difference is the manner of deployment of emotions that block feelings in either case. In the first case, overt repressive emotions can be used with minimal or no justification, whereas, in the second case, emotional inducements of various kinds must be offered. It is frequent in defensive pathologies for agents, directly using or affected by such a pathology, to inductively perceive cultural patterns, but to be unable to turn them into valid abductive conjectures about social change, variously because they cannot find the requisite internal will, social receptivity is inimical to the expression of that will, or generative schematization arising from abduction is inhibited.

The dissensual pathologies are ideological and regressive. In the critical social and normative sciences, the concept of ideology covers a wide span. In recent decades, it has fallen into disuse, assumed to have become an implausible universal thesis of the masking of reality by dominant groups. Ideology does not have to take the form of universal false consciousness; it can occur in any situation where symbolic power is being deployed to mislead and generate profound, unbridgeable opposition. Miller uses it in the relatively restricted sense of blocking collective learning in argumentation by hard-wiring differences. It can also be used to block reasoning in a more diffuse and general sense of unjustified preferences – that is, operating preferences that are literally not justified – for one group/party or another in public discourse. One particularly widespread manifestation in countries where English is the first official langauge is the use of ideology to defend a narrow and elitist version of an assumed permanent liberal order against anyone who might question or oppose it (Somers, 2008). In this type of assumed ideal order, consisting of the dogmatization of the ideal, inductive inferences are rigidly schematized, and the power of imagination is lost. This can sometimes, to some degree, be attributed to interests, but it is often the effect of a type of habitus that determines perceptual judgements and cognitive habits that may or may not follow definable interests. The other kind of dissensus pathology, regressive reasoning, involves a denial of the status of others and is well illustrated by the example given earlier (Chapter 11) of the dangers incurred by black males in wearing masks.

These core pathologies, called by Miller communication pathologies, described and elaborated upon here as reasoning pathologies, provide significant and relatively rare insight into how reasoning goes wrong. Extending beyond this insight in the first place is why it does, the question of what generates these pathologies, and, in the second, what are the implications? If reasoning in this non-formal, general sense can be shown to be at the heart of social stability and change, then a theory of society with normative intentions may be built around it, as was Habermas's original intention. For this purpose, it is necessary to identify more than these core pathologies of reasoning. It has to be shown more generally that the various pathologies that critical theory uses to diagnose social ills and injustices can be traced back directly or indirectly to patterns of reasoning. Moreover, it must be shown

*Critique and Reasoning Pathologies*   305

how such patterns of reasoning become embedded in the discursive and positional fields and the related cultural models of the earlier outlined societal ontology. The actuality that the ontology identifies has, in the first place, been generated by the actions of agents, consciously or unconsciously, intended or unintended, manipulatively or sincerely.

To Miller's account, it must be additionally shown that why agents reason as they do requires, first of all, understanding their embedding in positional fields. Such embedding does not mean that the social location of reasoners is fully determining, only that it has to be taken into account. Indeed, in some respects, contrary to the procedural turn of which Habermas is a main carrier, even if reasoning is fundamental, it cannot be supposed that its distortions and pathologies may be corrected without also correcting existing social arrangements. The time scales and complexity for attending to such corrections will exceed any time-limited procedural forum. In any case, the collective learning required will also be diffuse, practical, and even for long periods uncertain.

All of this complexity must be seen through the prism of a dialectical process of interchange between factual states of affairs and reflective learning, mediated through the generative power of phenomenal perception. In these circumstances, reflective learning of a fundamental kind can occur, but only if it is regulated by appropriate ideals and guided by appropriate logical forms within a general frame of democratization. This is a relatively autonomous process that is not procedurally regulated in any strict sense, nor foreseeably can it be. Reconstructing such a learning process as a shared enterprise between intellectual observers and agents is not a small task, and it amounts to specifying what Peirce and Dewey describe as the operations of collective intelligence (Bidet et al., 2013), ultimately from the normative standpoint of reasonable rationalization.

Continuing with the identification of reasoning pathologies, three further such pathologies that have widespread use in critical theorizing are also proposed. These are reification, alienation, and irrationality. Regarding reification, from early in the history of critical theory, in Lukács, Adorno, and Horkheimer, and building from Marx and Weber, instrumental reason was singled out as the empirically dominant form of reason, and in the critical tradition, in another way in Weber too, ascribed defined regressive import. Already, canonically in Lukács, the commodified form taken from Marx was coupled with Weber's thesis of the dominance of a spirit-less purposive rationality to create the characteristic abstract formality and hollowness of modern life (Lukács, 1972). There have been many iterations of this basic thesis since. The other side of the reification hypothesis, that which reification prevents or impedes, is most clearly expressed in Habermas's account of reason. He can only develop a thesis of reification as one that actually lies beyond reasoning in the form of the colonization of the lifeworld by the system. Systemic codes are still communicative, but they have become separated from the communicative action that reproduces the lifeworld. This approach enables him to preserve the 'positive' potentiality of communicative reason. The assumption of positive symmetry between communicative reason and the lifeworld preserves the long-standing idea of the 'purity' of reason

## 306 *Critique and Reasoning Pathologies*

and the reasoning on which it rests. The reifying intrusion of systemic codes appears to come only from the outside, something separated from reasoning per se, even if it is claimed that they originally were separated out from the sociocultural lifeworld.

There is considerable truth in this approach. What is at first a kind of innovation cognitive processing achieved through reasoning – the first steps towards the introduction of a money economy, for example – gradually becomes a symbolic and material reality of its own. As a fully-fledged medium, it may, over time, have a range of negative consequences. However, these negative consequences do not always simply happen on their own; they are supported by a general cultural structure that gives them oxygen and turns them from 'neutral' media forms to instead result in the suffering of some groups, including the diminution of their potential competences. Such consequences can be lodged in social arrangements by reified reasoning, applied to self, specific others, or forms of life generally. Hence, whereas reification frequently involves a type of institutionally organized collective suppression of potentialities for autonomous reasoning, a social pathology operating as a block on abduction, it also steps over to become a reasoning pathology. Here, it operates as an improper objectivation of contexts of life that should be the subject of communicative reflection in line with the various validity standards earlier outlined. The availability of money or power as media colonize reflective learning through the consequences of bad abduction, disorienting formation and use of ideals, and deficient or damaging action orientations. As held by both Peirce and discourse ethics, the human way of life has transcendental cognitive presuppositions that define human purposes. What these remarks on reification indicate is that while all the principles and associated purposes can be relatively easily identified as at work in society, there are many acute problems that impede reasonable equilibration between them as they become culturally embodied in forms of life.

A reified reasoning pathology may thus be understood as the gradual institutionalization of a kind of quasi-automatic, habitual process that grants hegemony to formal reasoning, resulting in the reifying consequences outlined by Horkheimer, where logical forms guide human relations that correspond to the logical appropriation of inanimate objects. The long-standing centrality of deductive certainty in formal logic is often taken by those espousing the interpretive turn in the human and social sciences as itself illustrative of reification. This is often coupled with a critique of the excessive attention attributed to decontextualized individual reasoning in the formal logical tradition. Even if this critique is ultimately inconsistent with the assumption of inter-operating logical categories where deduction has its place, there is still merit in the critique of the formal logical tendency to emphasize deduction working in tandem with routinized inductive premises. When coupled with social power imbalances in the selection of reasoning strategies and grounds of reason, this indeed does amount to reified reasoning since it excludes the influence of abduction as a type of conjecture – or modal projection – arising from autonomous qualities of feeling. Again and again, such reifying tendencies take their place in value-neutral technical prescriptions for the organization of society, precisely the kind of expedient that, taken to excess, has given the concept of rationality its bad reputation. Incomplete or selective use of reason – what Habermas in *TCA* calls selective rationalization, applied to Weber – is accordingly a just target of critique.

Alienation, a type of near relation of reification, canonically involves the separation of the practical mind from the suppressed power to engage in reflection, including self-reflection. For various direct reasons to do with imbalances of power or indirect reasons to do with socialization or situation, agents are abductively blocked – with Marx, their sensuous nature is inhibited. Such blocking of feelings leads to a corresponding inability to 'theoretically' search for adequate deductive rule systems to explain what is happening. Wright Mills's idea of the sociological imagination can be understood, given his deep familiarity with Peirce, as a type of abduction that could help agents break free of their lack of knowledge and sense of impotence (Mills, 1969; Mills, 2000). By implication, this is also a call for more comprehensive and inclusive sociological reasoning conducted by publics themselves with the aid of sociological concepts, that is to say, non-alienated reasoning. Forst has also advanced the classical Kant-inspired suggestion of viewing alienation as a condition of heteronomy, the inability to reason autonomously as a consequence of regarding the self as a mere means that has become artificially disconnected from the moral core of second nature (Forst, 2017). Honneth's idea of a second-order pathology, taking the form of reflexivity deficits, is also suggestive of an alienated condition. In this case, the alienation extends all the way from self-alienation to inability to respond to others to the inability to thematize social issues more generally (Honneth, 2004). Alienation in this case reveals abductive incapacities present in individuals, groups, and public.

Finally, the idea of a pathology of irrationality is strangely not given much attention in the recent critical tradition, though it was prevalent in the first generation. Lukács expresses it in a way that is highly suited to the present purpose in his *Destruction of Reason* when he speaks of the growth of irrationalism: 'The disparagement of understanding and reason, an uncritical glorification of intuition, an aristocratic epistemology, the rejection of socio-historical progress, the creation of myths, and so on are motives we can find in virtually any irrationalist.' (Lukács, 2021, 10). Irrationality as a reasoning pathology is therefore to be grasped as a type of enhanced nominalist sense of the particular and specific that asserts complete imaginative freedom beyond any collective powers of reflection. It particularly arises in eras of pointed crises, for which appellation the second and third decades of the 21st century abundantly qualify. In these conditions, there is a pronounced shift from justified, respectful pluralism, whose further potentials become salient in many social spheres, to an extreme type of individualist or group relativism. In logical terms, it involves the generation of radical conjectures that are confused and incapable of any kind of further logical explication or demonstration. It frequently operates therefore as non-reflexive dogmatism and has distinct affinities with aspects of consensus and dissensus pathologies.

## 308 *Critique and Reasoning Pathologies*

**Reasoning Pathologies in Practice: Second Outline**

I now turn to transposing these remarks on reasoning pathologies in critical theory to reflect more on the societal ontology outlined earlier in this text. So, interpreted in this context, the reasoning pathologies may be elaborated as follows, beginning with the two consensus pathologies, then the two dissensus pathologies, and the pathologies of reification, alienation, and irrationality, all as described above.

- Pathology of authoritarian reasoning with prescriptive presumed consensus: This assumes an already established consensus from which deviation is not allowed. Logically, this entails the deductive hegemony of some problematic ideals, such as that of hierarchy, that prescriptively organize the space of reasons, a space that is at best only nominally open within the form of this pathology.[1] Such reasoning frequently blocks attempts at discursive, and ultimately social, reconstruction. Settled consensus presumed at the level of norms (the institutional model) constrains variation through abductive schema formation. If the analysis is extended further into fields, it can be said that the positional field closes off variation in the perceptual field, and by so doing, blocks the exploration of validity in reasoning processes. Accordingly, abductive reasoning emerging from habits of feeling, and inductive reasoning associated with habits of volition and action, are both substantially blocked from being adequately thematized. The typical modalities of coordination include a combination of repressive hegemony and conflict, but repressive hegemony is preferred because the 'trick' of this pathology is to insist there is agreement even where there is not.
- Pathology of defensive reasoning, 'incorporating' forms of dissent into consent, preventing dissent from 'breathing': Defensive reasoning is potentially more open than authoritarian reasoning. It recognizes that there are forms of dissent, but it tries to subvert them through incorporation, recognizing it cannot always reach for the big stick of imposing authoritative consensus brooking no opposition. As such, there is recognition of disputation within the cognitive frame of relevance of ideals and less prospect for directly repressive ideals such as unjustified hierarchy or elite control. It generally entails blocking or inhibiting abductive and inductive inferences that could increase dissent. The recognition of dissent extends to assumptions about cultural models and fields. The perceptual field within the space of displacement threatens to open up new potentials for abductive schema-building, so every attempt is made to deploy the validity vested in existing cultural models to shut it down. Accordingly, the various habits of feeling, thought, and action allow a dispersed structure to some degree; that is, they do not have to tightly align. However, if defensive reasoning is strongly discursively challenged, a latent hegemony comes strongly to the fore, drawing off the modality of repressive hegemony. In these circumstances, the possibility of collective learning through exploring the nature of dissent is significantly diminished.
- Pathology of ideological reasoning, assumed permanent antagonism – hence dissensus-based – but frequently disguised: This assumes the permanence of

*Critique and Reasoning Pathologies* 309

antagonism and, accordingly, resistance to cross-perspectival learning. An example is the contemporary prevalence of a kind of free-market ideology that eschews anything but a minimal role for the state and more or less abandons to their fate the constituencies that rely on it (Somers, 2008). Accordingly, ideals tend to be disputed, as manifested in the highly fissured terrain of many contemporary societies. Disguise, in the classical ideological sense of manipulation, is typically used to hide real intentions. Where such disguise is used, it can lead to persuading constituencies that do not profit from certain ideals, for example, radical free market or 'pure' communitarian ideals, to believe that they do. Collective learning is often qualified by power-political considerations, where one-sided innovations create a new actuality that forces compromise. The coordinative modalities can variously be those of compromise, hegemony, or conflict, depending on whether the pathology is open or disguised, whether one of the poles is extreme or not, and the context of material and cultural opportunity structures present in the various fields. In this sense, collective learning can proceed initially in the line of the polarizing tendency, for example, neoliberalism. Like the defensive pathology, outlined immediately above, the ideological pathology entails a commitment to radical habit change. In particular, its goal is to block generative habits of feeling.

- Pathology of regressive reasoning, excluding or ad hominem type of dissensus-based argument: This type of pathology is closely allied to discrimination of all kinds. It denies the status of others so absolutely that they are no longer regarded as discourse partners but as belonging to categories that should not be tolerated. It is accordingly open in its rejection of excluded categories, as when racism becomes overt again after a period of being relatively subdued. When this pathology is dominant, only regressive collective learning is possible, as in how best to organize an exclusion-based campaign or how to narrate the 'lessons of history' in favour of the dominant, for example, white supremacism. It can have a powerful influence on the perceptual field and, consistent with its form of learning, uses mainly limited but still effective abductive schemata, such as advancing terms like 'invasion' or 'hordes' to describe asylum seekers, who are excluded by the device of dehumanization. Its commitment to ideals within the field of discourse is limited since the focus is more on breaking up established democratic patterns as well as seeking to direct politics towards one-sided and regressive versions of often anachronistic ideals. The cross-positional mediating power of these ideals is therefore highly limited, though they can be extremely effective in the positional field. In this field, this type of reasoning helps to restore 'traditional' hierarchies in the new circumstances of the present, often by pushing through one-sided legal-political norms. It seeks a thorough transformation of habits of all three kinds, feeling, thought, and action, so it is often radical in its pursuit of social change. The preferred coordinative modalities tend to be either hegemonic or conflict-oriented, with a greater emphasis on the latter. Neoconservative reasoning is its primary contemporary political expression.

310 *Critique and Reasoning Pathologies*

- Pathology of reification, instrumentalization, or selective rationalization: This pathology involves the assumption of the closing of the discursive field to that of means-end rationality and equivalent logical closure to only deductive-inductive considerations, the closing down phase spoken of earlier. Cognitive principles oriented to objective orientations such as efficiency, control, and effectiveness are foregrounded within the structure of ideals. These ideals accordingly evince the thematic hegemony of objective relations, where even democratic self-understanding is reified. This in turn vitally affects the inter-positional, co-ordinative cultural model (the SCM) that is forced onto this narrow ground. It can readily be seen how the ideological projection of the money medium and associated cultural beliefs in the last half-century has had a reifying effect, notably shifting normative arrangements, even subjective self-understanding, in a purpose-rational direction with major implications for the structuring of the field of positions. These changes have given much impetus to social theories that, in one way or another, emphasize the technology of organizing, such as those of Foucault or Luhmann. The general presumption of reified reason is to draw off codified sectoral rationalities (rationalization) without the transversal role of a wider communicative reason that would bring into play the normative ends of society. This wider sense of reasonableness, Peirce's logical socialism (Wartenberg, 1971), is dissolved into another of his terms, the articulation of the gospel of greed and its wide implications even for those who do not espouse it (Peirce, 1893). This idea is equivalent to the in-depth critique of the excesses of subjective reason in first-generation critical theory and is carried forward in *TCA* by Habermas's account of the degenerative colonization of communicative reasoning by systemic codes (Horkheimer, 1974 (1947); Condon, 2021; Kreide, 2023). Finally, abductive conjectures are highly restricted to extant system rationalities, and abductive schema-building accordingly makes possible only one-sided, 'selectively rational' collective learning.
- Pathology of alienated reasoning, reflexivity deficits among actors: This pathology focuses on those abductive deficits that lead to failure to effectively thematize directly experienced first-order social pathologies. The absence of thematization that would lead to generative schematization arises from conditions of hermeneutic injustice (Fricker, 2007), inadequate resonance (Rosa, 2021), and disempowerment. Alienation entails the blocking of habits of feeling that agents need to understand themselves, others, and society generally. The capacity for wide-ranging thematization is accordingly diminished, and instead further alienation may be generated as misunderstandings multiply in the various models and fields. The discursive field is accordingly characterized by identity-denial, or to speak with Honneth, denial of required relations of recognition. This can be understood as a failure to project cognitive principles, for example, dignity or legitimacy, to specific social groups. In terms of Peirce, the blocking of appropriate habits of feeling means that logical operations proceed mechanically, inappropriately deployed as formal rules rather than carrying the aesthetically informed imagination in its fullness, similar to Forst's Kantian formulation in this regard (Forst, 2017). Continuing the Kantian theme,

*Critique and Reasoning Pathologies*  311

collective learning is characterized by a regressive quality in being more subject to unchecked inclination than universal moral considerations. Appropriate ideal concepts are therefore not brought to the fore, and inappropriate ones take their place. The ratcheting effect of alienation accumulates in institutional models and in habits of action and volition that reproduce and extend first-order social pathologies of alienated experience. Such alienated experience crucially, both in the self and affecting others, is blocked from being reflexively thematized in reasoning processes.

• Pathology of irrational reasoning: This pathology has the characteristic of abductive validity claims being asserted that are not in any way inductively evaluated in any modal register, ranging from what is to what could be the case. Without such evaluation, considered in relation to cultural models and fields, irrational reasoning can postulate or contradict any ideal almost at will. Thus, there is no credible, authentic process of the ideal mediation of actuality. What is being sought in iconic resonance is to change the metaphors and images whereby objects are viewed, and where great inconsistency is often manifested between iconic constructions and their societal resonance and properly justified factual statements. Collective learning is often regressive, in the sense of hearkening back to earlier times, overtly or covertly. Accordingly, irrational discourse concentrates on the direct relationship between perceptual and positional fields, seeking to manipulate perceptions within the space of placement. Logically, premises have weak relations to conclusions, with sentiment rather than cogent inference as the main expedient. Irrationality as a reasoning pathology evinces mistaken or blithely tendentious inferential chaining or erroneous, incomplete, or over-optimistic premises.

This brief sketch of reasoning pathologies shows that when the focus is shifted from the certainties of formal reasoning, as it generally must be in practical questions, then the understanding of inferential operations looks very different. Such an account of reasoning allows insight into how domination enters into reasoning, the 'why' and the 'how' of bad reasoning. Bad reasoning extended over time will create unjustifiable norms and habits and embed them in symbolic models and spaces of placement in positional fields. These outcomes in turn will perpetuate bad reasoning. This dialectical formulation already indicates that bad and good reasoning coexist in the world, and each has its determining moment. Hence, it is theoretically-methodologically necessary to make bad reasoning as visible as good reasoning. Because of the entanglement of good, bad, and in-between reasoning, one critical task is to show they in part 'support' one another, as in the contemporary relationship of deracinated finance-capitalism and democracy. There are matters beyond reasoning in the capacity to feel and to perceive anew. All of this will indeed be helped by better procedures, but it will also require radical institutional change and recognition of the deepest sentiments of suffering and hope, some of which are currently only latent.

From the above account of pathologies, a number of general points may be made. The first is that the identified set of reasoning pathologies, which is very far

## 312   *Critique and Reasoning Pathologies*

from comprehensive, already provides significant tools for analyzing social situations from the perspective of the general societal ontology outlined in this text. The emphasis on logic and reasoning is designed to capture the modal quality of social reality, where reality is not just so to speak already there but permanently in a state of becoming. The direction of that becoming is critically influenced by reasoning processes and not just democratic reasoning processes. Accordingly, that state of becoming is far from decisively structurally fore-ordained, as it vitally depends on perception and reasoning processes in the perceptual and discursive fields and equivalent spaces of displacement and reasons. The second is that the 'classical' pathologies emphasized by critical theory, ideology, irrationality, reification, and alienation gain new life when elaborated as reasoning pathologies in the light of the modified validity standards of discourse ethics. The modal dimension is Peirce's thirdness in practice. Sociologically transmuted, it indicates capacities for progressive, general, collective learning and the enlargement of options. It accordingly changes the focus from the structural generation of social pathologies towards second-order reflexive pathologies, here following Honneth (Honneth, 2004). These second-order pathologies in the current account are fundamentally generative; beyond Honneth's account, they are reasoning pathologies in a space of reasons and part of the struggle over the direction of collective learning. They are accordingly immanent transcendent in a radical constitutive and reconstructive sense and cannot be securely related to deviations from established, reasonable ideals, as with Honneth. It might be said that Honneth's account is a moment in the process, but only one moment.

The third is that the emphasis on the self-understanding of societal members, as in Boltantki, Thevenot, and others, is complicated by the account of reasoning pathologies. How are we to think of the relationship between intellectual critique and such self-understanding in conditions where pathologies are powerful and widespread, like in the first quarter of the 21st century? This is even more challenging given that we know that modernity is replete with bad as well as good ideals and, viewed especially from a global perspective, with the unreasonable to a greater extent than the reasonable. Intellectual critique in these conditions should neither be seen as subordinate to ordinary self-understanding nor superior to it. It is distinctive in exploring the most general possible point of view from which to validly orient its operations. What modally forms in society is not always well-understood by society's members, and when it becomes a question of the collective gestation of the new, even less so. So the problem is less with the normative hegemony of the position adopted by contemporary critical theory than with the failure to sufficiently extend its legacy to future-oriented explorations on behalf of the cosmopolitan general public, insofar as it might be emerging and could be encouraged to further emerge. It is not so much a failure of the will in this latter respect, but the presence only of a partial theoretical-methodological capacity, partly because it has to some considerable extent set aside its sociological legacy. In self-criticism, I should finally say I have also evaded here the vital task of such theoretical-methodological explication. From exploratory examination, it is a task of great magnitude, and its fulfilment waits

Critique and Reasoning Pathologies 313

for another occasion. However, only through such an exercise can the complexity of self-organized collective learning by publics themselves be set in the context of intellectual and reconstructive critique, in which existing and emergent publics are absolutely central.

## Note

1 See Frankenberg on authoritarian constitutionalism and on authoritarianism as a pathology (Frankenberg, 2020).

## References

Apel K-O (1987) The Problem of a Macroethic of Responsibility to the Future in the Crisis of Technological Civilization: An Attempt to Come to Terms with Hans Jonas's "Principle of Responsibility". *Man and World* 20(1): 3–40.

Apel K-O (2007) Discourse Ethics, Democracy, and International Law: Toward a Globalization of Practical Reason. *American Journal of Economics and Sociology* 66(1): 49–70.

Benhabib S, Flynn J, Fritsch M, and Forst, R (2015) The Right to Justification by Rainer Forst. *Political Theory* 43(6): 777–837.

Bidet A, Boutet M, and Chave F (2013) Au-Delà le L'intelligibilité Mutuelle: L'activité Collective comme Transaction. Un Apport Du Pragmatisme Illustré Par Trois Cas. *Activités* 10(1): 1–46.

Calcaterra RM (2011) *New Perspectives on Pragmatism and Analytic Philosophy.* Amsterdam: Rodopi.

Condon R (2021) Reframing Habermas's Colonization Thesis: Neoliberalism as Relinguistification. *European Journal of Social Theory* 24(4): 507–525.

Forst R (2017) Noumenal Alienation: Rousseau, Kant and Marx on the Dialectics of Self-Determination. *Kantian Review* 22(4): 523–551.

Frankenberg G (2020) *Autoritarismus: Verfassungstheoretische Perspektiven.* Frankfurt: Suhrkamp.

Freyenhagen F (2015) Honneth on Social Pathologies: A Critique. *Critical Horizons* 16(2): 131–152.

Fricker M (2007) *Epistemic Injustice: Power and the Ethics of Knowing.* Oxford: Oxford University Press.

Habermas J (2003) *Truth and Justification.* Cambridge, MA: MIT Press.

Habermas J (2019) *Auch Eine Geschichte Der Philosophie.* Frankfurt: Suhrkamp.

Honneth A (2004) A Social Pathology of Reason: On the Intellectual Legacy of Critical Theory. In: Rush FL (ed) *The Cambridge Companion to Critical Theory.* Cambridge: Cambridge University Press.

Horkheimer M (1974 (1947)) *Eclipse of Reason.* London: Bloomsbury.

Horn C (2014) *Nichtideale Normativität: Ein Neuer Blick auf Kants Politische Philosophie.* Frankfurt: Suhrkamp

Kreide R (2023) Social Critique and Transformation: Revising Habermas's Colonisation Thesis. *European Journal of Social Theory* 26(2): 215–235.

Liszka JJ (2021) *Charles Peirce on Ethics, Esthetics and the Normative Sciences.* New York, NY: Routledge.

Lukács G (1972) *History and Class Consciousness: Studies in Marxist Dialectics.* Harvard MA: MIT Press.

Lukács G (2021) *The Destruction of Reason.* London: Verso.

McCarthy T (1993) *Ideals and Illusions: On Reconstruction and Deconstruction in Contemporary Critical Theory.* Cambridge, MA: MIT Press.

## 314 *Critique and Reasoning Pathologies*

Miller M (2002) Some Theoretical Aspects of Systemic Learning. *Sozialersinn* 3: 379–421.
Mills CW (1969) *Sociology and Pragmatism: The Higher Learning in America*. New York, NY: Oxford University Press.
Mills CW (2000) *The Sociological Imagination*. Oxford: Oxford University Press.
O'Mahony P (2013) *The Contemporary Theory of the Public Sphere*. Oxford: Peter Lang.
Peczenik A (2008) *On Law and Reason*. New York, NY: Springer.
Peirce CS (1893) Evolutionary Love. *The Monist*. 3: 176–200.
Pollock J (1987) Defeasible Reasoning. *Cognitive Science* 11(4): 481–518.
Ricouer, P (1965) *Fallible Man*. New York, NY: Fordham University Press.
Rosa H (2021) *Resonance: A Sociology of our Relationship to the World*. Cambridge: Polity.
Somers M (2008) *Genealogies of Citizenship: Markets, Statelessness, and the Right to Have Rights*. Cambridge: Cambridge University Press.
Strydom P (2019) On Habermas's Differentiation of Rightness from Truth: Can an Achievement Concept Do without a Validity Concept? *Philosophy and Social Criticism* 45(5): 555–574.
Toulmin SE (2009) *Return to Reason*. Cambridge, MA: Harvard University Press.
Wartenberg G (1971) *Logischer Sozialismus: Die Transformation Der Kantschen Transzendentalphilosophie Durch Ch. S. Peirce*. Frankfurt: Suhrkamp.
Watzlawick P, Bavelas JB, and Jackson DD (2011) *Pragmatics of Human Communication: A Study of Interactional Patterns, Pathologies and Paradoxes*. New York, NY: WW Norton & Company.
Zurn CF (2011) Social Pathologies as Second Order Disorders. In: Petherbridge D (ed) *Axel Honneth: Crtical Essays*. Leiden: Brill.

# Index

Note: Page numbers followed by "n" refer to endnotes.

abduction 35, 58, 64, 91, 96, 110, 126, 139–141, 150, 153–157, 163, 165, 168, 170–172, 177, 180, 182, 189–190, 196, 207–209, 226, 232, 242, 251–253, 255, 258–259, 262, 273, 286, 290, 295, 304, 306–307

abductive inference 148, 165, 171, 175

abductive schema 180, 186, 188–192, 197, 200, 208, 214n1, 218, 230, 232, 235, 238, 242, 246–247, 250–253, 256, 286, 291, 296, 308–310

achievement standard 34, 212

actuality 4, 12, 38, 75, 88, 126–128, 138, 144, 151, 156, 159, 164–166, 171, 178, 230–231, 253, 256, 266, 268–270, 286, 305, 309, 311

Adorno, T. 9, 11, 13, 57, 75, 107, 115, 118, 280, 290, 299, 305

affirmative dialectic 7, 11, 118

agent-level schema 187

Alexander, J. C. 3, 74–80, 120, 122, 125

alienation 7, 16, 60, 77, 127, 144, 160, 213, 260, 262, 294, 303, 305, 307–308, 310–312

antagonism 1, 56, 63, 280, 308–309

Apel, K. -O. 4–5, 7–10, 25, 32–33, 36, 50, 53, 99, 118, 168, 188, 197, 208, 211, 220, 223–225, 233–234, 236n1, 251, 256–257, 262, 265–266, 270–271, 273, 288, 290, 294, 299–301

Archer, M. 3, 69, 75, 89–94, 96–97, 100, 116, 120, 122, 125, 195

argumentation 8–9, 30, 34, 40, 42–43, 58, 65–66, 96, 129, 141, 148, 155, 157n3, 161, 164, 167, 171–172, 174, 180, 182, 185, 194, 198, 204, 209, 212, 217, 219, 232, 248–250, 252, 256, 266, 269, 273–274, 291, 300–301, 304

Atkin, A. 140

autonomy 11, 61, 65–66, 70, 75, 84, 87, 90, 119, 145, 147, 157n6, 182, 191, 197–198, 224, 232, 243, 247, 250, 279, 288

Azmanova, A. 107

Benhabib, S. 108–110

Bergman, M. 152–153

Between Facts and Norms (BFN) 19–20, 29–31, 216, 243, 265

Bhaskar, R. 89, 116

Boltanski, L. 60, 71, 117, 120

Bourdieu, P. 3, 37–38, 71, 75, 83, 89, 91–92, 94–101, 105, 107, 116–118, 120–122, 124–126, 130, 141, 163, 167, 176, 178, 191, 201–202, 206–207, 234, 241, 245, 285, 287–288; *Practical Reason* 99; *Science of Science and Reflexivity* 98

Brandom, R. 42–43, 146, 166, 168

Brunkhorst, H. 63

capitalism 22–23, 84, 103, 131, 210, 213, 280, 288, 301, 311

Chevalier, J. -M. 166

Cicourel, A. V. 72, 119–120

cognitive process 10, 34, 58–60, 72, 93, 95–96, 104, 142, 152, 165, 174, 200, 206, 209, 218–219, 230, 236n3, 238, 294, 306; dimension 94–95, 119–121, 262; mediated 94; nature 58–59; sociology 5–7, 10–11, 16, 42, 67, 74, 119, 131, 161, 175–176, 179

collective learning 4, 21, 24, 31, 33, 35–36, 41–42, 64, 77, 104, 106–107, 109–110, 151, 186, 209, 217, 225–226, 231–236, 238, 245–248, 252–253, 264–266, 268,

316 *Index*

277, 282–283, 285–287, 289, 291, 296, 298, 302–305, 308–313
communication 12, 18–20, 23, 27–30, 32, 37, 43, 45, 54, 56, 58, 60, 64–65, 72–73, 81–82, 85–88, 103–104, 119–120, 122, 128, 130, 140, 142, 145, 148, 151, 153, 160, 163, 167, 171, 185, 195, 198, 208, 210, 212, 230, 264, 269, 275, 284, 298, 300, 303–304
communicative epistemology 5, 25–30
communicative rationality 21, 26–29, 31–33, 104
conjecture 10, 12, 34, 58–59, 150, 154–155, 163, 165, 170, 174, 177, 181, 183, 187–191, 200, 208–209, 226, 232, 235, 242, 245, 251–252, 255–261, 263, 265–266, 268, 284, 286–287, 290, 295, 298, 304, 306–307, 310
consensual/consensus 22, 26–27, 33–34, 39–42, 44, 66, 80, 82, 101–102, 131, 147, 168, 181, 184–186, 212, 221, 227, 233, 239, 243, 245–246, 248–250, 263–264, 296, 303, 307–308
constructivism 23, 70, 84, 116, 206–211, 213, 247, 291
*The Contemporary Theory of the Public Sphere* (O'Mahony) 222, 236n4, 291n3
convergence-divergence 116–117
coordinative modalities 177–180, 184, 186, 243–246, 248–250, 265, 273, 309
co-responsibility 36, 197, 223, 263, 266–267, 270–271, 273, 294, 300
cosmopolitanism 63, 196
critical reflexivity 8, 52, 59–61, 63, 72–73, 78, 106, 121, 261, 285
critical theoretical sociology 11, 39, 130, 199, 285
critical theory 1–2, 4–13, 15–16, 18, 20, 22–25, 39, 41, 50, 52–53, 55–57, 60, 65, 71, 73–74, 101–106, 109, 115–118, 124, 127, 130, 136, 152, 161, 170, 172–173, 179, 186, 195–196, 199, 202, 204, 208–210, 213, 216, 218, 220–221, 224, 226, 228–230, 233, 240–241, 246–248, 252–253, 256, 258, 261–262, 264, 267–268, 272, 275, 279–291, 294, 300, 303, 305, 308, 310, 312
critique(s) actual 226, 229, 286, 293; disclosing 25, 106, 108, 125, 284, 286, 289; exposing 187, 261, 286, 289, 299; intellectual 261, 287–289, 312; negative 22–23, 41–42, 52, 81, 131, 195, 218, 269, 284, 286, 290–291; of reason 1, 2, 14, 15, 21, 49, 50, 52, 59, 99, 125, 127,

293–313; reconstructive 22, 40, 41, 282, 283, 289, 313; self-critique 1, 2, 4–5, 14, 60, 61, 73, 99, 148, 160, 213, 287, 312
cultural models: cognitive cultural model (CCM) 177, 180–185, 187, 196, 200, 203, 212, 217, 220, 228–229, 232, 238–240, 247–249, 251, 253, 256, 282, 291; institutional model (IM) 176, 186–188, 200–201, 204, 212, 227, 230, 232, 238, 240–241, 247–248, 273, 280; substantive cultural model (SCM) 184–187, 196, 200, 203, 212, 228, 232, 238–240, 248–251, 253; *see also* abductive schema

deduction 141, 154–157, 168, 171, 226, 255, 258, 264, 272, 295–296, 304, 306
deductive inference 148, 171–172, 175
definiteness 5, 58, 150, 155, 156, 164, 176, 190, 204, 240
democracy 2, 4, 6, 12, 16, 20–21, 32–33, 35–36, 40–41, 50–51, 75–76, 123, 130–131, 152, 160, 173, 180–184, 186, 194–196, 203, 219, 221–225, 227, 231, 239–240, 247, 267, 273, 275, 281–282, 285, 311
democratic conditions 64–65
democratic learning 32, 230
democratization 6, 10, 29, 32, 69, 222–224, 234, 265–267, 270, 285, 305
*Destruction of Reason* (Lukacs) 307
detranscendentalization 25–26, 30–36, 45, 46n2, 188, 229, 300
Dewey, J. 12, 144–145, 242, 247, 251, 267, 288, 305
dicent symbols 155, 165–166, 171
disclosing 8, 22, 25, 56, 106–108, 125, 274, 284–286, 289
discourse ethics 10, 21, 29, 31, 34–35, 40, 63, 65–67, 95–96, 152, 161, 188, 221–234, 236n1, 236n4, 238, 243, 249–250, 255–258, 261, 264–266, 268–269, 271–272, 287, 293, 297–298, 300–301, 303, 306, 312
discovery 8, 51, 53, 59–60, 88, 99, 123, 151, 155, 157, 170, 185
doubt-belief model 8, 97–98, 121, 181, 188, 198, 213, 230, 253, 286
Durkheim, E. 1, 41, 61, 70, 75, 78–80, 91, 101, 115–116, 122, 130–131, 145, 147, 150, 160, 162, 218, 261, 299
dysfunction 12, 187, 200, 213, 243, 293, 303

*Eclipse of Reason* (Horkheimer) 7
Eder, K. 42, 107, 252–253
epistemology 5–6, 10, 21, 22, 24–26, 36–39, 41, 50, 53, 55, 60, 63, 83, 84, 88–91, 97, 105, 109, 121, 126, 127, 141, 155, 162, 261, 282, 284, 287, 289, 307; *see also* communicative epistemology
epistemo-methodological activity 285–291
equality 2, 65, 106, 117, 147, 152, 164, 180, 182–183, 204, 212, 232, 249–250, 258, 296
expectations 86–87
explanatory 11, 50, 71, 165, 194, 200, 210, 218, 252, 283, 288, 290
exploitation 252, 301
exposing 100, 187, 261, 284, 286, 289, 299

fields: Bourdieu's account of 98–99; discursive 203, 228, 230, 232–233, 239, 241, 252, 298, 310, 312; perceptual 202, 229, 232–233, 308–309; positional 201–202, 205, 221, 229, 232, 241, 244, 247, 253, 274, 294, 298, 305, 308–309, 311; relational 125, 178, 202, 212, 269, 273; social 94–95, 101, 170, 178, 187, 201, 241
*Fin De Siecle Social Theory* (Alexander) 74–77
formal pragmatic theory 21, 27, 31, 34, 37–40, 43–44, 46n2, 59, 104, 226, 255, 260, 266, 275
Forst, R. 24–25, 63, 65, 74, 99, 105–110, 116, 118, 124–125, 130, 147, 164, 172, 181, 183, 233, 249, 252, 283, 299, 307, 310
Foucault, M. 87–88, 163, 165, 207, 251, 273, 289, 310
freedom 2, 16, 22, 24, 34–35, 70, 77, 83, 87, 102–104, 118, 120, 124–125, 141, 144, 151, 180, 185, 203, 208, 213–214, 240–241, 247, 251, 257–258, 260, 276, 296, 302–303, 307
*Freedom's Right* (Honneth) 103–104, 247

Gadamer 75, 149
globalization 223–224
Günther, K. 224, 269–270

Habermas, J. 3–10, 13, 15, 18–46, 46n2–46n3, 50–51, 54, 56–57, 59, 61–62, 65, 74, 76–77, 79–80, 84, 92, 97–101, 103–104, 106–107, 119–121, 127–128, 130, 132, 135–136, 139, 149, 154, 156–157, 159–161, 165–168, 170–172, 178, 181, 194–195, 197, 206, 211, 216–218, 222–227, 229, 233–234, 242–245, 247, 251–252, 256–257, 260, 262, 264–265, 267, 275–276, 284, 289, 291, 297–298, 300–301, 304–305, 307, 310; *Knowledge and Human Interests* 46n3; *Legitimation Crisis* 41; *Process Model of Political Will Formation* 243; *Truth and Justification* 31, 33–35, 38, 45
habit 14, 28, 51, 64, 91–92, 94, 97, 100, 135, 143, 153, 167, 174, 235, 251, 309
habitus 22, 37–38, 46n1, 62–63, 92, 94–95, 97–98, 100, 122, 124, 127, 170, 176, 178, 206–207, 241, 304
Hegel, G. W. F. 1, 31, 38, 41, 51–52, 55–56, 63, 83, 85–86, 97, 101–104, 115, 119, 121, 126, 142, 144, 248, 282, 284
Honneth, A. 4, 23–25, 40–41, 57, 65, 67, 74, 87, 101–106, 108, 116, 118, 123–125, 130, 144, 172, 195, 236n2, 247, 267, 270, 282–285, 298, 301–303, 307, 310, 312
Horkheimer, M. 7–8, 13, 26–27, 50, 75, 118, 276, 297, 299, 305–306, 310

ideal learning 253
*Ideals and Illusions* (McCarthy) 299
ideal theory 3, 12, 14, 40, 54, 59, 67n1, 102, 106, 109, 114, 125, 176, 229, 239, 259, 266, 284, 286, 290–291
immanent ideals 117, 128, 146, 172, 181–182, 187, 218, 238, 251, 265, 271
immanent limit 211–212, 270
immanent transcendence 6, 8–9, 15, 24, 30–31, 33, 35–36, 38–39, 42, 44, 46n2, 57–59, 62, 65, 67n2, 78, 81, 98, 103, 105–107, 115–118, 120, 130, 135, 146, 152–153, 163, 198–199, 204, 209, 229, 240, 242, 283, 288–289, 312
indefiniteness 176, 240
index 54, 136–139, 142–143, 156, 171, 179, 189, 200, 204–206, 241, 260, 270, 272
induction 141, 150, 154–157, 168, 170–172, 226, 255, 270, 272
inequality 23, 183, 200, 233
inference 15, 24, 43, 55–56, 78, 110, 143, 146, 148–150, 154–155, 163, 165–166, 169–172, 174–175, 187, 189, 202, 207, 230, 245, 261, 268, 273, 276, 294–295, 304, 308, 311
infinitesimals 164–165, 191, 275, 285

318  *Index*

injustice 15, 41, 45, 71, 81, 88, 107, 121, 186, 189–190, 200–202, 213, 244, 270, 280, 282, 290, 293, 301–302, 304, 310
inter-positional learning 232, 253, 270
interpretant(s) 14, 43, 82, 117, 122, 142, 166–168, 170–175, 180, 183–185, 187–188, 200, 250–251, 259, 262–264, 268, 295, 297; dynamic 168, 170, 171, 175, 180, 183–185, 187, 200, 250–251, 259, 268; final 167–172, 175, 187, 243, 251, 263; immediate interpretant 168, 170–171, 175, 183, 200, 250, 259; ultimate 180, 183–184, 251, 262–264
irrationality 305, 307–308, 311–312

justice 1, 8, 14–16, 25, 41–42, 45, 57, 66, 71, 76–77, 81, 88, 93, 107, 121, 123, 147, 160, 183, 186–187, 189–190, 196, 200–202, 213, 218, 226, 240, 244, 247–248, 280–282, 284, 290
justification 4, 8, 24, 31, 34–45, 52, 67, 73, 87, 106–110, 117, 120, 122, 124, 129, 132, 140, 143, 153, 157, 169, 172–173, 183, 185–187, 208, 211, 224, 228, 245, 249, 252, 260, 269–270, 276, 283, 286–287, 293, 296, 304

Kant, I. 1, 3–4, 8, 21, 24, 26, 30–32, 35–36, 41, 46n2, 51–53, 55–56, 59–62, 65, 73, 77, 81, 87, 94–95, 97–99, 102, 105, 109–110, 115–116, 119, 124–125, 131, 141, 145–149, 152, 162, 180, 188, 190–191, 194, 196–197, 203, 208–211, 213, 219–220, 222, 224, 226, 249, 253, 258–259, 261, 276, 283–284, 298–301, 307, 310
Kohlberg, L. 33, 95–96

left-Hegelian tradition 51, 53, 55, 73, 101–103, 105, 123, 135, 229, 300
Lenk, H. 220
Lizardo, O. 94–95
logic 7, 8, 10, 13, 15, 32, 35, 36, 42, 43, 45, 46, 51, 55, 56, 60, 61, 66, 75, 81, 83, 85, 86, 94, 96, 98, 99, 101, 102, 107, 116, 118, 122, 123, 135–137, 140, 145, 148, 151–156, 157n3, 163, 165, 167, 170–172, 185, 188–190, 197–198, 200, 203, 204, 216–221, 226–228, 230, 240, 242, 251, 259, 268–271, 274, 279, 280, 287, 289–291, 295–298, 300, 306, 312

Luhmann, N. 28, 46n1, 55, 73–74, 82–89, 115–116, 120–122, 130–132, 156, 206, 247, 279, 290, 310
Lukács, G. 103, 305, 307
Lynch, M. 71–72, 119, 121, 125

macro-social theory 22–25, 46, 73–74, 80, 89, 101, 105, 130, 194–195
Marx, K. 1, 6–8, 21, 38, 41, 63, 69–70, 83, 86–87, 89, 101, 103, 123, 125, 127, 130–132, 135, 144, 147, 150, 160, 162, 167, 203, 208, 210, 212–213, 218, 225, 248, 279–281, 283, 301, 305, 307
McCarthy, T. 229, 299
McNay, L. 74, 105–110, 115–116, 125, 127
Mead, G. H. 27, 91–93, 160, 162, 241, 251
mediation 6, 8, 12, 14, 23, 75, 91, 94, 101, 121–124, 130–131, 135, 145, 147–148, 150, 162–164, 200–201, 225, 232, 246, 276, 289, 311
Miller, M. 41–42, 192n2, 227, 233, 298, 303–305
Mills, C. W. 209, 260, 262, 307
modernity 6, 28, 45, 50, 66, 86, 104, 119, 213, 251, 280, 284–285, 302, 312
Moore, Jr B. 189–190
morality 21, 35, 83, 108, 154, 249, 272, 301
multi-perspectival vision of sociology 21
Munch, R. 78–82, 103, 105, 108, 118, 120–122, 125, 127, 129–131, 162, 227, 297

narcissistic reflexivity 95, 126
negative critical model 22
negative freedom 102, 125
neo-functionalism 74–75
Nesher, D. 189, 207
Nietzsche, F. 1, 52
nominalism 11, 137, 147, 169, 194, 198
non-ideal theory 109, 229, 284, 290
Nööth, W. 166
normative culture 108–109, 177, 183, 212, 265, 271
normatively relevant 3, 66, 153, 173
normative perspectives 66, 128–133

ontological construction 84, 126–127, 142, 144, 261
ontological radicalization 37
output schemata 177–178, 184, 186, 188, 197

Paolucci, C. 174–175
Parsons, T. 1, 22–24, 28–29, 41, 54, 69,
71–74, 79–81, 101, 108, 115–116,
118–120, 122, 127–128, 132, 208, 210,
212, 239, 261, 291
Peczenik, A. 296
Peirce, C. S. 4–5, 7–10, 12, 14–15, 19,
24, 28, 33, 35, 38–39, 42–46, 51,
55–61, 63–65, 67, 72, 80, 83, 85–87,
91–101, 110, 116–118, 121–123,
126, 128, 135–157, 157n1, 157n3,
161, 163–174, 176, 178–181, 183,
187–191, 195, 197–200, 203–204,
206–211, 213, 218–220, 225–227,
232, 235, 238, 241, 243, 247–248,
250–251, 255, 257–259, 261, 264,
267–271, 274, 276, 286–288, 290,
295, 297–301, 305–307, 310, 312;
extended mind and generals 145–148;
firstness 14, 58, 91–94, 105, 126,
128, 136–145, 147, 149–152, 154,
157n1, 170, 182, 189, 199–201,
204–209, 213, 220, 232, 235,
244–245, 268, 274; *The Fixation of
Belief* 168–169, 183, 187–188, 250,
286; logical theory 140, 226–227;
reasoning and symbolization 148–157;
secondness 14, 44–45, 55, 58, 93, 105,
126, 128, 136–145, 147, 149–152,
155–156, 157n1, 165–167, 169,
173–174, 176, 199–201, 204–205,
207, 209, 213, 220, 232, 235, 238,
245, 274; signification and potentiality
141–145; signs and categories
136–141; *A Sketch of Logical Critics*
169–170; *Sundry Logical Conceptions*
166, 179; thirdness 8, 14–15, 28, 38,
43, 55, 58, 88, 93–94, 105, 122, 126,
128, 135–144, 146–148, 150–151,
154–156, 157n1, 163, 165–168, 172,
174, 176, 190, 199–201, 203–205,
207–209, 220, 232, 235, 238, 246,
268, 274, 312
perceptual schematization 189–190
performative contradiction 4, 65–66, 96,
118, 290
*The Persistence of Modernity* (Wellmer) 31
Piaget, J. 33, 37, 94–95, 97, 100, 211,
243
pluralism 13, 66, 72, 120, 132, 222, 232,
240, 264, 279–281, 288, 296, 300, 307
positional learning 253
post-conventional 32–33, 95, 97

postmodernism 49, 73, 75
potential learning 32, 64, 255
pragmatics 10, 15, 31, 37–38, 40, 44–45,
59, 75, 78, 99, 120, 146, 149, 226, 255,
300

quality 26, 29, 31–32, 34, 40, 45, 52, 58,
66, 78, 86, 88, 91, 93, 107, 115, 118,
120–122, 127, 137, 140, 142–143,
145–146, 148, 163, 167, 189–191,
195, 197–198, 206, 208–209,
219–220, 222, 226, 232, 235, 239,
242–244, 257–258, 260, 267, 287,
302, 311–312

radical liberalization 223–224
rationality 2, 6–7, 21, 26–29, 31, 33,
37, 65, 69, 76–77, 79–84, 86, 89, 98,
102–104, 123, 125, 127, 132, 138–139,
159–161, 163, 169, 185, 218–220, 222,
258, 270, 293–294, 299–300, 302, 305,
307–308, 310
rationalization 6, 10, 12, 19, 26–27, 32–33,
37, 79–81, 104–105, 121, 125–128, 131,
144, 159–160, 166–167, 178, 189, 197,
211, 218, 229, 235, 238, 258, 268–269,
305, 307, 310
Rawls, J. 3, 54, 66–67, 67n1, 71, 76–77,
194, 224–225, 259, 265, 268, 281,
283, 291
reason/reasoning: abductive 236n3, 308;
actualization of 62–64, 102, 109, 127;
alienated 297, 310–311; bad 25, 44,
79, 213, 240, 298, 311; communicative
1, 3, 5, 10–11, 16, 18–25, 29–31,
36–39, 42–43, 45, 50, 55–67, 70, 74,
80, 103, 114, 131, 136, 149, 161, 178,
197–198, 216, 223, 227, 242, 283, 297,
305, 310; critique of 1, 2, 14, 15, 21,
49, 50, 52, 59, 99, 125, 127, 293–313;
cultural embodiment of 26, 30, 32, 39,
60, 174; defensive 308; ideological
308–309; inductive 58, 175, 190,
260, 271–273, 295, 308; inferential 9,
42–43, 59, 121, 129, 147, 151, 167,
187, 227, 295; instrumental 62, 132,
159, 305; intersubjective 13, 27, 42,
207, 276; pathologies 42, 60, 213, 260,
263, 293–294, 298–313; regressive
309; subjective 2, 6, 13, 26, 50, 60,
132, 160, 276, 297, 310; suspicion of
21–22, 49, 162; and symbolization
148–157

320  *Index*

reconstructive 22–24, 40–41, 115, 118, 213, 226, 259, 265, 269, 282–283, 286, 289–290, 312–313

reflexivity 3, 29, 49, 52–53, 56–58, 67, 69–110, 114, 120–126, 130–132, 135, 159, 208, 256, 261, 285, 294, 301, 307, 310

reification 7, 16, 40–41, 127, 144, 160, 213, 262, 270, 303, 305–308, 310, 312

relational 1–6, 8–11, 13, 15–16, 19–22, 25, 27–29, 34, 36–41, 43–44, 49–50, 53, 54, 56–59, 61–62, 72–74, 78, 81–83, 91–95, 97–106, 108–110, 116–117, 119–121, 123–129, 131, 135, 138–146, 148, 150–154, 156, 157n2, 160, 163–165, 167–168, 170–176, 178–179, 182–183, 185–190, 195–199, 201–205, 207–209, 212–213, 216–218, 221, 223, 227, 231, 232, 235, 238–240, 242, 243, 245, 248–249, 255–257, 259–261, 263, 268–270, 272–277, 280–282, 284–286, 288–290, 296–297, 301, 302, 306, 307, 310–312

Ricouer, P. 162, 302–303

Rosa, H. 174

Royce, J. 148

schema-building 175, 308, 310

schemata 14, 60, 64, 81, 94, 119, 128, 149, 152, 157n4, 168, 175–180, 183, 186–189, 191, 197–198, 214n1, 217–218, 220, 230, 232, 234, 238, 242, 246, 250–253, 276, 280, 294, 309

Schnadelbach, H. 1

Schutz, A. 29, 69, 71, 79, 120

second-generation critical theory 2, 7–9, 12, 60, 210, 221, 236n1, 253, 267

second-order pathology 307, 312

self-legislation 222–223

semantics 24, 37–38, 40, 44–45, 55, 148–149

social change 6, 10–11, 14–15, 24, 40, 42, 45, 54, 77, 90, 102, 104, 107, 118, 124, 132, 161, 173, 191, 208–209, 226, 249, 256, 262, 268, 280–281, 291, 304, 309

social freedom 102–104, 118, 144

social life, egalitarian coordination of 31–32

social ontology 10, 25, 84, 105, 109, 197–203; of communicative reason 36–39

social pathologies 40, 102, 105, 282, 298, 301–303, 306, 310–312

social process 61, 80, 164, 222–223, 241, 301

social theory 18, 23, 63, 74, 76, 78, 85–86, 93, 129–130, 173–174, 190, 195, 198, 204, 206, 221, 242, 273, 291, 301

societal development 91, 103–104

societal ontology 13–14, 41; component signs of 203–210; of critical reason 14–16; sign-mediation 5–6, 14–15, 64, 164, 195, 198–199, 203, 256, 289; validity and 227–228, 246–247

*The Sociological Imagination* (Mills) 209

sociological thinking 3, 24, 82

solidarity 16, 28, 62, 75, 78, 80–82, 101, 118, 122, 180, 195, 218, 225, 227, 232, 275, 277, 296

Stichweh, R. 85

structuration 37, 92–93, 210–214, 230, 273

structure-agency theory 74, 79, 89, 93

Strydom, P. 31, 34, 37, 42–44, 47n8, 57–58, 62, 66, 96, 110, 116–117, 146, 152, 175–176, 219, 226, 275, 283

subjectivation 124–126

subjective process 61–62

systemic codes 305–306, 310

systems theory 60, 83, 85, 88, 174, 186, 197, 234, 247, 291

thematization 227, 230, 310

theorematic deduction 155

*Theory of Action* (Munch) 80

*The Theory of Communicative Action (TCA)* 5, 7, 10, 15, 19–20, 22–23, 26–30, 32, 37–38, 40–46, 53, 62, 131, 149, 159, 167, 178, 195, 197, 216–218, 222, 224, 234, 242, 256, 265, 267, 284, 297–298, 305, 307, 310

Thevenot, L. 60, 71, 117, 120, 312

Toulmin, S. E. 7

Touraine, A. 46, 62, 92, 102, 125, 144, 157n6, 176, 178, 185, 239, 266–267

Tully, J. 288

validity:actual 226, 230, 262, 264–270, 274, 298; claims 15, 26–31, 33–34, 36, 38–40, 42–46, 62, 64, 139, 154, 157, 167–168, 170–171, 175, 208, 216–218, 221, 226–227, 229, 240, 242–243, 250–253, 258, 260–262, 275, 287, 311; conjectural 257–262, 267–268, 290; consensual 245; dissensual 245; hegemonic 245;

ideal 226–227, 262–263, 265, 267–268, 298; standards 6, 10, 13, 15, 34, 40–41, 65, 104, 118, 152, 162, 182, 186, 197, 208–209, 212, 218, 221, 226–227, 229–231, 233–235, 236n4, 238, 240, 243–244, 246, 253, 255–277, 279–280, 282–283, 287–291, 293, 297–302, 306, 312; transcendental 31, 34, 229

Weber, M. 1, 7, 19, 21, 26, 41, 69–71, 78–81, 91, 115–116, 127–128, 130–132, 144, 159–160, 162, 166, 218, 245, 260–261, 280, 305, 307
Wellmer, A. 31
Western liberalism 61
Wiener, A. 123
Wittgenstein, L. 8, 37, 55, 95, 98